D1338591

Toward an Urban Cultural Studies

HISPANIC URBAN STUDIES

BENJAMIN FRASER is Professor and Chair of Foreign Languages and Literatures in the Thomas Harriot College of Arts and Sciences at East Carolina University, North Carolina, US. He is the editor of the *Journal of Urban Cultural Studies* and the author, editor, and translator of book and article publications in Hispanic Studies, Cultural Studies, and Urban Studies.

SUSAN LARSON is an Associate Professor of Spanish at the University of Kentucky, US. She is Senior Editor of the *Arizona Journal of Hispanic Cultural Studies* and works at the intersections of Spatial Theory and Literary, Film and Urban Studies.

Toward an Urban Cultural Studies: Henri Lefebvre and the Humanities
Benjamin Fraser

Toward an Urban Cultural Studies

Henri Lefebvre and the Humanities

Benjamin Fraser

First published in 2015 by
PALGRAVE MACMILLAN®
in the United States—a division of St. Martin's Press LLC,
175 Fifth Avenue, New York, NY 10010.

Where this book is distributed in the UK, Europe and the rest of the world,
this is by Palgrave Macmillan, a division of Macmillan Publishers Limited,
registered in England, company number 785998, of Houndmills,
Basingstoke, Hampshire RG21 6XS.

Palgrave Macmillan is the global academic imprint of the above companies
and has companies and representatives throughout the world.

Palgrave® and Macmillan® are registered trademarks in the United States,
the United Kingdom, Europe and other countries.

ISBN: 978–1–137–49855–7

Library of Congress Cataloging-in-Publication Data

Fraser, Benjamin.
   Toward an urban cultural studies : Henri Lefebvre and the
   humanities / Benjamin Fraser.
        pages cm.—(Hispanic urban cultural series)
        Includes bibliographical references and index.
        ISBN 978–1–137–49855–7 (alk. paper)
        1. Sociology, Urban. 2. Culture. 3. City and town life. 4. Lefebvre,
   Henri, 1901–1991. I. Title.

HT151.F725 2015
307.76—dc23   2014037973

A catalogue record of the book is available from the British Library.

Design by Newgen Knowledge Works (P) Ltd., Chennai, India.

First edition: April 2015

10 9 8 7 6 5 4 3 2 1

for Abby

Contents

Acknowledgments

Although much of my previous work has been interdisciplinary in one way or another, this book in particular would not have been possible without the implicit and explicit encouragement of the scholars who have been my guides. First, thanks to Malcolm Alan Compitello and Susan Larson for showing by example that interdisciplinary work crossing the humanities and geography is worthwhile and important—even if it brings with it a specific set of challenges.

Thanks go, too, to those within Hispanic Studies who have been particularly open to new forms of scholarship—not only to the editors, boards, reviewers, and readers of the *Arizona Journal of Hispanic Cultural Studies* and the *Journal of Spanish Cultural Studies* but also those of forward-thinking journals such as *Hispania* and *Chasqui*. In addition to Malcolm and Susan, thanks go also to Eugenia Afinoguénova, Ed Baker, Francie Cate-Arries, Monica Degen, David William Foster, Daniel Frost, Rebecca Haidt, Christine Henseler, David Herzberger, Amanda Holmes, Sheri Long, Randolph Pope, Carlos Ramos, Nathan Richardson, Marcy Schwartz, Steven Spalding, Michael Ugarte, and David Wiseman, who in particular, in one way or another, have encouraged me to think differently about stretching the limits of disciplinary knowledge.

Thanks to Araceli Masterson-Algar and Stephen Vilaseca for agreeing to join me in forming the *Journal of Urban Cultural Studies*, and thanks to those who follow and contribute to that journal's accompanying multiauthored blog, urbanculturalstudies.wordpress.com. The esteemed members of the journal's editorial board also deserve my thanks. Most of all, I am grateful to Masoud Yazdani at Intellect, who supported the formation of that new interdisciplinary journal.

In particular, I am fortunate to have the welcoming colleagues I have found at East Carolina University (ECU) since starting on July 1, 2014. I must thank John Sutherland, John Stevens, Derek Maher,

Suzanne Powell, Sharon Peterson, Jason Walker, Denise Miller, Jone Letsinger, Renita Harley, and, last but not least, Bill Downs for making my transition so smooth; likewise, my colleagues in Foreign Languages and Literatures, and my fellow chairs in HCAS—particularly Jeffrey Johnson, Burrell Montz, and Gerry Prokopowicz—for their enthusiasm and goodwill. Thanks also to a great number of people at ECU— Cindy Putnam-Evans, Gina Betcher, Joseph Thomas, Laurie Godwin, and Joyce Newman, among many others—for their willingness to collaborate on future common projects, including forays into the digital humanities.

Chapters 5–7 each include significant portions of a previously published article, in minimally modified form, along with new material. Part of chapter 5 is reprinted from *Studies in Spanish and Latin American Cinemas*, formerly *Studies in Hispanic Cinemas*, 9.1—Benjamin Fraser, "A *Biutiful* City: Alejandro González Iñárritu's Filmic Critique of the 'Barcelona Model,'" pp. 19–34, 2012—with permission of Intellect Ltd. Part of chapter 6 is reprinted from *Emotion, Space and Society*, 4.1—Benjamin Fraser, "Re-scaling Emotional Approaches to Music: Basque Band Lisabö and the Soundscapes of Urban Alienation," pp. 8–16, 2011—with permission from Elsevier. Chapter 7 incorporates only a few pages of partial content from the *Journal of Gaming and Virtual Worlds* 3.2—Benjamin Fraser, "Why the Spatial Epistemology of the Video Game Matters: Mētis, Video Game Space and Interdisciplinary Theory," pp. 93–106, 2011—with permission of Intellect Ltd. I thank those publications for allowing me to reproduce that material—with minimal changes—in this book.

Introduction

The goal of *Toward an Urban Cultural Studies* is to provide a model for integrating two distinct strains of cultural inquiry—urban studies and cultural studies—as a concertedly interdisciplinary way of approaching the culture(s) of cities. Mobilizing the thought of French spatial theorist and urban philosopher Henri Lefebvre (1901–1991), it explores the ground common to both of these areas and, moreover, articulates in general terms a method for urban cultural studies research.

Both the advantages and the potential disadvantages of using Lefebvre's thought for this project stem from the very same core qualities of his oeuvre. His work was extensive (60–70 books), his books covered a wide range of subject matter, and this varied subject matter was examined in a compelling but often meandering style. In the end, he never shied away from grappling with the fundamental theoretical and philosophical problems of modern urban life under capitalism. While those who have often drawn from his work have certainly found it to be incomplete in certain respects, they have also shown that his core insights endure in the twenty-first century.[1] Moreover, the increasing interest in his work (recent re-editions, anthologies, new translations)—as well as the vast academic terrain to which it is being seen as relevant—testifies not merely to its relevance within and across disciplines but also to its versatility.[2] While it is significant that Lefebvre is arguably the twentieth century's most prolific urban thinker, it is perhaps just as important, given the task at hand, that his approach yields a loosely organized but cohesive framework for understanding urban culture. This approach is ultimately applicable to work by scholars bridging the humanities/social science divide, no matter what their city of interest. This introduction and the chapters that follow cull from Lefebvre's extensive work a relatively coherent set of questions surrounding the relationship of urban environments to cultural production in order to outline concerns central to the burgeoning, interdisciplinary area of urban cultural studies.

It is important to understand that the idea for this book developed organically out of two simultaneous circumstances. The first was shaped by the publication and reception of my earlier book *Henri Lefebvre and the Spanish Urban Experience: Reading the Mobile City* (Bucknell UP, 2011). A Hispanist by training, I had set out to compose a book that explored Lefebvre's substantial oeuvre more extensively, going beyond *The Production of Space* (English translation by Donald Nicholson-Smith, 1991)—the one book that single-handedly seemed to have captivated literary scholars from a range of language and area traditions—in order to dialogue with as many of his texts as possible.[3] My intention therein had been to use Lefebvre's thoughts on urban philosophy, urban modernity, and contemporary urban culture to explore representations of Spanish cities (namely Madrid and Barcelona) in select cultural products from nineteenth-century literature to the twenty-first-century videogame. My aim here, however, is notably different: I want to produce a text of potential interest to urban cultural studies scholars no matter what their area of expertise. Although I may refer in passing, during the second half of this book, to cultural products from my home discipline of Hispanic Studies, these references are intended to be representative of much broader trends throughout humanities fields, and I assume no knowledge of the disciplinary aspects of that field on the reader's part.

The second circumstance that has shaped this book is my concomitant commitment to the formulation of an urban cultural studies method. What I realized while writing that earlier book bridging Lefebvre's ideas with close-readings of Spanish cultural products was that, while literary scholars across many disciplines were increasingly dealing with topics germane to urban studies—the representation of cities in cultural texts or even the creation of the city itself as a cultural text (and sometimes both at once)—there seemed to be a reluctance among many of those scholars to fully digest social science research on those very same topics. There also seemed to be a reticence on the part of social scientists to engage questions of aesthetics from a humanities-centered perspective.

For a number of reasons discussed subsequently in the chapters comprising the first major section of this book, I came to believe that the work of Henri Lefebvre could potentially provide this burgeoning subfield of urban humanities research with a framework for understanding urban culture in general terms and, moreover, as a way of forging a more fruitful dialogue with social science fields where a growing number of scholars are also, of course, actively interested in investigating the culture(s) of cities. More important, I came to see that exploration of Lefebvre's urban thought might evince an urban cultural studies method. Such a method would not only be capable of providing a common ground for the work humanities scholars have already been producing over a number of years, it would also outline some central propositions around which to galvanize future scholarly conversations concerning the directions of this interdisciplinary and necessarily variegated field.

There are always limitations to this kind of work, of course. For example, it may thus be argued by some humanities scholars that the explicitly Marxian tenor and theoretical scope of the early chapters of this book, in particular, are distractions from the more pressing questions of the ins-and-outs of literary scholarship. Conversely, some Marxian scholars may complain that this book dialogues only insufficiently and indirectly with Marx's work itself, and that chapters 4, 5, and 6—which enter more fully into discourses that structure humanities scholarship (on literature, film, and popular music)—are themselves an unwanted digression. Chapter 7, on the topic of digital spaces, in general, and Digital Humanities work, in particular, may be received as a polemic by some scholars. This follows logically from the way in which public discussion of Digital Humanities is routinely accompanied by a globalizing discourse that touts its emancipatory potential to bring people together—one that has all too infrequently been left underanalyzed.

As many will understand, there are still other risks of publishing this kind of interdisciplinary work. Lefebvre scholars will necessarily find this book incomplete in many respects, and literary scholars may find the argument for Lefebvre's relevance unconvincing. It will undoubtedly be seen by some as not philosophical enough, not materialist enough, not literary enough, not geographical enough, and so on; it may be alleged that, taken separately, its humanities-centered insights and its presentation of Lefebvre lack novelty. To a certain extent, this is unavoidable if we are to begin a new kind of conversation about urban scholarship—which is to say that this book's flaws follow naturally from its basic premise and intended goal. This goal is precisely to fuse humanities (textual) criticism and Lefebvrian method—to point to their existing similarities and potential, interdisciplinary points of convergence—and not necessarily to provide insights that might change each discipline on its own terms. I must insist, however, that through forcing literary and cultural studies to think the city geographically and forcing geography to think the city artistically (in textual terms, defined from the perspective of the humanities), a new discourse may be forged whose sum is greater than its parts.

It is not hard to image that potential readers from sociology, geography, and other disciplines may find the very question of textual analysis—whether that text is a novel, poetry, music, film, videogames, or even a city itself—somewhat pointless. To wit: a prominent academic geographer (who shall remain nameless) based in a prestigious American university and directly inspired by Lefebvre's work—one who focuses explicitly on the notions of urban culture and urban struggles, in fact—once wrote me declaring that he saw nothing at all of value in the study of (cultural/literary) texts. As the chapters of *Toward an Urban Cultural Studies* progressively make clear, this attitude—certainly not one advocated by Lefebvre, and in fact directly contradicted by his work—itself reveals the very alienating structures that make a humanities-centered urban cultural studies method so necessary and so timely. This book's challenge and its potential, thus, stem from the fact that it is not solely about the humanities, nor solely about art, nor economics, politics, society, alienation, capital, criticism—it is, in the end, a text that attempts to take on the urban problem. And as an urban-centered work of interdisciplinary scholarship, it strives to find a way to force a confrontation between each of these areas. My fear is that it will not succeed in convincing specialists from a great number of disciplinary areas. But then again, given Lefebvre's own well-grounded suspicion of specialization, a Lefebvrian method *is not a method for specialists*. Instead, as we will see, it is a method for returning intellectual specializations to the totality from which they have been extracted by a certain conception of knowledge, one that arises—in his view—along with urban shifts particular to the nineteenth century.

Finally—in tribute to the philosophical dimensions of Lefebvre's own work and the purposely open spirit of his loosely defined method—another warning is necessary. The reader should be aware that this book does not explain, step by step, *how* to read literature and other cultural products from an urban cultural studies perspective, it merely explains *why* it is important to do so (note that later chapters provide brief and specific examples of possible ways of developing urban readings of film and popular music, for example). Instead of striving for a checked-box vision of cultural method, I have instead opted to underscore what general concerns we might take from Lefebvre's work in order to flesh out what this *how* may potentially involve in specific circumstances—whatever those may be. This is not merely a way of remaining open to potential future developments and aware of the vast and perhaps continually evolving set of varied "cultural texts." At the same time, this is a move to begin a conversation that is accessible to the widest range of researchers possible. If I have left anything out of the equation—and this is unavoidably the case—let this serve as an invitation to others working across the humanities–social science divide to join in the conversation. The newly created *Journal of Urban Cultural Studies* is one such venue for bringing such conversations the attention they deserve. There, or elsewhere, I invite further discussion.

Because I intend this book to span an interdisciplinary readership crossing both the humanities and the social sciences—and because I admittedly focus on the thought of Lefebvre in particular rather than taking a much more comprehensive approach—there are two fundamental topics that must be addressed, albeit briefly. The first is the notion of disciplinary friction in general, which boasts its own historical legacy and whose nuances will undoubtedly affect the reception of this book. The second is the wider cultural studies context within which this book's arguments are made. A full consideration of each of these topics would be out of place here; but, on the other hand, to ignore that some readers may not be familiar with them would be irresponsible. Accordingly, the remainder of this introduction turns, first, to an academic feud of sorts that goes by the name of the Snow–Leavis Controversy—which unfolded over 50 years ago as a way of broaching the general tensions surrounding interdisciplinary pursuits. Second, I concisely summarize the legacy and current state of cultural studies research in general terms and comment in particular on the place reserved in this context for discussion of the urban question. This is the question whose interrogation in truth constitutes the core of this book's subsequent chapters.

The Two Cultures: The Snow–Leavis Controversy

Because the Snow–Leavis controversy involved two high-profile personalities whose conflict raised the question of the distinction so often made between the sciences and the humanities, it can be of use in understanding those more contemporary interdisciplinary conflicts at the heart of urban cultural studies. Born in 1905, Charles Percy Snow is best remembered today as an advocate for disciplinary reconciliation—even if that legacy is not without its problems. While still young, he attended a school whose "strength was in science rather than in the traditionally more prestigious classics and humanities," completed the Intermediate Examination in Science in 1923, earned degrees in Chemistry in 1927 and 1928, and, after meritorious research in infrared spectroscopy, was elected Fellow of Christ's College, Cambridge, in 1930 (Collini 1993, xix–xx). Snow's scientific career, however, suffered a major setback in

1932 when his claim of having made an important scientific discovery was publicly proved faulty (Collini 1993, xx).[4] It was around that time that he published a detective novel (*Death Under Sail*), and two years later a second novel (*The Search*)—"These early efforts had been favorably reviewed, encouraging him to think of himself as a serious writer" (Collini 1993, xx). Over the next 30 years, Snow would write a series of 11 interlinked novels that "sold widely and were translated into several languages" (Collini 1993, xxi); the year 1945 thus marks the date of his separation from Cambridge, and by 1959 he had given up his transitional, part-time posts "to begin his third career as public figure, controversial lecturer, and pundit" (Collini 1993, xxi).

The Rede lecture—which Snow delivered on May 7, 1959, at the Senate House in Cambridge—marked the beginning of his "third career" and in many ways followed logically from his experiences. The title he chose for the lecture—"The Two Cultures"—centered on a concept he had introduced at least three years earlier and drew further public attention to the distance between what he referred to as "literary intellectuals" and "natural scientists" (Collini 1993, xxv).[5] Significantly, Snow (called Sir Charles, and later Lord Snow) thought of himself as straddling this divide—"By training I was a scientist: by vocation I was a writer," he would remark in the first paragraph of the lecture (Snow 1993, 1). Snow continued, stating his belief that "the intellectual life of the whole of western society is increasingly being split into two polar groups" and that this manifests itself also in "practical life" ("because I should be the last person to suggest that the two can at the deepest level be distinguished") (1993, 3–4). His goal of disciplinary reconciliation is, in this general formulation at the very least, laudable, and perhaps more so given the connection he makes between academic and nonacademic contexts.

In basic terms, Snow's argument has it that literary intellectuals and scientists persist in a state of mutual incomprehension. Nevertheless, Snow's lecture also reveals his clear personal identification with science over and against literature despite the seeming neutrality of his stated goal of reconciling the two cultures. This is evident even in his initial formulation of the question,[6] but more clearly, perhaps, in the elaboration of his position throughout the lecture. The first two arguments Snow makes, in fact, are that literary intellectuals should see the value of scientific optimism (1993, 6–7) and that the scientific opinion that equates literary authors with antisocial feelings should be upheld (1993, 8). More fundamentally, Snow defends scientism, stressing that "the scientific culture really is a culture, not only in an intellectual but also in an anthropological sense" (1993, 9) while, on the other hand, remaining suspicious of literary intellectuals and even coming to credit them with nurturing the "unscientific flavor" of the "whole 'traditional' culture"—a flavor that is "on the point of turning anti-scientific" (1993, 11). The division between these two cultures is particularly significant given that, as Snow adds, "It is the traditional culture, to an extent remarkably little diminished by the emergence of the scientific one, which manages the western world" (1993, 11).

The fact that Snow sided with science against literature—perhaps despite his reconciliatory intention—has already been acknowledged by critics who point to his disdain for "literary intellectuals" and their "snobbist and nostalgic social attitudes" (Collini 1993, xxiii). Admittedly, Snow regards scientists as out of touch with the literary/traditional culture—and admonishes them for their lack of familiarity with, say, Dickens or Rilke, as well as their lack of "imaginative under-standing" (1993, 11–14)—but, in the end, if scientists are "self-impover-ished," then literary intellectuals "are impoverished too—perhaps more seriously, because they are vainer about it" (1993, 14). Significantly, this asymmetricality of his argument drew much fire from those who were presumed to pertain to the culture of literary intellectuals.

It is thus not surprising that one of the most outspoken of Snow's critics was F. R. Leavis (1895–1978), professor of English at Downing College, Cambridge. Leavis himself was a forward-thinking intellectual who is most often remembered for having insisted—against disciplin-ary convention of the time—on the significance of newer writers such as James Joyce, D. H. Lawrence, Ezra Pound, and in particular T. S. Eliot. The year 1932 was a banner year for Leavis—whereas by contrast it was bittersweet for Snow—as it was then that he began his work as editor of the noted journal *Scrutiny*. By 1962, when F. R. Leavis was invited to give the Richmond lecture at Downing College, he was in many ways a larger-than-life figure, having arguably influenced in no small way the direction of twentieth-century literary study in Britain. Leavis used the occasion of the lecture, which he provocatively titled "Two Cultures? The Significance of C. P. Snow," as an opportunity to voice a strong response to Snow's perspective—one that has even been characterized as a "ferocious attack" (Collini 1993, xxix). Leavis certainly lambastes Snow in the Richmond lecture, calling into question both his identifica-tion as a literary intellectual and the quality of his novels (Leavis 1972, 44–45).[7] The intensity of Leavis's indictment—which surely seemed to have a personal tone—has frequently been taken as evidence of Snow's basic premise. That is, for many, it merely confirms first that these two cultures exist, and second that they are at the very least distant if not also antithetical or even inimical to each another. And yet, although there may be some truth to the claim that Leavis confirms the existence of the two cultures (as had Snow, of course, from his own side of the debate), it is shortsighted to think that his response to Snow's scientific bias is unwarranted or, worse still, to ignore that Leavis himself has his own reconciliatory goal in mind.

It is important to recognize that the heated nature of the Snow–Leavis controversy, nonetheless, overshadows many subtle points that are more worthy of our consideration. In his 1959 lecture, Snow takes humanists to task, likening lack of knowledge of the Second Law of Thermodynamics to never having read a work of Shakespeare (Snow 1993, 14–15). Leavis's later response insists that "There *is* no scientific equivalent of that question; equations between orders so disparate are meaningless" (original emphasis; 1972, 61). While it is tempting to see this as proof that Leavis will entertain no collaboration between the humanities and the sciences, we might read the comment not solely as a reflection on the current state of disciplinary isolation but, moreover, as a defense of the humanities that in fact complements what is, in essence, Snow's defense of the sciences. A more subtle position on "literariness" suggests that Leavis fears (rightly, in my own opinion) Snow's reduction of literature to a scientific worldview, but not that he is against science itself. In fact, as we shall soon see, he is not. This subtle position that I attribute to Leavis—which is insufficiently understood if it is taken to be merely "literary"—begins by recognizing the relative autonomy of aesthetic questions in the first pass before then moving to reconcile them with extraliterary discourse in the second—a progression that Snow's argument certainly cannot replicate.

In fact, from a certain perspective, Leavis's perspective is the more reconciliatory of the two in that it seeks to establish the importance of literary study on its own terms before bridging the distance between the humanities and the sciences. As implicit in Leavis's statement (above), disciplines—although we need to work across them—are not inter-changeable, not easily subjected to an identical logic or comparison. In this vein, it will just not do, Leavis implies, to hold literary study to scientific standards. We perhaps walk a fine line between accepting Leavis's denunciation of Snow as a literary interloper or impostor, on the one hand, and admitting Snow's point that Leavis speaks with an authority or a cultural capital that is perhaps all too easily associated with literary isolationism, on the other. It is important here, however, to distinguish between Leavis's authority and his intention. That is, although some critics have seen him as a literary isolationist, Leavis has gone out of his way to separate himself from that misperception, both in his legacy of a scholarship that sees literature not as a separate realm but as imbricated in "extraliterary" experience and also in comments where he deliberately rejects what he calls the "charge of literarism" that has been unfairly leveed upon him.[8]

With this in mind, it is easier to see the following: Leavis's assertion that there are not, in fact, two cultures has been misunderstood as an affirmation of the literary culture over and against the scientific culture. Yes, he insists vehemently that "there is only *one* culture; to talk of *two* in your way is to use an essential term with obviously disqualifying irresponsibility . . . It is obviously absurd to posit a 'culture' that the scientist has *qua* scientist" (original emphasis; Leavis 1972, 88, also 89), but we do well in recognizing that this is not a simple attack against scientific culture but a more global attack on the notion of isolated cultures in general. It is the distinction of two cultures that is his target, not the scientific culture per se: as evidenced in his subsequent statement that "We have no other; there is only one, and there can be no substitute. Those who talk of two and of joining them would present us impressively with the sum of two nothings" (Leavis 1972, 93). Given the way in which his views were commonly misinterpreted as a matter of course in a very public feud, he was later forced to definitely clarify that by one culture he did *not* mean a literary culture only (Leavis 1972, 158).[9]

In accordance with Henri Lefebvre's own thinking, to which we shall shortly return, the one culture with which Leavis is concerned is not the literary culture but a more complex culture enfolding the total human experience. When Leavis's remarks are considered within his critique of the disciplinary character of university structure, they gain further force and ultimately point toward the need to go beyond specialization. "Unlike Snow," Leavis writes "I am concerned to make it really a university, something (that is) more than a collocation of specialist departments—to make it a centre of human consciousness: perception, knowledge, judgment and responsibility" (1972, 63; also 98). It is possible to read the ire Leavis directs against the sciences as a complement to Lewis Mumford's own critique of the quantifiable logic of mechanization and industrialization (chapter 2, this book). Both thinkers clearly insist upon the irreducible, nonquantifiable character of the human (Leavis 1972, 151). But despite the contentious claims made by Snow that literary intellectuals in general (and quite plausibly Leavis in particular) are "natural Luddites" (1993, 22), Leavis still reserves a role for science in the future culture of creative collaboration he advocates.[10] He emphasizes, for example, that "A very strong, persistent and resourceful creative effort, then is desperately needed—a collaborative creativity to complement that which has produced the sciences" (Leavis 1972, 157). It must not be lost on the reader that this call for a "full human creativity" is of course, in essence, a call for reconciliation between the humanities and the sciences[11]—even if Leavis envisions this as a specific correction of the imbalance that gives greater priority to the latter. From this perspective, it is not that either Snow or Leavis is "correct" on his own, but rather that each launches a complementary call for reform—Snow (perhaps despite himself) from the side of the sciences, Leavis (uncompromisingly) from the side of the humanities.

Admitting the complementary aspects of Snow's and Leavis's views, we then move quite easily from Leavis's fears about the future of education to Henri Lefebvre's own critique of university and disciplinary structures. Leavis had written with a skeptical tone about the way in which computers were likely to affect instruction—responding to a specific article included in the *Times Literary Supplement* and asking, "What 'structured tasks,' for instance, are involved—could be, or should be—in the study of English literature?" (1972, 146–147). Leavis's commitment to humanism is evident here just as is his suspicion of mechanization and industrialization more generally. Implicit in his statement is his belief that a computerized education is likely to affirm a problematic and instrumentalized notion of knowledge and, likewise, that the study of literature in particular (just as the humanities more generally) cannot be so reduced (Leavis 1972, 147).

Of course, Leavis's skepticism of the very notion of "structured tasks" above resonates also with the perspective of critical pedagogues such as Gloria Watkins (bell hooks) and Paolo Freire, who denounce as "banking education" the notion of knowledge as a static deposit made directly into the mind of the passive student. Education, Freire writes, cannot be seen as "a set of things, pieces of knowledge, that can be superimposed on or juxtaposed to the conscious body of the learners" (1970, 72; also 1998; hooks 1994). These views on what hooks calls "education as the practice of freedom" (this phrase in the subtitle of her book is a clear homage to Freire's work) are—just like Lefebvre's—explicitly tied to the function of universities under a capitalist mode of production. Importantly, Lefebvre believed that a university was not a "warehouse" of knowledge (1969, 156). In *The Explosion*—the book he wrote in the aftermath of the events of 1968—Lefebvre states the insufficiency of this view in no uncertain terms when he writes, "What has to be abolished or transcended is primarily a view of learning as commodity and exchange–value, characteristic of the world of commerce and commodities—it views learning as a product that can be packaged and sold" (1969, 141; see also 2003a, 53–55).

There is no question that—for Lefebvre as well as for the present perspective—disciplinary structures affirm capitalist logic to the degree that they affirm knowledge as a product. The university, of course, as it became excruciatingly clear over the past three or four decades, does not exist outside of market relations—a fact whose consequences are legion.[12] What is worth reemphasizing here, of course, is that there is an immaterial, ideological complement to the material, economic forces that increasingly structure university life, a disciplinary specialization that accomplishes through the fragmentation and division of knowledge what the division of labor accomplishes in socioeconomic terms (Lefebvre 2003a, 60). The modern university, writes Lefebvre, "institutionalizes the social division of labor, helping to organize, nurture, and accommodate it. Isn't this the function assigned to the university today? To adapt itself to the social division of productive labor, that is, to the increasingly stringent requirements of the market, the technical division of intellectual labor and knowledge?" (2003a, 60). If it was at all possible to see this perspective as cynical in the 1970s, it is certainly less possible to do so today given the increasing market pressures affecting the nature of a university-level education.

Disciplinary reconciliation—if and when it is accompanied by a wider appeal—can be one strategy among many disalienating us from other alienating propositions inherent to capitalist modernity. When coupled with Lefebvre's specifically urban approach—his assertion that urban alienation trumps all other forms of alienation (explored in chapter 2)—interdisciplinarity goes beyond conceptions of knowledge as a "collection of objects—economy, sociology, history, demography" to grasp how urban thinking inflects all production and re-production (Lefebvre 2003a, 57). A Lefebvrian perspective on the Snow–Leavis controversy ultimately suggests that Leavis was right, there *is* only one culture, not two as Snow suggested. Moreover, as we will have chance to consider throughout the chapters that follow, Lefebvre's work suggests that this one culture that envelops all others is, significantly, an urban culture. It is to this question the remainder of this introduction now turns.

Cultural Studies and the Question of Urban Culture

It should be noted that this is hardly the place to reproduce, for the reader, either an extensive history of what goes by the name "cultural studies" itself or a summary of its general spirit. The former can be found in a large number of relatively recent volumes published over the course of the previous two decades (e.g., Turner 1990, 2012; Grossberg et al. 1992; Baker et al. 1996; Ferguson and Golding 1997; Morley and Robins 2001; Hall and Birchall 2006; Gibson 2007; Rojek 2007; Barker 2008; Grossberg 2010b). The latter is made particularly clear, I believe, in two privileged places—in a 1986 speech delivered by Raymond Williams (and included in the anthology *Politics of Modernism*) and in an essay by Henri Lefebvre himself, translated for the 1988 publication of *Marxism and the Interpretation of Culture* (edited by Lawrence Grossberg and Cary Nelson). What is clear to anyone working in the humanities at the start of the twenty-first century is that what cultural studies was, what it is—what it has become and what it may still be— are topics that have been extensively chronicled and debated in publications stretching back over many decades indeed. These topics may have even enjoyed attention for over a half of a century, in fact. Even this amount of time will seem insufficient if we include in our historical perspective the "precursors" of cultural studies in the 1930s, identified as such by Williams—that is, "all the people who first read what you could now quite fairly call 'Cultural Studies' . . .—from Richards, from Leavis, from *Scrutiny*—who were studying popular culture, popular fiction, advertising, newspapers, and making fruitful analyses of it" (2007, 55). Reasons are aplenty to consider that cultural studies—to the extent that it may be considered a disciplinary formation—has been engaged so thoroughly and by way of perspectives so diverse that it is better to no longer speak of it as a single, coherent, and internally homogenous approach. This is to admit that we now inhabit a curious moment of the history of cultural studies.

This current moment is clearly indebted to all of the rigorous work that has come before, critical directions that are far from obsolete, and whose influences endure in the present continuation of the cultural studies project. Any proper history of cultural studies would certainly include detailed explorations of the formation and legacy of Richard Hoggart and the Birmingham Centre for Contemporary Cultural Studies, the work of Stuart Hall (including the canonical anthologies *Policing the Crisis* [1978] and *Resistance through Rituals* [1993]), the development of Black British Cultural Studies in the 1990s and beyond (Manthia Diawara, Kobena Mercer, Paul Gilroy, Isaac Julien, and others), and the progressive fusion of cultural studies method with critical approaches to race, gender, sexuality, and disability studies, to name a few important directions. And yet, as Graeme Turner's perspective suggests in his recent *What's Become of Cultural Studies* (2012), it is possible in the current moment to see "cultural studies as a conjectural practice that is intrinsically interdisciplinary; while it is grounded in the body of theory that has developed as a result of the project of cultural studies and in particular the early work from Birmingham and the traditions flowing from it, it is also genuinely engaged in working across disciplinary and transnational territories which were not necessarily part of that history" (2012, 6).

As I see it, something has undoubtedly changed in the decade spanning 1990–2000. These years are noteworthy because they constitute the period of time separating the "Cultural Studies Now and in the Future" conference organized at the University of Illinois at Urbana-Champaign in April 1990 (which led to the 1992 volume edited by Lawrence Grossberg, Cary Nelson, and Paula A. Treichler) from the third international "Crossroads of Cultural Studies" conference "hosted at the legendary point of origin, Birmingham's Centre for Contemporary Cultural Studies, in 2000 [where] the Anglo-American expansion of cultural studies was probably at its peak" (Turner 2012, 1). It is just as clear that—now 15 years into the twenty-first century—further changes continue to unfold, changes affecting the way in which we engage cultural studies, the way in which we grapple with notions of disciplinarity and interdisciplinarity. These shifts permit scholars writing today to avoid unnecessary entanglements with a disciplinary history that is too complex, too broad, and too diverse to be reduced to a meaningful contextualization. Like Turner's volume, this book is not meant to be a comprehensive history of cultural studies, nor is it motivated by the need to engage the "rolling definition of what counts as cultural studies and what does not" (Turner 2012, 1), a need that clearly has become less pressing today and that Turner himself bypasses with good reason. I must acknowledge that there are clearly those who continue to regard cultural studies as a discipline despite its intrinsic attack on disciplinarity (see Turner 2012, 6–8). I insist, however, that while this matter may be itself worthy of exploration by disciplinary historians, it is not my concern here. I must echo Lawrence Grossberg, who suggests in the introduction to his *Cultural Studies in the Future Tense* (2010) that writing an "Introduction to Cultural Studies" is today a project of questionable value (1–3). I personally have no desire—neither here nor elsewhere—to engage cultural studies as a disciplinary formation. This does not mean that I have no interest in disciplinarity—far from it, in fact—only that what piques my interest is a specific and interdisciplinary urban question that has been seldom explored directly in any depth.

I want to acknowledge from the outset that the question of intersections between the humanities and the social sciences has certainly been driving much cultural studies research over the years. In many cases, the urban has figured into these discussions implicitly and, at times, even explicitly. I am aware that there have long been humanities scholars interested in the urban as a theme. In my home field of Hispanic Studies, for example, a conference held on the heels of the publication of Marshall Berman's *All that Is Solid Melts into Air*—in 1983—demonstrates this quite clearly.[13] Similarly, I am quite aware that cultural geographers, in particular, have been engaging humanities approaches more and more—with film being seen as increasingly important both at the curricular level and in published research. The full list of social science books that engage the city from a pointedly cultural perspective is too vast to mention here, of course, but the reader should be aware that significant work has been published in book form in recent decades, for example, by scholars Rob Shields (*Spatial Questions* [2013]) and Ben Highmore (*Cityscapes: Cultural Readings in the Material and Symbolic City* [2005]), who focus on Lefebvre, as well as such highly innovative books as those by Ash Amin and Nigel Thrift (including *Cities: Reimagining the Urban* [2002]), Rodolphe El-Khoury and Edward Robbins (*Shaping the City: Studies in History, Theory and Urban Design* [2003]), and Christoph Lindner (*Globalization, Violence, and the Visual Culture of Cities* [2009]). And despite the implicit and explicit relevance to cultural studies of the urban in these and numerous other works, I continue to assert there is still a disconnect between how humanities scholars engage the urban and how social scientists view cultural products. I say this as someone who has published in peer-reviewed venues from both the humanities and the social sciences. I must also make clear that it is this disciplinary distance that has motivated my creation of the peer-reviewed *Journal of Urban Cultural Studies*, whose first print/online volume (2014: 1.1, 1.2, 1.3) boasts a two-part Lefebvre-inspired inaugural editorial.

I am suggesting that the disciplinary disconnect structuring interdisciplinary work on cities persists even in the growing trend to bring humanities and social sciences work on urban topics together in what some see as the new field of Metropolitan Studies. Such programs at New York University, at University of California, Berkeley, and at the Center for Metropolitan Studies in the Technical University of Berlin, for example,[14] are potentially path-breaking. I am informed that culture in these programs is defined not only in terms of policy, urban design, cultural industries and economies, events, and institutions, but also in artistic terms. These programs may indeed boast a number of courses on music and literature, new media, and film—courses that are undoubtedly inspired by cultural studies methods—but my experience with what happens to the humanities in interdisciplinary contexts (cultural studies among them) has taught me a number of lessons. Chief among these lessons are the following: that a social science appropriation of the humanities is not in itself a triumph, that a mere willingness on the part of social scientists to look at the cultural products that have traditionally been at the core of the humanities is insufficient in itself. It is, rather, *the way in which cultural products are read* that is important. Often, cultural texts are turned into a message, they are reduced to content alone, without a full appreciation of how artistic form and structure in fact influence our understanding of content. Simply put, this is something that has traditionally been the domain of humanities scholars, and not necessarily social scientists.

It is not that social scientists are unable to grapple with aesthetics, but rather that their notion of aesthetics is at times—and I would say that this is particularly true for the vast majority of urban planners and urban geographers on top of the fact that it is still relevant for a range of cultural geographers, anthropologists, and sociologists—quite far from approaching what humanists talk about when they talk about aesthetics. Despite numerous exceptions to this, which may or may not be classified as "urban" in focus, and despite the fact that this reconciliation has been, in principle, a key part of its disciplinary method, in many cases cultural studies has been just as likely as social science fields to ignore *textual* artistic production for a larger-scale view of cultural production. In other words, I have written this book not to explore cultural studies in general, nor to prompt social scientists to engage the notion of culture (they are already doing so), but rather to correct for the fact that a humanities-inspired understanding of culture is absent in much of the interdisciplinary work on urban culture. This corrective is what I am calling urban cultural studies.

The chapters that follow chart out the common ground that can bring social scientists and humanists together in seeking to understand urban culture by focusing on the textual dimensions that so often seem peripheral to the field of urban studies proper. From where I sit, the way in which these "two cultures" of research—to appropriate Snow's term—are brought together in an analysis of the urban phenomenon is very important. When we look at cultural studies in general, there has been a tendency to devalue a possible equilibrium between humanities and social science approaches. Most often, individual scholars line up on one side or the other of the divide, recapitulating—to a certain degree—the schism between Snow and Leavis described above. That is, to mention one striking example, in the preface to Marjorie Ferguson and Peter Golding's *Cultural Studies in Question*, the editors frame their volume as a defense of social science–based cultural studies against the increasing reach of the humanities (1997, x). As a scholar from a humanities PhD program who was trained also in both cultural studies and geographical approaches, I hear in the editors' concerns modified echoes of the passions that flared during the Snow–Leavis controversy. But as an interdisciplinary scholar, I must admit that there is also, indeed, an element of truth in what Ferguson and Golding have to say.

That truth has to do with the power that "disciplinary" formations possess to inhibit the production of border-crossing intellectual work. There is some evidence of this in the humanities, where—on the whole, it is true—scholars may engage social science disciplines hesitantly, reductively, or else not at all, just as there is some evidence of it in the social sciences, where the humanities are viewed with suspicion, reduced to content, or else neglected entirely. These are the risks of any interdisciplinary scholarship as a whole that does not adopt a capacious view on the interconnection between what appear to be isolated and self-enclosed autonomous areas of human life.

What has motivated my writing of *Toward an Urban Cultural Studies* has been the need to carve out a particular kind of space for a humanities–social science collaboration in understanding the urban phenomenon. As the work of urban philosopher, spatial theorist, and cultural studies pioneer Henri Lefebvre is particularly well-suited for this endeavor, this book is simultaneously an exploration of his own particular brand of interdisciplinarity. Lefebvre's thought is relevant to interrogations of culture in the broad sense and to art in general, as is explored in the first section of the book that follows (titled "Theoretical Ground," which includes chapters 1–3), and also to discussions of literature, film, popular music, and digital forms of culture in particular—themes that are developed in this book's second section (titled "Textual Variations," which includes chapters 4–7). Because I feel it may be necessary to do so, I will end this introduction merely by stating unequivocally that this book has been written specifically with humanities scholars in mind, although it is my hope that social scientists will also find it valuable.

On then, toward an urban cultural studies.

PART I

Theoretical Ground

CHAPTER 1

Why Urban Cultural Studies?
Why Henri Lefebvre?

From the outset it is necessary to point out that any definition of "urban cultural studies" is likely to be as polemical as those of its two constituent parts—"cultural studies" and "urban studies." The meanings and significance of these terms themselves have been and continue to be hotly and widely debated within and across a number of increasingly interdisciplinary fields. And yet, taking a moment to sketch out the nature of the debates—even if briefly and in general terms—is necessary if we are to understand the current need for an urban cultural studies method, a method that might bridge both humanities and social science scholarship on the culture(s) of cities. The starting point for *Toward an Urban Cultural Studies* is, thus, to formulate a provisional definition of urban cultural studies. This requires, first, identifying a generalized, but also representative and relevant, thesis of cultural studies method and, second, subsequently applying this thesis to interdisciplinary research on the city in broad terms.

Continuing debates over the nature and relevance of "cultural studies" and "urban studies" involve a similar set of questions, or perhaps better yet a set of relationships. "Cultural studies," as Raymond Williams wrote in 1986 reflecting on its origins, consists of "the refusal to give priority to either the project or the formation—or, in older terms, the art or the society" (2007a, 152). This is to say that

> you cannot understand an intellectual or artistic project without also understanding its formation; that the relation between a project and a formation is always decisive; and that the emphasis of Cultural Studies is precisely that it engages with both, rather than specializing itself to one

> or the other... Project and formation in this sense are different ways of materializing—different ways, then, of describing, what is in fact a common disposition of energy and direction. (Williams 2007a, 151)

From this perspective, to take on a "cultural studies" method is thus to address the *relationship* between a project and its formation, between art and society. Of course, both in the present work and also in Williams's original text, this necessary simplification is intended as a point of entry into what is in reality a more complex set of questions. Put in a way that allows us to generalize this central thesis of cultural studies and apply it to interdisciplinary research on the city, the relationship in question is one between material conditions and cultural imaginaries. There is an understanding within cultural studies method that material conditions influence cultural imaginaries and that cultural imaginaries in turn influence material conditions—an understanding that each influences the other, at the very least, and that each may in fact even *include* the other. For a number of cultural studies theorists, the notion of culture as a process stands as a welcome correction to a legacy of instrumentalist applications of Marxist thought that subordinated culture as a "superstructure" to an economic base that was taken (somewhat short-sightedly) to be purely material.[1]

The case of "urban studies" serves as an interesting (and, perhaps, an inverse) point of comparison as regards the role of culture in urban research. A recent and prominently placed article, titled "What Is 'Urban Studies': Context, Internal Structure and Content," illustrates how culture is being undervalued, if not left out of the study of cities altogether. The authors of that article list the following seven subfields as constituting the "elements of the corpus of knowledge in the field": (1) Urban Sociology, (2) Urban Geography, (3) Urban Economics, (4) Housing and Neighborhood Development, (5) Environmental Studies, (6) Urban Governance, Politics and Administration, and finally (7) Urban Planning, Design, and Architecture (Bowen et al. 2010, 200). In this model of urban studies, culture is relevant only to the degree that it is seen as a concern of Urban Sociology or Urban Geography—and, of course, the possibility exists that it may not, in fact, be very much of a concern at all for some scholars in those fields. It is important to recognize that both disciplines are themselves sharply divided into two subgroups, consisting of those who do quantitative, statistical, "hard" research and those who do more qualitative, human, or "soft" research. Whether within sociology or geography, battle lines have often been drawn such that the quantitative "hard science" work on city infrastructures and built environments, on the one hand, has hardly been able to grapple with qualitative, theoretical, humanist, and even cultural explorations of urban life, on the other. Although there may be a number of urban studies departments or programs where culture is explicitly folded into the curriculum in one way or another, as a whole, this growing and highly interdisciplinary field, nonetheless, remains quite far from realizing a full structural or methodological integration of insights gleaned from cultural studies. In fact, the divisions within and across the disciplines associated with the most inclusive iteration of urban studies do little more than perpetuate the disconnect between the humanities and the sciences evident in the Snow–Leavis controversy (see this book's introduction).[2]

The use of the term "urban cultural studies" thus points to the subtle but meaningful shift of method that comes from resituating cultural studies research within an urban frame. Within this urban frame, what Raymond Williams called the investigation of "culture" and "society" is rendered as the investigation of "urban culture" and "urban society." Urban cultural studies, thus, seeks to explore the relationship between a project and its formation in the context of a necessarily and unavoidably urbanized (and urbanizing) society. Returning to Williams's definition (above), it must be said that "you cannot understand an intellectual or artistic [urban] project without also understanding its [urban] formation; that the relation between [an urban] project and [an urban] formation is always decisive; and that the emphasis of [Urban] Cultural Studies is precisely that it engages with both" (2007a, 151). In addition, there are a number of corollaries that follow from this proposition, each of which will be explored in turn here. For instance, it is important to recognize that urban cultural studies research is not limited to investigating the spaces of cities themselves—in opposition to spaces of the countryside—nor does it treat the built environment of urban locales in isolation from mental formations or matters of (urbanized) consciousness. Moreover, urban cultural studies—in the present formulation—insists on the relevance and value of close readings of cultural texts, whether those are traditionally literary texts, filmic texts, graphic novels, popular music forms (albums, songs, etc.), visual representations of the city (photography, digital media, video games, etc.), or any other concrete form of urban social practice whatsoever.

The approach that results from this proposition and its corollaries clearly underscores the importance of humanities scholarship. As such, it may be seen as an argument for reasserting the value of the humanities in what are perennially troubling economic times. But it is also worth emphasizing that its driving force is of a quite different character. Far from owing its genesis to the need for a timely response to the discourse centered on the perceived waning strength of the humanities, the urgency for formulating an urban cultural studies method has grown organically from existing struggles over the value and directions of interdisciplinary scholarship.[3] In this sense, there may be some who come to see the notion of an urban cultural studies—as it is outlined here—itself as an affront to the humanities, and perhaps even as a call to assimilate the humanities into the social sciences altogether. Make no mistake; those who would take this view end by betraying my intentions.

There are three important corollaries to the urban cultural studies proposition as it has been outlined above. First—as did Williams— urban cultural studies recognizes that the rural and the urban should be held in dialectical tension (Williams, *The Country and the City* [1975]; Lefebvre, *The Urban Revolution* [2003a]). Or as Louis Wirth of the Chicago School of Urban Sociology put it in his essay "Urbanism as a Way of Life" much more plainly (but no less significantly), "The degree to which the contemporary world may be said to be 'urban' is not fully or accurately measured by the proportion of the total population living in cities" (1938, 2).[4] This is to suggest that the progressive urbanization of society has resulted in a sea-change shift that affects individual areas spanning the entire globe—urban or not. Wirth continues:

> The influences which cities exert upon the social life of man are greater than the ratio of the urban population would indicate, for the city is not only in ever larger degrees the dwelling-place and the workshop of modern man, but it is the initiating and controlling center of economic, political, and cultural life that has drawn the most remote parts of the world into its orbit and woven diverse areas, peoples, and activities into a cosmos. (1938, 2)

This observation is necessarily more significant today than when originally written (over 70 years ago) given that we have passed the "tipping point" of urbanization. As of 2007, more than 50 percent of the world's population lives in cities. David Harvey's most recent book, *Rebel Cities* (2012), interestingly reports even that China's rural population has decreased from 74 percent to 50 percent over the period spanning 1990 and 2010, and he rightly emphasizes that "Though there are plenty of residual spaces in the global economy where the process is far from complete, the mass of humanity is thus increasingly being absorbed within the ferments and cross-currents of urbanized life" (2012, xv). In this context, it is quite hard indeed to deny that understanding urbanization and its cultural expressions is a worthwhile endeavor, or, for that matter, to suggest that rural populations somehow persist in the state of isolation or relative autonomy with regard to global urban processes.

Second, whether one gains insight from the canonical essay "The Metropolis and Mental Life" written by Georg Simmel at the turn of the twentieth century (2010; originally published 1903), or Harvey's relatively recent (and more *explicitly* Marxist) text *The Urban Experience* (1989; originally published 1985), the progressive urbanization of society has been accompanied by a corresponding urbanization of consciousness.[5] The material conditions of urbanization have evolved hand in hand with the development of an urbanized cultural imaginary. These two cohabitating aspects of contemporary urban life reveal a dialectical premise at work, one that is moreover, in general terms, embraced by a wide spectrum of urban thinkers. Certain spatial thinkers such as Lefebvrian urban theorist Harvey and Marxist urban philosopher Henri Lefebvre invoke a specifically (and in my view appropriately) Marxian avatar of this dialectical premise. Such thinking is also evident, to some degree, in the work of urban thinkers Lewis Mumford and Sharon Zukin, for example.[6] But Marxian or not, acknowledging this dialectical process remains a hallmark of approaches that attempt to think the city, broadly speaking. As Harvey notes, Robert E. Park— also of the Chicago School—once stated clearly that "indirectly, and without any clear sense of the nature of his task, in making the city man has remade himself" (1967, 3; quoted in Harvey 2012, 4).[7] I find there is no way of explaining the modern activity of urban planning that does not admit the following: that ideas about cities shape city plans, which physically shape cities, which in turn engender ideas about cities, and so on—forming a dialectical urban circuit of sorts. To think otherwise is to accept a very simplistic understanding of the planning process that renders it ideologically neutral. Such an understanding has been critiqued heavily by Richard Sennett (e.g., *The Conscience of the Eye* [1992]; *The Craftsman* [2008]; *Flesh and Stone* [1994]) and, of course, by Henri Lefebvre, as well, as the chapters of this book will explore (see also Fraser 2011a; Lefebvre 2003a, 1996). To think otherwise is also to perpetuate the discourse that privileges urban planning as a specialized activity that purportedly operates independently of wider social contexts, material conditions, and cultural practices.

Third, urban cultural studies seeks to bridge discussions of material conditions and cultural imaginaries in a broader social context. It achieves this both by asserting the importance of an interdisciplinary framework inspired by the potential and promise of urban studies—one that values both theoretical and practical knowledge of the city—and also by maintaining the humanities emphasis on cultural texts. This operation is rendered necessary by the current lackluster state of dialogue crossing the humanities/social science divide. Even in the best of cases, discussions of culture in Urban Sociology or Urban Geography writ large *may* (and, in fact, tend to) fall short of sustaining a rigorous engagement with the humanities.[8] In truth, neither of these two (inter)disciplinary discourses systematically reserves a privileged place for close "textual" readings of cultural products themselves (individual novels, films, albums, graphic novels, visual representations, digital media, etc.).

A brief look at the ambivalence of Harvey's engagement with literary and filmic texts in his own work (or, alternately, the relative lack thereof), for example, will illustrate what is at stake when working across disciplinary boundaries. In the essay "City Future in City Past: Balzac's Cartographic Imagination," for example, Harvey rightly points out that novels "have inspired the imagination, influenced conception of, for example, the city, and thereby affected material processes of urbanization" (2003, 24). And yet, he is not always so culture-savvy. When it came to discussing the cinema in *The Condition of Postmodernity*, he had famously suggested that film is "in the final analysis, a spectacle projected within an enclosed space on a depthless screen" (Harvey 1990, 308), a position that has provoked decades of sustained protests by cinema scholars.[9] He is right, of course, to argue that the "cultural turn has been accompanied by a certain depoliticization of academia in recent times" (Harvey 2003, 23). And yet, precisely what urban cultural studies (and cultural studies, more generally) has accomplished is a repoliticization of cultural inquiry—as Harvey himself admits on the same page, singling out the work by Williams, Stuart Hall, and Fredric Jameson as exemplary.[10]

The lack of an unambiguous, rigorous, and sustained engagement of the humanities areas with which urban theorists should be attempting to dialogue is troubling. This is not merely because it leaves the humanities out of the discussion (this is, after all, a conversation to which we humanists would very much like to be invited), but moreover because the humanities themselves are in fact central to what this discussion is all about. First and foremost, given the dialectical premise through which architects and planners come to form their own understandings of cities—concertedly, through their lengthy, formative education process, if not also necessarily, as routine consumers of cultural texts "on their own time"—it is shortsighted to think that their idea of what a city is (or should be) is not influenced by existing cultural representations of the urban. As Harvey himself has lucidly put it, "the architect is not an isolated monad" (2003, 24). Second, however—and perhaps more importantly—if we ignore the complex, formal properties of cultural products and thus avoid a deeper understanding of how cultural texts are produced, marketed, read, and interpreted, we threaten to reduce "culture" to a two-dimensional status symbol or sign of distinction. The result is that it becomes a mere epiphenomenal or "superstructural" moment divorced from the purportedly fundamental economic "base" of urban society. This reductive (and reified) view of culture is anathema, and moreover it is exactly what scholars have been struggling against for years by way of appealing to the concept of culture as process (e.g., Williams 1977; see this book's introduction, note 1; Lefebvre 2005).

From this urban cultural studies proposition—and the three corollaries outlined above—it can be seen that the present elaboration of an urban cultural studies method responds to a specific moment in interdisciplinary humanities/social science research. It addresses the growing number of scholars working on the culture(s) of cities from a number of disciplinary formations and outlines a way forward for future potential collaborations across these boundaries. The real argument for seeing the value of an urban cultural studies approach is that it is already being practiced, that it already exists—albeit in a diffuse, diasporic sense.[11] Currently, scholars engaging in topics germane to urban cultural studies are spread throughout various existing departmental and disciplinary structures. Such scholars are currently participating in university programs that run the gamut from Language (Chinese, Spanish, French, German, Italian, Japanese, Portuguese, English, etc.) and its ties with national and regional Literature (British, American, Latin American., etc.), to Area Studies (Asian Studies, African Studies, Middle-Eastern Studies, etc.), to Cultural Studies, Film Studies, Women's and Gender Studies, Critical Theory, Visual Studies, Popular Culture, and of course to Urban Studies, Urban Sociology, Urban Geography, Urban Anthropology, Architecture, City Planning, and even other areas such as Transport and Mobility Studies, Music Studies, International/Global Studies, Science Fiction Studies, Deaf Studies, the Digital Humanities, and so forth. The potential reach of an urban cultural studies method has been confirmed by numerous articles and book-length studies in the humanities that have linked cultural texts with urban theory. It has likewise been confirmed by social science publications focusing on the city that have reached out to incorporate, if not interrogate, cultural products from a variety of areas.[12]

As such, from a certain perspective, this book hardly represents a completely novel contribution to existing literature on the subject. Notwithstanding, it is indeed a first of sorts—in that it constitutes an attempt to begin a more overt, conscious scholarly discussion of the opportunities urban studies offers to unite the humanities and social sciences through discussion of the urban problematic. I believe that this in itself is a worthwhile enterprise. Moreover, what makes this book unique is that it attempts to communicate the significance and potential reach of this existing humanities/social science dialogue to a much wider audience than has been done before, and that it undertakes this endeavor through recourse to the oeuvre of one urban thinker in particular.

This book focuses on the work of Henri Lefebvre (1901–1991) with good reason. Lefebvre's engagement with the urban problematic is sustained, multidimensional, both intellectual and radical, interdisciplinary, historical, far-reaching, cultural, eclectic, and at its base philosophical and thus applicable to a variety of more narrowly defined investigations taking place the world over. His work captures some key and enduring insights into the urban phenomenon that range from questions of planning and design to conceptions of knowledge, the importance of movement, mobility, and rhythms, the nature of space and its relationship to temporality, the relationship between capitalism and the city, matters of pedagogy and university structure, the many forms of alienation in contemporary urban society, the question of scale, and even the problematic terrain of everyday life in which the logic of capital is embedded, internalized, negotiated, and perhaps even contested. Most important of all, Lefebvre's body of work—although extensive and seemingly infinitely variable in subject matter—in the end forms a complex but organic whole. At its base is a recalibrated notion of Marxian alienation and a respect for totality that allows the best grasp of the interconnection of all manner of individual problems central to the urban studies agenda.[13]

Choosing Henri Lefebvre—instead of, for example, earlier thinkers such as Georg Simmel, Frederick Engels, or Walter Benjamin (or for that matter Guy Debord, Manuel Castells, David Harvey, Marshall Berman, or Karl Marx, all of whom appear in Merrifield's *Metromarxism* [2002])—allows for multiple perspectives, but it also allows for scholars to "jump right in," to tackle questions central to more contemporary urban realities. That is—to zero in on a time period of crucial relevance—early-twentieth-century iterations of geography are important, but seem a world away from the more nuanced and more recent perspective elaborated by Lefebvre throughout the better part of that century. The great innovation of cultural geographers working at the turn of the nineteenth/twentieth centuries, for example, was to imbue the formerly quantitative study of landscape with a cultural character. When Carl Sauer—one of the founders of contemporary cultural geography—published the essay "The Morphology of Landscape" in 1925, geographers of the time generally accepted that cultural forms were determined by the natural environment. It was in this context that Sauer rightly asserted the notion of landscape as itself a cultural product.[14] We have come a long way since then, of course. Moreover, Lefebvre has fully digested these earlier insights and has created a variegated theory that explicitly confronts a number of specific moments in capitalist urban evolution, from the deployment of postwar capital and urbanism (*Critique of Everyday Life* [1991b, 2002, 2005], *The Urban Revolution* [2003a], among others) to the Irruption of Paris in 1968 (in *The Explosion* [1969] and writings on the Paris Commune of 1871) and back to nineteenth-century urban formations and epistemologies (*The Right to the City* [1996]; *The Production of Space* [1991a]) in the twentieth century. There is no reason to assume that his insights cannot be carried forward through the twenty-first century or even backward toward analyses of life in city environments in early modern contexts or even earlier still.

While concisely introducing a number of his more significant ideas and book projects here should not serve as a substitute for close readings of his texts or for reading the splendid critical studies of his work published in recent years (Elden 2004; Shields 2005; Goonewardena et al. 2008), continuing with such a format has the advantage of managing the expectations of the more general reader. I imagine this reader to be of one of two (or perhaps even three) types—(1) a scholar already doing work on the cultural representations of cities but based in a language, literature, or area studies program where training, publication venues, and evaluation criteria tend to be largely centered on the humanities as traditionally defined, (2) a scholar working on cities within a social science area (such as Sociology, Geography, Anthropology) where even the most qualitative approaches may tend to dialogue insufficiently with humanities scholarship, and perhaps even (3) a junior scholar or younger aspiring professional from any number of disciplines who is attempting to carve out a unique urban research area with which her or his senior colleagues and/or peers may be relatively unfamiliar.

As with my previous book, for those potential readers who may already be somewhat familiar with the work of Henri Lefebvre, I have attempted to explore ideas central to his thought that nonetheless go well beyond *The Production of Space* (1991a; originally published in French in 1974)—the work that has resonated most with Anglophone humanities scholars over the past two-and-a-half decades. My hope is that even readers who are extremely well-versed in Lefebvre's thought may encounter in these pages a fresh take on his texts—although it is nonetheless true that I have not written this book with such readers in mind. Above all else, the ideal implied reader of this book is part of a new generation of interdisciplinary scholars—whether graduate student or established professor working across research specialties—writing about the city from a cultural perspective. I imagine these readers to be as desperate as I have been over the years (with notable exceptions) to find a book that advocates a truly interdisciplinary approach to urban culture. This book's limitations, thus, follow logically from its approach. That is, I have tried to write both an urban studies text for the humanities and a humanities text for urban scholars. This may not be ideal, but I do believe that it is the best way to get an interdisciplinary conversation going.

Toward an Urban Cultural Studies, thus, investigates those questions pertinent to urban studies while continuing to insist upon the importance and relevance of carrying out close readings of cultural texts. It should be pointed out, too, given the vast variety of disciplinary perspectives to which this book appeals, that investing too heavily in performing those close readings themselves here would distract the general reader from the larger issues related to combining humanities and social science research (although the second half of the book makes a concerted attempt to explore the relevance of Lefebvre's thought for engaging in such an endeavor). Lefebvre's works—given their broadly philosophical engagement of questions pertinent to time and space, their relevance to both concrete political struggles and global capital shifts, and also their emphasis on specific questions of a theoretical nature that appear to have found a lasting place in academic discourse (not only the production of space but also scale, mobility, rhythms, everyday life—not to mention alienation, interdisciplinarity, and above all else the *right to the city*)—are an incredibly fertile ground for cultivating an urban cultural studies approach that is widely applicable to a range of perspectives.[15] This does not mean that there can be no other thinkers who are equally or perhaps even more important. It is simply the case that my previous and sustained engagement with Lefebvre's ideas has convinced me that they are much more rich than I even originally imagined. A Lefebvrian urban cultural studies is only one part—an important part to be sure, but one part nonetheless—of a larger move to understanding the culture(s) of cities at the widest of scales.

As a way of bringing readers who may be interested but uninitiated up to speed quickly, the second half of this introduction offer a series of vignettes of Lefebvre's life and work. These nine vignettes are organized around important concepts or events and mix in critical works on Lefebvre with discussions of his own texts. In the end, my goal here has not been to be exhaustive, but rather to produce concise summaries without sacrificing too much depth. There are, in fact, many different Lefebvres, each of which cannot exist without the others. The following Lefebvrian avatars are meant to serve a practical purpose. In effect, they are a vehicle for presenting some of the most enduring aspects of his legacy, and they have been arranged in a particular way so as to emphasize the connection of each with the next: there is Lefebvre, the taxi driver, the intellectual godfather of 1968, the urban revolutionary, the Marxist thinker, the spatial theorist, the philosopher, the critic of everyday life, the cultural critic, and even the pedagogue.

Lefebvre, Taxi Driver

Lefebvre was born in Hagetmau in the Basque Pyrenees in 1901 and later moved to Paris to attend classes at the Sorbonne in the 1920s. Publishing early translations of Marx and Hegel—and texts on Nietzsche, alienation, and dialectical materialism—in the 1930s, and taking part in the resistance in southern France during the Second World War, he defended his doctoral thesis on rural sociology in the early 1950s and soon found himself commuting to the University of Strasbourg as professor of ethics and later sociology (Shields 2011, 279; Stanek 2011, 20). In 1965, he moved to the University of Paris–Nanterre, where he became Director of the Institute of Urban Sociology and soon a noted figure associated with the student uprisings of May 1968. Although generally it is not the first thing mentioned about him, however, it is nevertheless quite significant that at one point Lefebvre (in his own words) "became (of my own free will) a taxi driver. And that was really a laugh! A huge volume could not explain the adventures and misadventures of this existentialist philosopher-taxi driver."[16] David Harvey is right to suggest that Lefebvre's "two years earning a living as a taxi driver in Paris" were surely "an experience which deeply affected his thinking about the nature of space and urban life" (1991, 426). The taxi-cab ride is, of course, a wonderful starting point for beginning to understand many of Lefebvre's hallmark ideas. First and foremost one must recognize the cab driver's evolving negotiation of both mental maps of the city and street maps of its built environment for transportation. Yet beyond this, from the perspective of the mobile taxi, the city itself appears to move, to shift, to flow—an undervalued if somewhat simplistic insight that nevertheless resonates with some of Lefebvre's more complex views on the city. Whether apprehended in action or in contemplation, for the taxi driver–philosopher, "The urban phenomenon is made manifest as movement" (Lefebvre 2003a, 174). This idea, in fact, constitutes one of the basic tenets of his analyses whether it is used to address the ills of city planning, the mobile character of urban knowledge, or even the class struggle.[17]

Lefebvre, Intellectual Godfather of 1968

Lefebvre's book *The Explosion* was written "at the end of May 1968" (1969, 11)—that is, in the wake of the uprisings by students and intellectuals who deigned to imagine another type of society beyond the exploitative class relations of capitalism. Scholar Eduardo Mendieta writes that "Without doubt, there is no philosopher who should be more closely associated with '68 than Lefebvre, especially if we recognize that this historical moment had to do with the explosion of the urban, and a concomitant assault on the colonization of everyday life by the technocratic forces of capitalist commercialization" (2008, 149). Lefebvre saw the Paris Commune of 1871—which had also captured Marx's eye, of course—as being an important touchstone for understanding the events of 1968 (Merrifield 2002, 86–88; also Kofman and Lebas 1996, 18)—and his legacy provides a way of uniting theory and practice as a basis for effecting social change in an urbanized and urbanizing society. Lefebvre was guided, in part, by Marx's dictum that the point is not to interpret the world but to transform it.[18] As Merrifield writes of Lefebvre's viewpoint, "speculative philosophy needed transcending in the name of action and practice...practice meant a humanist naturalism, a social practice, an analysis of pressing social problems, invariably economic problems, which called for practical solutions—invariably, *political* solutions" (original emphasis; 2002, 77). It is the spirit of this political-philosophical reconciliation that undergirds one of his more enduring turns of phrase.[19] Presciently completed in 1967 "to commemorate the centenary of the publication of Marx's *Capital*" (Kofman and Lebas 1996, 6; also Lefebvre 1996, 181), Lefebvre's earlier book

The Right to the City had emphasized that "the *right to the city* is like a cry and a demand" (1996, 158; also Purcell 2002; Attoh 2011).[20] In the end, we do well in recognizing the contemporary, twenty-first-century resonance of Lefebvre, as does Mendieta, who in effect anticipates the relevance of the French philosopher's work to future events such as the Arab Spring, the Indignado movement, and its Occupy Wall Street corollaries when he writes that: "The question of the urban, the project of the demand of the right to the city has become as urgent, if not more, than when Lefebvre proclaimed it in 1968" (Mendieta 2008, 151).

Lefebvre, Urban Revolutionary

Lefebvre established an important distinction between the "city" and the "urban" that is of primary importance for his urban theorizations.[21] Another way of phrasing this distinction is to emphasize, as he himself did, the distance between the "planned city" and the "practiced city": whereas the "planned city" was the static, geometrical, rational city as designed by urban planners from above, the "practiced city" was the dynamic city understood as a lived space, an inhabitable city.[22] In both *The Right to the City* and *The Urban Revolution*, Lefebvre takes pains to reconcile the modern bourgeois practice of city design with Marx's work on the commodity as outlined in *Capital* (Marx 1977; Lefebvre 1996; Lefebvre 2003a). As practiced by Baron Haussmann in Paris and by Ildefons Cerdà in Barcelona, both during the second half of the nineteenth century, the city was increasingly planned in the interests of and produced in the image of capital (Fraser 2011a, 2011b). Whole city blocks were demolished and reconstructed according to the logic of capitalist circulation as the city was envisioned first and foremost as a built environment for transportation.[23] As Lefebvre points out, this conceptualization of the city was predicated on a certain bourgeois formulation of knowledge itself—knowledge understood as a fragmented, spatialized set of facts that could be decomposed and recomposed, rearranged and reorganized at the whim of the bourgeois thinker or urban designer as so many objects in space (1996, 94–99; 2003a, 49).[24] Lefebvre frames the nineteenth century in particular as that time when the notion of cityspace as an exchange-value begins to trump the city as a use-value. In that context, bourgeois planners ultimately failed to create "an urban reality for 'users'" and instead produced the city as a site for exploitation by "capitalist speculators, builders and technicians" (Lefebvre 1996, 168). As this practice proliferates throughout the nineteenth and twentieth centuries, writes Lefebvre, urbanites become increasingly alienated from their urban environments and from their fellow city-dwellers, an observation that extends Marx's earlier thoughts on alienation to an urban milieu (Shields 2005). This situation necessitated, in his view, that the city be reclaimed as a use-value, from whence his idea of urban revolution.[25] Opposed to the practico-material fact of the city, Lefebvre thus asserted the notion of the urban as a site of encounter and thus simultaneously a nexus for struggle.[26] When examined in light of his engagement with a nondoctrinal Marxism, the urban phenomenon was also, for Lefebvre, a realm of possibility and a potential terrain for enacting social change.[27]

Lefebvre, Marxist Thinker

In light of Lefebvre's self-application of the moniker "Marxist philosopher" (Elden 2001, 2004, 2006b), the reader may rightly want to know more about the way in which Marx's writings inform his urban theory and spatial perspective.[28] Of course, to respond appropriately to such an insightful inquiry would itself require an entire volume.[29] (Note that Lefebvre himself wrote more than one book dedicated to the subject.[30]) At its root, however, Lefebvre's understanding can be characterized as a "humanist Marxism" (Merrifield 2006, xxi) just as an "open Marxism" (Charnock 2010, 1279, 1298n1), one that recognizes Marx's thought as both indispensable and nonetheless incomplete.[31] In the 1988 essay "Toward a Leftist Cultural Politics: Remarks Occasioned by the Centenary of Marx's Death," Lefebvre himself attempted a concise definition of "What is Marxism?"—running quickly through very general but divisive questions surrounding Marx's work and finally offering that "In order to understand the modern world, it is necessary not only to retain some of Marx's essential concepts, but also to add new ones" (1988, 77).[32] For Lefebvre,

> Marxism is an instrument of research and discovery; it is valid only if one makes use of it. Marx's thinking cannot be conceived as a "pure" object of knowledge; it is not an object of epistemological reflection, even less a gadget that one deconstructs and reconstructs in a kind of intellectual game. It becomes useful in understanding what has come to pass in the modern world if one tries to orient and transforms it...it is not a system or a dogma but a reference. (1988, 77)

Despite this seemingly fluid conception of Marxian thought, Lefebvre takes from his predecessor the notions of class struggle and the commodity but also political economy, mode of production, and the need to engage in (in order to go beyond) philosophy.[33] He also expands greatly on Marx's emphasis on the concept of alienation, an interest that is pervasive in the *Critique of Everyday Life* volumes (1991b, 2002, 2005) but that can be traced back to Lefebvre's 1936 volume *La conscience mystifée/Mystified Consciousness* (co-written with Norbert Guterman). Equally important, looking backward, is that Lefebvre contributes to the development of new concepts that Marx did not anticipate, such as "the everyday, the urban, social time and space" (Lefebvre 1988, 77)—concepts that are sorely needed to understand postwar urbanization in particular.

Lefebvre, Spatial Theorist

Lefebvre's recalibration of Marxism certainly has many dimensions, but it is widely accepted that above all else he sought to imbue it with an awareness of the importance of space (e.g., Soja 1980, 208; Merrifield 2002, 89; Merrifield 2006, Chapter 6; Elden 2007, 107; Harvey 2009a, 307). Lefebvre believed that "Marxism was...incomplete and uncompletable" (Burkhard 2000, 207) but nonetheless saw room for improvement regarding the spatial question specifically. Thus, one of his oft-repeated and key insights is that capitalism has survived throughout the twentieth century "*by occupying space, by producing a space*" (original emphasis; Lefebvre 1976, 21).[34] In response to this significant shift, Lefebvre elaborates a multidimensional theory and dialectical understanding of space, one that nevertheless elaborates upon the land–labor–capital trinity so central to Marxism (1976, 2006a).[35] Space for Lefebvre is conceived, perceived, and, most significant of all, actually *lived*—and he takes pains to underscore that "spatial practice is lived before it is conceptualized (1991a, 34). Furthermore, he fashions a spatial triad in which representations of space, representational spaces, and spatial practices each interact with the others. Thus, there are

1. *Spatial practice*, which embraces production and reproduction, and the particular locations and spatial sets characteristic of each social formation. Spatial practice ensures continuity and some degree of cohesion. In terms of social space, and of each member of a given society's relationship to that space, this cohesion implies a guaranteed level of *competence* and a specific level of *performance*.

2. *Representations of space*, which are tied to the relations of production and to the "order" which those relations impose, and hence to knowledge, to signs, to codes, and to "frontal" relations.
3. *Representational spaces*, embodying complex symbolisms, sometimes coded, sometimes not linked to the clandestine or underground side of social life, as also to art (which may come eventually to be defined less as a code of space than as a code of representational spaces) (Lefebvre 1991a, 33; also Harvey 1990, 218–219).[36]

From this perspective, space is no longer a mere static container or two-dimensional plane but rather a nuanced, dynamic social relation—and of course also a political battleground in which capital is deployed, accumulated, and resisted (Lefebvre 1991a, 190; 2003a, 40; Harvey 1996, 2005, 2006c; Fraser 2011a, 9–14; see also Soja 1980, 208).

Lefebvre, Philosopher

Undergirding Lefebvre's spatial recalibration of Marxism, of course, there is an extensive philosophical legacy.[37] This legacy is, in part, itself a Marxian one—in the sense that it reactualizes the philosophical thought of the early, Hegelian Marx. Like the early Marx, Lefebvre believes that philosophy is an ideology of sorts, obscuring if not concealing questions of social relations and power (Lefebvre 1976, 12). But—also like Marx—he emphasizes that philosophy cannot merely be vitiated outright, but rather that it must be engaged and shaped into a critique that goes beyond philosophy, that folds philosophy back into the material conditions of contemporary life and politics.[38] As Lefebvre writes in *The Urban Revolution*, "The philosopher and philosophy can do nothing by themselves, but what can we do without them? Shouldn't we make use of the entire realm of philosophy, along with scientific understanding, in our approach to the urban phenomenon?" (2003a, 64; also 1991a, 14).[39] Just as many have ignored the philosophical Marx, many have ignored the philosophical Lefebvre.[40] We do well in remembering that Henri Lefebvre's early years in 1920s Paris were spent among the group of "Philosophies" comprising not only Lefebvre but Georges Politzer, Norbert Guterman, Georges Friedmann, Pierre Morhange, and Paul Nizan (Burkhard 2000, 13–16; also Merrifield 2002, 72).[41] His identification as an "existentialist philosopher" (Shields 2011, 279) certainly relates to his experiences during those early years, but—as existing Lefebvrian criticism has shown—there is much to be gained from reading Lefebvre's work in tandem with such philosophical thinkers as Hegel, Nietzsche, Heidegger,

Descartes, and even—for that matter—Bergson.[42] The case of Bergson is a bit more complicated than these others—given that Lefebvre "hated Bergson's guts" (Merrifield 2006, 27)—with the Philosophies, most of all Politzer (see Burkhard 2000, 82–84), focusing much of their energy on attacking the philosophy of the 1927 Nobel Prize winner (curiously, Bergson won the prize for Literature). But Lefebvre's mobilization of a number of Bergsonian ideas—if not also in fact Bergson's philosophical method itself—makes this connection a fruitful area for appreciating the unavoidable philosophical dimensions of Lefebvre's work. While Bergson was certainly not a political philosopher, Lefebvre and others seemed to be comfortable accepting popular misunderstandings of his work that were pervasive at the time (see Fraser 2006b, 2008a, 2010). To give just one example here: Lefebvre's mistaken view that Bergson separated time from space (as expressed directly in Lefebvre 1976, 34; also Lefebvre 1991a) may have prohibited him from realizing that his own nuanced understanding of time derived, in essence, from Bergson's equally subtle position on temporality—with the only meaningful difference (albeit an important one) being that the complex relationship Bergson attributed to space and time was now explicitly reconciled by Lefebvre with capitalist social relations.[43]

Lefebvre, Critic of Everyday Life

The philosophical insights Lefebvre applied to the urban phenomenon (which itself should not be distinguished meaningfully from the rural sociology of Lefebvre's earlier years) resulted in a far-reaching critique of what he called everyday life—elaborated across three volumes spanning five decades (1991b, 2002, 2005) and perhaps also even a fourth volume (2006; published posthumously in 1992).[44] This critique followed somewhat logically from his early engagement—with friend and collaborator Norbert Guterman—of the Marxian concept of alienation. Scholar Rob Shields has explained Lefebvre's twist on Marx's original premise in this way:

> Marx had identified three forms of alienation. People could be alienated from their work and activities: they might be alienated from each other through excessive competitiveness, for example; and they might be alienated from their own essence, their "species being" or humanness, which meant that they misunderstood what it was that made them human...Lefebvre located these all-pervasive forms of alienation not just in the workplace but in every aspect of life. Estranged from our

activities, ourselves, and from each other, we still barely experience our lives, moving in a daze from obligation to obligation, programmed activity to programmed activity. (2005, 40)

In the first volume of the *Critique*, Lefebvre elaborated on this concept's multiple dimensions: alienation was at once economic, social, political, ideological, and philosophical (1991b, 249). Furthermore, these alienations were brought together under the banner of urbanization: "Urban alienation contains and perpetuates all other forms of alienation" (Lefebvre 2003a, 92). Inhabitants of both rural and urban areas affected by processes of capitalist urbanization were subjected to new alienations—from their environment, from their own cities, and in the postwar, particularly, from each other via "the sum total of consumer activities" (Lefebvre 2005, 2). As Shields points out, "The environment is commodified (air that is air-conditioned, water that must be purified, sun that must be filtered) and can be consumed (through purchase of the right technology, living in a favorable district of one's city or tourism)" (2005, 169; see also Harvey 1996, 298). Lefebvre (2002) invoked the phrase "the colonization of daily life" (as had Situationist Guy Debord 1961, 1995) to refer to the strategy of capital accumulation that came to characterize the postwar years: "capitalist leaders treat daily life as they once treated the colonized territories: massive trading posts (supermarkets and shopping centers); absolute predominance of exchange over use; dual exploitation of the dominated in their capacity as producers and consumers" (Lefebvre 2005, 26). This situation nonetheless meant that capitalism could be not merely critiqued in everyday life, but also resisted there as well.[45] Daily life can thus be conceived as both "an encounter and a confrontation between use (use-value) and exchange (exchange-value)" (Lefebvre 2005, 12). This insight has proved to be of crucial importance for cultural studies method and, right or wrong, has earned Lefebvre the title of "cultural studies pioneer."[46]

Lefebvre, Cultural Critic

Henri Lefebvre did not just contribute to the development of cultural studies method; he was also an astute cultural critic in his own right.[47] Nevertheless, a 2006 study points out, "Despite Lefebvre's involvement with questions of aesthetics, no significant scholarly attention has been given to his cultural theory within the history of Marxist art criticism or elsewhere" (Léger 2006, 144). One of the factors that has slowed acknowledgment of his interest in aesthetic questions has been his turbulent relationship with the French Communist Party (*Parti Communiste Français*—PCF)—which he sustained from 1928 to 1958. A popular line is that Lefebvre's interest in aesthetic matters came only as a result of party conflict, which may be true, in part. That is, in order to avoid censure (or because he was in fact being censured), he turned to writing on less overtly political topics: "it is worth noting that Lefebvre was also the official intellectual of the PCF at this time, mobilized in 1946 to critique existentialism's challenge to Marxism, and here playing a central role in a broader project of appropriating classical authors, that is, French cultural capital [books on Diderot or Rabelais, for example], for Marxist purposes" (Elden and Lebas 2003, xiii; see also Léger 2006, 145, who cites Poster 1975; Kelly 1982). But it is also true that he had been moving in literary and artistic circles for many years prior to joining the party, for example, as part of the Philosophies group, whose "collective written products" included "poetry, sociology and political economics, philosophy, history, novels, literary criticism and psychology" (Burkhard 2000, 28). One of Lefebvre's earliest articles written in the Philosophies period was on Dada—an article that in the end began a friendship with Tristan Tzara (Harvey 1991, 426; Burkhard 2000, 43). It is well documented that in the 1920s Lefebvre drank "wine and coffee with leading Dadaists and surrealists (like Tristan Tzara and André Breton)" (Merrifield 2002, 72; Elden and Lebas 2003, xvi). Somewhat less notably, for example, Lefebvre also wrote about Romanticism (Barth 2000, 24), published a defense of Proust's *Researche dus temps perdu* (Burkhard 2000, 39), and wrote a letter in support of Spanish novelist, poet, and philosopher Unamuno, who had been exiled under dictator Primo de Rivera (Burkhard 2000, 36–37; also 141–142). But this interest in aesthetic questions and things literary—sparked by life in 1920s Paris, developed as part of his experiences in the PCF—persisted well after his break with the party and can be seen in decisions both great and seemingly trivial. Lefebvre later worked in "collaboration" with the Situationists (Shields 2011, 280; also Kofman and Lebas 1996, 11–12; Ross 2004; Kitchens 2009), employed author Georges Perec to do fieldwork in 1960 and 1961 (Kofman and Lebas 1996, 15), and continued to write on aesthetic questions—most notably producing the book *La présence et l'absence* (1980). Lefebvre's interest in matters of art must not be forgotten if we are to forge an urban cultural studies method that dialogues with his work. In fact, "Lefebvre's concern with aesthetics is thus embedded within a broad conception of Marxism which does not conceive of art as an epiphenomenal concern; aesthetics is not separate from revolutionary politics" (Léger 2006, 143).[48]

Lefebvre, Pedagogue

Approached in light of work by critical pedagogues—such as Paolo Freire (1970, 1998) and bell hooks (1994), who have emphasized the importance, capitalist cooptation, and potential power of education (Fraser 2009a)[49]—Lefebvre's writings offer many similar lessons, suggesting the need for a more critical and more nuanced perspective on teaching and learning. His thorough critique of knowledge—particularly the nineteenth-century bourgeois foundations of modern scientific knowledge as discussed in *The Urban Revolution* (Lefebvre 2003a)—alone provides a basis for rethinking university education. Although this critique has been discussed elsewhere (e.g., Fraser 2011a, 19–23), it is worth noting that for Lefebvre the model of scientific knowledge of the world that becomes dominant in the nineteenth century (structured through compartmentalization and promoting the discourse of specialization) functions as an ideology. This is so because it tends to fragment each specialized area of knowledge off from the others, thus making impossible an apprehension of society's functioning as a whole—in sum, obfuscating the Marxian notion of totality. While much of this critique of knowledge is theoretical, Lefebvre mobilizes it to discuss, specifically, the limitations of disciplinary structures when taking on the urban phenomenon.[50] Lefebvre asks: "The problem remains: How can we make the transition from fragmentary knowledge to complete understanding? How can we define this need for *totality?*" (original emphasis; 2003a, 56). The answer, argues Lefebvre, is *not* to be found in simply grouping together objects of disciplinary (specialized) knowledge.

> Nor is it reasonable to assume that our understanding of the urban phenomenon, or urban space, could consist in a collection of objects—economy, sociology, history, demography, psychology, or earth sciences, such as geology. The concept of a scientific object, although convenient and easy, is deliberately simplistic and may conceal another intention: a strategy of fragmentation designed to promote a unitary and synthetic, and therefore authoritarian, model. An object is isolating, even if conceived as a system of relations and even if those relations are connected to other systems... The concept of the city no longer corresponds to a social object. (2003a, 57)

This perspective has implications certainly for the structure of urban studies programs and perhaps also for the structure of the university, more broadly speaking.[51]

But Lefebvre also makes reference to educational practices on a much smaller scale. Echoing what had been said by Freire, and anticipating what would be said by hooks, he emphasizes the classroom as a micro-cosm of capitalist society: "Pedagogical space is repressive. But the significance of this 'structure' goes beyond a merely local oppres-sion. Imposed knowledge, ingurgitated by the pupils and regurgitated in exams, corresponds to the division of labour in bourgeois society, and therefore sustains it" (Lefebvre 1976, 52).[52] In addition to serv-ing as a corpus of theoretical, philosophical, and geographical knowl-edge, Lefebvre's writings specifically advocate for an interdisciplinary reconciliation of technical knowledge (the applied sciences) and the humanities (philosophy, literary criticism).[53] Moreover, it is the urban phenomenon that offers the potential to overcome the fragmented view of knowledge that pervades contemporary life.

Ultimately, what an urban cultural studies method can take from Lefebvre is not merely a healthy respect for interdisciplinary research, in general, but also the need to recognize the complex nature of social problems, to philosophize and yet go beyond philosophy, to acknowl-edge the cohabitation of matters of both aesthetic and social importance, the significance of space for understanding the dynamics of capital, the primary importance of having an urban perspective, and even the need to reflect critically (politically) on our pedagogical practices and goals. The chapters that follow seek to reshape critiques culled from Lefebvre's numerous books into a format that might benefit urban cultural stud-ies scholars, aiding in the start of what may potentially be an ongoing interdisciplinary conversation.

Chapter 2, "Urban Alienation and Cultural Studies: Henri Lefebvre's Recalibrated Marxism," while it covers some of the same ground intro-duced above, does so via a more sustained dialogue with a greater num-ber of Lefebvre's texts—and with a different goal. The repetition there of certain ideas, concepts, and even quotations discussed up through this point is minimal, but also advantageous for those with little previous experience with the French philosopher's thought. More important, such minimal repetition is also, in fact, necessary—perhaps unavoidable if we are to see how each of these ideas and concepts is related to a pervasive focus on alienation. The notion of alienation is a significant focus that subtends many (if not all) of Lefebvre's critiques and that, ultimately, points toward the primacy of an "urban alienation." As such, the notion of urban alienation, in turn, becomes the basis for all other investiga-tions of the urban phenomenon, and more specifically of any and all attempts to approach urban culture in an interdisciplinary fashion.

Chapter 3, "The Work (of Art): 'Putting Art in the Service of the Urban'" turns mostly to Lefebvre's later book *La présence et l'absence*

(1980) in order to recuperate the aesthetic theorizations he describes as a theory of "the work." For Lefebvre, "the work" is a term that ultimately refers not only to the "work of art" but also to the "art of living," and of course the notion of the "city as a work of art" as well as the potential for a future urban practice that is unfettered by capitalist exploitation. Although the implicit ground for this discussion is Marx's own "ideal of a non-alienated 'artistic' form of production," which stems from his 1844 *Manuscripts* (Rose 1984, 79), here the work of art and its interpretation are approached in philosophical, methodological, and even historical terms, the latter through recourse to Raymond Williams's *Marxism and Literature* (1977). Williams's treatment of the ills of literary and aesthetic theory in effect allows us to see how Lefebvre's views on art and on disciplinary alienation can be applied to humanities study, in particular.

The next four chapters subsequently bring Lefebvre's general insights and specific reflections to bear on the novel, the film, the music album, and the notion of digital spaces. "The Urban Dominant: Everyday Life and the City in Textual Criticism" (chapter 4) paves the way for the next two chapters by using Lefebvre's own remarks on the novel to assert literary production as a site equivalent to the everyday and thus to argue for a Lefebvrian approach to specific genres of cultural texts. In particular, this Lefebvrian perspective foregrounds the inadequacy of many geographical invocations of literature (namely those of David Harvey) and returns to the notion of the "dominant"—as elaborated by Russian Formalist Roman Jakobson in particular—as a method for returning the individual text to the extraliterary urban world.

"The Iconic-Indexical City: Visions of Place in Urban Films" (chapter 5) suggests a complementary method for launching urban readings of filmic texts by melding the margins of film theory with Lefebvre's basic premise. In particular, this chapter goes beyond the arbitrary/conventional notion of the sign canonized by Saussurean linguistics more generally (and incorporated since the 1970s into much mainstream film theory) to explore the variety of signifying processes harnessed by the cinema. As such, it highlights the notion of iconicity (and indexicality) as a way of reconciling filmspace with cityspace. The final section of chapter 5 puts these insights to the test implicitly in a brief urban reading of the recent film *Biutiful* (2010) by director Alejandro González Iñárritu and starring Javier Bardem.

Chapter 6, "Listening to Urban Rhythms: Soundscapes in Popular Music," strikes a more theoretical note in textual interpretation but maintains the volume's characteristic dual emphasis on both textual criticism and the importance of the urban problematic. Here, it is Lefebvre's notion of rhythmanalysis that provides a point of departure for discussing the recent directions in interdisciplinary popular music studies that point to the materiality of sound and the imbrication of the musical text in an extratextual (but not unliterary) world. These insights are then briefly applied to a close reading of an urban-themed album by Basque band Lisabö as evidence for how urban cultural studies might retain an emphasis on urbanized consciousness even where analysis of sonorous texts cannot rely on musical representations of specific cities.

Chapter 7, "Representing Digital Spaces: Videogames, Geo-Humanities, and the Digital Humanities," brings the book to a close by taking on two relatively new interdisciplinary subfields—videogame studies and the digital humanities—specifically. Each of these is contextualized within a Lefebvrian, urban framework, and subsequent discussion raises the specter of the skepticism of technological advance voiced by F. R. Leavis. The end result is to return to the questions of university education and interdisciplinary scholarship highlighted in the introduction to this book that proved so compelling, also, for Henri Lefebvre himself.

In this way, *Toward an Urban Cultural Studies* underscores the relevance of Lefebvre's insights both generally and as they relate to specific genres of humanities texts—the novel, the film, the music album, the videogame, and potentially more (the graphic novel, collaborative developments in the digital humanities such as the relatively recent Hypercities project, etc.). At its base, this book argues for the opportunity offered by cultural texts to reconcile artistic questions with urban issues. In so doing, it actualizes an interdisciplinary connection that is the hallmark of Henri Lefebvre's career-long urban theorizations.

CHAPTER 2

Urban Alienation and Cultural Studies: Henri Lefebvre's Recalibrated Marxism

Following on the heels of a resurgence of interest in the work of self-proclaimed Marxist Henri Lefebvre (1901–1991) that has crossed disciplinary boundaries—passing from geography to the humanities—this chapter asserts the importance of the French scholar's recalibration of the notion of alienation for an urban cultural studies method. Tracing Lefebvre's multivalent development of alienation as at once economic, political, social, philosophical (Lefebvre 1991b, 2002, 2005, 2006a)—and, above all else, urban (Lefebvre 2003a)—the case is made for the centrality of the concept in urban cultural studies approaches that fuse urban theory with close readings of both traditional and nontraditional cultural products (literature, film, music, comics, videogames, etc.). This move builds on previous work on Lefebvre—dialoguing also with work by cultural studies pioneer Raymond Williams—in order to trace the French scholar's development of the original Marxian concept. In particular, it seeks to highlight what is at stake in discussions of a distinctly urban notion of alienation—reconciling that notion with the study of cultural production under capitalism—and ultimately to outline an urban cultural studies method in basic terms.

Any explicit attempt to reconcile Lefebvre–the "self-proclaimed Marxist" (Elden 2001, 809) with Lefebvre–the "cultural studies pioneer" (Goonewardena 2008, 6) must grapple with the primacy he affords the urban experience. Although Lefebvre's work was extensive and his subject matter quite varied,[1] this chapter prioritizes the French urban theorist's (reformulated, Marxist) concept of urban alienation, specifically, as an essential component of the themes of his *oeuvre* as a whole.[2] The result is an underappreciated take on Lefebvrian thought that, importantly, may be more consciously adapted to cultural studies analysis and ultimately to the outline of an urban cultural studies method.

The contributions by various scholars to the volume *Space, Difference, Everyday Life: Reading Henri Lefebvre* (2008, edited by Kanishka Goonewardena et al.) testify to the fact that interest in the prolific scholar's work is far from being in decline.[3] And yet, it is only recently that scholars have sought to bridge two divergent popular conceptions of Lefebvre—to wit: there has been a tendency to view the theorist "through the often mutually exclusive lenses of urban political economy and postmodern cultural studies" (Goonewardena et al. 2008, 6; see also Kipfer 2008, xxx). Particularly in Anglo-American scholarship—as Stuart Elden notes—the political and philosophical aspects of Lefebvre's work have been underrepresented (2004, 6). What has been the most recognized part of Lefebvre's legacy—and this is particularly so within humanities contexts—is his move to underscore the complexity of space. In this sense, he is most well known among scholars in literature departments as the author of *The Production of Space*, where he puts forth an oft-cited triadic model of space as conceived, perceived, and lived—a "spatial triad" that charts the entanglement of "spatial practice, representations of space and representational spaces" (Lefebvre 1991a, 33).[4] This model is invoked explicitly by Lefebvrian urban geographer David Harvey in *The Condition of Postmodernity* (1990, 218–219), and urban theorists such as Harvey, Edward Soja, and (in the Spanish context) Manuel Delgado Ruiz have been largely indebted to Lefebvrian method and his interrogations of the urban experience.[5] Nevertheless, the view of Lefebvre as a "spatial theorist"—while accurate in many respects— is also somewhat incomplete: as Lefebvrian scholars have emphasized, he was deeply concerned with the relationship between both space and time, particularly as it concerned the proliferation of capitalism.[6]

Here, rather than engage Lefebvre's reputation as a "spatial theorist" at length—and rather than risk a more comprehensive accounting of the philosophical significance of the urban philosopher's thought as a whole—I want to return to the Lefebvrian notion of "urban alienation" as a way of connecting Lefebvre-as-Marxist with Lefebvre-as-cultural studies pioneer. This chapter, thus, consists of four interdependent sections. The first section ("Lefebvre's Urban Appropriation of Marxian Alienation") returns concisely to Lefebvre's own reformulation of Marxian thought and to the role played by alienation in the development of his far-reaching urban theory. This serves as a brief reminder of the political and philosophical dimensions of Lefebvrian thought and simultaneously as a push for humanities scholars to go beyond the restrictive notion of Lefebvre as merely a spatial theorist in the simple sense. Alienation in fact forms an integral part of Lefebvre's numerous critiques of space, urbanism, everyday life, knowledge, and method and stems from the Marxian notion of the commodity. The second section ("Alienation and Urban Cultural Production") emphasizes this Marxian inheritance with an eye toward its appropriation by cultural studies scholars, specifically. The Lefebvrian concept of alienation is essential if we are to reconcile cultural products with each other, with the urbanized society in which they are produced and consumed and, moreover, if we are to formulate an urban cultural studies method.

If the second section points to the relative lack of attention routinely paid to matters of culture and to urbanization in Marxist analyses, the third section ("Mumford Versus Zukin: *The Culture(s) of Cities*") returns to two classic and relevant books (with similar titles) in order to continue the discussion of how a Lefebvrian (Marxian) perspective on the relationship of culture to the city can potentially counteract the urban alienation Lefebvre takes as primary. Reading Lewis Mumford's *The Culture of Cities* (1938) against Sharon Zukin's *The Cultures of Cities* (1995) with Lefebvre's key critiques in mind, one gains an appreciation of how traditional analyses of cities have tended to legitimize the basic (pernicious) assumptions of bourgeois planning culture—reifying the city in the process. The fourth section ("Toward a Lefebvrian Urban Cultural Studies") builds on this discussion to suggest an agenda for how Lefebvrian thought might be merged more fortuitously with the close study of cultural products themselves. Harnessing also the succinct definition of cultural studies offered by Lefebvre's contemporary, Raymond Williams (2007a, 151–152), the case is made that the task of the cultural critic is to persistently disalienate readers from the hidden relations of cultural production, relations that also alienate consumer and critic alike from the interconnected urbanized and urbanizing world which we live. In the end, urban cultural studies becomes an important arm in the attack on capitalist reification—which is, in the Lefebvrian framework, decidedly both material and mental.[7]

Lefebvre's Urban Appropriation of Marxist Alienation

It is still an underappreciated fact that Henri Lefebvre persistently engaged with Marxian thought throughout his entire century-spanning oeuvre (as reflected even in the titles of some of his works—*Le marxisme, Le matérialisme dialectique, Sociologie de Marx*, etc.). His perspective was that while many of Marx's insights remained indispensable, in the main, Marxian thought needed to be reformulated in order to become more closely attuned to the spatial character of contemporary capitalism and to the pernicious "colonization of everyday life" that was so essential to understanding postwar urban society.[8] The essence of this rereading of Marx—which Lefebvre himself described as a "new reading" (e.g., Lefebvre 1982, 3; also Elden 2004, 15), or alternately as an attempt to approach Marx "in a new light" (Lefebvre 1982, x)— was concisely encapsulated in a question he posed in *The Survival of Capitalism*. Lefebvre asked: "Should Marx's thought be accepted today *en bloc*? Or should it be globally rejected?"—his answer was simply "Neither" (1976, 10).[9]

One of the Marxian concepts that continued to capture Lefebvre's attention was that of alienation. In the process of re-theorizing Marxian alienation, Lefebvre nonetheless sought to update it for the twentieth-century urban realities lived by his readers. In this sense, his reconfiguration of alienation ultimately reflected his wider appropriation of Marx's thought, more generally speaking. The Lefebvrian project (subsequently continued in the work of Harvey, Manuel Delgado Ruiz, and others) strives to bring Marxian method to bear on something that the nineteenth-century thinker had not considered in depth—the uneven, spatial character of capitalism. Stuart Elden sustains that an interest in the notion of alienation was central throughout Marx's career,[10] and Rob Shields makes it possible to see this life-long pattern also in the thought of the French critic: "what unites all of [Lefebvre's] work—from his first to his most mature works—is his deeply humanistic interest in alienation" (2005, 2). This situation—Lefebvre's sustained engagement of the concept itself and of Marxian thought in general—is perhaps difficult to explore so concisely, but brevity is necessary as our present goal is somewhat distinct.

There are two aspects of Lefebvre's reappropriation of Marx's alienation that are of particular interest to the formulation of an urban cultural studies method. The first is—as Shields highlights as well—the way in which Lefebvre broadened the understanding of alienation, or at least how he explored dimensions of alienation that Marx had left as only potentialities. The second is Lefebvre's ultimate subordination of these forms of alienation to the urban problematic—something evidenced most clearly in *The Urban Revolution* where he notes that "Urban alienation contains and perpetuates all other forms of alienation" (2003a,

92). First and foremost, Lefebvre clearly saw his work as a recalibration of a Marxian critique of alienation. As he made clear in the first volume of *Critique of Everyday Life*—originally published in French in 1947—alienation is experienced, encountered, accepted, ignored, and negotiated all in the realm of everyday life (Lefebvre 1991b). Therein, he emphasized the multiple manifestations of alienation, noting that it is at once economic, social, political, ideological, and philosophical:

> Alienation has stripped life of everything which blessed its primitive frailty with joy and wisdom. Science and power have been acquired, but at the cost of many sacrifices (so much so that the very idea of human sacrifice was an "essential stage in man's progress"!). The human, stripped bare and projected outside of itself, was and remains at the mercy of forces which in fact come from the human and are nothing but human—but torn apart and dehumanized. This alienation was *economic* (the division of labour; "private" property; the formation of economic fetishes: money, commodities, capital); *social* (the formation of classes); *political* (the formation of the State); *ideological* (religions, metaphysics, moral doctrines). It was also *philosophical*: primitive man, simple, living on the same level as nature, became divided up into subject and object, form and content, nature and power, reality and possibility, truth and illusion, community and individuality, body and consciousness ("soul," "mind")...But man has developed only through alienation: the history of truth cannot be separated from the history of errors. (Lefebvre 1991b, 249)

The concept of alienation evokes, for Lefebvre, a dualistic splitting of experience that governs a person's external relationships (relationships with others, with his environment) but also an internal relationship—the relationship with himself or herself: "Alienation is defined not only as man's losing himself in the external material world or in formless subjectivity; it is also, and above all, defined as a split between the objectifying and the subjectifying processes in the individual, so that the unity between them is destroyed" (Lefebvre 1982, 10). Reading the lengthy quotation above (from *Critique of Everyday Life*, vol. 1 [1991b, 249]) together with the description following it (from *The Sociology of Marx* [1982, 10]), alienation is not so much *a single concept* as it is *a set of concepts*—or perhaps a multivalent and multifaceted force, an adaptive/adapting condition of capitalist modernity. "In fact," writes Lefebvre, "there are many alienations, and they take many forms" (2002, 207).[11]

Second, and more important, given the thrust of Lefebvre's work, these varied manifestations of alienation could not be separated in principle from the larger shift toward urbanization that had only accelerated since Marx's time. In *The Urban Revolution*, Lefebvre emphasized the importance of this shift with a sweeping statement that reflected his consistent commitment to an urban perspective on alienation (2003, 92). To paraphrase Rob Shields: this would mean that "people were alienated from their work and activities" in a necessarily urbanized/urbanizing context, that their relationships with each other were similarly inflected by specifically urban forms of alienation, and that the urbanization of society provided new opportunities for becoming "alienated from their own essence, their 'species being'" (2005, 40). It is even more useful, however, to see how the notion of "urban alienation" was equally expressed through key interdependent critiques suggested by Lefebvre's *oeuvre* as a whole: (1) a critique of static space, (2) a critique of modern urban planning, (3) a critique of alienation in everyday life, (4) a critique of knowledge, and (5) a critique of method. I address these critiques here only in passing, drawing attention to the resonance of each with the theme of urban alienation explicitly.

I start with the urban theorist's critique of static space (critique 1). Lefebvre's insistence that space is not merely a static container for experience (e.g., Lefebvre 2003a, 40, 48)—and that space is at once conceived, perceived, and lived (Lefebvre 1991a, 33)—is an attempt to harness the power of philosophy to "go beyond" it (Lefebvre 1982, 6–7), to reconstitute space as lived and confront "metaphysical" philosophy with the need for praxis. Just as the notion of "space as container" represents a particular conceptualization of space (and one that is, of course, deployed as an integral part of the capitalist production of space), certain representations of space in are truth alienated/alienating views of reality. "Conceptualized space"—which Lefebvre identifies as "the space of scientists, planners, urbanists, technocratic subdividers and social engineers, as of a certain type of artist with a scientific bent" (1991a, 38)—distances us from lived space. The theorist thus stresses that "Like all social practice, spatial practice is lived directly before it is conceptualized; but the speculative primacy of the conceived over the lived causes practice to disappear along with life" (Lefebvre 1991a, 33).

Moving into the urban theorist's critique of modern urban planning (critique 2), it is precisely this alienated, conceptualized view of space that drives the capitalist production of space. In *The Right to the City*, Lefebvre explores the modern triumph of the city as exchange-value over the use-value of urban spaces—a shift which he roots in the early nineteenth century (Lefebvre 1996, 167; cf. Harvey 1989, 199; Marx 1977). In its modern origins, the bourgeois science of urban planning saw the city as a series of objects, external to one another and situated in a static space, instead of as an ensemble of relations (see Lefebvre 1996, 94). Just as static space and conceived space were alienations (critique 1), the alienating practice of urbanism (critique 2) is equally suspect: "Urbanism is therefore subject to radical critique. It masks a situation. It conceals operations. It blocks a view of the horizon, a path to urban knowledge and practice. It accompanies the decline of the spontaneous city and the historical urban core. It implies the intervention of power more than that of understanding" (Lefebvre 2003a, 160; also Lefebvre 1969, 145). The characteristic alienation of urban planning becomes most clear in the distinction Lefebvre makes between the "practiced city" and the "planned city"—a contrast that reconstitutes the distance between lived and conceived space just as that between use-value and exchange-value (Lefebvre 1996).

Daily life (critique 3), Lefebvre writes, "can also be conceived as an encounter and a confrontation between use (use-value) and exchange (exchange-value)" (2005, 12). As it was necessarily encountered in everyday life, alienation became tangible in ways that Marx perhaps had not foreseen—necessarily as a consequence of the nineteenth-century triumph of exchange-value over use-value, but particularly rooted in the textures of life in postwar, twentieth-century capitalism. For Lefebvre, alienation was no longer solely relevant to the "domain of work."[12] Lefebvre recognized that "Capitalism represents the perfection of a system of alienation that pervades all aspects of life" (Shields 2005, 42); for example, continues Shields, the fact that "the environment is commodified (air that is air-conditioned, water that must be purified, sun that must be filtered) and can be consumed (through purchase of the right technology, living in a favorable district of one's city, or tourism)" (2005, 169). And yet, there is a double-edge to this imbrication of alienation in everyday life, as Andy Merrifield explains. For Lefebvre:

> Everyday life . . . possessed a dialectical and ambiguous nature. On the one hand, it's the realm increasingly colonized by the commodity, and hence shrouded in all kinds of mystification, fetishism and alienation . . . On the other hand, paradoxically, everyday life is likewise a primal site for meaningful social resistance . . . Thus radical politics has to begin and end in everyday life; it can't do otherwise. (Merrifield 2002, 79)[13]

Put somewhat simply, the ubiquitous alienation of everyday life, and particularly that of life in urban areas, thus paradoxically makes it possible for radical coalitions to form.[14] In his work *The Explosion: Marxism and the French Upheaval*, written in the wake of the events of 1968,

Lefebvre devotes a chapter to discussion of "Urban Phenomena" where he spells out the radical potential of confronting alienation in the city. The contradictions of the social and technological divisions governing labor and the reproduction of capitalism have been concentrated in urban environments (see also Lefebvre 1976, 19); thus, in the city, "The many forms of alienation are experienced obscurely and provoke muffled and profound anxiety. This is the source of the surge of spontaneity" (Lefebvre 1969, 98).

Lefebvre's fourth key critique can be seen as an attempt to show how a reified approach to cities—typified by nineteenth-century urbanism (critique 2)—is more broadly applicable to a general and fragmented and mystifying bourgeois view of knowledge (see also Lefebvre 1982, 59–88). Alienation, writes the urban critic, conceals a totality of interconnected relations as fragmented areas of "specialization and compartmentalization" (Lefebvre 1982, 22–23). Lefebvre writes also of the limitations of disciplinary structures in the context of the modern university (see Lefebvre 2003a, particularly 53–55; Lefebvre 1969, 41; more on this anon), but what is at stake is a more generalized (non–institution-specific) critique of fragmentary knowledge (see Lefebvre 1996, 95–96). Lefebvre was a thinker who "detested compartmentalization" (Merrifield 2006, xxxiii). The French theorist summed up the premise of the second volume of his *Critique of Everyday Life* by stating that:

> Knowledge must proceed with caution, restraint, respect. It must respect lived experience, rather than belabouring it as the domain of ignorance and error, rather than absorbing it into positive knowledge as vanquished ignorance... Understanding lived experience, situating it, and restoring it to the dynamic constellation of concepts; "explaining" it by stating what it *involves*—this was how the meaning of the work and project was expressed. (original emphasis; Lefebvre 2005, 17)

Certainly there is sufficient cause to root Lefebvre's notion of knowledge in the broader context of a Marxian dialectical thought, one which above all else values the proper formulation of questions themselves over the urgency of finding a final answer to those questions.[15] Lefebvre's knowledge is one that turns back upon itself, and he sees in Marx the model of an ironic thinker who questions what he himself knows.[16]

But it is in his later work *Rhythmanalysis*—intended as a fourth volume of the *Critique of Everyday Life* but published posthumously—that the French thinker fuses his critique of knowledge in general with a more focused discussion of the question of method. It is a matter, writes Lefebvre, of advancing a mode of thinking that eschews the fragmentary and spatialized bourgeois conception of knowledge. This "rhythmana-lytical" thinking (critique 5) is a clear contrast to what he calls "analyti-cal thought"—that is, a thought rooted in divisions and reified views of objects that have concealed shifting relations—and is grounded not in abstract concepts but rather in lived experience, corporeality, and tem-porality (Lefebvre 2006a, 20–22; also Elden 2006b). This novel way of thinking is in effect a disalienation, a way of attempting to reclaim lived space from its concealment by the alienating effects of conceptualized space (critique 1), urbanism (critique 2), the "colonization of daily life" (critique 3), and forms of knowledge in which static, fragmentary, and specialized/compartmentalized views have obfuscated an apprehension of movement and process (critique 4).

Despite the brief treatment that these five interrelated critiques have received here (and previously in Fraser 2011a), understanding them is essential for moving toward the formulation of an urban cultural stud-ies method. While this section has charted out the importance of urban alienation in Lefebvre's recalibrated Marxism, the next section moves on to matters of importance to the cultural critic, and in particular to the cultural studies critic. Ultimately, Lefebvre's recalibration of Marxian alienation and its extensive application to an array of questions grounded in contemporary urban life is of particular importance for the critic working in the subfield (or growing interdisciplinary realm) of urban cultural studies.

Alienation and Urban Cultural Production

Since it is one of the central pillars upon which Marxian thought is based, we do well in returning to Karl Marx's discussion of the commodity—but here with an eye toward how this notion has been appropriated by Lefebvrian perspectives. The first paragraph of Marx's *Capital* empha-sizes that "Our investigation therefore begins with the analysis of the commodity," and the opening pages, which chart the distance between use-value and exchange-value, are essential to any analysis of contempo-rary life under capitalism (Marx 1977, 125). Recalling Lefebvre's discus-sion of alienation above ("Alienation is defined . . . as a split between the objectifying and the subjectifying processes in the individual"; Lefebvre 1982, 10)—which of course follows from Marx's original premise—*Capital* opens with a discussion of how the commodity is itself split in two. Thus, there are two, very distinct but related, sides to the object:

> Every useful thing, for example, iron, paper, etc., may be looked at from
> the two points of view of quality and quantity . . . The usefulness of a

thing makes it a use-value. But this usefulness does not dangle in mid-air. It is conditioned by the physical properties of the commodity, and has no existence apart from the latter. It is therefore the physical body of the commodity itself, for instance iron, corn, a diamond, which is the use-value or useful thing. This property of a commodity is independent of the amount of labor required to appropriate its useful qualities. When examining use-values, we always assume we are dealing with definite quantities... Use-values are only realized in use or in consumption. They constitute the material content of wealth, whatever its social form may be. In the form of society to be considered here they are also the material bearers of... exchange-value.[17] (Marx 1977, 125–126)

It cannot be forgotten, of course, that labor power is also a commodity, and that the commodity logic of capitalism has been further applied to human beings with most disastrous effect, in the worst of cases reducing them to things. But the most important implication of this logic is that—whether applied to objects or human beings (for both Lefebvre and Marx, of course)—the apparent distance between the commodity's use-value and exchange-value necessarily expresses a social relationship.[18] "It is nothing but the definite social relation between men themselves which assumes here [in the fetishism of the commodity], for them, the fantastic form of a relation between things" (Marx 1977, 165).[19] From the vantage point of capital, the object seems to stand alone, apart from the social relations in which it is enmeshed.

Yet, the commodity reflects a more generalized social relationship that is historically riven through with alienations (e.g., of workers from their products, from other workers, and even from themselves)—alienations that, Lefebvre insists, are at once approachable not merely at the economic but also at the philosophical and everyday urban levels.[20] Clearly, it is of primary importance for Lefebvre (1996) that from the nineteenth century onward, the city itself has been subject to the same split between use-value and exchange-value endured by other commodities. On one hand, the city is a use-value for its inhabitants; on the other hand, it is viewed as an empty container for urban projects enacting the speculative activity of capitalists working alongside builders and governments. These actors are interested, after all, in creating a more favorable turnover time for investment rather than addressing the problem of creating livable cities, one that is more complex indeed (Harvey 1996, 2000; Lefebvre 1996, 2003a). Yet while the city is a privileged commodity under urban capitalism, it is not, in fact, the only commodity worthy of consideration, nor is it—under a Lefebvrian model of cultural studies—separable in principle from other commodities. The city is itself a cultural product—one constantly in the process of being constructed. As such, it is subject to the same logic of capital accumulation that all cultural products face, even if disproportionately given the increased urbanization of society and of capital (Lefebvre 1976; Harvey 1989).

Although the logic of capital suggests the ontological specificity of the product of labor—according to which we are invited to see the product of labor as a discrete "thing" that has an existence separate from our own[21]—from the perspective of a Marxian/Lefebvrian dialectical materialism, this view itself effects an alienation.

> The drama of alienation is dialectical. Through the manifold forms of his labour, man has made himself real by realizing a human world. He is inseparable from this "other" self, his creation, his mirror, his statue—more, his body. The totality of objects and human products taken together form an integral part of human reality. On this level, objects are not simply means or implements; by producing them, men are working to create the human; they think they are molding an object, a series of objects—and it is man himself they are creating. (Lefebvre 1991b, 169)

Production in general needs to be appropriately understood as a metaproduction or a reproduction: a reproduction of both social relations and the relations of production themselves. Despite the fact that Lefebvre takes a moment to bemoan how diluted the concept has become, "production" retains a specific meaning in his thought that is consistent no matter what type of product it is used to characterize.[22] This consistency stems from the notion of totality. While not all production is the same, all production is—as the above quotation from *Critique of Everyday Life* (vol. 1) makes clear—a reproduction of social relations, relations that are unavoidably structured by capitalist urbanization. We reaffirm the importance of the Marxian concept of totality by seeing cultural products as embedded in a more general process of cultural production.

Understood broadly, cultural inquiry must proceed by giving priority to the role of urbanization in analysis of the capitalist mode of production: as Lefebvre points out, "the urban phenomenon has had a profound effect on the methods of production" (2003a, 167; also Lefebvre 1976). This is one of Lefebvre's fundamental insights and has been carried to new heights by figures such as David Harvey (2012) who see urbanization as central to contemporary capitalism. While earlier Marxism saw industrialization as constituting the core of capitalist relations, Lefebvre saw that urbanization was inseparable from the "survival of capitalism" throughout the twentieth century and that, in retrospect, industrialization in fact had been the forerunner of urbanization.[23] In his work on the urbanization of capital and the urbanization of consciousness, Harvey has expanded upon Lefebvre's critique, noting that "The reproduction of capital passes through processes of urbanization in myriad ways. But the urbanization of capital presupposes the capacity of capitalist class powers to dominate the urban process" (2012, 66).[24] In constructing this argument, however, he has also had to go against the grain of orthodox economic theory and even Marxist economic theory to do so. He writes that "in fact the structure of thinking within Marxism generally is distressingly similar to that within bourgeois economics. The urbanists are viewed as specialists, while the truly significant core of macroeconomic Marxist theorizing lies elsewhere" (Harvey 2012, 35).[25] While Harvey's reading of urbanized capitalism may take the Lefebvrian study of capital, production, speculation, and circulation in new directions, it nevertheless stays true to the French philosopher's original insight regarding the priority granted to the processes of urbanization.[26]

Lefebvre's original insight held that because the mode of production has become urbanized, all social relations—and alienations—offer only partial understandings if they are understood outside of this urban framework. Understood within the whole of his work, this assertion merely updates the evolving historical relationship between production and modes of production to potentially comment on our contemporary urban realities. In the early work *Dialectical Materialism* (originally published in 1938), he had written that "Living men still do not fully understand their essence and their true greatness. The analysis of the production of man by himself shows that all the philosophical definitions of man's essence correspond to moments of that production" (Lefebvre 2008, 143). If society has become urbanized—if the capitalist mode of production has been urbanized—it follows that contemporary explorations "of man's essence" must directly take on the urban nature of that "essence." This is not to say that our essence is indeed urbanized, for we are far more than that[27]; only in failing to deal with the urban as a formative influence, a structuring paradigm, and perhaps also a context for potentially liberating practices, we fail to grapple with the key urban moment in which we currently live. The point is subsequently to unmask the errors of thinking that stem from holding too fast to this "urbanized essence" while also remembering that "urban alienation contains and perpetuates all other forms of alienation" (Lefebvre 2003a, 92).

Following from Lefebvre's reconfigured Marxism, the notion of cultural production must be restored to its urban context. Applied to cultural studies—particularly a cultural studies that takes on the task of

sustaining the humanities tradition of close readings—this means recognizing that in fashioning cultural products, human societies refashion
themselves and replicate (or potentially contest) the logic of urbanized
capital. Cultural products beg the question of cultural production more
generally and in fact—if cultural inquiry is guided by the fundamental
concept and reality of alienation—may potentially lead us back into
urban social relations from the analysis of things. Cultural inquiry must
accept this as a basic tenet, a dialectical premise without which it necessarily risks assuming a reifying view of cultural production if not also
becoming a stale tool of historical periodization.[28] It bears repeating
that there is much to be gained by going beyond the borders of the text
itself in humanities scholarship.[29] "Going beyond the borders of" is not,
however, equivalent to "dispensing with." This movement beyond the
text is, in fact, absolutely crucial if we are to restore cultural products to
the urban context in which they are produced and consumed.

Understanding the effects of alienation is central to an urban cultural studies approach, even if many of these will necessarily seem to
be somewhat obvious. First, individual cultural products appear to
us to be separate from urban society. Lefebvre's work on the distance
between spaces of work and spaces of leisure throughout the twentieth
century is applicable to the cultural landscape of marketing as well.[30]
Such products (we are told implicitly by marketers) as novels, films,
music, videogames, and so on promise a world of escape, a world of pure
entertainment and leisure. But this view is an error and an alienation.
Moreover, do we not *consume space* itself when we read, watch, listen
to, or play these products, much as the tourist *consumes leisure spaces*?
Whether the space referenced in these products is identifiable on a map
(Madrid, Paris, etc.) or not (e.g., science fiction spaces that nevertheless
dialogue with existing and potential spatial imaginaries), we consume
it all the same. To believe otherwise is to accept another erroneous view
of space that Lefebvre's work directly contests—the view holding that
space is merely a material entity or an empty container for action, unin-
flected by mental conceptions and representations and ungoverned by
the dialectical process of spatial production. The standpoint alleging
that culture reflects material conditions is a first step in accounting for
this error, but is ultimately insufficient, as this reflection is only one
part of the equation.

Lefebvre's approach represents a significant overhaul of a reified
view of culture and suggests the continuing importance of the contemporary urban context. In his own terms, his perspective "precludes
reducing society to the economic and the political, and modifies the all

too famous controversy over 'base and superstructure' by putting the emphasis on the social" (Lefebvre 2005, 16). He not only takes Marxists to task for ignoring aesthetic questions,[31] he also emphasizes that art has the potential to "transfigure" society.[32] Moreover, Lefebvre elaborates on this perspective by mentioning the city specifically:

> Thus it is necessary to take up again not only aesthetic theory but also the project according to which art succeeds in transfiguring practical reality, because it does not consist of a simple passive reflection of that reality... Art metamorphoses reality and this metamorphosis returns to reality. Thus, the transformation of the world is not only a realization of philosophy but a realization of art. This development of the Marxist project would take into account the city as a work—everything that peoples and enriches urban space, with all that this implies. The city is a work of art and a practical realization of art. In this way, Marxist aesthetics would be taken up again, not merely as a theory of art, but as a practice that creates. (1988, 83–84)

By reconciling aesthetic matters with Marxist analysis—and by infusing Marxian thought with an appreciation of the significance of the urban phenomenon—Lefebvre (2003a) attempts to account for the ills of an entrenched and alienating bourgeois view of knowledge that divides the world into so many separate spheres that seem to each possess their own internal logic and to subsequently assert, unquestioned, their own relative autonomy with respect to the others.

Moreover (and second), individual cultural products also appear to be separate from each other. That is, the bourgeois compartmentalization that Lefebvre so despised[33] has encouraged a "specificity thesis" whereby scholarly traditions draw hard lines between novels, film, poetry, music, videogames, and so on. This does not mean there are no meaningful differences between and among these distinguishable art forms, but rather that these meaningful differences do not mount a serious challenge to the fact that the capitalist (urban) mode of production serves as a context common to them all. One of Lefebvre's articles from 1988 includes a lengthy meditation on culture that is instructive in this regard:

> It so happens that the word "culture" also evokes a magical image for me, that of Sleeping Beauty. She does not doze on flowers and on fragrant grass but on a thick mattress of texts, quotations, musical scores—and under a vast canopy of books, sociological, semiological, historical and philosophical theses. Then one day the Prince comes; he awakens her

and everything around the forest comes to life along with her—poets poetizing, musicians musicking, cooks cooking, lovers loving, and so on. Singers? Songs? Yes, they are a part of culture, yet they must not be considered in isolation but within an ensemble that also includes dance, music, cartoon strips, television, and so forth. Moreover, culture is not merely a static palimpsest of texts, it is lived, active, which is what the fable of the wakened princess suggests to me. (1988, 81–82)

This "fable," in fact, speaks to both of the alienations that may be accounted for and counteracted by the proper formulation of an urban cultural studies method. In it, cultural products of all stripes are not merely taken as part of a single ensemble (heterogeneous and complex), but also spring to life in that very moment when "sociological, semiological, historical and philosophical" knowledge is itself awakened, and not a second later. This temporal simultaneity seems to suggest that neither social knowledge (or rather, knowledge external to the text) nor culture as "a static palimpsest of texts" receives priority—both are of equal importance.

In this way, the skill of the urban cultural studies thinker, then, shall be measured on a scale privileging a total approach.[34] Lefebvre's (Marxian) notion of total humanism ultimately provides a model for moving from alienating, partial views of cultural production to grasp a complex but unified whole. As the next section explores, however, the notions of culture and city have themselves been difficult to blend in urban analysis, even where humanities scholarship has been left out altogether. In the end, since "adding" humanities scholarship to cultural studies of the city is (for some) considered an extra step, it helps us to understand how a nuanced view of culture itself has been historically left out of scholarship on the city, and thus alienated from the urban problematic.

Mumford Versus Zukin: *The Culture(s) of Cities*

Looking at the way in which the notions of cities and culture have been combined by previous academic treatments can help us understand what is at stake in the formulation of an urban cultural studies method that draws from the humanities. The two texts I return to here are of value not merely for their titles but due to the way in which they have been central to fomenting two different, but overlapping, academic discourses on the city. *The Culture of Cities*, written by Lewis Mumford and originally published in 1938, has been widely cited by scholars interested in cities from a variety of disciplinary perspectives. Today, it remains a classic text of urban studies, understanding this interdisciplinary field in the widest possible sense.[35] The book is broadly reflective of a humanistic approach to cities that offers some important lessons, lessons gleaned from circumstances that are both historic and material. Nevertheless, its insights are themselves somewhat conditioned by their own (prewar) historical context.[36] Sharon Zukin's text *The Cultures of Cities* (originally published in 1995), on the other hand, reflects the wide diffusion of new critical thinking about cities that developed in the wake of the Second World War. The perspective here is just as humanistic as Mumford's—although, significantly, it begins from much of a different stance regarding the motors of urbanization than does that earlier book. As Zukin writes in the book's concise preface, hers are "very different concerns from those that animated Lewis Mumford's classic work *The Culture of Cities*, whose title inspired mine. Though his book and mine are both concerned with urban design, democracy, and the market economy, for me the very concept of culture has become more explicit and problematic" (1995, x). The thematic similarities of both books, which are mentioned here concisely by Zukin, should not be overlooked—but neither should their differences. Moreover, in the end it is Lefebvre's perspective that implicitly provides us with a way of assessing the distance between the two perspectives. Emphasizing capitalist urbanization as the logical outcome of previous industrialization and establishing the importance of culture in no uncertain terms—rescuing it from the pitfalls inherent to a still-hegemonic "base-superstructure" model (Lefebvre 2005, 16)—Lefebvrian analysis illuminates how to move forward by combining city, culture, and the humanities.

The most essential similarity of the two texts is a quality common to what are, in the end, two distinct methodological approaches. It needs to be emphasized that neither Mumford nor Zukin, strictly speaking, takes an instrumentalist approach to the city. That is, for each, the city is more than a mere architectural fact—it is for Mumford "the form and symbol of an integrated social relationship" (1970, 3),[37] while Zukin notes that "Real cities are both material constructions, with human strengths and weaknesses, and symbolic projects, developed by social representations" (1995, 46). Even in Mumford there is a concerted effort to think the dialectic—"Mind *takes form* in the city; and in turn, urban forms condition mind" (original emphasis; 1970, 5). For both thinkers, the city becomes not merely *one way* but rather *the privileged way* of assessing human social relations.

Nevertheless, there is a certain friction produced in the act of reading each text against the other—*The Culture of Cities* against *The Cultures of*

Cities. One can say that Mumford's work is an important starting point for understanding the urban transitions that took place in the wake of nineteenth-century industrialization, but that Zukin's reading is essential for understanding twentieth- and twenty-first-century urban realities. It is also fair to say that Mumford effectively and consciously denounces the pernicious effects of industrialized capital while Zukin takes on those of a capital that is urbanized, specifically. To a certain extent, the approach employed in each case supports a predetermined conclusion. Mumford views the big city as a problem and probes large-scale practices and their effects, coming to critique existing planning perspectives and to favor managed decentralization.[38] Zukin perhaps accepts the big city well enough on its own terms, but—employing a focus on visual culture and concrete public spaces—favors a more nuanced interrogation of how urban environments like museums, restaurants, parks, and shopping malls become battlegrounds, asking "How do we connect what we experience in public space with ideologies and rhetorics of public culture?" (1995, 46). The conclusion reached by the first perspective indicates that the urban flaws created by nineteenth-century industrial capital should be better managed and cities better designed for the good of humanity[39]; the second, that as a space of encounter, the city will long be the site through which we must negotiate urban fears and contest urban inequalities.[40]

In essence, each thinker approaches both the city and the potential of the urban environment from a distinct perspective. Mumford views the large city with suspicion and treats urban planning with a certain optimism that persists despite his rigorous critique of its traditional ills.[41] Famed antiurbanist Jane Jacobs notably saw Mumford as a kind of counterpoint to her approach (and he saw her in much the same way).[42] In her *Death and Life of Great American Cities*—in a discussion of "orthodox modern city planning and city architectural design"—she directs readers to Mumford for "a sympathetic account which mine is not" (1992, 17). On *The Culture of Cities*, specifically, Jacobs writes that Mumford's book "was largely a morbid and biased catalog of ills. The great city [for Mumford and others] was Megalopolis, Tyrannopolis, Nekropolis, a monstrosity, a tyranny, a living death. It must go" (1992, 20–21; also 207). Mumford remains convinced that planning can be a boon on cities (e.g., Mumford 1970, 375–376), writing that "genuine planning is an attempt, not arbitrarily to displace reality, but to clarify it and to grasp firmly all the elements necessary to bring the geographic and economic facts in harmony with human purposes" (1970, 376). *The Culture of Cities* sought, in part, to rectify a situation in which "current thinking about cities [had] proceeded without sufficient insight into their nature, their function, their purpose, their historic role, or their potential future" (Mumford 1970, ix). His critique of the science of city planning is that it was mechanistic, that it had been out of touch with "organic events and organic patterns" that were the central occupation of humanity and humanness (Mumford 1970, 149). The key issue, as Mumford saw it, was that the mechanistic logic of industrialization (1970, 149–50) had been carried over to the process of building cities—a historico–material connection embodied in the extension of the railroads from the mines to industrial centers (1970, 150, 159). But Mumford understands neither how the characteristic ideological fragmentation of bourgeois knowledge fed this very material problem (Lefebvre 2003a, 1996) nor how the relations of capital are decisive in both realms. Notwithstanding, his calls for reform—centered around the possibilities for renewal of urban environments—had a lasting (if also uneven) effect on planners.[43]

At the time, Mumford's concerns seemed reasonable to many and were perhaps only made more easy to digest by his well-intentioned appropriation of rhetoric that advocated a universal humanism. He was certainly "conscious of cities as places of human habitation" (Preston and Simpson-Housley 2010, 317) and saw in them a starting point for assessing our state of civilization (or barbarism). Ultimately, however, his understanding of culture lacked nuance and—as Zukin saw well—was insufficient to make sense of an urbanized, postwar capitalism (1995, x). Generally, Mumford saw large cities as a threat to "culture." Because the word was, for Mumford, a generalized indicator of human prosperity, he employed it in a very general way—thus the reader is invited to accept problematic notions of "non-metropolitan culture," "human culture," "advanced cultures," and "cultural impoverishment," which are, after all, somewhat vague (1970, 335, 327, 347). On the other hand, culture in Zukin is fundamental, and although she insists that the notion of culture is "unstable"—there is no comparison with how generally (and vaguely) it is used by Mumford.[44] For Zukin, culture is inseparable from relationships of power: it is a "powerful means of controlling cities," a "source of images and memories," a "set of architectural themes," the "unique competitive edge of cities," and the fuel for "the city's symbolic economy" (1995, 1–2). While "culture" was for Mumford a large-scale, global attribute of human societies (and not for that reason any less univocal), for Zukin it is inherently multivocal, fluid, and heterogeneous—a "dialogue" involving "material inequalities" that are necessarily rooted in concrete places even if influenced by large-scale processes (Zukin 1995, 290).

In *The Cultures of Cities*, Zukin even points to Lefebvre's triadic understanding of space (Lefebvre 1991a, 33) as an explicit source of inspiration (Zukin 1995, 293). The fact that this reference comes late in the text and is unaccompanied by a more extensive dialogue with Lefebvre's urban thinking might distract the reader from what is in reality a very Lefebvrian approach. Zukin goes out of her way to establish the notion of "Culture as an economic base" (1995, 11–15), saying that "we cannot speak about cities today without understanding: how cities use culture as an economic base" (1995, 11; cf. Lefebvre 2005, 16). She stays true to a cultural studies method by interrogating both the cultural and the political-social at once, recognizing that, although cities may influence and direct "the force field of culture" (Zukin 1995, 147), "Taking a materialist approach compels us to look for structures of power outside the cultural field. At the very least, we must look for structured coherences between cultural and other kinds of power" (1995, 291). In the end, Zukin's text is attentive throughout to that question so dear to Lefebvre, "Who has the right to the city?" (Lefebvre 1996; cf. Zukin 1995, Chapter 1).

For that matter, of course, many of Mumford's thoughts on the city clearly resonate with remarks made by Lefebvre, even if his method is dissimilar (note that the French philosopher does not seem to reference the author of *The Culture of Cities* as often as he would Jacobs—if he even does so at all). This is true from both a general perspective— unsurprisingly, all three deal with the classic notion of the organic city (Mumford 1970, 6; Jacobs 1992, 433; Lefebvre 1995, 116)—and, in addition, even at the sentence level.[45] For example, Mumford's invitation that we "Approach more closely the paleotechnic town: examine it with eye, ear, nose, skin" (1970, 191) reads today as a companion to Lefebvre's call that "[the rhythmanalyst] thinks with his body, not in the abstract, but in lived temporality" (2006a, 21).[46] And reciprocally, Lefebvre's idea of the city as, in a sense, musical—"[the rhythmanalyst] will come to 'listen' to a house, a street, a town, as an audience listens to a symphony" (2006a, 22)—is itself foreshadowed in *The Culture of Cities* where Mumford writes: "Through its complex orchestration of time and space, no less than through the social division of labor, life in the city takes on the character of a symphony: specialized human aptitudes, specialized instruments, give rise to sonorous results which, neither in volume nor in quality, could be achieved by any single piece" (Mumford 1970, 4; cf. Jacobs' idea of the "sidewalk ballet"; Jacobs 1992; Fraser 2012a).

In the end, the contrast between Mumford and Zukin—the distance between *The Culture of Cities* and *The Cultures of Cities*—nevertheless provides twenty-first-century scholars with a number of insights that are of interest to an urban cultural studies project motivated by Lefebvre's urban philosophy. Ultimately, the dissonance between Mumford's and Zukin's texts points to the twin relationship of cities to capital, and of capital to culture. To wit: it is now widely understood—although opinions regarding the significance of this fact may vary greatly—that the city is not merely the *seat of capital* (Mumford 1970, 228) but also the *project of capital*—something that Mumford fails to explore in detail, given that his ire is directed disproportionately toward the "paleotechnic" mechanism that accompanied industrial development. Mumford's perspective amounts to what Lefebvre would call "partial knowledge" (1996, 95–96), not a total view of urban society—although his work is paradoxically structured by claims to universality.[47] His approach is dismissive of both individualism and socialism, saying that each is "equally oppressive to a good society" (Mumford 1970, 455, 454–458), and in the end he leaves the topic (and urban reality) of alienation out of the equation.[48] In its place, Mumford offers a narrative of personal responsibility—"Though the common instruments of production have increased the human basis for association, the breakup of coherent value-systems has undermined the possibilities for unified action" (1970, 378). Nonetheless, the attention he devotes to the large-scale matters of city planning cannot be ignored, nor can his historical interest in the material, urban consequences of unchecked nineteenth-century capitalist industrialization. Zukin, on the other hand, although she perhaps bypasses the relevance of this important accounting of "paleotechnic" urban history, offers a politically committed critique of more contemporary urban realities, insisting that "Claims about the power of symbols are not independent of claims about political and economic power" (1995, 292). Without this commitment, even the most humanistic interpretation of cities risks co-optation by the unapologetic (Lefebvre would say "triumphant and triumphalist") notion of capitalist modernity (Lefebvre 1995, 3); and, of course, without an understanding of urbanization's forerunner industrialization, our assessment of the contemporary urban problem will necessarily be incomplete and insufficient.

Reading Mumford along with Zukin provides us with a corpus of urban knowledge that stands out for its historical view of the city, nuanced view of culture, political commitment, and philosophical potential—all which are, in fact, complementary to the work produced by Henri Lefebvre throughout the twentieth century. Mumford and Zukin each articulate directions of urban studies that each form one part of the equation. In Lefebvrian terms, they outline the alienating dissonance between a vibrant urban culture and a staid culture of urbanism, both of which await the assessment of contemporary urban critics.

Toward a Lefebvrian Urban Cultural Studies

In order to articulate what an urban cultural studies might look like, it is first important to take a moment to reflect upon the enormity and complexity of the urban phenomenon, and also upon the insufficiency of currently existing disciplinary frameworks for grasping the totality of the urban experience. As Lefebvre's take on the urban phenomenon suggests, the key question hinges on the difference between a system and a method. In *The Urban Revolution*, he notes that the city is irreducible to a system or a semiology (Lefebvre 2003a, 50) and bemoans the limitations of approaches that boast of being able to divide the urban phenomenon—defined in terms of its "enormity and complexity" (46)—into a manageable if large number of subfields. He writes that the complexity of the urban phenomenon "makes interdisciplinary cooperation essential. [It] cannot be grasped by any specialized science" (Lefebvre 2003a, 53). But there is a more fundamental problem with the proposal of accumulating disciplinary approaches, a problem with grouping them together as a way of understanding the urban phenomenon:

> Every specialized science cuts from the global phenomenon a "field," or "domain," which it illuminates in its own way. There is no point in choosing between segmentation and illumination. Moreover, each individual science is further fragmented into specialized subdisciplines. Sociology is divided up into political sociology, economic sociology, rural and urban sociology, and so forth. The fragmented and specialized sciences operate analytically: they are the result of an analysis and perform analyses of their own. In terms of the urban phenomenon considered as a whole, geography, demography, history, psychology, and sociology supply the results of an analytical procedure. Nor should we overlook the contributions of the biologist, doctor or psychiatrist, or those of the novelist or poet... Without the progressive and regressive movements (in time and space) of analysis, without the multiple divisions and fragmentations, it would be impossible to conceive of a science of the urban phenomenon. But such fragments do not constitute knowledge. (Lefebvre 2003a, 48–49)

"But such fragments do not constitute knowledge"—as Lefebvre makes clear, the fragmentary character of knowledge, which becomes institutionalized as disciplinary specialization, stems from and reproduces the social division of labor (2003a, 60).

As long as disciplinary conceits structure our approach, no degree of systematic collisions will yield an understanding of the "totality" of the urban phenomenon (Lefebvre 2003a, 53–54, 58–59); no "collection of objects—economy, sociology, history, demography" can reconstitute the complexity of the urban phenomenon (Lefebvre 2003a, 57). The question remains, "How can we make the transition from fragmentary knowledge to complete understanding? How can we define this need for *totality?*" (original emphasis; Lefebvre 2003a, 56). Only a loose method, and not a strict system—for Lefebvre this is an important distinction—can shed light on the complexity of the contemporary urban experience. Provided that it does not fall into the traps of either becoming a systematized science or of becoming a sort of urban boosterism—that is, uncritically cataloging and touting the uniqueness of the varying urban cultures that have been inflected by capitalism's tendency to replicate a serial homogeneity (Harvey 1996, 2000) in its occupation of spaces (Lefebvre 1976)—an urban cultural studies method such as the one articulated throughout this book should be able to address also the need for a "total" synthesis of theory and practice that is so central to Lefebvre's recalibrated Marxism (see Lefebvre 1982, 27).

As a way of shifting the topic of discussion to the praxis of cultural critique, it is necessary to return to alienation. One of the basic Lefebvrian insights regarding (a recalibrated Marxian notion of) alienation is that in everyday life human relations appear in the guise of relations between things. In *Dialectical Materialism*, the French thinker writes that

> Human relations seem to be nothing more than relations between things. But this is far from being the case, or rather it is only partly true. In actual fact the living relations between individuals in the different groups and between these groups themselves are made manifest by these relations between things: in money relations and the exchange of products. Conversely, these relations between things and abstract quantities are only the appearance and expression of human relations in a determinate mode of production, in which individuals (competitors) and groups (classes) are in conflict or contradiction. The direct and immediate relations of human individuals are enveloped and supplanted by mediate and abstract relations which mask them. (Lefebvre 2008, 80)

To properly understand the relationship between the cultural critic and the static cultural text, it is necessary to realize that the boundary of the text is only the conceptual limit for a reified—an alienated—view of culture. Properly understood, the relation in question is not one between the critic and the product to be analyzed, nor even between the critic and the artist as necessarily mediated through the work of art. Instead, it is a matter of seeing that the significance of criticism comes from a simultaneous interrogation of both the work of art and its social context. Cultural studies analysis, thus, seeks to resituate the cultural product within the context and terms of human relationships. This may seem a commonplace for many, but certainly not all, contemporary readers (note, of course, that this has not always been the case; cf. Williams 2007b, 165), but I wish to make another subsequent leap in articulating what I call an urban cultural studies framework inspired by Lefebvrian thought.

My focus here, however, is on a very particular form of cultural critique, one that goes by the somewhat chimerical name of cultural studies. Whereas there appear to be many invocations of cultural studies—that is, arguments abound over whether the term evokes a political commitment, one specific intellectual inheritance or another, or merely a generally anesthetized appeal to "culture"—I find the definition offered by Raymond Williams to be the most convincing and the most succinct. In his view, cultural studies consists of "the refusal to give priority to either the project or the formation—or, in older terms, the art or the society" (Williams 2007a, 152). This is to say

> that you cannot understand an intellectual or artistic project without also understanding its formation; that the relation between a project and a formation is always decisive; and that the emphasis of Cultural studies is precisely that it engages with *both*, rather than specializing itself to one or the other... Project and formation in this sense are different ways of materializing—different ways, then, of describing, what is in fact a *common* disposition of energy and direction. (original emphasis; Williams 2007a, 151)

The mention of "energy and direction" is quite important (and relevant also to Lefebvre's own articulation of a rhythmanalytical method; see Lefebvre 2006a; also 2002, 2005). Facing a static cultural product, the critic's task is thus to return from what is effectively an abstraction, an alienated extraction, to the shifting relations that at once underlie its production and reception in a given context. That context—as Lefebvre's *oeuvre* makes clear—is an inherently urban context.[49]

What makes a Lefebvrian cultural studies different from, say, a cultural studies grounded in the work of Williams (see Gorak 1988;

Williams 2007a; Seidl, Horak, and Grossberg 2010a) is its explicit confrontation with the necessary primacy of the urban theme. Williams' dual-reading/reconciliation of what he called "culture" and "society" (2007b: 163–165) effectively becomes a simultaneous reading of both "urban culture" and "urban society."[50] Seen from the vantage point of a (somewhat traditional but newly reconfigured) literary and cultural studies grounded in textual criticism, the task of the urban cultural studies critic is thus to venture across and outside of the boundary of the individual work of art to grapple at once with the realities of urbanization and its alienating effects.

At their base, the methodological aims of a Lefebvrian urban cultural studies maintain a close relationship with those of Williams's view of cultural studies (albeit inflected more explicitly by questions pertaining to the urban problematic)—thus, in the dialectical process of uniting work and world that is synonymous with the praxis of scholarship, we disalienate ourselves from the dogmatically fictional approach to texts just as we also disalienate ourselves from the seemingly factual immutability or "givenness" of our collective extrafictional experience.[51] Notwithstanding, we perhaps do well also in returning to Lefebvre's critique of the fragmentary—"specialized/compartmentalized"—understanding of the role played by academic disciplines. To the degree that criticism is a part of an ongoing process of learning—and this is most definitely so, whether conceived as scholarly conversation, as an indirect catalyst, or a direct influence on students, or as a conversation taking place at the scale of community—it must eschew the progressive encroachments that capitalism has made into the realm of education (paradoxically—a realm whose autonomy from other aspects of life itself owes to the bourgeois fragmentation of knowledge discussed in Lefebvre 2003a, 1996). Effectively allying himself with critics such as Paolo Freire and bell hooks (a.k.a. Gloria Watkins) who have denounced a style of "banking education" inflected by the capitalist reification of knowledge (see Freire 1970, 1998; hooks 1994; Rowland Dix 2010), Lefebvre similarly wrote that "An educator is not a mere conveyer, nor is the institution called 'university' a warehouse" (1969, 156) where learning can be reduced to a product in accordance with the capitalist logic of exchange (141).

In this sense—and by way of conclusion—the essential relevance of "alienation" to the formulation of an urban cultural studies method can be approached in three overlapping disalienations. First, methodological disalienation: in the reconciliation effected between "urban culture" and "urban society" (*a la* Williams), there operates a potential disalienation of specialized disciplinary knowledge. Second, a disalienating view of cultural products: novels, films, music, comics, and so on, acquire new meaning to the extent that they are restored to the shifting urbanized and urbanizing environment in which they are necessarily produced and consumed—what is at first an alienated object (cultural product) becomes a part of urban cultural production. Third, a disalienation of the learning experience (Freire, hooks, Lefebvre): where knowledge itself becomes not a capitalist "deposit" but rather a process of folding the individual learner back into the movement of a necessarily complex urban society. Building on this discussion, the next chapter looks even more closely at the relationship between artistic discourse and the urban phenomenon in theoretical terms.

CHAPTER 3

The Work (of Art): Putting Art at the Service of the Urban

This chapter continues to think through the fundamental question posed by Henri Lefebvre: "How can we make the transition from fragmentary knowledge to complete understanding?" (Lefebvre 2003a, 56). One way to answer this question is to see how alienation structures the way in which we divide the social world into so many isolated areas that communicate insufficiently with one another, if at all. Understanding how alienation plays out with regard to both artistic and critical experiences, specifically, is crucial if we are to realize a future reconciliation of capital with culture. My reading of Lefebvre's work suggests that the formulation of an urban cultural studies method requires an aesthetic theory as its base—one that can account for the overlapping but distinct roles of the *thing*, the *product*, and the *work of art*. The French philosopher's late text *La présence et l'absence* (1980) provides lengthy and nuanced meditations on the relationship of these terms, in the process building on his previous discussions of art and the urban. As such, it provides a way of thinking through the value of aesthetic questions while also remembering that, from a Lefebvrian–Marxian perspective, culture is not at all a realm separate from the various other areas of contemporary life (Lefebvre 2005, 16; Léger 2006, 143), even if it may appear as such an autonomous space due to ideology, alienation, and the structure of the modern university, which reinforces and aids in naturalizing this perspective.

This move to recover the aesthetic theory operative throughout Lefebvre's work is in itself a considerable shift from now classic Marxist perspectives on aesthetic matters—perspectives that, for example, have tended to emphasize art as "systematization of feelings in form" or that reduce the question of artistic style to being "conditioned by the course of social life" (Bukharin 1972, 101; 105). In one way or another, in fact, much previous Marxist art criticism has traditionally asserted something of the following sort—that "directly or indirectly, art is ultimately determined in various ways by the economic structure and the stage of the social technology" (Bukharin 1972, 107), a notion from which Lefebvre's theory of the work of art diverges considerably. It was necessary for Marxist thought to break with the idealist (and thus alienated) understanding of works of art as, for example, "*autonomous* and subjective facts; almost as phenomena in their own right, out of time, out of space, out of absolutely all the conditions of their genesis, of their birth" (original emphasis; Barbaro 1972, 161). And yet, in lauding social realism over other styles of artistic production (e.g., Gyorgy Lukács), and in subordinating art to a determining economic base through models of reflection and/or mediation (discussed by Raymond Williams, below), much Marxist aesthetic theory in practice reduces the power of art and separates it from questions that are more-than-aesthetic.[1] The advantage of Lefebvre's Marxian theory of art is that it notably reasserts the powerful potential of art while in effect dissolving the border between aesthetic matters and contemporary urban life more broadly considered.

To reassert Lefebvre's thoughts on art in the present context is not merely to signal the complexity of twentieth-century Marxism's relationship with culture more generally.[2] It is also to recognize the fact that the French theorist, in many different ways, placed art at the center of his thinking. The brief vignette titled "Lefebvre, Cultural Critic" (included in chapter 1) concisely established the importance of art, artists, and artistic discourse for Lefebvre during his early years, and this chapter now builds on that vignette by turning to the substantial arguments he elaborated in his 1980 text regarding the "work of art" specifically. Though some critics have been right to note that Lefebvre's more canonical books have tended to push aesthetic questions to the side (e.g., Léger 2006), it is important that we resist the temptation to divide his work into two subcategories (aesthetic topics and nonaesthetic topics). Such a division would merely replicate the characteristic fragmentation of bourgeois knowledge he so patently rejected. In fact, rejection of this very dichotomy is central to what I will call his "theory of the work (of art)." More important, Lefebvre's thoughts on art do not constitute an entirely new direction in his writing but, instead, follow logically from his theses surrounding the "colonization of everyday life" as elucidated over the three-volume *Critique of Everyday Life* (1991b, 2002, 2005—and other works, e.g., *Everyday Life in the Modern World*

[2007], *Rhythmanalysis* [2006a]). These thoughts are also intimately relevant to his thoughts on the city itself. Art is thus as good a place as any to enter into more complex discussions of capital, value, and exchange. Ultimately, Lefebvre believes that art can and should serve a disalienating function, one that might be carried over into other areas of urban thinking.

In *The Right to the* City, Lefebvre writes that "To put art at the service of the urban does not mean to prettify urban space with works of art... Leaving aside representation, ornamentation and decoration, art can become *praxis* and *poiesis* on a social scale: the art of living in the city as work of art... In other words, the future of art is not artistic, but urban, because the future of 'man' is not discovered in the cosmos, or in the people, or in production, but in urban society" (1996, 173). In short, to put "art at the service of the urban" is to reunite it with the urban phenomenon—to reconcile it with the city from which the bourgeois discourse of specialization has traditionally alienated aesthetic questions. The value of Lefebvre's perspective is that it explicitly outlines a model in which humanities texts (novels, music, poetry, paintings, etc.), cities, and urban practices all play into the designation of "works (of art)". As such, it potentially leads us toward a radical reformulation of contemporary urban life. Contemplating the French philosopher's perspective, this chapter asserts that to interrogate the notion of art in contemporary capitalist society is simultaneously to look more closely at questions of method and of disciplinary practice. As in the previous chapter, the underlying Marxian concept of alienation is crucial to this endeavor. Alienation holds the key to understanding how art has been defined in opposition to other areas of contemporary life and, moreover, how it also offers the opportunity to grasp urban life as a totality. Our journey toward totality will cover three interrelated levels: the work of art, the criticism of art, and the urban as art.

The first section of this chapter—"Art: The Thing–Product–Work"— explores these three terms as discussed by Lefebvre, relating them to his understanding of the urban phenomenon more generally and also to a humanities-centered notion of cultural production. Importantly, Lefebvre defines "the work" in his discussion quite broadly—so as to fold together both the idea of the city as a work and also the more traditional notion of "works of art" ("poetry, music, theater, the novel, etc.," Lefebvre 2006b, 237). It is important, however, to build on his discussion to make some of the connections between these two areas more concrete. In doing so, this section emphasizes that his theory of the work follows from the Marxian notions of use- and exchange-value and is irreducible to a single set of norms. Crucial to this discussion is the nuanced Lefebvrian distinction between the product and the work. The former is loosely equivalent to an exchange-value, while the latter is better understood as an outcome of what he calls the "creative capacity" of the artist.

The second section—"The Critic: Disalienating Humanities Scholarship"—marks a shift from the realm of the artist to the realm of the cultural critic. It is my take that much of what Lefebvre suggests is—in the best of cases—true of the creation of art criticism or even humanities scholarship. Although the situation of art continues to be as complex as Lefebvre imagined, here I want to maintain the emphasis on both the potential *value* (not the *exchange-value*) of art and the potential *value* (not the *exchange-value*) of humanities criticism. As is so often the case in Lefebvre's own work, here the notions of alienation and disalienation are critical to understanding how humanities scholarship either resigns itself to remaining a "product" or becomes (partially, ephemerally) a "work." Moreover, if criticism is to realize itself as a "work" lies, humanities scholarship must shake off the bourgeois assumptions that—even 40 years after the publication of *Marxism and Literature* by Raymond Williams—continue to dog the language and literature fields as a whole.

The third section—"Totality: Art at the Service of the Urban"— builds on previous sections to establish what the urban phenomenon itself can offer as art and how "the art of living in the city as a work of art" can shed light on the common goal that underlies both the study of humanities texts and the study of urban culture, more broadly speaking. A reconfigured Lefebvrian notion of Marxian totality emphasizes the potential pitfalls of alienating discourse for the cultural critic. It also makes it possible to move from the "creative capacities" of both artists and critics to the urban environment as a site for encounter and play against the instrumentalized discourse of rational urban planning. This last section of the chapter points toward what is to be gained from combining art and philosophy. As such, it provides an important backdrop for the closer engagements with humanities texts carried out in the second major section of this book (the four chapters labeled "Textual Variations").

Art: The Thing–Product–Work

Lefebvre's *La présence et l'absence* is addressed to those seeking a "new path."[3] It is a book, he says, written for philosophers ("perhaps"), and for artists ("without a doubt")—with the caveat that we keep in mind how "artists and art today form part of the culture industry" (Lefebvre 2006b, 229). The need for a more theoretical treatment of "the work (of art)" thus stems from the fact that "the vast majority of artists play with the ambiguity of the 'work-thing-product' and have no interest in elucidating their differences" (Lefebvre 2006b, 229–230).[4] Although the distinction between thing–product–work is part of an age-old discussion—in one single paragraph Lefebvre references Christianity in general but also Kant, Hegel, Marx, Nietzsche, Schelling, Schopenhauer, and Heidegger (2006b, 234)—the urban thinker makes it clear that the majority of philosophers have tended to discuss one term at the expense of the others and in lieu of elaborating on their connections.[5] Understanding the relation of each term to the others—and ultimately understanding the central role of "the work"—is of great importance for the formulation of an urban cultural studies method. While there is no need, Lefebvre insists, to draw hard lines between the three terms of "thing," "product," and "work," we do well in seeing how each suggests a different perspective on the same complex contemporary reality analyzed by Lefebvre.[6] While it is possible to define each term quite briefly, this section will subsequently spend more time on the nuanced relationship of the "product" to the "work" in particular.

To begin, the "thing" is—historically speaking—the object as received from nature.[7] Of course, given Lefebvre's Marxian inheritance, it makes sense to see the thing, in a simple sense, also as the physical object or, to a certain degree, the use-value of that object. The perspective suggested by the moniker of "thing," then, points to a set of properties retained even by those "things" that have been (re)fashioned by human activity.[8] The notion of the "product," on the other hand, necessarily presupposes that very human activity itself (also, of course, a social activity), and as such, it might be loosely equated with the exchange-value of the object. From a certain perspective, both the "thing" and the "product" (taken together) are complementary, pointing to that nuanced split internal to the Marxian notion of the commodity addressed briefly in chapter 1 (and, of course, more extensively in Chapter 1 of *Capital*).[9] But the "product" shares much with the "work" as well. In fact, Lefebvre emphasizes, "the product is situated between the simple thing itself and the work produced by an artist" (2006b, 235).[10] From this assessment, it seems to follow that there exist products that are not works—but that works are *necessarily* also products, just as works and products are necessarily things in the simple sense. From this it follows a "product" is only a "work" to the extent that it is irreducible to the logic of capital, and yet the "work" is always (by definition) susceptible to partial if not total appropriation by that logic. In this light, a dynamic model is needed in order to approach the notion of "work." Lefebvre's dynamic model asserts that "differences appear [between the product and the work], but without breaking the nexus. Production and creation are considerably distinct, but creation presumes-explains production and the productive process" (2006b, 267).[11]

Even though the notion of the "work" is, in principle, inextricable from the "product," Lefebvre points out that individual thinkers have privileged one over the other: for example, the product over the work (in Marx), or the work over the product (in Nietzsche) (Lefebvre 2006b, 235). It is clear that understanding the tension between the "product" and the "work" is particularly important for Lefebvre. This tension becomes evident in the context of contemporary capitalism, which presents certain challenges for what Lefebvre calls the "creative capacity of works" (2006b, 235). Just as he previously argued in *Critique of Everyday Life* that postwar capitalism had crushed natural rhythms by introducing serial homogeneity and monotonous repetition into everyday life (e.g., Lefebvre 2005, vol. 3), here he points out that "capitalism and statism have crushed the creative capacity of works" (Lefebvre 2006b, 235).[12] In such a context, "The product is separated from the work... Relegated to the periphery, sometimes taking it as a favored place, creative forces are condemned to failure: impotence, sterility" (Lefebvre 2006b, 235–236).[13] This insight has significant consequences regarding not merely the context in which works are produced, but also the potential (contestatory) meanings they may hold in that very context.

Lefebvre's distinction between the product and the work, in a way, recapitulates the nuanced relationship between use-value and exchange-value so central to Marx's *Capital*. Once again, however, the French theorist does this by building on and going beyond traditional Marxian thought. Lefebvre's theory suggests that the work (of art)—just as is the case with the commodity—is itself necessarily riven through by a contradiction. Yet, just as the object was (partially) reconstituted as a use-value once it acquired an exchange-value, the product understood as a work—if and to the extent it is conceived as such—similarly has two faces. In this case, "the work" is simultaneously a product while also having a second aspect that is irreducible to exchange. Lefebvre insists that "The work has no price, even if it is sold" (2006b, 251)—which is to say that although the "product" is sold, likely (somewhat necessarily) *because* of its connection to its cohabitating other (the "work"), the "work" is nonetheless irreducible to this exchange.[14] "Even if a market exists," Lefebvre continues, "the work *escapes the economic in a way that is (always) fictitiously-real.* The artist realizes himself and realizes the work in spite of economic, social and political factors . . . Thus, *the work restores use-value*" (original emphasis; 2006b, 251).[15] In particular, this insistence by Lefebvre that "the work restores use-value" requires further consideration.

Upon closer examination, what might be called the second aspect of the "work" (the aspect by which it differs from the product) both is and is not a use-value in the traditional sense (the sense acquired through exploration of the "thing–product" tension). That is, this second aspect or "restored use-value" of the work inhabits a space that extends—in principle, even if only partially and of course ephemerally—beyond the logic of capital. This does not mean that capitalist logic and accumulation strategies cannot reappropriate "the work" and effectively reintegrate it into the circuits of capital; only that the "work" retrogrades and is reconstituted as a "thing–product" to the degree that "the work" or aspects of "the work" are so reappropriated. Thus, for as long as it exists as such, "the work" is the producer of value itself (*the work* and *value* coincide for Lefebvre [2006b, 229]). This is not the case of the simple "thing" that is always–already awaiting actualization as a product embedded in capitalist relations. There is, thus, a radical potential in "the work"—in Lefebvre's view—that is not possessed by the "thing" or the "product." This should not be surprising to readers who are generally familiar with Lefebvre. After all, it is the "work [as] a reality and a concept [both] borne of humanism" that marks the beginning of the "new path" of questioning he outlines in *La présence et l'absence.*[16]

Lefebvre's theory of "the work" is important for urban cultural studies scholars in that it potentially provides a radical way of understanding the dialectical (urban) relationship between capital and culture by privileging the notions of commodification and resistance, specifically. This characterization may be taken as optimistic by critics—a description which need not imply a judgment although it will be accompanied by such in many cases. That is, a whole tradition of (traditional) Marxism views culture as a dead-end that can only reaffirm the logic of capital. Yet critics holding on to this view either misunderstand Lefebvre's work as a whole or disagree with it. That is, if Lefebvre's cultural theory of "the work" seems optimistic, his urban philosophy was equally optimistic—optimistic in the sense that he persistently pointed to the possibility for disalienation that was contained within the many and multifaceted alienations of contemporary urban society (Lefebvre 1991b), and optimistic in that he pointed to the potential of an urban society that would transcend the logic of capital and realize a total and totalizing change in the nature of contemporary life (Lefebvre 2003a). More important, given the purpose of the present book, the Lefebvrian notion of "the work" provides a way of recuperating the goals of humanities scholarship and reconstituting them as a fundamental part of an urban cultural studies method. It is key to this shift of perspective that Lefebvre rejects a market-based understanding of culture (2006b, 236–237). He refuses to equate culture with product or to reduce work to being merely a product. But it is crucial that he simultaneously creates a theory of "the work" that is broadly applicable to both humanities and social science scholarship, irreducible to a single set of norms, and indicative of the (alienating) limitations placed on bourgeois knowledge by the social division of labor from the nineteenth century onward.

First, it is essential to take note of Lefebvre's concertedly broad view of "the work" (2006b, 237). The "work" is both individual and social (Lefebvre 2006b, 238)—a position that recalls a traditional Marxian skepticism of the individualist myth of capitalist society (see also Harvey 2006b). Even though "the work" is a concept irreducible to the "work of art" specifically, this "work of art" continues to be the prime example of the "work" more generally speaking (Lefebvre 2006b, 238). Lefebvre clearly states that art—which he defines in a way that naturally speaks to humanities scholars focused on cultural products ("poetry, music, theater, novels, etc.," 2006b, 237)—is thus not the limit case of his concept of "the work," but is instead an essential, representative case. Moreover, he writes, it is a case that in fact constitutes the basis for all thoughts about more broadly defined understandings of "the work."[17] By this Lefebvre means to reference his idea that the city itself is potentially a work of art—or reference, as he had written earlier, the notion of "the art of living in the city as work of art" (1996, 173). Because this phrase itself—as with other commonplaces touting the "organic" nature of city life, the metaphor of the city as a body (organic metaphor), the city as a symphony, ballet, or as a set of flows (see Fraser 2009a, 2011a, 2012a; also above, chapter 1)—necessarily takes on the tenor of the context in which, it is asserted, we do well in clarifying what Lefebvre means by this.

It is useful to read Lefebvre's comment against (or along with) the insistence by famed urban thinker Jane Jacobs that "a city cannot be a work of art" (1992, 372).[18] In her 1961 salvo titled *The Death and Life of Great American Cities*, Jacobs took on the shared assumptions of the urban planners of her day, who advocated large-scale solutions far divorced from the realities that cities were lived spaces (i.e., use-values) and who were largely sympathetic to a certain distanced (alienated) artistic view of the city as a product. In that 1961 book, Jacobs wrote that "To approach a city, or even a city neighborhood, as if it were a larger architectural problem, capable of being given order by converting it into a disciplined work of art, is to make the mistake of attempting to substitute art for life" (1992, 373; see also Fraser 2009a, 2011a, 2011b). The notion of the city as a work of art was—and of course still is—hegemonic among planners who approach the city as a ordered geometrical realm or object of beauty, and whose interests, of course, tend to dovetail with those of speculators, builders, and capitalists (Lefebvre 1996; Sennett 1992, 1994, 2008; cf. Olsen 1986). Yet context is everything. When Lefebvre insists this very thing—that the city *is* *indeed* a work of art—he is paradoxically saying the same thing Jacobs intended when she asserted that the city *was not* a work of art. In each case, the city is being reclaimed—by both Lefebvre and Jacobs—as an inhabited and habitable space, a realm unfettered by the staid designs of conceptualized space, constructed instead on the basis of unpredictability, encounter, movement, improvisation—we can say that for both Lefebvre and Jacobs the city is a space that is, in a word, *lived*.

Lefebvre's broadly applicable premise regarding "the work," then—he calls the city itself a work on numerous pages (e.g., 2006b, 239–239, 242, 244)[19]—leads him beyond the boundaries of the text itself toward urban realities. He thus forces a confrontation between multiple—sometimes competing—understandings of the work of art. When Lefebvre invokes the phrase "the work of art" in reference to the city, specifically, he is acknowledging and contesting the primacy of reductive, urbanistic views of city life—views which continue to divorce the conceived from the lived and assert the triumph of the exchange-value of the city over the use-value of the city (Lefebvre 1996, 2003a, 2006b). He simultaneously points to the potential of urban life. This potential is synonymous with what the city *could* be (and perhaps already is, although only partially and ephemerally) if the use-value of the city were to be *restored* (*a la* Lefebvre 2006b, 251) by shifting the city itself along the dialectic from "product" toward "work."

As equally privileged elements of Lefebvre's theory of "the work (of art)," both humanities texts and the city itself have the potential to become radically transfigurative of urbanized society. This is true, of course, only to the degree that they harness the lived and eschew the conceived, fully assimilating Lefebvre's (1991a) dictum that space is lived before it is conceived. This insistence amounts to a rudimentary method that—phrased in these general terms—is equally applicable to what we normally take to be two widely divergent sets of circumstances: problems of literature and of culture on one hand, and problems of urban life on the other. Lefebvre's emphasis on lived experience in what might provisionally be called his more spatially oriented books (e.g., 1991a, 1996, 2003a) is in fact the complement to his insistence on the creative capacity of artists in *La présence et l'absence*. Thus, just as we must put the lived at the center of our understanding of spatial production and of our approach to cities, it is equally important that "art, the project, the work, begin with experience (poetry, music, theater, the novel, etc.) subsequently incorporating knowledge, and not the other way around" (Lefebvre 2006b, 237).[20] And after all—as Lefebvre himself argues—it is the bourgeois specialization of knowledge that encourages the error of thought that takes these two sets of circumstances to be divergent in the first place; it is an adherence to specialization that, significantly, becomes decisively entrenched during a period of formative urbanization and urbanism (Lefebvre 1996, 2003a; Fraser 2008a, 2011a).

The second advantage of Lefebvre's view of "the work," which follows from the first, requires much less discussion—but is not for that reason any less important. In addition to being defined quite broadly— thus being applicable to both humanities texts and cities themselves—it is a theory that is accompanied by a specific approach: "The theory of the work implies a respect with an ethical reach. Works, in the same way as experience, should not be approached without care and precaution. As such, our theory does not take it upon itself to give instructions. It has neither a normative nor pedagogical aesthetic. It must shed light on a creative practice" (Lefebvre 2006b, 238).[21] This open attitude and distrust of system is, of course, an attribute of Lefebvre's philosophical thought in general, and one that tends to manifest itself in discussions of any number of various topics.[22] Given that Lefebvre sees no reason to reduce his thoughts to a set of norms or instructions, it would be counterproductive and moreover inappropriate to do so here. Nonetheless, echoing Lefebvre, it is important to understand how the alienating limitations of bourgeois knowledge—from the nineteenth century onward, rooted in the social division of labor—themselves attempt to restrict the nature and potential of "the work."

The next section will thus elaborate on what I have pointed to above as the third advantage of a Lefebvrian theory by exploring how "the work (of art)" is restricted by the current state of humanities scholarship. This argument will require turning, once again, to the complementary work of Raymond Williams as a way of understanding the modern formations of literary study. From this perspective, the critic exercises a function that is traditionally circumscribed by the limits of bourgeois knowledge. By and large, such bourgeois knowledge alienates the work of art from its social, political, and economic contexts through the discourse of literary specialization. This engagement with literary specialization should be taken, of course, as a representative case for narrowly specialized cultural inquiry more broadly considered.

The Critic: Disalienating Humanities Scholarship

Below, in this section, we will soon return to the topic of what Lefebvre calls the "creative capacity" of the artist, and then—in the final section of this chapter—its relation to Lefebvrian discussions of both city life and literature (i.e., culture, broadly considered). Before taking that step, however, it is important to see how scholars have traditionally maintained the boundary between these two areas of thought through recourse to the alienating discourse of specialization. There is a wealth of material on this subject awaiting consultation by interested scholars. I suspect that those grounded in literary fields are acutely aware of this issue no matter their perspective on it, and whether they recognize it to be, in fact, a manifestation of alienation or not.[23] Given the Marxian dimensions of the present work—and of Lefebvre's oeuvre as a whole—it makes the most sense to return to a fundamental (if oft-ignored) text that some 40 years ago attempted to disalienate literary scholars from the pernicious effects of their own disciplinary specialization.

That text is Raymond Williams' *Marxism and Literature* (1977). Therein, Williams begins by introducing the basic concepts of culture (11–20), language (21–44), literature (45–54), and ideology (55–71), before looking in turn and in greater detail at cultural theory (Part II: 75–141) and literary theory (Part III: 145–212). Much as does Lefebvre, Williams regards the way in which the base-superstructure opposition has been typically (mis)interpreted throughout the development of Marxian method with some degree of skepticism (1977, 75–82; cf. Lefebvre 2005, 16). Adopting this skeptical view, Williams attempts to go beyond the difficulties that have traditionally dogged the use of this base-superstructure opposition (formed by what are two abstract categories) through a "relational emphasis" (1977, 79) that unites "(a) institutions; (b) forms of consciousness; [and] (c) political and cultural practices" (77). On account of these basic methodological similarities, it becomes appropriate to use Williams's text to further the present discussion of Lefebvre's ideas. And yet this move is not merely appropriate, it is also necessary, given that *Marxism and Literature* offers a critique of disciplinary method that prioritizes aesthetic study. Unlike Lefebvre—who nonetheless suggests numerous disciplinary critiques, and whose texts prove to be more relevant to the construction of an interdisciplinary urban cultural studies method, specifically—Williams delves into the history, motivation, and ills of literary and cultural theory in detail. He exposes the alienations inherent to disciplinary practices, doing so from a decidedly Marxian perspective.

Dovetailing well with Lefebvre's elaboration of Marxian method throughout the *Critique of Everyday Life*, Williams points out that Marx's understanding of culture was clearly either rooted in his nineteenth-century capitalist context—such that it badly needed to be updated—or else was insufficiently developed. The example Williams provides is succinct, accessible, and broadly applicable to contemporary postwar contexts, generally speaking. "There is a footnote in the *Grundrisse* in which it is argued that a piano-maker is a productive worker, engaged in productive labour, but that a pianist is not, since his labour is not labour which reproduces capital" (Williams 1977, 93).[24] Williams then launches from this anecdote to assert a more capacious definition of materiality (1977, 94). This sentiment is, course, one that readers can very easily identify with Lefebvre's contribution to Marxian thought—not merely in that it functions as timely update of Marx but, moreover, also as it alludes to the more generalized inadequacy of much previous Marxian thought to theorize "everyday" culture in particular.[25] But it may also be taken as a warning of sorts for aspiring or established cultural critics.

As Williams points out, traditional Marxist perspectives have approached art through insufficient frameworks, frameworks in which art is either a "reflection" or a "mediation" of social reality.[26] Williams considers the somewhat more nuanced understanding of "art as mediator" of social reality to be subject, in essence, to the same criticism as the notion of "art as reflection."[27] Reflection establishes a "basic dualism" between base and superstructure, and "Mediation, in this range of use, then seems little more than a sophistication of reflection"—thus, "it is virtually impossible to sustain the metaphor of 'mediation'...without some sense of separate and pre-existent areas or orders of reality" (Williams 1977, 99).[28] In the end, Williams regards mediation, in a sense, as the lesser of two evils: "To the extent that it indicates an active and substantial process, 'mediation' is always the less *alienated* concept" (emphasis added; 1977, 99). The use of the word *alienated* in this passage is not merely fortuitous, but rather a sign of Williams's concerted engagement with that Marxian notion that is most relevant, also, to the urban cultural studies critic.

Following from Lefebvre's recalibrated Marxism (chapter 2), alienation permeates our contemporary (urban) social environments, our relation to others, to our work, our world, and even our relationship with ourselves. It also necessarily structures the way we categorize our knowledge about the world and thus the abstract categories through which we make sense of that world and reproduce its value structure. While the next section of this chapter will look at the divisions across disciplines—their alienation from one another—the remainder of this second section will interrogate the ways in which literary and aesthetic disciplines are routinely alienated internally, through the discourse of specialization. This means understanding that within the specialization of the study of art (as opposed to economy, politics, sociology, etc.), literature is seen as distinct from other aesthetic investigations (Williams 1977, 145). But this also entails taking a closer look at literary study in particular, understanding that its most ingrained method is in fact predicated on cleaving itself off from the wider economic, political, social world. With these explorations in mind, we will then be able to understand what challenges await the urban cultural studies critic, specifically, in attempting to cross disciplinary boundaries in pursuit of a disalienated approach to contemporary urban life.

First, Williams explains that the development of aesthetics as a "theory of perception" arose "in the eighteenth and especially the nineteenth century [as] a new specializing form of description of the response to 'art'" (1977, 150). This aesthetic theory focused "initially the perception of beauty; then the pure contemplation of an object, for its own sake and without other ('external') considerations; then also the perception and contemplation of the 'making' of an object: its language, its skill of construction, its 'aesthetic properties'" (Williams 1977, 150).[29] This move, of course, itself may have developed as an antidote to the rapidly growing hegemony of the commodity form, in which—as Williams points out—certain notions of instrumentality and utility were essential (1977, 151).[30] But there is a paradox here, he makes clear, in that by attempting to affirm the noneconomic value of art with respect to the ascendant commodity culture, this eighteenth/nineteenth-century aesthetic theory cleaves the artistic work from its social context. In the process, the artistic work becomes isolated in line with the very divisive logic of capital, which replicates the social division of labor in a fragmented model of human knowledge (Williams 1977, 153–154; cf. Lefebvre 1996, 2003a). (Note that, in particular, the significance of Lefebvre's theory of the "thing–product–work" as elaborated in *La présence et l'absence* lies in the fact that it turns its attention toward resolving this problem—or rather toward maintaining the nuances inherent within it.) Williams's 1977 book was written, in part, precisely in order to correct the excesses of this interpretive shift, reconciling the aesthetic with the material and calling into question their distinction: "we have to reject 'the aesthetic' both as a separate abstract dimension and as a separate abstract function ... At the same time we have to recognize and indeed emphasize the specific variable intentions and the specific variable responses that have been grouped as aesthetic in distinction from other isolated intentions and responses" (Williams 1977, 154).

Second, Williams explains how literary specialization arose more or less in tandem with this aesthetic specialization, how it stemmed from the same causes and motivations and produced similar conclusions. Taking on "the historical development of the concept of 'literature': from its connections with literacy to an emphasis on polite learning and on printed books, and then, in its most interesting phase, to an emphasis on 'creative' or 'imaginative' writing as a special and indispensable kind of cultural practice" (1977, 145; also 147), Williams emphasizes the seeming distance of the literary from the aesthetic and the challenge thus awaiting any "social theory of culture." Such a theory must consequently contend not merely with one specialization but instead with two, and thus also with the divisions between them both (Williams 1977, 145).[31] "The theoretical problem is that two very powerful modes of distinction are deeply implanted in modern culture. These are the supposedly distinctive categories of 'literature' and of 'the aesthetic.' Each, of course, is historically specific: a formulation of bourgeois culture at a definite period of its development, from the mid-eighteenth to the mid-nineteenth century" (Williams 1977, 145). Even within literary studies, the movement of an alienating bourgeois logic that severs the social world into manageable (Williams uses the term "useful"), isolated fragments of specialized knowledge continues to operate on a micro level: dividing literature into genres ("poetry, drama, novel") and subforms ("'lyric,' 'epic,' 'narrative'") and distinguishing also between literary and nonliterary writing (Williams 1977, 146). In reality, of course, both the aesthetic and the literary specializations are coetaneous, and each has its own subspecialties that await further critique. Most important, whether it is with regard to literary studies or aesthetic theory, the fragmented logic accompanying specialization has become crystallized in criticism and, in fact, "has done significant harm" (Williams 1977, 146).

With Williams's remarks in mind, let us now return to Lefebvre's emphasis on the "creative capacity" of the artist. Because Lefebvre's understanding of the radical opportunity confronted by the artist who begins with experience is equally applicable to the critic, it is thus doubly worthy of our attention. The notion of "creative capacity"—by which Lefebvre means something quite specific—offers a way of discussing the potentially disalienating aspects of the artist's activity, but also of the cultural critic's activity, provided that it, too, harnesses this "creative capacity." We saw earlier that Lefebvre suggests that the artist begin with experience (2006b, 245).[32] This is to adopt the perspective of artistic production as a (potentially) creative and not a (merely) productive act—as a way of reiterating the previously discussed, nuanced Lefebvrian distinction between the "product" and "the work." Lefebvre makes clear that exercising a creative capacity requires that the artist adopt a different perspective. S/he cannot remain "in experience" for long periods of time, instead, "The creator of works finds in experience an initial inspiration, a vital and original impulse" (Lefebvre 2006b, 246).[33] It is important to recognize here that, although the term "experience" seems simple enough on its own, understood in light of the French philosopher's extensive oeuvre, the command to "begin with experience" is equivalent to advocating a more complex methodological premise.[34] Specifically, for Lefebvre, "starting with experience" means that the artist necessarily roots her or his creation in a complex yet immediate world—a realm of multiplicity where cultural, economic, political, and social concerns all cohabit with one another, each inextricable from the rest.

That is, starting with experience or—to use the phrase made popular in Anglophone circles with *The Production of Space*—starting with space as it is *lived* (and not merely *conceived* or *perceived*), the artist creates a "work" that folds what are (for the fragmented bourgeois intellect) separate spheres of activity into a single if variegated whole. It follows that if the "work" loses its connection with experience, if it becomes "autonomous," it risks merely "producing or reproducing the conditions of its autonomy" (Lefebvre 2006b, 244).[35] As Lefebvre insists, "That which merely *is* economic, technological, ludic, quotidian, etc., cannot but be a representation or a product, and distances itself from the work" (original emphasis; 2006b, 244).[36] What he refers to using the name of "creative capacity" in fact corresponds to the ability to simultaneously overcome the many alienations of contemporary life. From this perspective, one part of any Lefebvrian definition of art might be that a creative product acquires the status of a "work" through a characteristic blending of two or more areas of contemporary life that are routinely regarded as separate. Such a Lefebvrian definition of art is in itself disalienating and thus interdisciplinary in a radical sense.

An instructive example of what this might mean in practice can be found in street art and graffiti, although the second major section of this book will explore what it means for other kinds of cultural texts to be subjected to the Lefebvrian notion of "the work"—particularly those kinds of texts that are of interest to scholars working in the humanities. For now, however, we do well in looking merely at a case that might be representative of the way in which social scientists are more likely to engage urban culture. This is the case of street art/graffiti. In downtown Baltimore in 2012, concretely, there is a street artist going by the name of Gaia who has created some work on Howard Street as part of his "Legacy Series."[37] "Affixed to the façade of a forgotten building, the rendering of [Harry] Weinberg looks out onto a parking lot of the opposite block. That entire square block was once one of Weinberg's holdings, and the fact that it's now a parking lot serves as a testament to what little Weinberg had done for Baltimore's revitalization. Gaia's artwork is a reminder of this disastrous tale," writes a blogger in a post reflecting the push of a larger research project about "street artists as catalysts for change."[38] Without venturing too far into notions of artistic intention or degrees of social awareness on one hand, and without reducing the work of art to its inspiration on the other, in fact, one can easily see that Gaia begins with "experience"—a lived experience of Baltimore, to be specific. That is, he begins with the material spatialization of the contemporary city and the material political, the social, the economic aspects that accompany this complex urban situation. Grounded in Lefebvre's loosely defined and pointedly interdisciplinary theory of art, one might say that the painting of a billionaire investor's face on the side of a boarded-up building thus becomes a "work" precisely because it brings the political, the social, and the economic into direct resonance with the artistic—and of course also with the urban (which unites them all). This move is radical in the specific sense that the artist has detached from a number of alienations that would have pushed him to see the artistic, the social, the political, the economic as separate areas of experience, and has also, in this way, gone beyond an urban alienation (which for Lefebvre [2003a, 92] trumps all other forms of alienation).

Let us take this case more representatively of the nature of the Lefebvrian "work (of art)" in general, and we will see that the creator's efforts yield a "work" and not merely a "product" (in part) because it serves as a fulcrum for reconciling alienated, specialized areas of experience with one another. This is an act of—in a word—disalienation. Significantly, Williams, for his part, reaches somewhat similar conclusions regarding what he calls "creativity" toward the end of *Marxism and Literature*, although his theory is not as nuanced as Lefebvre's regarding this topic specifically. Nonetheless, for Williams, creativity, too, is implicated in material social processes and has an essentially far-reaching and reconciliatory character: "For creativity relates, finally, to much more than its local and variable means. Inseparable as it always is from the material social process, it ranges over very different forms and intentions which, in partial theories, are separated and specialized" (1977, 211).[39] Lefebvre's theory of "the work" is much more thorough than Williams's concluding remarks in that it charts out in what way, specifically, creativity brings its "locality" into relation with much, "much more." Lefebvre's theory also specifies precisely how we might better understand the range and relationship of creativity to separated and specialized "forms and intentions" (in both cases, by way of its essential disalienations). The movement effected by the creation of "the work" is also explained by Lefebvre as a twin-reconciliation: he affirms that the creator of works "realizes a double creation: that of knowledge by way of experience, and of experience by way of knowledge" (Lefebvre 2006b, 246).[40]

It is essential to see that the Lefebvrian notion of "creative capacity" is as equally applicable to the creator of artistic work as it is to the creator of critical work. To situate the critic outside of the aesthetic realm is not only to deny his or her inherent potential for creation (or "creative capacity") but also to effect yet another of the fragmentations that Williams and Lefebvre both eschew. This is not to say that the context of the critic is no different from that of the artist, nor that there may not be additional issues with which to contend. In a certain sense, however, just like those of the street or graffiti artist, the efforts of the creator of critical work may come to constitute a "work" and not merely a "product" (in part) based on the degree to which this critical activity breaks down the separating walls of alienated areas of specialized knowledge. In the case of cultural criticism of novels, films, music, digital spaces, etc., it is the critic, and not merely the artist, who has the responsibility of reconciling these various alienated spheres (returning the political to the social, the cultural to the economic, etc.). Moreover, the creator of critical works must also "start with experience"—with urbanized capital and urbanized consciousness, with everyday life and its increasing commoditization, and with the multiple realities of alienation that structure both thought and the everyday. As in the case of the artist, that which the critic creates will ideally employ the cultural (artistic) as a way of linking areas that are alienated from one another in the urban phenomenon. Ultimately Lefebvre asserts that "The work of art and the artist together propose to exalt experience, and even to transfigure it" (2006b, 247). It follows that criticism may either seek to do the same, or else (consciously or not) to reaffirm existing alienations that prevent an apprehension of the totality of contemporary urban life.[41] If radical art strives for interdisciplinarity as a path toward disalienation, then so too must radical criticism strive for interdisciplinarity.

Totality: Art at the Service of the Urban

The Marxian notion of totality—by which critics usually mean to reference "Marx's over-all analysis of capitalism"—is perhaps traditionally explained in economic terms (Kolakowski 2005, 256). Leszek Kolakowski, for example, in his essential text *Main Currents of Marxism*, broaches the subject by invoking *Capital* (vol. 2) and writing that

> Throughout history material forces have dominated human beings, and in considering capitalist society each separate element must be related to the whole and each phenomenon treated as a phrase in a developing process. In *Capital* Marx more than once recalls this global aspect of his method of inquiry. No economic act, however trivial, such as the buying and selling that occurs millions of times a day, is intelligible except in the context of the entire capitalist system. (2005, 256)

Referring also to the *Grundrisse*, Kolakowski makes it clear that this notion of the whole, even for Marx, need not remain "untouched by theory" (2005, 257). But totality acquires an entirely new character when viewed through Lefebvre's extended critique of Marxian alienation and his reconfiguration of the base-superstructure model of capitalist society. To trace the relevance of alienation to matters not merely economic but moreover philosophical, social, political, urban, aesthetic, and disciplinary, for example—as Lefebvre does in *Critique of Everyday Life*, *The Right to the City*, *The Urban Revolution*, and even *La présence et l'absence*, to name just a handful of instances—is to reconstitute totality as much more complex indeed.

Viewed in light of the urban thinker's five nested critiques of static space, modern urban planning, alienation in everyday life, knowledge, and method (from chapter 2), Lefebvrian totality retains the traditionally Marxian emphasis on economics, but acquires multiple dimensions that were underdeveloped in Marx's original thought. Grounded in yet going beyond Marx, Lefebvre characterizes capitalist modernity as a totality broken into pieces: "In order to become more explicit, a multitude of capacities and forces—some ancient and others more recent—*became autonomous*, each one going its own way, affirming itself on its own, imposing itself or attempting to impose itself on the others and totalizing itself through its own strength" (2006b, 242).[42] In this passage, Lefebvre takes it upon himself to "enumerate these capacities and activities"—a group in which he includes "the economic," "the *political* and later the *state*," "science and knowledge," and finally "art" (original emphasis; 2006b, 242). Because Lefebvre's vision of totality explicitly forces a confrontation between each of these areas, in considering his theory of the "work (of art)" as we have done, we are simultaneously pushed further along toward consideration of what he calls, in the *Critique of Everyday Life*, the "art of living." We are thus pushed onward toward the city as a work of art, and finally toward what might be called the art of living in the city. This is to move, ultimately, toward a reconstituted urban society that, through emphasizing social needs alongside the notions of play and the unpredictable against the limitations of an instrumentalist capitalism, ends by returning the city to urbanites as a use-value and a lived space—in short, returning the urban to its inhabitants as a "work." In fact, elsewhere the Lefebvrian "right to the city" is framed precisely as "The right to the *oeuvre*" (1996, 174).[43]

Seasoned readers may recognize echoes of Marx in these basic Lefebvrian notions. It is true that what Marx, in his 1844 *Manuscripts*, termed the "ideal of a future non-alienated 'artistic' form of production" (Rose 1984, 79) inspires, more or less directly, Lefebvre's concentrated interest not only in the "work (of art)" but also in his vision for the realization of an "urban" society (note that this is not merely an "urbanized" or "urbanistic" society).[44] In this way, both Lefebvre's theory of the work of art as outlined in *La présence et l'absence* (1980) and what are, for him, its logical consequences express something that was undertheorized (but not untheorized) in Marx. "Although Marx had spoken of a future form of non-alienated labour in terms of artistic activity in his *Economic and Philosophic Manuscripts* of 1844, he had not yet offered a fully developed analysis of art as a form of economic production subject to the demands—and alienations—of other forms of production" (Rose 1984, 79).[45] In this sense, Lefebvre picks up where Marx left off.[46] We do well in seeing the relationship of Lefebvre's theory of creative capacities to areas that are traditionally seen as having few ties to aesthetic matters. In this tracing, this movement of thought, there is an opportunity to flesh out the recalibrated Marxian notion of totality, ultimately reconstituting it in specifically urban terms.

To start, the creative "work" is not merely a "product," Lefebvre argues, precisely because it liberates itself from the division of labor. The "work"

> frees itself from the division of labor, although it results from a labor. For this reason, it is not a product. The creative effort seems (in a fictitiously-real way) freed from coercions, from limits, from separations. Apparently the artist does everything by himself; he dominates his time and his space, as a consequence, through the work, the space and the time of all. He works (a lot, sometimes without rest) without it seeming like he works (as it is with the poet); he acts in a space of representations that neither ties him nor drags him to an illusory surface. The work appears to "produce" his time, his space, his affirmation and his force. (Lefebvre 2006b, 251)[47]

A previously mentioned essay assessing Lefebvre's underappreciated engagement with aesthetic questions can help us to understand further that for the French philosopher "art is the product of a specific kind of work that characteristically struggles against the division of labour in an attempt to grasp the 'total' content of life and of social activity" (Léger 2006, 151).[48]

Nevertheless, Lefebvre himself also makes this connection clear through his assertion that the work of art—once again the creative work as opposed to the product—always yearns for the totality: "No work— neither the work of art properly understood, nor the city and second nature etc.—can realize itself without reuniting all of the elements and moments, without constituting a totality" (Lefebvre 2006b, 244).[49] Lefebvre writes in the same way about the work of art as he already had regarding everyday life itself. In the *Critique of Everyday Life*, the French philosopher had written of "the art of living":

> The critique of everyday life has a contribution to make to *the art of living*...In the future the art of living will become a genuine art, based like all art upon the vital need to expand, and also on a certain number of techniques and areas of knowledge, but which will go beyond its own conditions in an attempt to see itself not just as a means but as an end. The art of living presupposes that the human being sees his own life— the development and intensification of his life—not as a means towards "another" end, but as an end in itself. It presupposes that life as a whole— everyday life—should become a work of art. (Lefebvre 1991b, 199)

Here we can see, unsurprisingly for many, that Lefebvre employs the same method to approach what might be taken as (through an alienating perspective) two separate areas of experience. Despite the considerable temporal distance between these two texts (*La présence et l'absence*, originally from 1980; *Critique of Everyday Life*, originally from 1947), the notion of art nonetheless retains the same value and potential.

There is something of a "creative capacity" that must be actualized whether in the work of art or the art of living itself; there is an act of creation that "will not be reducible to a few cheap formulas": "Recipes and techniques for increasing happiness and pleasure are part of the baggage of bourgeois wisdom—a shallow wisdom which will never bring satisfaction. The genuine art of living implies a human reality, both individual and social, incomparably broader than this" (Lefebvre 1991b, 199).[50] The fact that Lefebvre here characteristically underscores the tension between the individual and the social is important when considering, as he does, that the city is also a work of art. Scholar Sara Nadal-Melsió has noted that "The Lefebvrean city functions like the aesthetic expression of the body in space—a work of art—that produces knowledge as well as history" (2008, 165). Just as the work of art yearns for totality, so too does the city as a work of art.[51] But Lefebvre makes clear that "the city has been and continues to be the supreme work, the work of all works" (2006b, 161).[52] The "urban form" is thus the site of encounter, movement, and flow in which totality may be realized through creative practice.

In the face of the instrumentalist paradigm of urbanism, this creative urban practice is necessarily made possible by being grounded—just as with the creation of the work of art—in "experience." In *The Right to the City*, Lefebvre writes of what it means to return to experience in the context of the city:

> To *inhabit* finds again its place over habitat. The quality which is promoted presents and represents as *playful*. By *playing* with words, one can say that there will be *play* between the parts of the social whole (plasticity)—to the extent that *play* is proclaimed as supreme value, eminently solemn, if not serious, over-taking use and exchange by gathering them together. And if someone cries out that this utopia has nothing in common with socialism, the answer is that today only the working class still knows how to really play, feels like playing, over and above the claims and programmes, of economism, and political philosophy. How is this shown? Sport and the interest shown in sport and games, including, in television and elsewhere, the degraded forms of ludic life. Already, to city people the urban centre is movement, the unpredictable, the possible and encounters. For them, it is either "spontaneous theatre" or nothing. (original emphasis; 1996, 172)[53]

And just as it had in the discourse of art, returning to experience—here, for Lefebvre—means returning to the realm of the senses. Marx himself, of course, had advocated generally for the power of the senses, from which modern man had been progressively alienated through the intellection and instrumentalized knowledge that had accompanied the rise of a commodity culture (this will be the point of departure for analyzing popular music in chapter 6). Much of Lefebvre's theorizations harness the power of the senses, specifically, as a revolutionary force. Although this is perhaps most obvious in *Rhythmanalysis* where sound and smell are given equal importance to visual matters in approaching the city as always in movement, it is also a crucial component of the *Critique of Everyday Life* more generally speaking.

Yet the move to return to experience, to return to the senses—whether in the work of art, the art of living, or the city itself seen as a work of art—is not an end in and of itself. Or rather, what is significant about these returns is that they are all movements of disalienation. In the *Critique*, Lefebvre writes that "The art of living implies the end of alienation—and will contribute towards it" (1991b, 199). Thus, when urban living is taken to be an art—a creative practice complementary to or suggested by the creation of the work of art—this means simultaneously moving beyond the "partial determinisms" of alienation toward urban totality.[54] In this way, Lefebvre explains, art and philosophy must work together if the urban problematic is to be resolved.[55] Philosophy itself, in fact, has the power to think totality, writes Lefebvre.[56] But similarly, philosophy cannot accomplish this on its own, for it runs into certain obstacles.[57] As Lefebvre writes, "Philosophy cannot realize itself without art (as model of appropriation of time and space), accomplishing itself fully in social practice and without science and technology, as means, not being fully used, without the proletarian condition being overcome" (1996, 176).[58]

We have only now arrived at the possibility of explaining what Lefebvre means by "putting art in the service of the urban." The significance of this phrase can be seen only after discarding an alienating view that obfuscates how art has been assimilated into the existing, rational project of urban planning. That is, there is, today, a certain commonsensical meaning to combinations of "art" and "the city" that the vast majority of city dwellers have no doubt internalized after over a century of efforts to "prettify urban space." Art—mostly, but not purely through architectural modifications and built environment improvements—is frequently harnessed by speculators and capitalists investing in urban projects as part of the practice of intercity competition. But Lefebvre does not mean to invoke art in this way—as a product—but to underscore quite a different notion of art—as a "work." He believes that, taken together, philosophy and art can illuminate a future for urban practice that succeeds in moving the production of urban space beyond the concerns of turnover time, capital accumulation, and the city as exchange-value: "art can become *praxis* and *poiesis* on a social scale: the art of living in the city as work of art" (Lefebvre 1996, 173). Through the dual-lens of art and philosophy, the city is not an exchange-value but a use-value, a lived space for its inhabitants who are—potentially—empowered to reshape its produced space based on more broadly social needs.

There are many barriers to effecting this change. Some of those barriers are being challenged in social practice in the city itself through direct action, coalition building, and the fostering of community forms that take on capitalist alienation specifically. Others are being challenged in social science fields that draw on culture within anthropological, sociological, geographical frameworks, suggesting that we pay closer scholarly attention to those areas of social life that have been traditionally seen as marginal or "less material" in essence. And, of course, humanities scholars who reconcile texts with contexts, the texts as representations with lived experience as a representation, do the same. As the subsequent section of this book attempts to make clear—and as an illustration of the affinity between the "work (of art)" and the "city as work (of art)" that is so important for Lefebvre—humanities texts are privileged places for beginning an interdisciplinary and disalienting approach to urbanized society. In a general sense, cultural texts render attitudes and assumptions about urbanized society concrete in a way, allowing them to be discussed, debated, and potentially discarded, contested, and/or reformulated. To undertake such an investigation is to make the identification of alienating propositions—and thus disalienation of those propositions—possible. Urban cultural studies is motivated by a disalienating proposition, the need to disalienate scholars and consumers of urban cultural products of the notion that this city is (only) a thing or also (merely) a product, and return it to them as a work. But more specifically, as the next four chapters will address, cultural texts of all genres foreground the importance of both spatiality and temporality through their formal properties. From this perspective, space and time become less abstract and thus more investigable in novels, films, popular music, videogames, and so on. Although Lefebvre was certainly not completely satisfied with his aesthetic theory (Léger 2006, 160)—and although, moreover, he did not fully urbanize his aesthetic theory—pushing for the articulation of a Lefebvrian urban cultural studies requires identifying in general terms how his work might shed light on analyses of specific kinds of humanities texts.

PART II

Textual Variations

CHAPTER 4

The Urban Dominant: Everyday Life and the City in Textual Criticism

Lefebvre made an important statement in *The Right to the City*: "Philosophy cannot realize itself without art (as model of appropriation of time and space)" (1996, 176). This chapter builds on both the spirit of this comment and the discussion of the intersection of artistic discourse and the urban phenomenon begun in the previous chapter, charting out a model of how to approach cultural works from the perspective of the urban cultural studies method. Before going further, however, the reader must understand that the inclusion of this statement in chapter 3—on "The Work (of Art)"—was part of a larger goal. In brief, this goal was to outline a Lefebvrian theory of art: sustaining the French thinker's emphasis on alienation, asserting that aesthetic matters are inseparable from other (political, social, economic) concerns, drawing attention to the limits of disciplinary (traditionally literary) approaches to art, and underscoring the power and potential of the "creative capacity" of both the artist and the critic, ultimately as a challenge to existing alienated views of a Marxian-inspired notion of totality. By outlining this Lefebvrian theory of art, I suggest—Lefebvrian thought suggests—that there is a correlation or resonance between an emancipatory production of art and an emancipatory production of everyday life—and of contemporary urban life (Lefebvre 1991b, 1996).[1] Reimagining (or for some scholars, continuing to imagine) the study of literature from a perspective grounded in Lefebvre's musings on everyday life has the added advantage of facilitating increased interdisciplinarity: as Lefebvre writes, "the study of everyday life affords a meeting place for specialized sciences" (2007, 23; also 22).

Similarly, understanding the significance of the statement that "Philosophy cannot realize itself without art" requires that the reader go beyond a number of previously discussed and short-sighted views: both on Marxism in general and on Lefebvrian thought in particular. It is helpful to summarize those views before moving forward. First, for example, it has not been uncommon for scholars to approach Marx purely as a political economist, marginalizing his engagement with philosophy and exercising the function of a harmful economic reductionism (see Elden 2004). Such economic reductionism—as others have suggested—may, in fact, betray Marx's own intention. But it is wholly unnecessary to entertain debates over intentions when we are dealing with (1) Lefebvre's own loose or "open" mobilization of Marxism (e.g., Lefebvre 1988) and (2) the fact that twentieth-century (and twenty-first-century) capitalism has effected a sea change of sorts yielding situations that were, even for Marx, largely unanticipated. This sea change makes it necessary to place the question of urbanization as central and to widely recognize the insufficiency of a base-superstructure model to account for the complex interactions of contemporary culture and capital (Jameson 1999; Lefebvre 2005; Harvey 2012; see also Fraser 2014). Lefebvre, in fact, counters the notion that Marx may be reduced to either merely a philosopher or purely a political economist most directly in his assessment of the spirit behind the first volume of the *Critique of Everyday Life*, which he later maintained "challenges both philosophism and economism, refusing to admit that Marx's legacy can be reduced to a philosophical system (dialectical materialism) or to a theory of political economy" (2007, 30).

Second, there is the short-sighted view that reduces Lefebvre to a "spatial theorist" in the simple sense—as if spatial matters were separable from time, history, and so on, a position Lefebvre vehemently opposed and that recent scholarship has sought to correct (e.g., Elden 2004, 169–210; Fraser 2011a, 2008a).[2] Lefebvre undoubtedly made it clear that philosophy had its limitations, that it risked exercising merely an ideological function. But he also stressed many times that, properly reconfigured, philosophy nonetheless had a role to play (e.g., Lefebvre 1996, 2003a). In particular, this assertion is relevant to the crucial center of Lefebvre's rearticulation of Marxian thought—the multifaceted concept of alienation (chapter 2), which in essence actualizes Marx's own philosophical thinking and extends it to a wider range of contemporary matters.[3] Far from a call for abstract (disembodied) philosophical contemplation, Lefebvre's is a call to turn philosophy against the "colonization of daily life" (2002); that is, to reconcile philosophy with the city (and the urban) and, of course, also with the discourse of art.

As he mentions in *Everyday Life in the Modern World*, "Either philosophy is pointless or it is the starting point from which to undertake the transformation of non-philosophical reality, with all its triviality and its triteness" (Lefebvre 2007, 13). To philosophize in this way is not to distance oneself from reality through abstract thought but inversely to seize abstract thought, now turned against itself, as a way of returning to the experience from which we are routinely alienated.

With these considerations in mind, it is appropriate to take one further step—a step that brings us face to face with the individual humanities text. Following from Lefebvre's statement, the key question here is: if "philosophy cannot realize itself without art (as model of appropriation of time and space)," how, then, does art in fact appropriate time and space? And what, for example, can we learn from this spatiotemporal appropriation? A provisional answer to this question is "nothing." This is to say, we learn nothing from art's appropriation of time and space if we limit "meaning" to the text itself—that is, to the product. But understood as an oeuvre, as a "work" of art—with the Lefebvrian caveat that both the city and even everyday life are also creative works—there is a natural affinity between art and city that makes such textual interrogation meaningful and even crucial. Time and space are the common axes along which urban studies and cultural studies may establish a fruitful dialogue. Moreover, this chapter suggests that space and time are rendered investigable (visible, audible, tangible, assessable) in the cultural text (here, the literary text, but just as equally in filmic or other humanities texts) in a form that may be present but unacknowledged in everyday life. As this statement has great potential for being misunderstood, some clarification is necessary.

Make no mistake—certainly cultural texts are routinely harnessed (if not also intended) to affirm alienation rather than disalienate; yet the dual proposition that held for everyday life, which Lefebvre asserted was a site of both exploitation and resistance, is also applicable here. Literary criticism may (knowingly or unknowingly) implicitly affirm exploitation just as it may also constitute resistance in an explicit sense. To believe otherwise, in fact, is to reify the cultural text and constitute it somehow seemingly beyond the webs of capital in which it is enmeshed. It is important that we not reduce the cultural text to being merely a servant of capital. Lefebvre's theory of the work as discussed in chapter 3 (particularly the nuanced distinction between the "product" and the "work") is highly important in this regard: in that it preserves the primacy of the dynamic relationship between commodification and resistance that makes humanities scholarship so worthwhile an endeavor. It may be repeated that all works are products, but that not all products are works. If humanities scholarship remains acutely aware of this relationship, then investigation of the way in which space and time are appropriated through cultural texts can be an important arm in much broader debates over the way in which space and time are harnessed by capital "outside" of the work. For the urban cultural studies critic, then, the investigation/criticism of the cultural text is not an end in and of itself, but instead a crucial starting point for a critique of urban society—a critique that must necessarily pass through stages: of the work of art, of the criticism of art, of the city as work, and of the future of the city. To actualize this project and its stages—stages that may certainly be simultaneous—is to see the value of Lefebvre's extensive work and to call immediately upon the potentially disalienating function of interdisciplinarity.

The first section in this chapter ("The Urban Dominant") returns to a concept theorized by Roman Jakobson—and Russian Formalist literary criticism more generally—and modifies it for application to urban cultural products. Now recast under the augurs of an urbanized mode of capitalist production, "the dominant" provides a way of reconciling cultural analysis at the level of the text with the extratextual spatial realities and urbanized consciousness that necessarily influence the work of art's production and reception. Specifically, urbanized space and time are the very hinge making this reconciliation possible. Discussion turns briefly also to the relationship Lefebvre establishes between space and time—despite the popular and reductive conception of the thinker as merely a "spatial theorist"—and to how this philosophical insight is sustained in David Harvey's own Lefebvrian neo-Marxism. The goal of using the notion of an "urban dominant" here in rethinking the approaches of Lefebvre and Harvey is to refine the stated aim and role of the urban cultural studies critic. Far from merely fusing political economy and culture in general terms—a fusion that, in Harvey's nonetheless valuable work, in particular, remains relatively unconvincing for the typical humanities scholar—the urban cultural studies critic must work to sustain the value of close textual reading in the face of geography's generalized and disciplinary suspicion of the "text."

The second section ("Everyday Life and the City in Textual Criticism") begins by positing a complementary relationship between the Russian Formalist concept of "the dominant" and the Lefebvrian notion of everyday life. This relationship hinges on the boundary of the text itself. Both function to restore the individual text to the world from which it has been routinely alienated by deeply ingrained schisms (between the aesthetic and the political, the artistic and the economic).

Lefebvre's remarks on the everyday are, in fact, made alongside affir-mations of the importance of literature for understanding space itself. Seeing how Lefebvre himself situates literature along with philosophy as elements of his spatiotemporal thinking then leads into discussion of the presentation of everyday life and the city in literature. Moreover, following up on the lessons learned from the limits of Harvey's approach to texts in the first section of this chapter, it is important to see that the city as described in literature (and by extension in film and other cultural products)—while important—is not enough if we are to avoid reducing cultural texts to two-dimensional products or reified, static representations. This approach functions as one way of advocating for the restoration of cultural texts now understood as "works" to the Lefebvrian "work" that is the city itself.

The Urban Dominant

Urban cultural studies critics have the luxury, today, of being able to look back upon a long history of literary theory and select those aspects of previous approaches that may potentially aid in the stated goal of uniting analysis of both literary and nonliterary spaces. As suggested earlier, it is likely that not all previous approaches will have something to offer, and it is certain that the excesses of literary criticism may be safely discarded. Such excesses may be briefly identified concisely: on the one hand, there is the notion that there exists an isolated, aesthetic, literary realm uncomplicated by political, social, and economic inflec-tions; on the other hand, there is the idea that aesthetic matters may be completely reduced to being reflections or expressions of political, social, and economic problems. There is one concept in particular I would like to recuperate here as part of an urban cultural studies method. Surely it is not the only concept of value that may be taken from previ-ous approaches—and I hope that future engagements of urban literary criticism will seek out those other worthy concepts. Yet this section will address only the Russian Formalist concept of the "dominant"— fleshing out its potential relationship with Lefebvre's urban thinking, specifically.

It is important to note that there is a considerable degree of variation amongst the literary theories of the Russian Formalists, broadly con-sidered, which should not be overlooked (e.g., Mayakovsky, Jakobson, Shklovsky, Eichenbaum, Mukarovsky, Tynyanov, Tomashevsky, the Moscow Linguistic Circle, OPOJAZ, the Prague Linguistic Circle)— and that it is likely that reception of this range of work by contemporary

Anglophone audiences has necessarily been influenced by the association of the group with New Criticism (Cleanth Brooks et al.; see
Jameson 1972). While there may be important differences between the
Russian Formalists and the New Critics, generally speaking, both "aim
to explore what is specifically *literary* in texts" and advocate "a detailed
and empirical approach to reading" (original emphasis; Selden 1986, 6).[4]
In the end, the present interest in forging a Lefebvrian urban cultural
studies specifically means that there is little to be gained here by exploring either the similarities or the divergences of the groups in greater
depth.[5]

   Instead, by postulating the relevance of the formalist concept of "the
dominant" for urban cultural studies, I emphasize how it has been elaborated by one thinker in particular—Roman Jakobson (1896–1982).
Jakobson's perspective is significant as he judged the concept to be "one
of the most crucial, elaborated and productive concepts in Russian
Formalist Theory" (1987, 41).[6] Simply put, the dominant is "the focusing component of a work of art: it rules, determines, and transforms
the remaining components" (Jakobson, quoted in Selden 1986, 15).[7]
As originally theorized, different artistic movements were said to have
distinct dominants.[8] Thus, for example:

> The dominant of Renaissance poetry was derived from the visual arts;
> Romantic poetry oriented itself towards music; and Realism's dominant
> is verbal art. But whatever the dominant may be, it organises the other
> elements in the individual work, relegating to the background of aes-
> thetic attention elements which in works of earlier periods might have
> been "foregrounded" as dominant. (Selden 1986, 15)

From this perspective, the dominant must thus be evaluated, Jakobson
insists, "within the framework of a given literary period and a given
artistic trend" (1987, 41). Within this specific context it is a "leading
value" (Jakobson 1987, 42), and as such "The dominant specifies the
work" (41). Significantly, also, the notion of the dominant as developed
by the Russian Formalists was wrapped up in a dynamic, historical view
of the development of literature.[9] This dynamic and socially contextualized perspective on artistic production—which is perhaps more characteristic of the later periods of Russian Formalism—is often ignored by
characterizations that reduce what is quite a complex body of work to a
notion of *literariness* that ends with the boundaries of the text.[10]

   It is important to recognize that artistic works are not created in a
vacuum, nor are they created by individuals who exist outside of wider

social relationships: to make this argument would be to reproduce the individualizing discourse of capitalist ideology. And while the need to contextualize analysis along historical axes in particular remains an imperative, the concept of "the dominant" requires an update of sorts if it is to be mobilized within a Lefebvrian understanding of urban modernity. That is, rather than pursue a strictly formalist view that links different dominants with distinct artistic movements—a view that may, in effect, risk affirming what Fredric Jameson (1981) has called the bourgeois need for periodization—we do well in seeing that, from a Lefebvrian perspective, a dynamic view of the dominant can be more fruitful if it is linked to the urbanized character of the contemporary capitalist mode of production. This acknowledgment does little more than expand upon the original insight by Jakobson that there are many uses of the term itself. He originally wrote of the dominant as a concept that was applicable to a series of scales of progressively larger scope: "We may seek a dominant not only in the poetic work of an individual artist and not only in the poetic canon, the set of norms of a given poetic school, but also in the art of a given epoch, viewed as a particular whole" (Jakobson 1987, 42). In the present case, by extending the scale of his insight further toward that of the urban (the urban now "viewed as a particular whole")—that is, in effect, by reading Russian Formalism against Lefebvre's urban thought—we do for the dominant what Lefebvre did for the Marxian concept of alienation: we prepare it for commentary on a set of interdisciplinary and specifically urban relationships that Jakobson did not fully anticipate.

Moreover, there are many similarities between Jakobson's discussion of the dominant and Lefebvre's discussions of art more generally that make it seem quite reasonable to extend the original concept in this way. As is the case with other Russian Formalist thinkers, Jakobson seems to share with Lefebvre a concern in returning the work of art from an alienating, purely aesthetic discourse to a position where it is relevant to the whole of society.

> Equating a poetic work with an aesthetic, or more precisely with a poetic, function, as far as we deal with verbal material, is characteristic of those epochs which proclaim self-sufficient, pure art, *l'art pour l'art*. In the early steps of the Formalist school, it was still possible to observe distinct traces of such an equation. However, this equation is unquestioningly erroneous: a poetic work is not confined to aesthetic function alone, but has in addition many other functions. Actually, the intentions of a poetic work are often closely related to philosophy, social didactics, and so on.

Just as a poetic work is not exhausted by its aesthetic function, similarly the aesthetic function is not limited to poetic works. (original emphasis; Jakobson 1987, 43)

Jakobson's emphasis on the multiple functions of a poetic work is not surprising when we consider that one of the goals of the Russian Formalists in general was to assess "how the 'literary' is distinguished from and yet intimately related to the 'extra-literary'" (Selden 1986, 7). The Jakobson–Tynyanov theses of 1928 were key to this endeavor, in that they sought to relate what they called a "literary series" with a "historical series" (Selden 1986, 19), a complex undertaking that perhaps squares in general terms with Lefebvre's own nuanced understanding of the "work of art."[11] In fact, "Jakobson added the interesting idea that the poetics of particular periods may be governed by a 'dominant' which derives from a non-literary system" (Selden 1986, 15). While these dynamic aspects of Jakobson's thought may be reconfigured for mobilization by an urban cultural studies, it is important to go beyond the rigidity with which he regarded such notions of genre and period (e.g., Jakobson 1987, 45).[12] This does not mean dispensing with the idea that a novel is different in many ways from a film, or from popular music, or from a videogame. Instead, this push recognizes the need to interrogate those differences at the level (or stage) of textual analysis and fold them into a wider urban framework in the context of a cultural studies method.

Reconfiguring the dominant to function within an urban framework is one way to reconcile textual humanities analysis with the central concerns of urban studies. This potential for reconciliation is strengthened by the fact that the literary elaboration of the concept of the "dominant"—as developed by Jakobson, for example—shares much with the more contemporary work of spatial thinkers. In both cases—whether inside the text, outside of the text, or across the boundaries of the literary/extraliterary—there is a common thread that selects one element among many as a privileged point of entry into complex and necessarily dialectical questions. Many (Anglophone) readers of Lefebvre's theorizations, for example, have been tempted to see the privileged role of "space" throughout his work as a dominant of this sort—and yet the understanding of Lefebvre deployed throughout this book suggests that a better choice of dominant would be urbanization itself (i.e., urbanized space and time; urbanized consciousness). In his *Postmodernism: Or, the Cultural Logic of Late Capitalism*, Jameson—who, therein, dialogues insufficiently with Lefebvre's writings as a whole—nevertheless yields a comment of great relevance for the current discussion:

for Lefebvre, *all* modes of production are not merely organized spatially but also constitute distinctive modes of the "production of space" ... even though other modes of production (or other moments of our own) are distinctively spatial, ours has been spatialized in a unique sense, such that *space is for us an existential and cultural dominant, a thematized and foregrounded feature or structural principle* standing in striking contrast to its relatively subordinate and secondary (though no doubt less symptomatic) role in earlier modes of production. (second emphasis added; 1999, 365)[13]

Jameson's characterization of Lefebvre's work reproduces the tendency of Anglophone critics, outlined above, to see the French theorist's work as "spatial"—but he has notably added the further modification that space is not merely a dominant, but a "cultural" dominant.[14] The critic's use of the phrase "cultural dominant" in his characterization of Lefebvre's theory—which unavoidably echoes the Russian Formalist concept—is fortuitous because it actually effects the connection between literary and nonliterary matters underscored by the Russian Formalists in general, and by Roman Jakobson in particular.[15]

On the heels of Jameson's comment, it can now be said that the central idea of this chapter is that in literature it is *urban space-time* that constitutes the dominant—a constructive factor that subordinates other elements or rather (to return to and reappropriate the phrase authored by Louis Wirth) draws those other elements "into its orbit" (Wirth 1938, 2). This spatiotemporal *urban dominant* must be necessarily reconciled with the urban character of contemporary capitalism by the urban cultural studies critic. That is, in light of Lefebvre's urban thinking, it makes sense to admit that contemporary poetics are necessarily influenced by the processes of urbanization, processes that have been harnessed by capitalism for some two hundred years (Harvey 1989, 199; Lefebvre 1996). The philosophical dimensions of Lefebvre's oeuvre, in particular, provide an understanding of how the hallmark feature of capitalist urban production has been its characteristic use of space and time.[16] As a way of contextualizing the spatiotemporal urban dominant of cultural analysis, the remainder of this section briefly explores the relationship between time and space first as envisioned by Henri Lefebvre and next as elaborated by Lefebvrian thinker David Harvey, with an eye toward (1) the need to draw text and city together into a single, if complex, analysis and (2) the possible pitfalls of such an endeavor.

Contrary to popular belief, Lefebvre's urban theory is not merely a spatial theory but rather a theory that asserts the importance and cohabitation of both space and time.[17] In line with his stated suspicion of abstract categories (and of abstract philosophy—but not philosophy altogether), Lefebvre is interested in both spatiality and temporality as they are experienced directly and simultaneously as they are meditated through the alienations of contemporary capitalism, specifically. In *The Production of Space*, he reflects intermittently on the close relationship between the two, making such statements as: "Time is distinguishable but not separable from space" (1991a, 175); "time is known and actualized in space, becoming a social reality by virtue of spatial practice. Similarly, space is known only in and through time" (219); and "the history of space should not be distanced from in any way from the history of time...It begins, then, with the spatio-temporal rhythms of nature as transformed by social practice" (117). These remarks—and the nuanced philosophical position from which they spring—have been frequently misinterpreted or even ignored by critics framing Lefebvre not as an urban thinker but as a spatial theorist (for such an account of previous criticism, see Elden 2004; Fraser 2008a, 2011a).

Moreover, in the *Critique of Everyday Life* (volume 3), for example, Lefebvre explores the disastrous effects of capitalism on both space and time, which he characterizes as the "splintering of space and time in general homogeneity, and the crushing of natural rhythms and cycles by linearity" (2005, 135).

> On a watch or a clock, the mechanical devices subject the cyclical—the hands that turn in sixty seconds or twelve hours—to the linearity of counting. In recent measuring devices, and even watches, the cyclical (the dial) tends to disappear. Fully quantified social time is indifferent to day and night, to the rhythms of impulses. (Lefebvre 2005, 130)

Because temporality under capitalism is quantified (just as space is itself homogenized and subjected to partitioning), time thus seems to be reversible, an illusion which tends to suppress tragedy and even death (Lefebvre 2005, 133). Time for Lefebvre is "projected into space through measurement, by being homogenized, by appearing in things and products" (2005, 133; see also 2002).[18] From this unfortunate situation, asserts Lefebvre, there arises the need to reestablish time as irreversible—a need that is fulfilled, albeit ephemerally and cyclically, through everyday life in such popular forms as music, dance, and of course the festival. Throughout his oeuvre, in fact, Lefebvre attempts to rescue time and space from the "social relationship" through which they are mediated by capitalist relations. In *The Urban Revolution*, he writes that "The relation between time and space that confers absolute priority to space is in fact a social relationship inherent in a society in which a certain form of rationality governing duration predominates. This reduces and can even destroy, temporality" (2003a, 73–74). These insights led Lefebvre, of course, to assert the value of what he called "rhythmanalysis"—a concept introduced in the *Critique of Everyday Life* (volume 2), and elaborated upon in writings that were posthumously published as the eponymous book, *Rhythmanalysis*.

Understood in reference to these hallmark spatiotemporal principles, David Harvey's perspective on space and time under capitalism is soundly Lefebvrian—with the caveat that their elaboration pushes Harvey to dialogue with capitalist space-time in a much more concertedly (economically) materialist way than had his French influence. It remains true that Harvey's work on space is undoubtedly (at times) just as philosophical as Lefebvre's: "Space as a Key Word" (2006c); the last essay of Harvey's *Spaces of Global Capitalism* is a notable example of this, as are extensive passages of *Justice, Nature and the Geography of Difference* (1996). It is also true that Lefebvre's perhaps more persistently philosophical approach does not preclude Harvey's tendency to engage Marxian political economy but arguably complements it. There are numerous similarities between the two thinkers to note, of which I will mention only a few here in passing. It is significant, for example, that Harvey specifically cites the value of Lefebvre's triadic model of spatial production (e.g., Harvey 1990, 218–219) and employs it quite frequently even if indirectly. Similarly, Harvey's account of how capitalism has imposed certain rhythms on everyday life (e.g., 1989, 171; 1990, 201) follows logically from Lefebvre's position, even if it is hard to imagine Harvey writing something along the lines of Lefebvre's *Rhythmanalysis*. And finally, Harvey's account of space-time compression in reference to the turnover time of accumulation-driven capitalists emphasizes not absolutes but embodied human practices (1989, 2000).[19] In both cases, the contradictions inherent to the capitalist mode of production are central to the discussions each sustains, as are their shared commitments to a reconfigured Marxian thought capable of thinking the urban. In this regard, it is also possible to say that while Lefebvre tends to emphasize the notion of alienation, Harvey perhaps emphasizes the more seemingly material aspects of class division; and yet it must be seen that both alienation and class divisions are parallel manifestations—simultaneously cause and effect—of the contradictions that underlie capitalist modernity.

That being said, Harvey's take on capitalist spatiality-temporality is just as complex as Lefebvre's in that it is a dynamic model allowing for space-time to be absolute, relative, and relational according to specific sets of circumstances (2006c, 125). In "Space as a Key Word," Harvey writes that

> we need to take the concepts of space and space-time to a deeper level of complexity. There is much in this description that escapes the Lefebvrian categories but refers back to the distinctions between absolute space and time…relative space-time…and relational space time. Yet we cannot let go of the Lefebvrian categories either. The constructed spaces have material, conceptual and lived dimensions. (2006c, 133)[20]

Much like Lefebvre, Harvey in fact frequently dwells on the philosophical dimensions of "The Social Construction of Space and Time" (1996, 210; also 53) while simultaneously pushing for a Marxian thought that emphasizes political economy through dialectical thinking. The strengths of this approach are many—but the clear weakness of his approach (perhaps unintended) has reared its head in discussions of art and aesthetic matters.[21] On the one hand, his thinking quite naturally lends priority to "aesthetic and cultural practices," which he believes "are peculiarly susceptible to the changing experience of space and time precisely because they entail the construction of spatial representations and artefacts out of the flow of human experience" (Harvey 1990, 327).[22] On the other hand, of course, his own assessment of these aesthetic and cultural practices has at times lacked nuance.[23] While the work of both thinkers is of great importance for urban cultural studies work, the distance between Harvey and Lefebvre has to do precisely with the value, complexity, and potential role of the humanities in investigating the nature of urbanized society.

Following up on one (certainly important) aspect of Lefebvre's work, Harvey is concerned to interrogate "the ways in which aesthetic and cultural trends get woven into the fabric of daily life" of urbanized capitalism (1990, 347). But what about the inverse—how daily life gets woven into aesthetic and cultural products in their capacity as representations? Taking on this aspect of cultural production under urbanized capitalism, an approach which is set up by Lefebvre's theorizations in the *Critique of Everyday Life*—and perhaps even more directly in *La présence et l'absence*—is the goal of the urban cultural studies critic in the present humanities-centered formulation. Part of the reason that Harvey's journeys across the boundaries of the literary/filmic text frequently remain so unconvincing for the humanities scholar may have to do with a suspicion regarding the notion of text. In *Justice, Nature and the Geography of Difference*, he voices a complaint that might be taken as representative of the distance between disciplinary cultures, a distance that from a Lefebvrian perspective reads precisely as the product of an alienating, specialized bourgeois formulation of knowledge.[24]

> In geography, for example, we now find cities, landscapes, bodies, and cultural configurations being interpreted purely as texts. Even the institutions, powers, social relations, and material practices at work in producing, say, *urban life gets reduced to texts* in a totalizing gesture that is both extraordinary and startling given the anti-totalizing rhetoric of many of those engaging in the *reduction*. (emphasis added; Harvey 1996, 87)[25]

When read in light of his entire oeuvre and contrasted with Lefebvre's views, Harvey's fear and insistence that urban life cannot be viewed as a text—in contrast to Lefebvre's comments in *The Right to the City* (1996) (and note the curious use and repetition of the word *reduced/reduction* in Harvey's wording above)—cannot but be interpreted as a question regarding disciplinary alienations.

For the geographer—for some geographers, but certainly not all geographers—it seems, texts are (only) static, (only) reflective of society, (only) reducible to content. Lefebvre, for one, does not subscribe to this erroneous proposition. It is not that texts by themselves reduce experience to a flattened two-dimensionality (this view affirms a curious reification of the text as a thing as has been suggested), but that scholarship itself (as a social relation involving text and world), in fact, risks doing so when it is not clear about its method. This is true both of humanities and geographical scholarship. In *The Right to the City*, Lefebvre himself goes so far as to directly compare the city to a text, even suggesting that we "read the city" as a text. Lefebvre explains that the city "is situated at an interface, half-way between what is called the near order (relations of individuals in groups of variable size, more or less organized and structured and the relations of these groups among themselves), and the far order, that of society, regulated by large and powerful institutions (Church and State)" (1996, 101). Thus if the city and the urban are to be understood as a "text" (1996, 108), as Lefebvre argues, it is simultaneously necessary also to read both below and above the text, highlighting what the theorist calls the "double morphology [of the city] (practico-sensible or material, on the one hand, social on the other)" (112). From this perspective, Lefebvre's engagement with the concepts of "levels and dimensions" (e.g., in *The Right to the City* and in *The Urban Revolution*; see Fraser 2008a, 2011a) can thus also be seen an attempt to explore the complexity of the city as an appropriately multidimensional text.[26]

Harvey's own analyses of literary works (e.g., in Balzac; Harvey 2003, 2006a) and by extension his analyses of films such as *Blade Runner* and *Wings of Desire* (Harvey 1990) may elucidate well if somewhat routinely how individual characters experience and thus embody/represent/express the effects (e.g., the space-time compression) of urbanized capitalism and urbanized modernity. But what these analyses lack is an understanding of literature (i.e., culture) as a work of art. In the end, the question is whether Harvey analyzes the work, or merely the product (Lefebvre 2006b)? Returning to Raymond Williams's reflection on the definition of cultural studies discussed earlier in this book, does Harvey really give "equal weight" to the project (art) and the formation (society) (Williams 2007, 152)? Furthermore, the urban cultural studies critic must ask what do we gain—and, perhaps more importantly, what do we lose—if our view of texts becomes purely instrumentalist? Make no mistake, if texts are read purely as reflections/expressions of society (and therein lies the true *reduction*)—even if they are read in accordance with a theory of social change such as Harvey's recalibrated Marxism—they are thus read according to the instrumentalizing, homogenizing logic of capital. This may not seem to be the case for literary perspectives foregrounding political economy, which may be more attentive to class power than to its correlate concept of alienation. But from a more broadly defined Lefebvrian perspective emphasizing the fundamental and complex role of alienation (and the role of urban alienation in particular), this is indeed the case. Read against Lefebvre's theory of the work (of art), Harvey's inability to see depth and/or potential in the work of art may in fact say something about our ability to imagine a different society.[27] Which is to say that both Jameson's critique of the "spatial" cultural dominant in *Postmodernism* and Harvey's similar critique of "aesthetic and cultural trends" now "woven into daily life" are merely one (important) part of a more complex interrogation of culture.

On account of what is, in effect, the hesitancy of some geographers to venture across the border of the cultural "text" itself, resulting scholarship is incapable of seeing in literature and in film anything but content and themes—that is, reflection and expression (cf. Williams 1977).[28] There is, from this point of view, no discussion of the relationship between content and form (inside the text); and without form (without discussion of *literariness*—now folded back into extraliterariness and thus into an entire political, social, economic world), there can be no meaningful discussion of art, aesthetic matters, or the Lefebvrian concept of the "work." The end result of such a move is a truncated understanding of the literary and cultural imaginary. Of course, what Harvey lacks in artistic (textual) sensibility he more than makes up for through insights relating to political economy; but nonetheless, moving forward we must insist on the need for a textual practice that employs the representation of urban space and time (as both content and form) as a way of dialoguing with extratextual notions of space-time. In practice—given current university and disciplinary structures—this may be to suggest a slightly different task for the urban cultural studies critic than for the urban political economist. But urban cultural studies method as put forth in this book is itself a product of the need to disalienate the one from the other. Significantly, the notion of the spatiotemporal urban dominant ultimately provides a way of linking the humanities with the social sciences without reducing works of art to mere products.

Everyday Life and the City in Textual Criticism

Although the above formulation of an urban dominant is one way to move toward linking literary with extraliterary spaces, the Lefebvrian concept of everyday life offers the same opportunity under a different guise. Lefebvre's own elaborations of everyday life persistently connect literary with nonliterary questions and as such continue to push for that reconciliation of life and art advocated by Jakobson and the Russian Formalists. In the end, both of these views are complementary. That is, the analytical shift produced by introduction of "the dominant" was carried out beginning within the literary text and moving toward extraliterary realities, while the shift produced by Lefebvre's concept of everyday life was begun outside of the literary text and pushes us toward literary discourse. In both cases, the boundary between the cultural (literary/filmic) text and world is blurred so as to constitute an arm of urban cultural studies methodology.

We know from previous chapters that Lefebvre took quite a broad view of art and that he was intensely interested in aesthetic questions from his early years throughout his life and career. In this context, the present effort to harness his theory in order to suggest an approach to specific cultural texts is not a misuse of his work but an extended application of it to an area important to humanists. That Lefebvre himself saw the value of this sort of humanities-centered cultural interrogation itself is clear for those familiar with his earlier work with Norbert Guterman, his writings during the interwar years, his positions in literary and artistic circles and as the active cultural critic of the PCF, and also his later work both on his own and in collaboration with Guy Debord and the Situationists. But it may nevertheless surprise the reader to know that Lefebvre's interrogations of space are carried out simultaneously with his interrogations of literature.

To see how closely related these seemingly disparate concerns actually were for Lefebvre, we need turn only to *The Production of Space*. In an oft-read but certainly underappreciated passage that appears early on in that book, Lefebvre wonders what might be the starting point for a theoretical attempt to account for the relationship between "ideal space" and "real space" (1991a, 14). Here, he defines these terms concisely (if, in my estimation, provisionally) by saying that the first "has to do with mental (logico-mathematical) categories" while the second "is the space of social practice" (Lefebvre 1991a, 14).[29] In this passage, he not only discusses the need for and the limits of philosophy (also Lefebvre 1996, 2003a; Fraser 2008a), but also introduces the potential relevance of literature to spatial discussions as well. This detail has, unfortunately, sometimes been left out of discussions of this passage, but it deserves our attention nonetheless.

> What about literature? Clearly literary authors have written much of relevance, especially descriptions of places and sites. But what criteria would make certain texts more relevant than others? Céline uses everyday language to great effect to evoke the space of Paris, of the Parisian *banlieue*, or of Africa. Plato, in the *Critias* and elsewhere, offers marvellous descriptions of cosmic space, and of the space of the city as a reflection of the Cosmos. The inspired De Quincey, pursuing the shadow of the woman of his dreams through the streets of London, or Baudelaire in his *Tableaux parisiens*, offer us accounts of urban space rivaling those of Victor Hugo and Lautréamont. The problem is that any search for space in literary texts will find it everywhere and in every guise: enclosed, described, projected, dreamt of, speculated about. What texts can be considered special enough to provide the basis for a "textual" analysis? (Lefebvre 1991a, 14–15)[30]

It is certainly *underappreciated* that one of the first places Lefebvre turns—in the very moment in which he launches an interrogation of *The Production of Space*—is to literature; but in the current circumstances, perhaps a better word would be *crucial*. From this quote we may take some insights, insights which—despite the fact that Lefebvre himself pushes them to one side—nonetheless resonate with his own concerns and, more important, contribute strongly to the interdisciplinary push for an urban cultural studies method. Moreover, we must remember that Lefebvre's nuanced relationship with literature may be (and I believe *is*) just as complex as his relationship with philosophy. That is to say, although Lefebvre seems to discard philosophy in this passage as a starting point for spatial investigations, as we have seen he nevertheless takes it to be essential (Elden 2001, 2004; Lefebvre 2003a; Fraser 2011a). In the same way that philosophy must be reconfigured to deal with Lefebvre's urban thinking, we must reconfigure literary study for the same purpose.[31] Significantly, to explore this reconfigured literary terrain is at once to actualize other aspects of Lefebvre's own thinking (the importance of aesthetic questions, alienation/disalienation, critique of disciplinary specialization).

The first insight Lefebvre offers in this passage, one that may be taken as a starting point for urban cultural studies, is the fact that "literary authors have written much of relevance, especially descriptions of places and sites," which is to say that, as many scholars are already aware, the urban cultural studies critic does not merely see in literature *what s/he wants to see* (for a number of possible reasons) but at once also responds to *what is already there*. From the present perspective, it is relatively unsurprising to find this to be the case. That is, if the reader encounters in individual (novelistic) texts "places and sites," "the space of the city," and "accounts of urban space," this can be easily explained by adopting one of a number of interrelated perspectives. One (existential–perennial): the brute fact of the city and its role in human social development considered from the widest of angles, something that the contemporary writer in particular must struggle to avoid and that merely becomes more conspicuous through its absence.[32] Two (historical–dynamic): the progressive concentration of urban populations throughout the nineteenth century specifically, a process coterminous with the proliferation of literature and the novel in particular as a manifestation of cultural (national) bourgeois activity. And three (capitalist mode of production): the Lefebvrian (reformulated Marxist) proposition that humankind's activities must be understood in relation to their historical context, namely the mode of production that inflects all social expressions, and in the present situation, the importance of the urban for this contemporary capitalist mode of production (Lefebvre 1976; Harvey 2012). The point here is merely that at the most immediate level, approaching literature from an urban perspective is, in many ways, a relatively uncomplicated act. That is, to approach literary production from a nonurban framework, in fact, requires the effort (or an unanalyzed internalization) of mobilizing alienating disciplinary propositions such as those denounced (without reference to the urban specifically) by Raymond Williams (1977).

The second insight to take from Lefebvre's passage cited above stems from his remark that "The problem is that any search for space in literary texts will find it everywhere and in every guise: enclosed, described, projected, dreamt of, speculated about" (1991a, 14–15). There are, it is quite important to emphasize, a number of humanities scholars currently working with urban themes who would not—who do not—see this extensive proliferation of spaces in literary texts as a problem (Lefebvre does view this as a problem). Instead, it is precisely the richness of how the urban experience is presented in literary texts that makes the formulation of an urban cultural studies paradigm so potentially worthwhile for literary scholars. Of course, one does well in seeing that Lefebvre's reasoning here—his identification of this as a problem—seems to be rooted in his subsequent and stated quest for "special texts." This search for works that "can be considered special enough to provide the basis for a 'textual' analysis"—in my own view—speaks much more to the not unproblematic issue of disciplinary consensus on canon formation than it does to the value of interdisciplinary urban cultural studies scholarship per se.[33]

Lefebvre's emphasis on "special texts" is disappointing and—for our purposes—distracting; and yet, by considering it further it becomes possible to see that his perspective on literary matters seems out of line with his thoughts on everyday life, possibly indicating that he has been tempted by the very alienated bourgeois views of disciplinary specialization that he critiques in other writings. We do well in considering further how Lefebvre's views on everyday life elsewhere might enrich his thoughts on literature—thoughts that after all, in *The Production of Space*, are quite limited, given that his aim there differs from the central premise pursued in his work on everyday life. Lefebvre in fact does write on the connection between everyday life and literature in the underappreciated book translated as *Everyday Life in the Modern World*, discussing Joyce's *Ulysses*, specifically:

> The momentous eruption of everyday life into literature should not be overlooked. It might, however, be more exact to say that readers were suddenly made aware of everyday life through the medium of literature or the written word. But was this revelation as sensational then as it seems now, so many years after the author's death, the book's publication and those twenty-four hours that were its subject matter? And was it not foreshadowed already in Balzac, Flaubert, Zola and perhaps others? (2007, 2)

It is clear that Lefebvre considers *Ulysses*—in line with generations of literary scholars who have produced a specific kind of literary canon—to be a "special text" worthy of consideration. And, of course, he is perhaps not wrong to see it this way, given that during a specific urban moment, *Ulysses* charted a new course for the contemporary novel (Lefebvre 2007, 3).[34] Perhaps *Ulysses*, as Lefebvre suggests above, placed the quotidian at the center of the novel in a way that had never been done before, even if in this it was foreshadowed by earlier authors (Balzac, Flaubert, Zola, etc.). But it is helpful to distinguish between the plausible notion of the existence of "special texts," on the one hand, and the potential for useful (potentially disalienating) literary criticism, on the other. That is, if it is indeed worthwhile to read *Ulysses* for how the novel places the everyday at its center, it is potentially just as worthwhile to critique novels that have not constituted the everyday as a privileged realm of experience—precisely because they have *not* done so.

In this respect, it is significant that Lefebvre himself recognizes everyday life as constituting a reference for films and literature, broadly considered. "Films and literature use everyday life as their frame of reference but they conceal the fact, and only expose its 'objective' or spectacular aspects. Writing can only show an everyday life inscribed and prescribed; words are elusive and only that which is stipulated remains" (Lefebvre 2007, 8). It is reasonable to assume that even if films and literature conceal the everyday—and in fact, *especially if they conceal it*— they are worthy of literary criticism.[35] Thinking otherwise requires that we forget the lessons already gleaned from Lefebvre's Marxian reconfiguration of alienation (chapter 2) and his theory of the "work (of art)" (chapter 3), namely, that Marxian method strives (perhaps above all else, in fact) to disalienate the urbanite (the consumer, the reader) from his or her life and work, from the everyday, and from that nebulous but important concept that Lefebvre calls "lived experience."

There is no avoiding the fact that for Lefebvre there are texts he regards as being at "the level of mere literature," a phrase he invokes in *The Production of Space* by contrast in order to argue for the greater relative value of literature produced by the Surrealists in particular (1991a, 18). In his estimation, the Surrealists—who "sought to decode inner space and illuminate the nature of the transition from this subjective space to the material realm of the body and the outside world, and thence to social life" (1991a, 18)—made a concerted attempt to go beyond the traditionally alienated and alienating, bourgeois view of literature. All the better. Moreover, we do well in extending this assertion to the literary products fashioned by a number of avant-garde movements worldwide. But it is here that the now deeply ingrained bias of the literary critic against authorial intent—a bias that has sometimes been used, unfortunately, as a way of separating author from social context—plays potentially not an alienating but a disalienating role.[36] That is, yes, literature—just as is the case with any number of other areas of social life that are routinely approached as partial knowledge, alienated fragments of a fluid if complex totality—potentially alienates us from everyday life. But the presentation of everyday life in literature has, just as does everyday life in the modern extraliterary world according to Lefebvre, two sides. Far from merely being categorically reducible to (or severed from) authorial intent, literary works are both the site of alienation and also the site for resistance (echoing Lefebvre 2005). Furthermore, for the literary critic (from the perspective that prioritizes resistance), there is value in the act of seeking to unmask literary alienation just as there is value in exploring those (perhaps "special") literary works whose authors set out concertedly to disalienate their readers from existing alienations.

In this question of authorial intention, there are echoes of Lefebvre's own nuanced theory of the product–work; that is, works of art are, as discussed in chapter 3, from a certain perspective, products that serve a disalienating purpose. While disalienation *may seem to be* inherent in the work itself, it is yet another social relation. It is appropriate to ask whether the work even exists outside of an individual, who in turn is nothing without the social. From this perspective, and although this is nevertheless a meaningful distinction that will undoubtedly deserve the thorough critic's attention, it is more important that this act of disalienation occur than it is that it be essentialized as pertaining to one moment or another (the moment of artistic production vs. the moment of artistic interpretation).[37] In *The Production of Space*, Lefebvre admits that literary texts as signifying practices are bound to certain limitations, limitations that are transcended "in and through the work in space [as spatial practice]" (1991a, 222). Although he does not discuss criticism of individual texts here, it nonetheless makes sense—from a Lefebvrian perspective informed by familiarity with a greater range of his oeuvre—to see literary criticism as potentially disalienating. That is, art criticism is disalienating to the extent that the critic links the signifying practices of the text with extraliterary spatial practices—this is, of course, the primary interdisciplinary goal of urban cultural studies, properly considered.

It is perhaps fair to say that one may explore literature just as Lefebvre proposes that we explore everyday life. In both cases, the notions of

space and of time (what, in this chapter, I am calling the "urban dominant") are of primary importance.

> [T]hus we assert our decision to explore *recurrence*. Everyday life is made
> of recurrences: gestures of labour and leisure, mechanical movements
> both human and properly mechanic, hours, days, weeks, months, years,
> linear and cyclical repetitions, natural and rational time, etc.; the study
> of creative activity (of *production* in its widest sense) leads to the study of
> re-production or the conditions in which actions producing objects and
> labour are re-produced, re-commenced, and re-assume their component
> proportions or, on the contrary, undergo gradual or sudden modifica-
> tions. (original emphasis; Lefebvre 2007, 18)

If "everyday life is the object of philosophy precisely because it is non-
philosophical" (Lefebvre 2007, 17), literature may be the object of the
study of everyday life precisely because it is *not* everyday life.[38] That
is, one important question may be, how does *recurrence* in the novel
diverge from *recurrence* in everyday life—particularly with regard to a
given space or set of spaces? We do well in recognizing, also, that to the
extent that a novel portrays everyday life in all its depth, it may present
the reader with chance encounters akin to those realized in the unpredictability of city-life—only that these encounters are alienated, reified,
paginated, ready not only for consumption but also for consideration
and critique, something which may, in fact, be an advantage for readers
willing to think through a Lefebvrian critical project.

In the introduction to this chapter, I have written "that space and
time are rendered investigable (visible, audible, tangible: assessable) in
the cultural text (here, the literary text, but just as equally in filmic or
other humanities texts) in a form that may be present but unacknowledged in everyday life"—and here it is worth turning to how Lefebvre
presents what is, to my mind, a similar idea. In the third volume of the
Critique of Everyday Life (originally published in French in 1981, just one
year after his extensive consideration of representation—*La présence et
l'absence*, 1980), Lefebvre makes a prescient point for the literary critic:

> Everyday discourse consists in spoken word; voices emit it. It is writ-
> ten badly. When literary discourse seems to approximate it, it is in fact
> transcribed and transformed by being transposed. In everyday discourse,
> as opposed to literary writings, the denotative predominates. This does
> not contradict an earlier analysis: connotations feature in daily life only
> when they are reduced to the denotative, immediately linked as values
> and implicit evaluations to the words used and objects referred to. This

impoverishes yet clarifies the discourse, giving it the appearance of a chain of signifiers such that it can be followed, recalled, even inverted. (2005, 70–71)

Two points follow from the connection established by Lefebvre regarding everyday discourse and its manifestation in literary discourse. The first is this: if everyday discourse is transcribed in literature, it is significant to determine how and why it is so transcribed; and the second, if it is transfigured and transformed in literary discourse, toward what end is it changed through this transposition? The answers to these questions, of course, will vary as the work itself varies (genre, author, context, language, and so on). In addition, if everyday discourse is thus "impoverished if clarified" in this way (making it possible to "follow," "recall," and/or "invert" it), other everyday matters must be similarly inflected upon transposition to the literary realm.[39] In every case (discourse or not) such matters are rendered inert (fixed, objectified) and in this way alienated from their extraliterary context, such that the very possibility of literary criticism requires a dynamic (and necessarily individual-social) movement to reunite these newly fixed forms with their absent referents.

While the reader may or may not be very familiar with the investigation of everyday life in the literary text, s/he will have doubtlessly come across scholarship that looks at the representation of the city in literature. By this I mean to reference not the studies of cities in literature by geographers (Harvey 1990, 1996, 2006a; mentioned above) but instead those written by literary-trained critics in particular. It bears repeating that much may come (much has already come) of the reconciliation of specific cities that are, to use Lefebvre's wording, "enclosed, described, projected, dreamt of, speculated about" in literature with their extraliterary referents (e.g., Madrid, Paris, Berlin, Beijing, Buenos Aires, etc.) (1991a, 15). Just as the city has long captured the imagination of authors, it has also captured the attention of literary critics.[40] Needless to say that it is outside the scope of this book to provide a history of criticism on the representation of city in literature—although that is surely a worthwhile endeavor that would require a book-length text of its own. We can readily accept that the city does appear in literature, but we do well in assessing the significance of this appearance—which is to say that the view we adopt regarding space in general delimits, to a certain extent, the range of perspectives we may adopt on the city in literature.

For example, the seemingly common-sense view that space is an empty container—criticized directly by Lefebvre[41]—finds its way into literary criticism to the extent that cities are seen by the critic as mere backgrounds to whatever human drama is taken as the "true" concern of the author. That is, the critical perspective that sees certain (perhaps "special") works of art as being in a sense timeless or as somehow amounting to universal statements on the generalized "human condition"—to the extent that they ignore the spatial (oftentimes, necessarily *urban*) context of the work—do little more than carry this simplistic and erroneous conception of space over to the realm of critical textual practice.

Another erroneous understanding of space is what Lefebvre criticizes as the notion of the city as an object—against which he mobilizes the distinction between the city and the urban. The first is a static set of structures, while the second is a dynamic relationship that is constantly being shaped and reshaped through practice. Neither is right or wrong, of course, both operate simultaneously—the first, writes Lefebvre, espoused by developers, capitalists, and speculators harnessing the geometrical, static spatial vision that has for hundreds of years been the fundamental building block of urban planning; the second, an alternative vision potentially relevant to if not already underlying all manner of social struggles over cityspace, struggles that at once involve the whole of social life. The reified view of the city as an object has its complement in criticism that envisions the city in textual practice as separate from the narratological practice in which it is enmeshed. In the end, as we will see by discussing an essay by literary scholar Franco Moretti (2010), this tempting proposition of some literary criticism risks replicating in textual analysis the very separation between the urban and the aesthetic that Lefebvre's critique of alienation warns us against. Moretti's essay is significant and worthy of our consideration precisely because it seems to have appealed to a wide range of scholars working on the city (the essay has been included as part of *The Blackwell City Reader*, second edition, which is presumably used as a textbook in numerous university-level courses focusing on the urban problem).

One of the central propositions of Moretti's essay (of which only an excerpt appears in the *City Reader*) seems to be this: "It is essentially through *description* that the city penetrates literature, and literature our perception and understanding of the city. To convey information about the city, the text must stop the story, temporarily suspend the action, and describe places and spaces" (original emphasis; 2010, 309). Moretti's assertion is not without its own value and may in fact be (more) fruitfully applied to forms of generic literary criticism.[42] His defense of literariness is not completely unwarranted—"Literary description is not a replica of something else" (Moretti 2010, 309)—particularly since he builds on that concept, going beyond the borders of the text to think the urban. This move, after all, is seemingly in tune with the Russian Formalist notion of the extraliterary, what I have called the spatiotemporal urban dominant. Yet the essay also suggests what is a central problem of interdisciplinary criticism more generally. That is, it is frequently convenient to adopt a simplistic understanding of the city in literary criticism, just as it is frequently convenient for geographers to reduce the "literary" to mere content or themes. The larger issue is that one discipline routinely engages with another only if it can reduce the second to the status of an uncomplicated object. For Moretti, "the city is ultimately and above all a spatial entity where the value and meaning of every component—human or other—crystallize in the form of objects, houses, entities that can be variously described and classified" (2010, 309).[43] It seems that the tendency is for literary studies to reify the city while geography reifies the text—in each case, dialectical thought is unable to cross the border between text and world without producing isolated objects restricted by disciplinary framing. If urban cultural studies is to be dynamic and interdisciplinary, analysis of the city as it appears in works of art directly is only the first stage, for there is also the analysis of urbanized consciousness (second stage), and of course the unity of text and world (third stage). These stages must occur simultaneously in textual analysis.

Returning to Moretti's original quotation that the city appears in literature "essentially" through description, it is important to point out that the presence of the city in literature cannot be merely reduced to intermittent descriptions that interrupt the narrative, as he states.[44] Moreover, the direct and specific place-bound correlation between textual city and extraliterary city (e.g., novelistic Paris vs. "real world" Paris) need not exist if we are to enact an urban cultural studies method. Such a method, after all, also admits the reality of urbanized consciousness (Harvey 1989; Simmel 2010), as well as the relationship between urban and rural spaces (Williams 1975; Wirth 1938). The modern evolution of the city—as Lefebvre, Harvey, Simmel, Wirth, Benjamin, De Certeau, and a host of other urban thinkers agree—has impacted our contemporary consciousness to such a degree that urban analysis of literature should be possible even when the context for the work is neither urban, nor rural, nor even earthly (e.g., in the case of extraplanetary science fiction).

As I have argued in another article (Fraser 2012b), the city thus appears in novels not merely through description (which is, of course, often reduced to content by literary and nonliterary scholars alike) but moreover necessarily through the structural qualities of the literary work. Although description is important—and although description itself must be seen as a vehicle for other literary elements—the urban cultural studies scholar must be wary of reducing the novelistic appearance of these cities to description alone. Nor should description be taken as a relatively unproblematic aspect of literariness. From this perspective, even interpretations of the city itself as a literary theme and as a symbol of modernity risk failing to fully separate themselves from this static, objectified vision of the city. As Burton Pike has written in *The Image of the City in Literature*, "As an image, the city is too large and complex to be thought of as only a literary trope. It has a double reference, to the artifact in the outside world and to the spectrum of refractions it calls into being in the minds of the author and reader" (1981, ix).

There is a way forward, of course, one which is deceptively simple, and for which we need not insist (as Lefebvre had in *The Production of Space*) upon the existence of "special texts."[45] This way forward for urban literary criticism—seen as one part of a larger urban cultural studies method—presumes the notion of the spatiotemporal urban dominant as way of connecting intra- and extraliterary spaces. From this perspective, both special and other literary texts can be read for how they describe spaces and places, reading these descriptions in the context of the novel as a work of art and joining intra- and extraliterary concerns to elucidate the nuanced connection between "ideal space" and "real space." In broad terms, speaking in this chapter of the spatiotemporal urban dominant has really been a way to outline and establish a set of questions that guide a Lefebvrian perspective on artistic production. The result of this endeavor amounts to a set of guidelines (not norms), one possible way for the urban cultural studies critic to approach art through close readings while reconciling the work with urban society. Even when read in light of Marx's early works, the term production involves creations like "social time and space" (Lefebvre 2007, 31). Social time and space may not normally be visible under (alienating) everyday conditions—but the estrangement offered by the literary text and its capacity for concrete representation allow for the viewer to see and assess the social relationships surrounding space and time. Social space and time thus appear in the work of art not merely as content, theme, and symbol but also as structure and form.

It follows that a Lefebvrian understanding of literary study carries within itself the potential for analyzing texts other than those that have traditionally been the bread and butter of humanities scholarship. That is, the spatiotemporal urban dominant may be applied also to other visual and auditory texts: works such as films, popular music, videogames, and digital spaces, even if in each case we must adjust our scholarship accordingly to account for the variations intrinsic to the notion of genre.

CHAPTER 5

The Iconic-Indexical City: Visions of Place in Urban Films

In the previous chapter, we saw how Lefebvre's hallmark urban thinking blends with textual criticism as one possible direction of an urban cultural studies method. Such criticism, of course, is also explained by Raymond Williams as that which gives equal weight to the project (art) and the formation (society); and by Jakobson and the Russian Formalists as that which folds the literary back into the extraliterary (through the notion of "the [reconfigured, *urban*] dominant"). Following logically from discussion of an "urban dominant" that serves to preserve the nuanced "literariness" or artistic value of texts while reading them in relation to the complexities of urban/urbanized society, this chapter turns specifically to film in order to construct a similar argument. In a sense, the interdisciplinary links between film studies and geographical approaches have perhaps been somewhat more fruitful than the intersection of literary study and spatial theory. This chapter thus offers—in part—an explanation of why that may be the case. It explores what the potential pitfalls of geographical takes on film are and, most importantly, how film theory can be better harnessed in future interdisciplinary approaches to the city in cinema. This is not intended to be an exhaustive take on the matter, but rather merely one more push toward thorough collaboration between the humanities and the social sciences on artistic matters in urban contexts.

This chapter's first section ("The Cinematic Sign and Film's Spatial Properties") takes as its starting point the accumulating body of work on geography and film (by, e.g., Aitken and Zonn 1994; Hopkins 1994; Clarke 1997; Dear 2000; Cresswell and Dixon 2002) and attempts to reconcile this with key insights provided by film theorists such as Peter

Wollen (1972), Siegfried Kracauer (1968), Béla Balázs (1970), Pier Paolo Pasolini (1988), and Stephen Prince (1999). While the former spatial thinkers have presumably begun their investigations from an urban ("extratextual") perspective, the latter's musings have been grounded in discussion of aesthetic matters of form, structure, and interpretive method. It is significant, however, that in each case the border between artistic text and urbanized/urbanizing world has been successfully traversed. In particular, the semiotic notions of iconicity and indexicality explored in detail by selected film theorists—while not always integrated explicitly into geographical studies of filmic works—nevertheless offer an implicit way of bridging the concerns of each perspective. These notions are, in fact, particularly relevant for urban cultural studies approaches.

The second section of this chapter (*"Biutiful* Barcelona: An Urban Cultural Studies Reading"*) digests the insights of the first section while mobilizing them implicitly in approaching a recent movie that received notable international attention. Launching an urban cultural studies reading of Mexican director Alejandro González Iñárritu's *Biutiful* (2010), the case is made that the film functions as a complement to theoretical critiques of urbanism such as that of Lefebvrian theorist Manuel Delgado Ruiz, specifically. The director's choice of Barcelona for the location of the film's diegetic action as well as for the place of its production makes it possible to read the struggles of immigrant and marginalized characters in the film against the widespread, triumphant image of Barcelona as a "model" European destination city in extrafilmic discourse. Moreover, I suggest there is a necessary relationship between the film's primary urban theme—analyzed at the levels of both content and form—and its numerous secondary elements, including even a supernatural narrative arc. The importance of this section is that it provides a practical example of what (one variant of) urban cultural studies scholarship might look like—of what it means to retain the notion of film as a nuanced work of art while using an interdisciplinary framework as a way of drawing even the most seemingly disparate, individual aesthetic qualities of that work into relation with the urban problematic, which is now primary. The interdisciplinary and urban reconciliations effected through this sort of urban reading are to be understood as a Lefebvrian attempt to disalienate each discipline from the other.

The Cinematic Sign and Film's Spatial Properties

Just as literature is insufficiently understood by frameworks that reduce it to intended and received message, neither can the film text be seen as solely the static product of the artist's move to communicate an idea. In all works of art, in fact, there are aspects or qualities of the work that escape this instrumentalist paradigm, which is to say that we broaden the communicative model of artistic production by going beyond the notion of authorial intent. The perspective of the filmmaker is still important, however, and, as the second section of this chapter insists, can be folded into a much larger argument about meaning and film form. Nevertheless, film theorists have asserted that in cinema, specifically (as opposed to literature), there is a precision or overdetermination of the cinematic image that is lacking in—or merely distinguishable from—the nature of the verbal signs that constitute prose texts. Thus, the filmmaker necessarily deals with the "real world" in a way that differs from the way in which, for example, everyday life figures in the literary text. As we will see, this difference is properly understood as a qualitative shift emphasizing distinct aspects of the signifying process.

It is useful to begin with a distinction between literary and cinematic works by Italian filmmaker and critic Pier Paolo Pasolini, taken from an essay titled "The 'Cinema of Poetry,'"

> [The filmmaker] chooses a series of objects, or things, or landscapes, or persons as syntagmas (signs of a symbolic language) which *while they have a grammatical history invented in that moment*—as in a sort of happening dominated by montage—*do, however, have an already lengthy and intense pregrammatical history*... This is probably the principal difference between literary and cinematographic works (if such a comparison matters). The linguistic or grammatical world of the filmmaker is composed of images, and [filmic] images are always concrete, never abstract. (original emphasis; 1988, 171)

As Pasolini himself suggests, this distinction between the literary and the cinematographic may not in fact matter. That is, I choose to see this distinctiveness of the cinematic image as complementary to distinctive aspects of other genres of artistic production, aspects that—as indicated in the previous chapter—matter greatly at the level of textual analysis, but in every case are resolved or fully integrated as the urban cultural studies critic folds the work back into the urban/urbanizing world. This does not mean that these artistic (in part, genre-inflected) distinctions can or should be ignored by the cultural critic, of course. In this way the urban cultural studies project exercises a potentially disalienating activity—but cultural work cannot be disalienating without passing from one fragmented area of knowledge to another, and it cannot pass from one fragmented area to another if it merely skims the surface of one discipline. That is, if we do not understand the work of art on its own terms (aesthetically, hermeneutically), we reduce it to being merely another artistic product and in practice merely affirm the notion of a separate realm of aesthetic matters.

Pasolini's assertion is, in fact, echoed by numerous other film theorists with similar insights. These insights hinge on the nature of the cinematic image as a multivalent signifier that has not only arbitrary but also iconic and indexical aspects. When read on the heels of the previous chapter's discussion of the spatiotemporal urban dominant, the iconic-indexical aspects of the film constitute a complementary way of joining the levels of textual and extratextual analysis in an urban reading of film texts. It is important to recognize that these aspects of film have been traditionally marginalized by much canonical film theory, which "since the 1970s has tended to place great emphasis upon what is regarded as the arbitrary nature of the signifier-signified relationship, that is, upon the purely conventional and symbolic aspect of signs"— and this in lieu of exploring its iconic and indexical aspects (Prince 1999, 99).[1] In spite of this symbolic bias, however, as Peter Wollen has explained in the essential text *Signs and Meaning in the Cinema*,

> The cinema contains all three modes of the sign: indexical, iconic and symbolic. What has always happened is that theorists of the cinema have seized on one or more of these dimensions and used it as the ground for an aesthetic firman . . . In the cinema, it is quite clear, indexical and iconic aspects are by far the most powerful. (1972, 125, 140)

In practical terms, what this means for the critic who may be relatively unfamiliar with film studies is that, as Pasolini puts it in simpler language, the semiotic code of cinema is not the semiotic code of *language*, but is instead the semiotic code of *reality*.[2] Given that the notion of reality is often taken to be self-evident and potentially misinterpreted, we do well in exploring what this means.

In the present invocation, "reality" does not invoke a contrast between a world of representation and a world of things—but rather, returning once again to Lefebvre's assertion that philosophy has a role to play in discussion of art—a world in which there is dialectical movement between these two poles of experience (the idea and the thing, ideality and materiality, etc.). It is fundamental to see that these two poles of experience are a part of our arguments over art, politics, society, economics, and even language itself. In film studies, the somewhat eclectic lineage of film theorists implicit here (Pasolini, Prince, Balázs, Kracauer,

Wollen) suggests that reality is itself both representation and material force—a nuanced perspective maintained, as we have seen in the work of Lefebvre whether pertaining to spatial production or even artistic work. Wollen's tripartite classification of the cinematic sign itself potentially explains this progression from materiality: the indexical as a material trace of the thing itself through the use of light in cinematography; the iconic as the force of this material trace to evoke resemblance; and the symbolic value of this resemblance, which is necessarily structured by arbitrariness/convention along an individual–social axis. We will return to these three parts of the cinematic sign at the close of this section. For now it is important to stress how much film theory of recent generations has devalued the indexical and iconic aspects of film precisely because of a bias inherited from the study of language. It is not that film is not language or that it shares no affinity with language, but rather that it is not *merely* language in the simple sense. This is to assert that linguistic study has itself been biased against recognizing the iconic or indexical aspects of languages, aspects that endure nonetheless.

The fact that film theory since the 1970s has privileged arbitrary signification over iconic and indexical aspects of cinema semiotics (Prince 1999, 99) is not surprising when read in terms of the hegemonic Saussurean bias of linguistic signification itself. Ferdinand de Saussure famously held meaning in language to be almost completely explainable through recourse to the arbitrary/conventional link between signifiers and signified, and his approach became synonymous with the marginalization of those aspects of linguistics not explained by this model. The *Course in General Linguistics* compiled by his students during the early twentieth century all but ignores iconicity/indexicality in natural languages and briefly references onomatopeia as little more than a footnote before pressing on to emphasize the arbitrariness of language throughout (Saussure 1983). This tradition has been continued by, for example, Noam Chomsky, whose drive for a universal grammar ignores the iconic/indexical, or, in the words of Wollen, "banishes the ungrammatical into outer darkness" (1972, 124). The truth is that many contemporary researchers have sought to correct for Saussure's oversight, emphasizing the roles that these formerly marginalized aspects of signification have even in natural languages. Ivan Fónagy, for example, asserts that "Iconicity, far from being a marginal kind of verb play, is a basic principle of live speech, and more generally, of natural languages" (1999, 3); and Linda Waugh—together with Roman Jakobson—has made significant contributions regarding iconicity and lexicon (Jakobson 1965; Jakobson and Waugh 1979; Waugh and Newfield 1995). These contemporary scholars not only show how crucial the iconic elements we associate with onomatopoeia are for language (the latter is the most frequently recognized iconic form of language), they also discuss other kinds of linguistic iconicity such as phonesthesia (i.e., words ending in –ash [crash, bash, flash, stash, for example] all share the characteristic of quickness).[3] All this is merely to make clear that the compulsion to focus on the arbitrary nature of the filmic sign over its iconic and indexical aspects seems to be a consequence of literary scholars trained in a particular tradition, scholars who transpose their modes of analysis from the linguistic code of narrative to the visual text.[4]

Stephen Prince's underappreciated essay "The Discourse of Pictures: Iconicity and Film Studies" (1999) is notable in that it provides a strong argument for rescuing film studies from this decidedly Saussurean (arbitrary/conventional) linguistic bent. It cannot be ignored that his perspective squares nicely with work by numerous other film theorists whose analyses similarly call for folding the film text back into the larger world. Filmmaker and critic Béla Balázs, for example, emphasized the expressive qualities inherent to the image itself as a way of returning the filmic work of art to reality, noting that the notion of art as separate from reality is in some ways conditioned by existent and variable social relationships.[5] There is also Siegfried Kracauer who saw film as the "redemption of physical reality" and asserted that everyday life, in particular, is prioritized by cinema.[6] Interestingly given the present effort, in one instance Kracauer even turns to the writings of Lewis Mumford—discussed in the first section of this book—in order to underscore this property of cinema: "Without any conscious notion of its destination, the motion picture presents us with a world of interpenetrating, counterinfluencing organisms: and it enables us to think about that world with a greater degree of concreteness" (1968, 299; original citation in Mumford 1934, 340).

In every case, the point is that films are not, as much popular and theoretical discussion of film seems to suggest, reducible to explanation by way of the language of art alone; nor, of course, are they mere reflections of extraliterary reality. This assertion, of course, has its complement in Lefebvre's comments regarding the work of art more generally and is relevant to remarks made by a host of other cultural critics. Among them, Susan Sontag is a notable example, given that she noted in her influential essay "Against Interpretation"—critiquing a purely mimetic theory of art—"what is needed is an erotics of art" (1969, 23). In subverting the representational bias of much structuralist film theory, the indexicality/iconicity of film contributes to answering Sontag's call for an erotics of art by returning the artistic work to the fluid and corporeal life from which simplistic representational models have distanced it. Prince's essay, in particular, may prove to be crucial as a starting point for a more thorough linkage of research on film within both geography and the humanities—precisely because it is the iconic/indexical dimension of the filmic image that has long motivated a critical geography of film, underscoring the intimate relationship between filmspace and extrafilmic city-space in preparation for urban readings.[7]

Moreover, Prince's insights dovetail nicely with Peter Wollen's classic remarks on the multifaceted nature of the cinematic sign (as above: iconic, indexical, symbolic) and in essence account for many of the disciplinary polemics that have surged up in recent years as cultural geographers have turned increasingly to film in their investigations. Attempting to address a change in approach to understanding such hallmarks of geographical thought as landscape and region, Tim Cresswell and Deborah Dixon have asked, "Why do so many geographers, either in their research or in their teaching, engage film?" (2002, 1).[8] We might take the following statement as a sign of the basic premise of their co-edited volume titled *Engaging Film*:

> In more conceptual terms, geographers have deployed film as a mimetic of the real world, such that people and places can be represented in as authentic a manner as possible to peers and students; a series of images and sounds that relay intersubjective meanings; a medium that allows investigation of the production of dominant ideologies; and a site of resistance, in which the stability of any meaning is open to critical scrutiny. (Cresswell and Dixon 2002, 1)

Their perspective is somewhat nuanced, but nonetheless points to crucial problems involving the simplistic understanding of other disciplines often implicit in interdisciplinary approaches. To wit: in the introduction they take on "two major epistemological stances brought to the study of film" (Cresswell and Dixon 2002, 1) as a way of contextualizing the essays included in their nonetheless valuable volume. Although the discussion of these two stances is relatively brief (2–4), it is immediately apparent that theirs is a drive to go beyond the notion that film is a "representation of reality" (2). Yet while their goal of undermining a static understanding of representation is a worthy one, in the process, however, they refrain from engaging more thoroughly with existing film theory. The result is that they risk turning the humanities discipline they would appropriate into a mere object serving to reinforce another discipline's insights.

To explain: it is clear that in assessing the originality of their own perspective, Cresswell and Dixon's worthwhile conclusions are nonetheless limited by the correspondence the authors establish between the notion of the "representation of reality" and a perceived *essentialist* position on film that they hope to dislodge. That is, their approach is limited *because* it is sketched out by way of overly concise references to filmmakers and theorists such as Sergei Eisenstein, Andre Bazin, and Siegfried Kracauer[9] and *although* it is complemented by mention of previous Marxist film analysis, which they seem to regard not merely as more political but also as more nuanced than the former (Cresswell and Dixon 2002, 3). The authors make it clear that in contrast to these other approaches they take to be essentialist or essentializing, theirs is antiessentialist:

> Clearly, these and other Marxist-inspired approaches to the study of the representations that make up our everyday world have reinvigorated the study of popular culture in general and have recognized the particular significance of film as one of the most ubiquitous and visceral sources of such representations. Yet, over the past decade, a radically different epistemological understanding of representations has emerged that has had an equally great impact on geographers' engagements with film. Under the rubric of *antiessentialism*, writers as diverse as Bakhtin and Bhabha, Butler and Bauman, Derrida and Deleuze, and Lyotard and Kristeva have transformed...geography's engagement with film. (emphasis added; Cresswell and Dixon 2002, 3)

As evidenced above, Cresswell and Dixon go so far as to suggest that they are engaging a very recent turn of events—one that they even refer to as a "dissolution of the reality/representation divide" (2002, 3)—and they also suggest, perhaps, that this dissolution may be particular to geography or else to the theorists they mention specifically. Evidence of this is their statement that "Films are no longer considered mere images or unmediated expressions of the mind, but rather the temporary embodiment of social processes that continually construct and deconstruct the world as we know it" (Cresswell and Dixon 2002, 3–4).[10] What may seem to be a relatively innocuous statement for the reader from geography is sure to come as a shock to many a humanities scholar. That is, while I have come across many literary approaches I judge to be conservative, disciplinary, and perhaps even outdated, I challenge anyone to find a literary scholar—or perhaps less likely still, a film scholar—who considers a (literary or filmic) text to be a "mere image" or an "unmediated expression of the mind."

Keep in mind that I do not wish to critique either the method or the results of the editors of *Engaging Film*, a book whose contribution is laudable and appropriately complex; I merely want to use their introduction as a way of drawing attention to a curious quality of much interdisciplinary research—a quality discussed also at the end of the previous chapter in relation to literary study, specifically. The point here is once again related to disciplinary structures: the fact is that while the nuances and complexities of social interactions are no doubt present in geographical research more generally, geographers' engagement with humanities texts has been at times reluctant to admit that same level of nuance and complexity in the work of humanities scholars. The result is that such interdisciplinary criticism is insufficient and ultimately incapable of forging a truly interdisciplinary conversation on urban matters. This fact has practical consequences.

First, cultural geography is not—in relation to neither film nor literature—in the position of having to reinvent the wheel. The reconciliation of on-screen and off-screen space effected even by the geographers whose work is cited in the introduction to *Engaging Film* is at times explicitly grounded in previous work familiar to literary scholars. There is, for example, the notion of what semiotician Iuri Lotman called a "two-fold experience," where the film's observer participates in "simultaneously forgetting and not forgetting that the experience is imaginary in origin" (Hopkins 1994, 57; reading Lotman 1976, 17).[11] And second, to the degree that geographers refuse to thoroughly engage with insights from the humanities—or vice versa—disciplinary knowledge persists in an alienated state decried by Lefebvre, potentially affirming the fragmentations effected by bourgeois knowledge and preventing a grasp of Lefebvrian (Marxian) totality in the consequences this has for disciplinarity. While the consequences of remaining entrenched within disciplinary conceits influence not only scholarly work but also scholarly (university) life and everyday life more generally (passing along the scales from individual to disciplinary to social practice), I leave consideration of those matters for another time. It is most important, here, to recognize that the complexity of the cinematic sign as theorized by film scholars can be brought to bear on geographical film analysis explicitly, and on analysis of the city in/on film in particular.

Jeff Hopkins, whose essay "Mapping of Cinematic Places: Icons, Ideology, and the Power of (Mis)representation" appears in one of the collections mentioned by Cresswell and Dixon, provides a great example of how this can be accomplished. In the following passage from Hopkins's essay, the scholar mobilizes the three aspects of the filmic sign highlighted by Wollen (iconic, indexical, symbolic) using the example of the city itself as cinematic semiotic:

> For example, let us imagine one frame in a documentary film depicting a wide-angle shot of a city skyline. Is the film image an icon, an index, or a symbol? How strong might be the impression of an "almost real" film city, and how much effort might be required to "willingly suspend" one's disbelief that the film city is merely a projected image of light and shadow rather than an actual city? The film city is signified by all three semiotic processes. The projected image is an iconic sign because it convincingly represents or resembles what viewers visually experience, or might expect to experience, as a city in the everyday material world. The image is also an index because it has causal connection to the material world. The skyline on the screen has been created by light reflecting off a "real" city and hitting raw film stock to produce a representation on the film of the city. The city image may also be read as a symbol of any one of a number of socially constructed conventions: adventure, mystery, progress, temptation, and so-forth. Because it is a documentary film, a so-called "live–action" authentic record of actual events using real people and objects in an actual space and time . . . spectators are more apt to accept the film city as real, which will lesson the effort necessary to suspend their disbelief. (1994, 53)

It seems to me that Hopkins' remark is fundamental for urban cultural studies theorists who want to think the urban using film texts as their point of departure. This does not mean always differentiating and discussing all three aspects of the cinematic sign (although that may be ideal); but it does mean recognizing that even where interdisciplinary geographical-cultural critics have not explicitly discussed filmic signification or film theory—such as in various essays published throughout edited books such as *Engaging Film: Geographies of Mobility and Identity* (Cresswell and Dixon, 2002), *Place, Power, Situation, and Spectacle: A Geography of Film* (Aitken and Zonn, 1994), *The Cinematic City* (Clarke, 1997), and *Cinema and the City* (Shiel and Fitzmaurice, 2001), among others—they have nonetheless necessarily (and unavoidably) built upon this iconic/indexical relationship between cities within filmspace and extrafilmic cityspace.

The way forward for interdisciplinary research—and in this case, interdisciplinary research that places the urban problem at its center—involves being able to actively take stock of the contributions of multiple disciplines. The method advocated as part of an urban cultural studies approach does not accept the alienating proposition that the humanities are fragmented from or irreconcilable with the social sciences, nor does it accept that either aesthetic matters or more-than-aesthetic social relations can be considered in simplistic terms. Urban cultural studies reads cultural texts in their context, but it does so not by ignoring or going beyond their aesthetic complexity but by preserving and folding that complexity back into what is a similarly complex social world. The next section provides an example of just such an urban cultural studies film reading with the understanding that there are multiple paths to these textual-contextual scholarly reconciliations (or as Cresswell and Dixon aptly put it, echoing much film theory, integrations of the "reel" with the "real"). As might be expected, of course, this urban cultural studies reading integrates Lefebvre's insights—but it is more important to see that it attempts to give equal weight to both art and society, the project and the formation, the artistic and extraartistic qualities of the text.

Biutiful Barcelona: An Urban Cultural Studies Reading

After so many years of international applause for Barcelona's monumental and spectacular built environment, at long last Alejandro González Iñárritu's *Biutiful* (2010) shows, as this section explores, not a dystopic future Barcelona but the dark underbelly of the Barcelona that already exists. Instead of the acclaimed "model" Barcelona we have the "real" Barcelona (in the sense of the term as employed by Zizek; see the 'Introduction' in Kay 2003)—that is, the drab, grimy city full of labor inequality, the collusion of police with multinationals, the reality of sickness (here: the protagonist's cancer), and the lack of real possibilities for the immigrants who come from abroad hoping to make a better life for themselves and for their families. In light of the writings of Barcelona-based Lefebvrian urban theorist Manuel Delgado Ruiz (1956–), the filmic image of the Catalan capital presented in Iñárritu's film[12] calls attention to the distance between self-congratulatory discourses of Barcelona as the modern city *par excellence* on one side, and the injustices faced by so many of its urbanites on the other.[13] *Biutiful* manages this at the levels of both content and form: by focusing on immigrant and marginalized characters throughout the film; by largely frustrating the viewer's predictable expectation for glimpses of the city's triumphant and monumental architecture; by privileging interiors throughout; through subtle yet poignant camera movements that shift attention from the "model" city back to the "real" city; by mobilizing a wealth of props that depict images of sea life—a way of compensating for and simultaneously drawing attention to the viewer's lack of visual access to the Mediterranean (and thus to Barcelona as destination city); and ultimately even by the integration of a spiritual/supernatural narrative arc that captures the protagonist Uxbal's gradual crossing over into the beyond—a storyline that ultimately serves also to reinforce the theme of urban immigration/marginalization.[14] During the discussion of each of these elements—and true to the spirit of what I am calling urban cultural studies method—this reading consistently emphasizes that it is the primary urban theme of the film that brings together its disparate secondary characters and subplots.

From this perspective, the choice of Barcelona both as the diegetic setting for *Biutiful* and as the location of its filmic production must be understood as being in no way casual. In extrafilmic discourse, the intriguing case of Barcelona is today widely invoked by both sides of a very polemical conflict over what cities should be—many planners and architects label the "Barcelona model" a triumph of urban design while many urban critics see it as a product of what Henri Lefebvre has denounced as capitalist modernity's "enthusiastic (triumphant and triumphalist) consciousness" (1995, 3). Manuel Delgado's insistence in his recent work on the "Barcelona model" (2007b)—a concept cleverly respun by Mónica Degen in her labeling of Barcelona as the "top-model" city (2004a, 2004b)—voices a disdain widely held by those who see an enormous gap between triumphalist and majestically touristic images of contemporary cities and the class differences, social inequalities, and even the quotidian suffering requisitely hidden by the slick images promoting what many call intercity competition (see Harvey 1996).

To see how *Biutiful* paints a picture at odds with the triumphalist idea of the "modelo Barcelona," it is helpful to ground a reading of the film's formal qualities and content in the urban criticism of Delgado—which specifically addresses topics ranging from the urban built environment itself to immigration and difference. The present urban cultural studies approach may seem "too urban" for traditional film critics and too "cultural" for many scholars working in the more quantitative and historical field of urban studies proper, but I insist that in seeking to understand Iñárritu's most recent film, it is necessary and perhaps even unavoidable to force a confrontation between these two discourses. The present Delgado-inspired urban reading of the film thus underscores that *Biutiful* is, throughout and in the final analysis, a compelling and unique film foregrounding the human costs of spectacular urban modernity.

It is significant that director Alejandro González Iñárritu himself has said that *Biutiful* has "little to do, at least in conceptual and structural terms" with his earlier films *Amores perros* (2000), *21 Grams* (2003), and *Babel* (2006) (quoted in Deleyto and del Mar Azcona 2010, ix; also 121–140). Although the context for this comment is a discussion of *Biutiful*'s linear storyline and its focus on the main character's subjectivity (as contrasted with the complex narrative structures of those previous films; ibid., see also Podalsky 2011; Smith 2006; Tierney 2009), another difference is that the city is now not only a backdrop for human struggles but an inextricable part of the film's urban critique (on the urban setting of *Amores perros*, see D'Lugo 2003; Thornton 2003; Gregori 2006; Kantaris 2008). Much has been written, of course, on the relationship between film and cities; and such volumes as those edited by Stuart Aitken and Leo Zonn (*Place, Power, Situation and Spectacle: A Geography of Film*, 1994) and by David B. Clarke (*The Cinematic City*, 1997) are foundational in this regard (see also Mennel 2008; Webber and Wilson 2008). Rather than dialogue more extensively with this tradition as I have elsewhere (see Fraser 2006, 2008a, 2010a), here I prefer to delve further into Delgado's theory of the urban itself (discussed in even greater depth in Fraser 2007a, 2008a, 2010, 2011a) and reconcile it with a close textual reading of the film. Nonetheless, Larry Ford's general assertion in his contribution to the Aitken and Zonn volume—that "the role of cities in film gradually changed over time from serving as mere background scenery to acting as the equivalent of major characters in many stories" (1994, 119)—is of great relevance. With this in mind, it is easy to see that Barcelona is undeniably recognizable as the film's co-protagonist, along with Javier Bardem's lead character named Uxbal.

One of the film's strengths is that, despite a consistent focus on Bardem's character, there are numerous secondary characters whose subplots become closely and carefully intertwined with Uxbal's necessarily urban experience. One reviewer summarizes *Biutiful* by writing: "Uxbal and his morally suspect brother Tito (Eduard Fernández) are a pair of half-baked hoods who profit from Barcelona's black market, taking money from Chinese Sweatshop owners and Senegalese street vendors to pay off the city's corrupt police officers" (Feaster 2011, 36). Uxbal's contacts with such secondary characters as sweatshop co-owners (and lovers) Liwei (played by Jin Luo) and Hai (Taisheng Cheng), sweatshop worker Lili (Lang Sofia Lin), Senegalese street vendor Ekweme (Cheikh Ndiaye), and his wife Ige (Diaryatou Daff) are particularly emphasized as Iñárritu allows each character's experience to reflect the greater dehumanizing forces of capitalist urban modernity in Barcelona. These experiences are tragic, indeed: Liwei and Hai's business comes to an abrupt end, precipitated by Uxbal's purchase of what are nonetheless faulty gas heaters for the workers; Hai eventually murders Liwei in a hotel room after the business fails and after his wife and family have likely become aware of his extramarital affair; Lili, her child, and a score of other Chinese immigrant workers die from gas inhalation, locked in the factory where they sleep nights in cramped conditions; Ekweme is beaten and arrested by the police, being eventually deported and separated from Ige who he urges to remain behind; and even Uxbal himself struggles to juggle his roles as father and separated husband with the bribes and black market business ventures undertaken with his brother, ultimately falling to an end-stage cancer in the film's final sequences.

In *Biutiful*, these seemingly disparate human tragedies acquire an accumulating force as manifestations of a decidedly urban problematic where the value of human relationships is consistently subordinated to the rule of exchange. Urban theorist Delgado has written of Barcelona as being "un artículo de consumo con una sociedad humana dentro [an article of consumption containing a human society]" (2007b, 11), and in this light, the film crafts a critical view of the reified and consumed city as product, this time as seen from the inside of the packaging. The director relies heavily on interiors, which dominate throughout the film as a way of underscoring the small-scale stories of the immigrants and street vendors who struggle from day to day just to make ends meet. We are frequently shown, for example, the locked and cramped basement room where Lili and her child sleep with other Chinese immigrants to awaken regularly at 6:30 for a demanding day's work at an underground sweatshop, just as the insides of apartments predominate (those of Uxbal, of Tito, of Uxbal's estranged wife Marambra, of his spiritual mentor Bea, the small space Ekweme and Ige share with numerous other immigrants). When exteriors are indeed shown, the scenes alternate between still shots of empty street corners at dusk (e.g., in the area of the Chinese sweatshop) and vibrant daytime sidewalks crowded with people. Regardless, shots of the streets during the day (of Uxbal, the children, Marambra) are often shot at such an angle so as to crop out the sky. The vibrant sidewalk scenes play an important role—as when Ige picks up the children from school, for example. The crowds of people moving to and fro during the day offer a complement to the desolate night streetcorners, thus emphasizing the human city, the practiced city—implicitly in line with the emancipatory notions of the sidewalk ballet/"eyes on the street" that famed antiurbanist Jane Jacobs (1992) wrote about in her *Death and Life of Great American Cities* (a similar evocation of Barcelona occurs in José Luis Guerín's film *En construcción*; see Loxham 2006).

Delgado has himself linked Jacobs' vision of the life of the streets with his greater critique of contemporary urban design.[15] In his prizewinning book *El animal público/The Public Animal*, he goes so far as to claim the street is "la patria de los sin patria [the country of those with no country]" (1999, 209), invoking Hannah Arendt while suggesting that the exile and the foreigner are those who best express civic values (ibid., significantly enough, on the book's concluding page). It is in the street where every moment sees the production of what he calls the "integration of incompatibles" (Delgado 1999, 208; my translation[16]). Walking the city-streets, in Delgado's view (just as for Jacobs and Michel de Certeau before him), defies symbolically and, often in practical terms, the necessarily static poses of much identity politics. Delgado evokes the pedestrian as a transient, uncodified, "stateless," being whose shifting from place to place makes him or her hard to pin down and identify. Though *Biutiful* makes it equally clear that this "statelessness" enjoyed by the transient pedestrian is necessarily ephemeral (e.g., through the scene of the police raid in the Plaça de Catalunya that rolls down the Ramblas and ends in Ekweme's deportation), the life of the streets shows through as the basis for a potential alternative urbanism that might humanize the city, embracing difference and once again asserting the priority of the city as use-value over the bourgeois legacy of the city as exchange-value (Lefebvre 1996).[17]

Biutiful's persistent focus on interiors and on the ephemerality of street life—the human city, what Delgado (1999, 2007a) and Lefebvre (1991a, 1996) call the "lived city"—presents a stark contrast with the triumphalist view of Barcelona as a monumentally architectural and touristic Mediterranean destination. The dehumanizing experiences of these marginalized secondary characters—working in sweatshops or on the streets, living in poverty, and under exploitative conditions—point to the characteristic fate of a greater number of urbanites trapped inside a city that is essentially a product for sale to tourists and multinationals.[18] Iñárritu's film is, thus, important not only for the interior sets on which it chooses to focus but also for the specific type of exterior it largely eschews. The viewer is generally frustrated in his or her expectation to see pleasing general shots of what is possibly one of the most photographed and "beautiful" European cities. The most notable or recognizable public spaces of Barcelona, if they appear at all in the film, are significantly portrayed only as "sites of conflict" (Delgado writes that "el espacio urbano es ante todo espacio para el conflicto [urban space is above all a space of conflict]," 2010, 138).

For example, the monetary arrangements between Uxbal and the municipal police prove to be of little importance when a raid is made on Senegalese street vendors selling their wares in a particularly touristic area of the city. A shot relatively early in the film effects a subtle camera tilt downward from the Nike logo on the store window to the vendors below, set up outside the multinational's shop located in the capital, rich Plaça de Catalunya. This movement directly underscores the contrast between the city as exchange-value and the city as use-value so key to Lefebvre (1996) and later Delgado (2007a, 2007b). Later, the dramatic police-raid sequence makes it clear that this seemingly "public" space in the city is partial to a certain definition of the public—that a more democratic notion of public is always–already subject to the uneven laws of capitalist competition. The sequence is notably filmed with disorienting handheld cameras as a way of capturing the danger and violence of the hunt as police chase down the vendors—using brutal force. One part of the chase highlights Ekweme who, while trying to escape, is hit in the face with a nightstick as he rounds a corner. A subsequent mobile close-up of his feet only—Uxbal's point of view (POV)—as his limp body is dragged away initially leaves it open to interpretation as to whether he has been knocked unconscious or perhaps even killed. Although part of this chase sequence takes place as the vendors run down Barcelona's famed Ramblas departing from the Plaça de Catalunya, this touristic staple of the Catalan capital is purposely obscured on screen through an excessive traveling frame and a dizzying handheld camera, such that little visual appreciation of the area's characteristic painted performance artists or sanctioned vendor stalls is possible. In this sequence, the Ramblas and the Plaça de Catalunya are used not as touristic spectacles but instead, in line with Delgado's view of the city, as first and foremost a "site of conflict"—whether understood in terms of immigrants versus police, multinational corporations versus street vendors, or more appropriately, both at once.

Just as importantly, the film's images of Barcelona's triumphant and characteristically "modern" architecture are either nonexistent or else marred by references to human tragedy. Establishing shots of recognizable parts of the city are few and far between, amounting collectively to a minute's duration at most in a film that lasts over two hours. Late in the film, for example, we see a brief high-angle shot of nineteenth-century urban designer Ildefons Cerdà's Eixample district illuminated at dusk with lights of car traffic visible.[19] Another important but brief establishing shot of a familiar if touristic and monumental Barcelona similarly occurs late in the film: a pan initially capturing the recently constructed Torre Agbar building[20] and Antonio Gaudí's still unfinished Sagrada Familia and moving left to rest finally on the rightward gaze of Javier Bardem's Uxbal, who sits in a hospital chair gazing through a window as he receives a cancer treatment. This subtle but poignant pan-left functions as a cinematic redirection allowing the viewer to contrast the city's monumental architecture and triumphalist touristic skyline with the quotidian human stories of marginality and illness that form the basis of Iñárritu's film. Similarly, Barcelona's famed Olympic village (see McNeill 1999) can be seen briefly and likewise late in the film— but even then, as will be discussed in subsequent paragraphs of this section, in a way that explicitly points to the human tragedies that are the hidden cost of urban renewal in international cities such as Barcelona.

Biutiful's aforementioned crucial camera movements—both subtle (the tilt, the pan) and not so subtle (dizzying mobile frame and handheld camera)—function to force a filmic confrontation between two widely divergent conceptions of the modern city. Manuel Delgado writes extensively on these two perspectives (in the process explicitly following urban theorist Henri Lefebvre's distinctly spatial reappropriation of line of Marx's reflections on the nature of capital).[21] In an essay titled "La ciudad levantada/The City in Revolt," Delgado writes that the city has—throughout the twentieth and into the twenty-first century—become so controlled by exchange-value and so neglectful of use-value that the "city dramatizes, then, the perennial conflict between two models of urban society": one a bourgeois model driven by capitalist development that "detests conflict" and the other a home for "the exploited and the excluded" (Delgado 2010, 139–140; my translation[22]). Iñárritu's *Biutiful* persistently dramatizes the distance between these two opposing forces: on the one hand, the bourgeois Barcelona intent on securing a spot as a destination city for both tourism and capital within the international market, and on the other, the Barcelona comprised by the workers and immigrants who are withheld access to this dream (cf. Castells and Mollenkopf 1991; Riis 1890).

This dualistic contrast between Barcelona as a bourgeois "model" city and as a city of the exploited can also be understood in terms of a more theoretical framework: Delgado's Lefebvrian stress on the importance of the "practiced city" over the "planned city." This opposition between the city as it is lived on the ground and as it is designed from above in the interests of capital accumulation comprises the key thrust of Delgado's urban critique (1999, 182). It is the practiced city that holds the potential to combat the compromised (with respect to capital) perspective of contemporary urban designers and also to help craft a more inclusive city, one more attentive to the needs, realities, and heterogeneity of its inhabitants (see Delgado 1999, 182).[23] Just as the planned city is opposed to the practiced city, so too is the bourgeois city opposed to the city of the exploited, and the dehumanizing capitalist city to the city as a lived space. *Biutiful* carries the spirit of Delgado's critique to the screen, illustrating that the vital human essence of the city such as that found ephemerally in the streets is nonetheless persistently "subordinated to urbanism." Maintaining an emphasis on Delgado's urban theory, it is necessary to explore the film's nuanced presentation of the Mediterranean (and thus its subversion of the touristic image of Barcelona) before bringing its supernatural aspects with its capitalist critique in a reading of the first and final sequences of the film.

Numerous books and articles published over the years make reference to the perennial refashioning of the city by an urbanism that Joan Ramon Resina has recently called *Barcelona's Vocation of Modernity*. Scholars have frequently commented on the ills of Barcelona's urban planning—in reference to the nineteenth-century plans of Ildefons Cerdà who designed the city's Eixample in 1859 (Cerdà 1867; Goldston 1969; Epps 2001, 2002; Resina, 2003, 2008; Fraser 2011a, 2011b) just as to preparations for the 1929 World's Fair (Vázquez Montalbán 1990; Epps 2001; Fraser 2008c) and the creation of the Olympic City for the 1992 Games (McNeill 1999, 2002; Degen 2008) (also see Hughes 1992; Hall 1997; Corominas i Ayala 2010). Notwithstanding, the "modelo Barcelona" is applauded as part of a view that prioritizes the concept of what Delgado (2007b) denounces in his introduction as "La ciudad-negocio [The City-as-Business]": he writes that "Quien ansía ocupar Barcelona y avasallarla es, hoy, un capitalismo financiero internacional que aspira a convertir la capital catalana en un artículo de consumo con una sociedad humana dentro [What anxiously desires to occupy and subdue Barcelona is, today, an international financial capitalism that aspires to convert the Catalan capital into an article of consumption with a human society inside]" (2007b, 11). An important component of Barcelona's international fame and marketability as a destination city is, of course, its proximity to the Mediterranean Sea.

To fully appreciate how Iñárritu's onscreen presentation of a decidedly bleak urban environment approximates Manuel Delgado's denunciation of a "model" Barcelona—as an article fit for consumption—it is necessary to turn to the film's nuanced dialogue with the Mediterranean, which, although it is persistently denied onscreen representation, is presented indirectly through frequent ocean imagery on props and sets, and also through its association with the film's mobilization of the color blue (the color most often associated with the water). These stylistic decisions on the part of the director nonetheless point to the conspicuous absence of the Mediterranean Sea, heightening the significance of its appearance in a crucial sequence late in the film and eventually intersecting even with the theme of worldly death and, necessarily given the plot circumstances, of supernatural connection with the world beyond.

The meaning of the film's rich formal aspects (props, sets, color palette) cannot be considered in isolation from *Biutiful*'s primary emphasis on the human costs that undergird the perceived success of the "modelo Barcelona." For example, Iñárritu's film employs an often drab palette, perhaps to emphasize the lack of opportunities that exist for his marginalized urban characters—and yet, within the context of that often drab palette, the color blue acquires a special resonance, heightening the film's sympathetic portrayal of its marginalized and even tragic immigrant characters. Blue objects haunt the film—the cabinets in the medium Bea's apartment, and the stones she gives to Uxbal; the blue bag brought to the train station by the Senegalese immigrant Ige when she thinks of leaving Spain; the underwear worn by Liwei—the younger lover and business partner who is later brutally murdered by Hai in a hotel room—and, not least of all, the blue sweatshirt worn by Uxbal as his own death grows nigh. In this way, the color becomes synonymous with social marginalization just as it is a poetic way of redefining Barcelona as a city of "others"—a city, as all cities, defined by difference either in the sense of a diverse community (Jacobs 1992; Harvey 1996, 2009b; Esposito 2009) or the implicit contrast with the presumably more homogeneous structures of life outside urban areas (e.g., now classic work on the city by Wirth 1938; Simmel 2010). The color blue, of course, enjoys a rich history as the symbol for deep sadness and melancholy such as that experienced by *Biutiful*'s numerous secondary characters, and it is perhaps fortuitous in this sense that Iñárritu himself has remarked in an interview conducted during the production of his 2010 film that "*Biutiful* is like the blues: a long, melancholy note" (quoted in Deleyto and del Mar Azcona 2010, 126; translation by the authors). It would be shortsighted, however, to ignore that the color draws its signifying power also from the proximity of the Mediterranean Sea itself. And if the director's comments are any indication, the sea does not just symbolize an escape from generalized earthly woes, but—for him—more specifically an escape from the spatial territorialism of advanced capitalism. In that same interview, Iñárritu remarks: "When I go to the seaside, what I find hypnotic about the sea, what is truly relaxing, is that there's no property. If an idiot decided to build a brick wall in the sea, if the technical possibility existed, I'm sure all the G-8 countries would erect a barrier in the sea" (quoted in Deleyto and del Mar Azcona 2010, 139; translation by the authors; cf. the Lefebvrian dictum from *The Survival of Capitalism*—that capitalism has survived throughout the twentieth century by "producing space, by occupying a space," 1976, 21).

The sea appears on screen more often in *Biutiful* as a motif than as a filmed image—in props/sets including the large fish sticker in Uxbal's shower, the aquarium nightlight in his children's room, the painting of the boat jarringly (but diegetically) shot early in the film, the fish stickers on the cabinets in Marambra's kitchen, and the exterior wall-art of a large slick shark devouring what appears to be older graffiti. These references to the sea—and thus to freedom from property, the rule of exchange-value, and the misery experienced by Barcelona's immigrant underclass—serve as an intermittent reminder that a better life lies just outside the reach of the film's secondary characters. The children Mateo and Ana, as Marambra says so poignantly, "Nunca han salido de este barrio [Have never left this neighborhood]"; and similarly, Uxbal says that the bipolar Marambra has never heard "el ruidoso mar [the noisy sea]" despite Barcelona's location on the coast of the Mediterranean itself. The film-goer's visual experience of onscreen Barcelona parallels this lack of access to the beach, and thus drives home the film protagonists' collective lack of hope. Simply put, *Biutiful* largely frustrates the viewer's predictable expectation to see the Mediterranean—with one important exception.

This exception occurs late in the film. After the Chinese workers die from gas inhalation while asleep, locked in the basement room of the sweatshop, we learn that their bodies have been taken out to sea and dumped offshore so as to avoid repercussions that might harm Hai's business deals. Nonetheless, the cadavers soon wash up on shore—as we learn from an intercalated news report. Cut to a tranquil sealine and a mobile frame passing ethereally over the rhythmic waves to a sandy beach where the bodies recall beached whales seen on television by Uxbal earlier in the film.[24] Perhaps the most memorable scene of the film (with the exception of the images comprising the beginning and end of the film's ring composition, discussed below), this one holds true to Iñárritu's decision to show not Barcelona as architectural triumph and Mediterranean destination city, but Barcelona as a façade draped over human tragedy. A view of what might otherwise be a symbol of hope, freedom, escape, and of course leisure—the Mediterranean sea itself—is thus delivered instead as a jarring reminder of the daily tragedies underscoring urban life.

As stated earlier in this section, I regard the distance between the "modelo Barcelona" and the "real" Barcelona, one which in reality makes the city's success possible, as the primary theme of the film. And yet there are secondary themes that complement this one—a fact that makes it so much easier to regard *Biutiful* as a complex film. The distance between the two Barcelonas (whether pristine image versus underbelly; planned city versus practiced city; the bourgeois city versus the city of the exploited) parallels (1) the baroque interplay between appearance and essence highlighted by the film's ring composition just as it does and (2) the contrast between life and death as seen through the supernatural aspects of the film.

Those sequences with which the film begins and ends (comprising its "ring composition") highlight the opposition of outer beauty and inner essence—just as does the title *Biutiful* itself, of course. The first words the viewer hears in *Biutiful* are spoken by Uxbal's daughter Ana who asks "¿Es de verdad? [Is it real?]" as we see a close-up of her hand touching the ring on her father.[25] The dialogue foregrounds the question of the "reality" of beauty, just as the camera juxtaposes the human hand—through labor, the source of all wealth in capitalist societies—with the ring, a symbol for the products of that capitalist labor. Here, we see the hands, the ring, but no faces, no shots of either Ana or her father—a decision that has imbued the scene with a certain subjective, and even poetic effect. If the shot is indeed a POV shot, then it may either be Ana's, Uxbal's, or perhaps even a shared POV (an interpretation that is more plausible given the supernatural slant of the film as a whole, and the finale in particular). The final sequence of the film returns to and reimagines this same initial dialogue and question ("¿Es de verdad?"), although from a different perspective, one that is (not unproblematically) more objective. As opposed to the film's beginning, in the final sequence, we see not a close-up but instead contextualized mid/mid-long shots of father and daughter resting in bed, while Ana touches the ring. At the side of the bed sits Uxbal's double, indicating that he is passing on into death. This passing is itself intriguing and is rendered poetically by Iñárritu who fuses previous moments in the film together on screen—a poetic amalgam of Uxbal's memory of his own father spawned by a photo, his son's interest in owls, and previous discussion of a trip by his wife and daughter to the snow-covered Pyrenees. Along with the visual presentation of these images, the final and the initial sequence of the film both include audio of what might very well be the sounds of the "ruidoso mar [noisy sea]" itself. The effect of the shift made from the beginning of the film (a disjointed close-up POV) to the ending (the contextualized, more objective mid/mid-long shots) in the portrayal of what is actually a single moment in time is to highlight the human story behind the hands we initially see. The ring itself, while indeed still an object and symbol of "*biuti*," requires less of our attention as we focus instead on the human relationship between Ana and her father Uxbal. In this sense, the film's ring composition highlighting death parallels the film's urban preoccupation—its emphasis on the human relationships behind the shimmering myth of the Barcelona model—human relationships that, of course, through labor, have made that very myth possible.

The theme of death also foregrounds the notion of belonging, which is in turn so central to Delgado's contemporary urban criticism. The lost souls, and eventually Bardem's Uxbal, do not belong to the world of the living anymore, just as Ekweme, Ige, Liwei, Lili, and her child presumably do not belong in a Barcelona that nonetheless profits off of their labor. The fleeting sense of community established between Uxbal and Lili/Li, and between Uxbal and Ige; the volatile portrayal of the family relationships between Ana/Mateo and Marambra, between Uxbal and Marambra, and between Uxbal and Tito; all of these are nothing in contrast with the portrayal of a Barcelona that does not tolerate difference and discourages a sense of belonging to place. Significantly, a number of the film's climactic scenes foreground so-called "nonplaces"—for example, the hotel where Liwei is murdered and the train station where Ige struggles with the decision either to return to Senegal or to remain in the Catalan capital.[26] The central characters of *Biutiful* are subject to this particular capitalist refashioning of city-space, in which under the illusion of homogeneity—effecting the "absence of difference"—marginality is policed in the modern city so that space may be sold as a tourist destination or as an attractive business location (Lefebvre 1991a; Philo and Kearns 1993; Harvey 1996; Fraser 2010).

In this context, lacking an identity—going unidentified—becomes a way of momentarily evading the codification that aids in the selling of city-place. Delgado writes of the urban pedestrian's "right to anonymity," wherein the apparent lack of identity is, in fact, a protection of sorts that, in theory, makes it possible for individuals to momentarily evade the systems of control that increasingly play a role in the reproduction and vigilance over the shared spaces of the city.[27] With this in mind, *Biutiful* suggests that there are only a handful of ways to escape the excessive codification of identity, the concomitant cleansing of city-space, and, of course, also the modes of social exploitation to which the city's urbanites are routinely subjected. Uxbal's passing into the other world—and the fate of the film's Chinese immigrants—intimates that the city's persecution of marginality may end only in death. Another alternative is shown through the narrative arc of Ekweme, who is forced to accept deportation as a solution to the struggles he encounters in the Catalan capital. And Ige faces an uncertain future in Uxbal's apartment in which she may even take on the not-unproblematic role of mother to his children Ana and Mateo. In the end, whether it is seen as a stunning human story or as a supernatural narrative, all readings of *Biutiful* must grapple with the dehumanizing effects of what Joan Ramon Resina calls *Barcelona's Vocation of Modernity*.

CHAPTER 6

Listening to Urban Rhythms: Soundscapes in Popular Music

In *Spaces of Hope*, Lefebvrian urban thinker David Harvey notes the way in which Marx had "grounded his ontological and epistemological arguments on real sensual bodily interaction with the world" and proposes that "The contemporary rush to return to the body as the irreducible basis of all argument is, therefore a rush to return to the point where Marx, among many others began" (2000, 101–102).[1] Harvey's discussion—unsurprisingly if the reader has been attentive to the ways in which his Marxism differs in emphasis, but not in its foundation, from Lefebvre's own Marxian thought—turns quickly to political economy and to notions of class, labor, and production. While Harvey provides valuable insights, it is instead Lefebvre whose Marxian development of the themes of embodied being under capitalism lends itself to a closer examination of the aural cultural product.

As we saw earlier in this book, it is the concept of alienation that constitutes the core of Lefebvre's recalibrated Marxian project and that, through the twin concept of disalienation, provides a way of returning to *experience*—a way of reuniting individuals with the totality of a social realm that is routinely fragmented according to capitalist logic. At a philosophical level, this pernicious fragmentation severs mental from physical realities (e.g., ideology on the one hand, material goods on the other); at a practical level, it breaks mental realities up into knowledge areas of specialized character and fragments material realities through the division of labor; from a spatial perspective, it both affects the categories that influence our conception of space and also our perception of an uneven geographical development, obscuring the complex unity of *lived* space (Lefebvre 1991a, 1996, 2003a). Because it underscores a dialectical approach, Lefebvre's reconfigured Marxism emphasizes the potential of effecting transformative change across both the mental and material realms at once—bucking the reductive interpretation of Marxism as merely a materialist critique in the simple, economic sense. While temporality had long been a key aspect to his dialectical thinking, in his later years specifically, however, he asserted that there was a visual logic to capitalism that could be subverted by turning to the other senses—in particular, hearing.

Because Lefebvre's remarks on music, listening, and the aurality of rhythms came relatively late in his career, this chapter necessarily turns also to a number of other thinkers whose thinking about music—although they are perhaps not directly indebted to Lefebvre—squares with his emphasis on embodied experience, his appeal to interdisciplinarity, his acknowledgment of the complexity of aesthetic and cultural realities, and the disalienating spirit of his work as a whole.[2] Following the example of cinema in the previous chapter, it would be just as possible to advocate a musical criticism of songs that take cities as their theme or topic, or for that matter an approach that sees specific cities as linked to the musical imaginaries of certain songs or bands, even where that connection is not explicit. Both of these examples would surely be welcome when carried out in accordance with the general principles of an urban cultural studies method, and in fact, I have attempted musical criticism of the second type in a co-authored essay on Joy Division and the city of Manchester published in *Punk & Post-Punk* (Fraser and Fuoto 2012). In this chapter, however, I have chosen to provide an alternative form of urban popular musical criticism—one that contributes to theoretical discussions but that is no less interdisciplinary, nor for that matter any less textual.

The first section that follows ("Rhythmanalysis: Music, Emotion, and Sound") turns to the mode of critique that Henri Lefebvre referred to as rhythmanalysis, offering an explicitly interdisciplinary perspective through which he pointed to a more embodied theoretical practice. This mode of criticism should be understood as a complement to and not a substitute for more critically distant analyses that tend to downplay the capacity of music to move us all. Lefebvre's lifelong interdisciplinary project is well suited to this endeavor, and particularly well suited is the volume *Rhythmanalysis*, published posthumously in 1992, and intended as a fourth volume of his *Critique of Everyday Life* (see Lefebvre 2006a, viii).

Building on recent studies that have linked music, emotion, and geography, the second section of this chapter ("Lisabö's Soundscapes of Urban Alienation") looks at the musical production of the Basque post-punk band "Lisabö" across their four albums: *Ezlekuak* (Bidehuts 2007), *Izkiriaturik aurkitu ditudan gurak* (Metak 2005), *Ezarian* (Esan Ozenki 2000), and the EP *Egan Bat Nonahi* (Acuarela 2002). Melding musical (cultural/textual) studies with a range of geographical and urban theory, this analysis takes on both the sonic immediacy and the lyrical content of the band's music in an attempt to rescale emotional approaches to the notions of space and place to an urban level. Ultimately this reading of Lisabö's emotional soundscapes highlights the role (and omission) of emotion in the production of urban places and simultaneously suggests that our emotional connections with music might form the basis for an embodied musical criticism engaged with space and place at the level of the urban.

Rhythmanalysis: Music, Emotion, and Sound

To the extent that Lefebvre's rhythmanalytical project is a logical continuation of his distaste for traditional philosophy, it is foreshadowed even more generally in his earlier work (1991a, 117; 2002, 130, where he even terms it "a new science"). While very much in tune with his earlier rejection of overly analytical approaches, Lefebvre's later writings elaborated upon the method of "rhythmanalysis" he had already introduced in volumes two and three of the *Critique* and signaled a further departure from the reductive notion of knowledge commonly pursued by traditional criticism. Of course, Lefebvre borrowed the term from Gaston Bachelard, who had in turn borrowed it from writer Lucio Alberto Pinheiro (Lefebvre 2006a, xiii, 9). In Lefebvre's appropriation of the notion, rhythm became a way of reconciling the body ("each segment of the body has its rhythm," 2006a, 38), with larger processes ("The body? Your body? It consists in a bundle of rhythms...But the surroundings of the body, the social just as much as the cosmic body, are equally bundles of rhythms," 2006a, 80).

Viewing with suspicion the critical distance that continues to subtend traditional disciplinary knowledge, Lefebvre articulated his method by drawing extensively upon musical metaphors and sonorous realities. This move functioned as a way of restoring a traditionally distant critical perspective to the world from which it has been detached. Sound is in no way peripheral to Lefebvre's new science, as he underscores in the chapter of *Rhythmanalysis* titled "Music and Rhythms" (2006a, 57–66)—and his fundamental incorporation of the sonorous is manifest from the start of the book's first chapter. Therein, the geographical philosopher who is so often fond of emphasizing relational triads (Hegel's "thesis-antithesis-synthesis," Marx's "economic-social-political," 2006a, 12) suggests an appropriate triad for use in rhythmanalysis: "melody-harmony-rhythm" (12). The importance given to this relational triad underlies his discussion of such concepts as measures (2006a, 8), harmonics (60), musical time (64), of arrhythmia, isorhythmia, polyrhythmia, eurhythmia (16, 31, 67), and more generally of rhythm throughout the volume. While the rhythmanalytical method was at once biological, psychological, social, urban, political, metaphysical, and, to use Lefebvre's own assessment, medical, historical, climatological, cosmological, and poetic (2006a, 16), it was also musical.

Ultimately, Lefebvre uses the notion of rhythmanalysis to combat the tendency of thought to think in terms of space alone and not time.[3] For the rhythmanalyst,

> nothing is immobile. He hears the wind, the rain, storms, but if he considers a stone, a wall, a trunk, he understands their slowness, their interminable rhythm. This *object* is not inert; time is not set aside for the *subject*. It is only slow in relation to our time, to our body, the measure of rhythms. An apparently immobile *object*, the forest, moves in multiple ways: the combined movements of the soil, the earth, the sun. Or the movements of the molecules and atoms that compose it (the object, the forest). The rhythmanalyst calls on all his senses. He draws on his breathing, the circulation of his blood, the beatings of his heart and the delivery of his speech as landmarks. Without privileging any one of these sensations, raised by him in the perception of rhythms, to the detriment of any other. He thinks with his body, not in the abstract, but in lived temporality. (original emphasis; 2006a, 20–21)

Thinking not in the abstract but with the body presents challenges for traditional analysis, which must now open itself up to alternative ways of knowing. In his estimation, the paradigm of traditional intellection strove for a pure and even disembodied knowledge, through prioritizing visual knowledge, that which can be observed from a distance. Rhythmanalysis, although it does not completely lack a visual component, downplays it. Lefebvre subverts the hegemony of the visual field, embracing the tactile, embracing sensations and especially sound, the act of listening (the rhythmanalyst "hears the wind," above). Recognizing the significance of sound is a particularly important way for the researcher to plunge into the mysteries of time, and Lefebvre's text returns time and time again to the act of listening. As Lefebvre elaborates, "The object resists a thousand aggressions but breaks up in humidity or conditions of vitality, the profusions of miniscule life. To the attentive ear, it makes a noise like a seashell" (2006a, 20); and also "[the rhythmanalyst] will come to listen to a house, a street, a town, as an audience listens to a symphony" (2006a, 22; cf. Mumford 1970; chapter 1, this book). Rhythmanalysis constitutes an attempt to reach the corporeal and the sensible,[4] both the tactile and more important, given the present attempt, also the sonorous.

Recent years have seen the proliferation of numerous studies in cultural geography that implicitly or even explicitly invoke Lefebvre's rhythmanalytical project. For example, Reena Tiwari uses Lefebvre's method to construct what she calls "experiential maps" of the city (2008, 289), and Fraser Sturt (2006) even applies it to the maritime archaeology of prehistory. Tim Edensor and Julian Holloway look at the multiple rhythms (some institutionalized) of the tourist experience, highlighting the audio narratives of the coach drivers (2008, 491–493). Other articles have taken advantage of the concept of rhythmanalysis to look at such topics as street performance and street life in London (Highmore 2002; Simpson 2008), sidewalk talk on Calle Ocho in Miami (Price 2007), the rhythms of breakfast in a city café (Laurier 2008), and sound and the television-viewing experience (Obert 2008) as well as other aspects of the sonorous realities of city life (Fortuna 2001, 1998; Rihacek 2006).[5] Nevertheless, it is appropriate also to apply Lefebvre's notion of rhythmanalysis to a humanities-driven analysis of musical texts themselves. Read in tandem with his critique of capitalist spatial production (Lefebvre 1976, 1991a, 1996, 2003a), the effect of Lefebvre's remarks on music and the audible is to suggest that we might understand space differently through sound. "[Music] gives itself above all else in return for a time: in return for a rhythm" (2006a, 60).[6] In time, in rhythm, contradiction and conflict are not subjected to the univocal logic that sustains, for Lefebvre, the production of space.

In using Lefebvre's insights to comment upon sonorous texts, we must also grapple with the intimate connection between music and emotion. As has been noted by an increasing number of theorists writing across traditional disciplinary boundaries, emotions are not merely a surface disturbance of human experience but are instead an essential, if oft-ignored, aspect of our thought and cultural production. Over the past decade, scholars from geography in particular have worked to "tap into the emotional content of human affairs" (Wood and Smith 2004,

533) and to see the relevance of emotions to spatial understandings and practices (Anderson and Smith 2001; Ettlinger 2004; Wood and Smith 2004; Tolia-Kelly 2006). This "emotional turn" has often proved to be a way of recalibrating the dualistic Cartesian schism between thinking and feeling—as Joyce Davidson and Christine Milligan concisely state in a compelling editorial, "there is little we can *think apart* from feeling" (original emphasis; 2004, 523; see also Bondi 2002, 7).[7] At the same time, a parallel shift in disciplinary orientation has highlighted the significance of music to issues of space and place, often intersecting with this focus on emotional geographies and highlighting musical experience as both individual and community practice. It is in this vein, for example, that Ben Anderson (2005) has looked at the experience of music in domestic everyday life; John Connell and Chris Gibson (2004) at the more global phenomenon of "world music"; George Revill (2005) at "folk music"; and Frances Morton (2005) at Irish traditional music. As Anderson, Morton, and Revill suggest in their editorial introduction to a special issue of *Social and Cultural Geography*, scholars have moved beyond "music or sound as textual objects" toward musical practice and performance as a way of legitimizing "the multiplicity of ways in which musics are experienced, produced, reproduced and consumed, and to foreground the relationships between the physical presence of sound and the flow of sensory impressions" (2005, 640). Broadening the approach to music in this way has in effect appropriately challenged another dualistic posture that risks conceptualizing the sonorous and the musical merely as an immaterial representation of a more fundamental tangible and material world.

Just such a dualistic posture has been similarly rejected by recent work at the intersection of sound and cognition that has pointed out the intimate connection that exists between music, emotion, and the brain. As popular neuroscience authors Daniel J. Levitin (2006, 251–252) and Oliver Sacks (2007, x) agree, music may have been very important, evolutionarily speaking. As both authors underscore, there is an interesting and direct link between emotion, sound, and motor activity, owing to the fact that not all of the connections between the inner ear and the brain run to the auditory cortex—some run directly to the cerebellum. Sometimes called the "reptilian brain" (2006, 174), Levitin writes: "The cerebellum is central to something about emotion—startle, fear, rage, calm, gregariousness [and is] now implicated in auditory processing" (187). In this context, the opportunity thus presents itself to approach the connection between emotion and music not merely as a surface disturbance of human experience but rather as a fundamental relation impacting both thought and action.

Not surprisingly, this recent biological and neurological argument for the importance of sound resonates with a growing body of geographical scholarship that has already been engaging sound at a deeper level. The theorist who has most directly synthesized emotions, music, and geography is perhaps Susan J. Smith (1997, 2000, 2001, 2005; see also Wood, Duffy, and Smith 2007), who formulates a key question, effectively turning the ocularcentric nature of knowledge production on its ear. Just as when she argued that "sound is as important as sight for the project of geography" (1997, 502), Smith provocatively asks, "What would happen to the way we think, to the things we know, to the relationships we enter, to our experience of time and space, if we fully took on board the idea that the world is for hearing rather than beholding, for listening to, rather than for looking at?" (2005, 90). Smith's question points to the opportunity presented in musical performance to reconcile both dualistic categories and divergent scales of experience. She writes that "it is through their capacity to tie the personal to the political, the aesthetic to the material, the emotional to the social, the individual body to the collective enterprise that performers make their place in the world" (2005, 111). Actualizing just this sort of reconciliation, the literature on music and geography has grappled just as much with theoretical and philosophical issues as it has with concrete expressions of place and identity, exploring the dialectical relationship that exists between sonorous realities and material practices.[8]

Interest in such subjectivity formations has very often reverberated through the scales of the individual, the community, the region, and of course the national (Wood 2002; Davidson and Milligan 2004; Anderson 2005; Hudson 2006), but has less frequently been directed toward the urban scale. Appropriately, here I engage in a rescaling of our approach to music, emotion, and geography through a sustained look at (or rather a "listening to") the musical production of the contemporary Basque band Lisabö. Their four albums, *Ezlekuak* (Bidehuts 2007), *Izkiriaturik aurkitu ditudan gurak* (Metak 2005), *Ezarian* (Esan Ozenki 2000), and the EP *Egan Bat Nonahi* (Acuarela 2002), are best engaged at the scale of the urban, as an expression of and a reaction to an urbanized consciousness. Building on the discussions begun in chapter 2 of the present book, I want to show how the band's variegated emotional soundscapes function as a complementary soundtrack to theoretical approaches to urban alienation. This rescaling, specifically entailing a shift from the national to the urban, is not a negation of previous work, but an acknowledgment of the multiple and socially negotiated scales of experience (Marston 2000).

At the same time that this chapter attempts to rescale musical scholarship and suggest the relevance of an urban-centered approach, it is also an attempt to return to the notion of music as a cultural product—not in the traditional sense denounced by Wood as a way of ignoring music's connection to space and place (2002, 59)—but here as a way of supporting a recalibrated understanding of the role of the humanities in investigating the connection between music, emotion, and place. As is evident from recent interest in the resonance of music with issues of space and place (Connell and Gibson 2003), music is certainly a commodity and a social practice, a hybrid artifact tied into processes of identity formation and global exchange. Yet while music certainly does not exist "beyond the worlds of politics, commerce and social life" (Connell and Gibson 2003, 18), it is nevertheless important to assert our emotional connection to music and to see that there is a role reserved for humanities-centered close readings of musical texts in urban cultural studies criticism. That is, it is important to assert that recorded musical "texts" and the connections formed with them by listeners are no less emotional than performances. Susan McClary and Robert Walser cogently report on what they term the "staggering" (1990, 283) problems of reconciling music as a cultural artifact with social organization, noting also that "music is an especially resistant medium to write or speak about" (1990, 278; see also Wood, Duffy, and Smith 2007, 885). As Simon Frith's work suggests, part of the challenge of writing about music involves displacing the hegemonic position long enjoyed by lyrics in discussions of musical signification (1988, 105–106, 120–121; 1996a, 158–182) and compensating for the fact that scholars have more frequently taken to analyzing the structural and formal qualities of a piece of music rather than tackling the "the qualities of immediacy, emotion, sweat [which are] suspect terms in both the library and the classroom" (Frith 1996b; quoted in Smith 2005, 108). And yet it should be noted that Frith's position clearly does not advocate abandoning lyrical content or the analysis of formal qualities altogether. Given the difficulty of writing about the elusive qualities of sound, lyrics—especially when complemented by a substantial attempt to address nonlyrical aspects—provide one appropriate pathway among others into the meaning of music, a direction pursued even by Frith himself in his works.

Appropriately, the second section of this chapter seeks to work from a middle ground, grappling simultaneously with Lisabö's music as a cultural product and as a point of entry into urbanized consciousness. This effort thus simultaneously treats Lisabö's albums as cultural products and also as theoretical (musical) texts in their own right, blending a close reading of the band's musical texts with a nod to larger urban questions. In tune with broadly accepted tenets of literary/cultural studies, this blended and somewhat unconventional approach succumbs neither to the intentional fallacy that seeks to reveal the "essential" meaning lurking behind a cultural product nor to the facile distinction between the form of a given work and its content. Instead, this chapter underscores the band's recorded musical production as a whole and frames it as a complex musical representation, and also a contestation, of urban alienation. This focus on the richness of recorded music itself should be seen as a complement to lucid analyses of live music performances and national musical communities by Anderson, Revill, and Morton (2005) and others.

With all this in mind, the next section of this chapter thus approaches the relevance of music to identity formation loosely, both stepping back from the tendency of reading music too closely in relation to identity politics and simultaneously (if paradoxically) contextualizing the band Lisabö within a Basque tradition of punk/post-punk. Stepping back from the need to see their music in terms of (Spanish or even Basque) national identity but admitting the potential of music to contribute to theoretical discussions of the urban, it explores how the musical and lyrical content of the band's albums intersect with the work by a number of theorists on urban alienation and so-called "nonplaces." In the end, discussion emphasizes the notion that criticism on music and place need not eschew the very emotional enjoyment of music it so often sublimates beneath a theoretical veneer of analytical objectivity. Instead, as my reading of Henri Lefebvre's "rhythmanalysis" suggests—grounded in the connection between music and emotion underscored by neuroscience and drawing upon the work of Henri Bergson (see Fraser 2010, 2009b)—there is reason to acknowledge that the listener in fact comes to coincide with the sounds s/he hears. Listening to Lisabö's music—and from Lefebvre's perspective sound more generally—returns us to the realm of temporality, making contradiction and conflict audible, encouraging emotional connections with place and calling into question the sight-bound logic that drives the capitalist production of urban space—that is, the notion that the city is (re)produced as exchange-value in the form of a particularly visual spectacle.

Furthermore, the intimate qualities of our relationship to music suggest that we might approach it with a greater degree of critical intimacy than other areas. In the introduction to the volume *Music and Emotion: Theory and Research*, Patrik N. Juslin and John A. Slobada draw attention to what they call "evaluative processes" "the determination, or awareness of music as eliciting liking or disliking; preference; emotion and mood; and aesthetic, transcendent and spiritual experiences" (2001, 4). Music does not merely mean something cognitively, it also *does* something. This perspective emphasizes the intersection of emotion, the body, and place. The body itself is a place, as suggested by Lefebvre's elaboration of rhythmanalysis, as we will discuss by returning to his predecessor Bergson's statement that affect as a real action occurring where it is felt. This is not to say that (less textual) geographical analyses of musical production as a cultural practice are inappropriate, but rather that a complementary engagement of music might arise as a way of folding the humanities and the social sciences together. In this engagement, the critic does not momentarily ignore the power that music has to move us, attempting to formulate a detached and therefore more objective perspective. Instead, acknowledging the emotional connection we have with music becomes the starting point for an understanding of theoretical issues, more broadly conceived. All too often—given the close link between emotion and music—criticism reconciling music and space adopts a distancing perspective, a clinical approach that functions only within a sterile void of emotional detachment. As Wood, Duffy, and Smith lucidly point out, "Even academic musicologists such as Cook (1999), McClary and Walser (1990) and Shepherd and Wicke (1997), for example, are critical of the extent to which, within their own musical disciplines, scholars have distanced themselves from the sensual and emotional experience of participating in, or practicing and creating, musical events (whether as performers, listeners, or audience members)" (2007, 868). While analytical distance has its place, there is a way of maintaining a deep level of theoretical commitment while engaging music from a closer distance, thus preserving the emotional capacity of music to please or displease us as listeners—something from which even the critic is not immune. The point, however, is to use our intimate connection with music to rethink the urban phenomenon. If, as Tia DeNora has argued, music has the power to "reorient consciousness" (2003a, 59–82; also 2003b), then Lisabö's emotional soundscapes offer to reorient consciousness in tune with the multifaceted critique of urbanization made possible by Lefebvrian theory.

Lisabö's Soundscapes of Urban Alienation

Betwixt, between and across the Pyrenees—the mountain range separating Spain and France—there lie the seven lands of the Basque Country, or *Euskal Herria* as it is known in the Basque language. None other than noted cineaste Orson Welles (the director of *Citizen Kane* and *The Magnificent Ambersons*) traveled there in the 1950s as part of a BBC television series titled *Around the World*. Placing his camera "directly on an international border" of a "little-known corner of Europe," Welles presents us with visual anchors for what have become the standard images of a traditional representation of Basque life—an agricultural-based village, traditional berets called *boinas*, rural feats of strength, and the varieties of Basque ball games from which contemporary *jai alai* developed. The director films the Basque Country in black and white, adding his own voiceover narration, and he seems entranced by what appears to be an authentic culture—yielding a televised platitude that would make today's students of Anthropology cringe. But for all his flaws, Welles is right on the money when he remarks: "The people who live here are neither French nor Spanish; Basques are what Basques are."

Perhaps the most important part of "what Basques are" comes from their language, *euskara*. In today's era of international musical commodities—in which many bands on the Iberian peninsula find it easier to make a buck singing in English rather than in their own languages of Castilian (Spanish), Catalan, or Galician, for example—Basque band Lisabö's decision to sing in *euskara* sets them apart. The band members themselves have remarked that their rejection of English is a protest "against the English-language monopoly in music and in all areas. A total monopoly in this globalized world where other cultures are hidden from the fucking cultural and commercial monolith of English and the United States." Lisabö's appeal goes much further than that, of course. First, there is their difficult heavy rock sound, which draws from both punk and post-punk roots—its weft and wane oscillating between thick, heavy guitar progressions and loosely knit ethereal digressions. Next, there is the band's characteristic lyrical intensity, vocals in Basque screamed or whispered against the punctuated meter of a drum kit (or, at times, even two). But there is also the equally challenging subject matter of their songs.

On the stand-out album *Ezlekuak* (Non-Places, 2007), the song lyrics tend more toward an urban sociology, or an anthropology of life in today's cities. In the process, they stray far from the traditional reliance of the genre on the personal lives and emotions of disaffected youth. In fact, the album's title seems to be ripped straight from French anthropologist Marc Augé's 1995 book *Non-places: Introduction to an Anthropology of Supermodernity* (or the work of French urban thinker Michel de Certeau, before him). "Nonplaces," as described by Augé, are places such as hotels, airports, shopping malls and the like—cleansed and sterile environments that discourage our emotional connections to place. As in much punk and post-punk, Lisabö's music is full of message, above all, a distrust of the urbanization and suburbanization that has characterized the postwar years in both Europe and the United States. But in contrast to groups such as Arcade Fire—whose albums, *The Suburbs* (2011) in particular, might be seen as supporting an idealized image of a rural past—for Lisabö there is no easy way out of the problems inherent to urbanized modernity.

This is not Welles's traditional Basque country—peacefully nestled in the rolling green hills and arid pastures of northern Spain—but another perspective on "who Basques are." One of the oldest living languages in Europe, Basque is not a Romance language like (Castilian) Spanish, Portuguese, or French. The Basque people and their language existed long before the Roman Empire, and they survived more recent conflicts in a state of relative autonomy if not—some would say—isolation. Throughout the entire twentieth-century Spanish dictatorship of Francisco Franco (1939–1975), *euskara* was officially outlawed, and even today it is still a somewhat threatened minority language on the Iberian peninsula. Yet with Spain's post-1975 transition to democracy, you can now read novels in Basque—like Bernardo Atxaga's *Obabakoak* ("Things that Happened in Obaba," published in 1989, available in English translation)—and, of course, you can listen to Basque music— really cacophonous and compelling Basque music.

Lisabö's decision to sing in *euskara* itself is undeniably a part of who they are, but their music says things that language cannot fully express. These are not easy songs: they are built up through thick sheets of sound, accompanied by a language with which few listeners are familiar, and to top it all off, enigmatic lyrics that pack a theoretical punch (lyrics that are translated into Spanish, English, and French in the album's liner notes). But you do not have to be a student of anthropology or sociology to appreciate what they are driving at. At their core, these are songs of urban decay and rot. It is just that they have got a bit more edge than the urban realities evoked by Joy Division's implicit representation of Manchester or The Clash's essential *London Calling*. For example, at the end of the last song on the album—"Theory of Tiredness" (*Nekearen Teoria*)—Lisabö's singers bring the album to a close by belting out the following lyrics against screeching guitars, steadily marching baselines and a chaotic crescendo: "I know perfectly well that this one isn't the most appropriate hotel. I know perfectly well that traffic never takes a break and that painting falls off the walls. It's just fear, nothing else.

The non-places. (Nik jakin badakit heu ez dela hotelik aproposena. Jakin badakit, nik, zirkulazioak ez duela sekulan atsedena hartzen eta pintura paretetatik erortzen dela. Beldurra da, besterik ez. Ezlekuak)." This is another perspective on "who Basques are." Basques are also city dwellers, subjected to the same miserable and haunting urban realities as the rest of us, and willing to think, sing, and even shout about it—loudly.

The band was founded in 1998 in Irun, a town in the northern province of Gipuzkoa, by members Ivan (drums), Imanol (guitar and vocals), Karlos (base and vocals), and Javi (guitar and vocals). While the band's makeup has changed over time to include others (such as Aida, Maite, Eneko, Ionyu, and Martxel), its sound has remained relatively consistent across its three full-length albums and one EP, including a collaborative album (*Izkiriaturik Aurkitu Ditudan Gurak*; LP, 2005) where the group collaborates with a number of other bands who sing also in French, Polish, and Spanish. Incorporating aspects of musical styles that have been labeled as punk, post-punk, emotional hardcore, and noise, Lisabö's songs oscillate between heavy crashes and ominous silence, grating drives and melodic progressions, throughout maintaining a consistently high level of intensity. The addition of a second drum set in 2000 notably heightened the aural intensity of their music, which was described in a 2001 music review as "disquieting and threatening" (Luna 2001).

On the question of musical influences, Lisabö's oscillation between driving crescendos and haunting lulls owes a great deal to the legacy of such small-label bands as Fugazi, June of 44, Godspeed You Black Emperor!, Low and Shellac—all of whom were singled out for praise by the band members themselves in an interview (Jorge X, 2002). The *Ezlekuak* album, in particular, is a roller-coaster ride that deserves recognition as a coherent "concept album" in the true sense of the term. The eight songs hold together as if a single recording: each track bleeding into the next, familiar themes and dynamics cropping up again and again. Holding them all together, lyrically, is their persistent focus on the absence of emotional connections that so often comes with harsh urban conditions. The listener is thrust into a barren musical terrain of lonely crowds, highways and bridges, gas stations and beggars, toilets and television, darkness and death—a land that is so beautifully full of horrors that you cannot bring yourself to leave it. One of the most significant qualities of their musical sound stems from Lisabö's consistent use of the Basque language. My reading sees the band's use of Basque as a musical and political decision that testifies to both an attentiveness to the material realities of place and also a refusal to engage the excesses of the limiting discourse of identity politics on the (Spanish or even Basque) national scale.[9]

It is first important to acknowledge the extensive literature built up concerning the dialectical tension between what numerous critics have termed place and space. To highlight just one such example, Lefebvrian geographer David Harvey (1996, Chapter 11) moves "From Space to Place and Back Again" in order to locate the notion of place at the intersection of both material and immaterial processes. He concisely states the basic premise of this line of thought: "Place, in whatever guise, is like space and time, a social construct" (1996, 293). Many other theorists have likewise approached the production of places in both material and immaterial terms, noting that places are caught up in a tension that exists between the particular and the universal. For example, there has been extensive debate of late surrounding how the differentiation and socially constructed notion of scale intersects with processes of identity formation (see Marston 2000; stemming from Taylor 1982; N. Smith 1984; more recently Howitt 2003; Brenner 2004, 9–11). The characteristic tension involved in the negotiation of the notion of place (the tension between the particular and universal) is all too easily reduced in one direction or the other. Appealing too much to universality results in the danger addressed through David Lloyd's (1997) now classic understanding of the exclusion inherent to transitions from nationalist movements to state structures. On the other hand, lauding the particular at the expense of universality can lead to the danger of a myopic conservatism/traditionalism that encourages a restrictive notion of difference.

Even such a brief presentation of particularity and universality is useful in that it allows us to push further into the more fluid notion of place engaged through Lisabö's music. It is significant, in this regard, that the band both continues and contests the legacy of Basque punk music. Shortly after the death of Spanish dictator Francisco Franco on November 20, 1975 (during the period known as the "destape"/ the "uncorking," known also as "la movida"), Basque punk flourished "in those areas of Euskadi [The Basque Countries] which were exposed to strong urbanization and industrialization, to internal segmentation and marginalization" (Lahusen 1993, 266). Just as in the tradition of the gritty and socially conscious origins of American punk, such Basque punk groups were similarly committed to overtly political content. Lisabö's more recent music, however, succeeds in striking a middle ground between the explicitly political punk movement of the 1980s (according to Lahusen, a movement that coincided in many respects with the aims of the various strains of Basque nationalism) and a new generation of popular musicians on the Iberian peninsula who prefer to sing almost exclusively in English instead of their native Basque, Catalan, Valencian, or even Castilian Spanish (some of these such groups include Maple, Zeidun, No More Lies, Standstill, Half-Foot Outside, many of which have released albums with the labels Acuarela [Madrid] or bcore [Barcelona]). Certainly the advantages of singing in English are apparent—in all probability such a decision would contribute to a larger fanbase, wider appeal and distribution, and ultimately greater album sales (see Berger and Carroll 2003).

Defying the directly political content of more traditional punk music, Lisabö's song-lyrics are more often than not enigmatic, such as in the first track of their *Ezarian* album (the band's debut release) titled "Narrazti gizakiaren sehaska kanta [Cradle song of the reptile man]" where the words are delivered in a faint Basque whisper: "Egizu lo maitia, ez izutu Egizu lo Ez dut ez eskurik. Eskurik laztantzeko. Ez dut ez besorik. Besorik zu besarkatzeko. Eta ezin zu hitzez maitatu. Mutuak ezin kantatu. Egizu lo maitia, ez izutu. Egizu lo. [Sleep love, don't fear. Sleep. I have no hands. No hands to caress you. I have no arms. No arms to hug you. And I cannot talk to you of love. The dumb do not sing. Sleep love, don't fear. Sleep.]"[10] Significantly, the lyrics of songs on all four of the band's albums are throughout delivered in Basque, with the exception of infrequent phrases in English and the songs in Spanish, French, English, and Polish on the collaborative album *Izkiriaturik aurkitu ditudan gurak*.

It is important here to return to Frith's assertion that "the academic study of popular music has been limited by the assumption that sounds somehow reflect or represent 'a people'" (1996a, 269). Taking on Lisabö as a Basque band requires a more subtle approach than the hard lines of identity politics proper are able to provide. While the band conserves some of the musical inheritance of previous Basque punk, it also manages to break away from the tradition of explicit politically charged lyrics. The decision to sing in Basque is itself thus neither an essentialization of nor a retreat from the place-bound histories of the Basque countries, with which the band has linguistically maintained a metonymical connection. This more subtle position on the "Basqueness" of the band means that the critic is no longer fettered by the need to have Lisabö speak for an entire "people" (whether considered to be region or nation), and may instead attend to the particularities of their musical/lyrical production. Adopting this perspective allows the album to contribute to theoretical debates over the capitalist production of urban space through musical/lyrical production that splendidly renders the realities of urban alienation in audible form.

Returning briefly to the notion of urban alienation as discussed in the first major section of this book is important as a way of contextualizing the reading that follows. In *The Urban Revolution*, Henri Lefebvre makes the lucid comment that "Urban alienation contains and perpetuates all other forms of alienation" (2003a, 92), a remark which is best understood in relation to his critical project as a whole. Throughout his works, the twentieth-century philosopher and geographer sought to recalibrate Marxism to more closely grapple with contemporary relations of capital—and the two entwined areas of Marxian thought upon which he expanded most were spatiality and alienation. In his other works, Lefebvre argued for a multifaceted understanding of alienation as at once economic, social, political, ideological, and philosophical (1991b, 249) and pointed to the legacy of modern urban planning as being itself a form of alienation. City planning, he argued, was predicated on a reductive bourgeois conception of knowledge that was harnessed in the act of a top-down approach that failed to create "an urban reality for users"—instead, it constructed the city in the interests of "speculators, builders, and technicians" (1996, 168). Capitalism survived the twentieth century, he later argued, with the complicity of city planning "by producing space, by occupying a space" (1976, 21). The priority Lefebvre assigns to urban alienation thus needs to be understood as a qualitative change in the whole of postwar experiences in the advanced capitalist countries, one that is just as relevant to the production of space as it is to the pattern of history described by Lefebvre (1991b) as the dialectical oscillation between alienation, disalienation, and new forms of alienation.

Of course, Lefebvre was not the only one to write about the alienation implicit in the urban experience. Georg Simmel's classic 1903 essay "The Metropolis and Mental Life"—which has since achieved foundational importance within the developing multidisciplinary tradition of urban studies—complements Lefebvre's analysis. Simmel observes the burgeoning formation of a specifically urbanized consciousness at the dawn of the twentieth century, noting that "The psychological basis of the metropolitan type of individuality consists in the *intensification of nervous stimulation* which results from the swift and uninterrupted change of outer and inner stimuli" (2000, 150). As a necessity wrought of the confrontation with the overstimulation and fast pace of city life, the "deeply felt and emotional relationships" of small town life are effectively rendered obsolete. Simmel thus characterizes a newly urbanized consciousness in terms of the adoption of what he calls a "blasé attitude"—a "state of indifference" required in dealing with the chaos of urban life. Reconciling Lefebvre's perspective on the primacy of urban alienation with Simmel's explicit characterization of urban life in terms of emotional deficiency requires that we pay attention to what various critics have called "nonplaces." Tellingly, these spaces where capitalist production has cultivated an atmosphere of emotional detachment constitute the title of Lisabö's most recent album *Ezlekuak* (2007). The following discussion thus engages the album as an angry response to urban alienation in general and to the emotional deficiency of the nonplace in particular.

In the critical interdisciplinary literature on the space–place dialectic, there is, perhaps, no concept as intriguing as that of the "nonplace." The term reaches us today after having been popularized by the French anthropologist Marc Augé, who dedicated an important work to exploring the nonsymbolic space (2005, 87) of "the real non-places of supermodernity" (99).[11] Michel de Certeau had previously noted that the nonplace "is a space devoid of the symbolic expressions of identity, relations and history: examples include airports, motorways, anonymous hotel rooms, public transport . . . Never before in the history of the world have non-places occupied so much space" (Certeau quoted in Bauman 2000, 102; see Certeau 1988, 103–105). The critic of modernity Zygmunt Bauman uses the term "nonplace" more generally, almost coming to equate it with places of consumption that are characterized only by "tamed, sanitized" differences—"the comforting feeling of belonging—the reassuring impression of being part of a community" (Bauman 2000, 99). His description of these "nonplaces" gives them the power and privilege of being able to influence subjects. Nonplaces themselves thus "reduce behavior," they "colonize ever larger chunks of public space and refashion them in their own likeness" (Bauman 2000, 102). Nonplaces are best understood as proxies for places, created to satisfy one specific need rather than privileging multidimensionality and manufactured in such a way as to constrict or limit human behaviors and even to encourage or discourage emotions, thoughts, and patterns of relating.[12]

On Lisabö's provocatively titled album *Ezlekuak* (2007), two songs in particular make reference to such emotionally barren sites. The song "Nekearen teoria [The theory of tiredness]" immerses a reference to a hotel within a stream-of-consciousness style meditation on alienation fear and darkness. "Beldurra da, besterik ez, sexual, gosea, iluntasunari eusten, tinko oratzen hutsuneari. [It's just fear, nothing else, sex, hunger, holding on to darkness, holding to the void tightly.]." The hotel is not a dwelling but a stop along the way that encourages no emotional attachment, as we saw above in a quotation from this song reproduced earlier in this very chapter. The song's remaining lyrics make reference to the pervasive emotion of fear, wailing creatures, the quick passing of time, and, though it all, the ongoing presence of nonplaces: "Ezlekuak, oraindik, orain [The non-places, still [adverb], now.—*my modified translation*]." In "Alderantzizko magia [Inverse magic]," the lyrics again specifically reference nonplaces, this time using more disturbing images:

> Ezlekuak, eskuko marren bitartean. Gaixo bati bisita lez, erditzeko leku bat iragaten duzu. Ezpainak josi ondoren, kartetan aritu ginen butano-kamioi hartan. [Nonplaces, among the lines of the hand. Like visiting a sick person, you cross a place to give birth. After sewing our lips, we played cards in that butane gas-truck.—*my modified translation*]

As elsewhere, the lyrics are delivered in a controlled yet anxious and evenly punctuated shout that occasionally breaks into a yell or a scream, even pointing directly to the erasure of identity: "Nork lapurtu dizkizu hatz-markak? Ezlekuak, eskuko marren bitartean. [Who has stolen your fingerprints from you? Non-places, among the lines of a hand—*my modified translation*]." Where the image of a hotel (a classic representation of the nonplace, according to Certeau) with peeling paint was used in "Nekearen teoria [The theory of tiredness]," here the lyrics point alternately in direct and indirect terms to the cleansed environment of the hospital. The song closes with the lines: "Ezlekua, enigma, obsesioa eta argazkia. Itsaso-kaian labain egin du nortasunak. [The non-place, enigma, obsession and photography. Identity has slipped into the seaport—*my modified translation*]."

Furthermore, in many other songs off of the album *Ezlekuak*, Lisabö points less directly to nonplaces through references to urban worlds devoid of meaningful interpersonal connections and emotional belonging. The song titled "1215. katean [On Channel 1215]" depicts a man lost in himself watching television; "Sekulan etxean izan ez [Never have been at home]" explores the reality of "Inon ez gustura, nahiz ta lurrak egiten duen argi gure begien aurrean. [Feeling comfortable nowhere, though the floor shines in front of our eyes.]"; "Bi minutu [Two minutes]" describes the ubiquity of alienation recalling the classic imagist poem on the modern experience by Ezra Pound (1913) titled "In a Station of the Metro."[13] The remaining songs similarly point to the cold, cleansed environments of modernity, as in "Hazi eskukada II

[A handful of seeds II]" where the lyrics juxtapose the emotional significance of a handful of seeds to a series of barren sites: "Nahiz ta meazuloan, museoan, harreralekuan, lantegian, putetxean, bulebarrean, haitzuloan, ispilu-gelan, aldarean, espaloi distiratsuetan, gure begiek etengabe hazi-eskukada eskatu. [Although in the mine shafts, in the museum, in reception, at work in the whorehouse, in the boulevard, in the cave, in the mirrors room, in the altar, on the shiny sidewalks, our eyes ask continuously for a handful of seeds—*my modified translation*]." The content and form of these songs work together to engage a distinctly urbanized and urbanizing consciousness that produces nonplaces, discouraging emotional attachments to place.

The band's earlier releases certainly resonate with this more recent focus on nonplaces. Both *Ezarian* (2000) and Lisabö's EP *Egun Bat Nonahi* (2002) make a point of highlighting the extreme isolation that characterizes the modern experience. This lyrical content—this denunciation of modern alienation and the growing trend of producing spaces unreceptive to establishing and maintaining emotional connections—resonates with the formal musical structure of the band's songs as well as the sonic immediacy of its blaring sound. Take the song "Gezur Erraza [Simple Lie]" (from the *Ezarian* album), for example, where after a lulling intro extending well past the two-minute mark, an unannounced wave of thunderous screaming, accompanied by drums and loud guitar, suddenly shouts "Lehen erraza zen guztia, zaila bihurtu zen. Gezur erraza. Ez zen inoiz aise izan hitz egokiak aurkitzea, biluztea, egia absolute guzti horietatik alde egitea. [Everything that before was so easy has become difficult. The simple lie. It was never easy to find adequate words, to bare oneself, to flee from all those absolute truths]." Over and over, the band's lyrics return to a familiar range of questions, asking whether there is room for a complex and rich emotional life in a capitalist modernity that alienates the individual.

Lisabö's masterful oscillation between sheets of thick amplified rock and waves of distant ethereal chaos is best understood as a specific type of emotional reaction to the frustrating isolation and rapid changes wrought of a modern experience that—in many cases—is driven by an emphasis on consumers over people. Consider the song "Goiz euria [Early morning rain]" (from the EP *Egun Bat Nonahi*) where one male and one female voice simultaneously chant the following lyrics in unison over a sparing drumbeat and thin layers of ambient noise:

Bagoaz anaitasunari oraindik beldurra dion desfilean bulego, biltegi, pabilio, idazkaritza, ikasgela, dende gainontzeko eremu hesituetara gure hatsa eta izerdiz eta keinuz eta begiradez zitaltasunez goxotasunez ere tarteka ezjakintasunez uneoro zein ezinegonez inertzi amankomun neka-garri nardagarriaz gure mugimenduak elbarritzera prostituzioari maita-sunari baino zilegitasun gehiago emanaz konbentzioei ausardiari baino legeei zuzen bideari baino komunikazoia gezurra da komunikazioaren garaian [We march in the parade that still fears brotherhood towards the bureaus, stores, pavilions, secretary's offices, classrooms, shops the rest of the closed spaces to mutilate our movements by our breath and sweat and gestures and looks misdeeds sometimes sweetness as well as both by ignorance and restlessness all the time by tiring abominable common inertia giving more rightness to prostitution than to love to conventions than to courage to laws than to justice communication is a lie in the era of communication].

The effect of the two singers, one male the other female, singing the same lyrics but with seemingly no emotional connection either to their own words or those of the other, is to at once critique the lack of com-munity between the two and hint through this absence to the possibil-ity of a future reconciliation.

The trend of Lisabö's lyrics overall is to critique the demands of an instrumentalist society that prohibits the development of deeper emo-tions, encouraging only those that can be merged with capitalist accu-mulation strategies, the production of needs, and the products sold to satisfy them—and of course how these processes are produced in articu-lation with the (re)production of space itself. The band's emotional and musical response is an angry one that can be clearly heard upon listen-ing to the their albums—even if it is one only insufficiently described through academic writing, which is, after all, a visual and not an aural medium (McClary and Walser 1990; on the difficulty of writing about music, above). As scholar Victoria L. Henderson so lucidly writes in the article that she calls her guarded defense of anger (2008, 29), it is important "to defend anger because it can locate blame for injus-tice and tends, more than other emotions, to motivate punitive and/ or preventative demands against the unjust treatment of others" (30). Moreover, "The argument that anger is incompatible with democratic process stems from a tradition which considers emotions to be disrup-tive of, rather than collaborative with, reason" (31). Anger can in fact work together with hope, she argues, and may as such, Henderson sug-gests, be a key component of effecting social change. Lisabö's anger—stemming as above from the band's theoretically informed critique of urban alienation—is not merely heard but also actually felt by listening to the band's music. This is not to say that music represents emotional states, but that it simultaneously induces them to an extent—that music not merely means something but that it *does* something.

For Lefebvre's unacknowledged influence on Henri Bergson, emotion was itself an action ("Affection differs from perception in that it is real instead of virtual action," *Matter and Memory* 1912, 57). Although explored by Bergson over a century ago, this perspective turns out to have quite a contemporary resonance, even with recent work by Deborah Thien who coins the phrase the "motion of emotion" (2005, 451; see also Bergson 2001, 44; Fraser 2009b). Following as much from Bergson's writings as from the immediate experience of listening, Lisabö's loud crashing sheets of sound both produce a bodily effect on the listener, inducing a state of tension, as they simultaneously *suggest* (in the Bergsonian sense, above) the emotion that motivated the music—namely a mixture of the haunting experience of a pernicious urban alienation and an angry response to that alienation.

In a sense, the alternately hot-and-cold, heavy-and-soft character of Lisabö's music—its more grating sequences taken together with its more melodic ones—reflects a number of such dualisms: not only the distance between passive acceptance of urban alienation and angry critique but also that between love and desire, the individual and the community, places and nonplaces, and between the sense of belonging characteristic of the home and the emotional deficiency of the hotel mentioned in their lyrics. The contrast between the highs and the lows of the band's sound point not to a simplistic unity, but rather, paradoxically, to the possibility of the resolution and reconciliation of opposing but complementary forces. In light of Henderson's defense of the democratic potential of anger, Lisabö's musical production is the complementary inverse of hope, pointing critically and consistently to a world in which individuals are able to connect with one another, and where the production of space does not hinder this process.

There is even reason to consider the potential of Lisabö's music being harnessed in reshaping city spaces. In a recent essay published in *Emotion, Space and Society*, Janet McGaw and Alasdair Vance conclude first that those who are "emotionally robust" have a greater capacity to shape the city but also that the social and physical environment of urban places may affect the emotional state of individuals for the worse: "It seemed that while my collaborators exhibited emotional deficits that affected their capacity to shape the city, the city, in turn, was complicit in shaping their emotional states" (2008, 68). Understood in relation to this dialectic, the Basque band's robust emotional soundscapes not only reflect the emotional deficits that shape the city but also function as a potential contestation of those deficits. Henri Lefebvre believed that the dialectical reshaping of such a world required not merely changes in social relations but also, as Lefebvrian geographer Harvey writes concisely, "new ways of thinking and feeling" (1990, 322). Part of this challenge is to find a place for emotion in scholarship itself as an antidote to that instrumentalization of knowledge the theorist labels as "analytical." Lefebvre's notion of "rhythmanalysis," discussed earlier in the chapter, functions precisely as this antidote to traditional scholarly "analysis."

In the context of Lefebvre's emphasis on listening and his suspicion of the visual, Lisabö's albums provide a way of hearing the sounds of urban alienation—of hearing the haunting echoes of today's urban non-places rather than seeing them. Their songs thus invite a rupture with the visual logic of the capitalist production of space. Whereas the latter routinely elides conflict through the presentation of seemingly pleasing environments that are destined to be consumed visually, the band's albums articulate that conflict powerfully and immediately in sonorous terms. In "Sekulan extean izan ez [Never have been at home]" off the *Ezlekuak* album, the lyrics reference an emotional state of "Inon ez gustura, nahiz ta lurrak egiten duen argi gure begien aurrean [Feeling comfortable nowhere, though the floor shines in front of our eyes]" (also in "Hazi eskukada II [A handful of seeds II]" where the singer uses the phrase the "espaloi distiratsuetan [on the shiny sidewalks—*my modified translation*]"). Their songs' lyrics return again and again to the alienated distance of urbanites from their feelings: in "Murgilduta [Submerged]" (off the *Ezarian* album) noting the impossibility of achieving love ("beti amodiozko ametsak [always dreams of love]") or even happiness ("Zoriona itsasoko arraign handiena da soilik [happiness is just the biggest fish in the ocean]"). Ultimately, Lisabö consistently points to a disconnect that results from the fact that feelings have little or no place in the cleansed environments of modernity. For example, in the song "Ideiak itotzen dira [Ideas are drowned]" (*Ezarian*) the singer notes "Galtzen dira sentimenduak [Feelings are lost]" but also contradictorily, "eta nik denbora osoan maite zaitut [and I . . . all the time, I love you]."

This disconnect and contradiction is evident even more powerfully in the actual sound of Lisabö's rhythms—including both the musical and structural elements of their compositions and also their emotional components. The dualistic character of their oscillating sound resonates with the apt characterization of modern urban life made by Georg Simmel whereby the overstimulation of the city necessitates adopting a blasé attitude. Just as the heavy sections of their music contrast with complementarily lulling sections, a confrontation with the chaos of the urb is juxtaposed to the detachment required of the urbanite. In this way, periods of emotional engagement thus contrast with the state of indifference that for Simmel was necessary for urban life or, according to Lefebvre, the urban alienation that trumps all other forms of alienation. Many times, on their albums, the listener is brought slowly from a detached state of indifference to a more visceral engagement with a song, as happens with the first track from the *Egun bat nonahi* EP, "Gau minean [In the midst of the night]." After an initial 25 seconds of silence, a lone guitar begins to patiently intone a minor interval before carefully accentuating a range of notes. The drums and base come in only at the 1'20" mark, adding definition to a subdued but sharp middle-section (approximately 1'20"–2'57") and leading into a period where each beat is more highly punctuated and where the music has grown noticeably louder. Initial whispers (2'51") then give way to voiced lyrics that are soon complemented by counterpoint lyrics delivered in a muffled scream by another distant singer (3'45"). The two voices engage in a manner of call and response over an extended period of time, while the intensity of the song builds (3'45"–5'50"), subtended by the repetitive brush of a bow against a stringed instrument. Finally, at the end of the song, the musical structure is slowly dismantled piece by piece, layer by layer as if a scaffolding somewhere is being broken down for transport (5'50"–6'31). The third and last song on the EP, titled "Egunaren begietan [In the eyes of the day]," initially suggests a return to the theme of the first song in its tone and instrumentation, although the subsequent unmuffled delivery of the lyrics soon enters a cacophonous range unreached in the first track. Taken together, these songs are typical of the band's musical style as a whole. In each case, there is an attempt to recalibrate the emotions of urban life—to reorient the consciousness of the urban listener who has been split in two by alienating forces that oppose indifference to engagement in an explicitly urban context.

The opportunity is for the listener of Lisabö's music to coincide with a song and thus to participate in an attempt to draw the urbanite out of her or his alienation and force an engagement with the original chaos of the city. While the lyrics interrogate the future (in "Zer eigteko gai gara? [What things are we capable of?]," *Ezarian*), their music, as does all music, thrusts us into temporality itself, pointing—through lyric content and artistic, musical form—both to the inadequacy of current urban realities and also to the possibility of future action. Listening to music is potentially a subversion of the visual and spatial order of contemporary urban capitalism, in that contradiction may exist in time—in temporality—in a way that is impossible in space. These contradictions involve the dualisms of engaging with or detaching from the urban experience, of embodied feeling versus of analytical thinking. Lefebvre noted capitalism's "crushing of natural rhythms and cycles by linearity" (2005, 135), from which comes the illusion of time as reversible. "Time is projected into space through measurement, by being homogenized, by appearing in things and products" (2005, 133; see also 2002). This asserts itself the need for restoring the irreversibility of time, Lefebvre argues, through dance, the festival, and through music. At a fundamental level, the act of listening to music reaffirms the reality of the temporal, reinforcing that the world is always in movement and this only appears to be static when subjected to an analytical framework. For Lefebvre (and for Bergson), music delivers us into time from space. It is there—in music, in temporality—that emotions dwell. And where there are sounds and emotions, as geographers and neuroscientists seem to agree, there can be the momentum for changing our urban realities.

In closing, the musical production of the Basque band Lisabö provides a compelling introduction to engage the production of space at the urban scale. Connecting with scholarly work on urban alienation, nonplaces, and emotional geographies, their heavy/soft songs chart out a new path in contemporary popular music on the Iberian Peninsula. Their unique position among various musical styles—bringing together postpunk, emotional hardcore, and perhaps even the musical style known as noise, and within and beyond the tradition of Basque punk—points to an inclusivity that posits a larger notion of community without adhering overtly to a particular identity formation (Basque, pan-European). Critiquing the characteristic alienation of today's urban spaces implicitly and even explicitly (through dialoguing with the critical literature specific to the "nonplace"), rejecting the commodification of desire, and the categorical rule of exchange-values, they suggest a loosely defined emotional community—a community centered around the hope for a more emotionally connected world not yet realized and motivated by an angry rejection of the staid and lifeless places that are commonplace in today's cities.

If, as David Harvey has written, explicitly evoking the Lefebvrian tradition, "Materiality, representation and imagination are not separate worlds" (1996, 322), then Lisabö's necessarily oral/aural engagement of Basqueness is neither an essentialist reduction of the place-bound history of the Basque country nor an uncritical acceptance of larger-scale engineered European identities. The band thus positions itself at the level of the urban, at intersection of place and space, of the particular and the universal, in a dialogue that—while angry and full of uncertainty—nonetheless evokes the complex process through which place is imagined, produced, represented, and contested. The result is a hard-hitting emotional soundscape that, "inquietante y amenazador [disquieting and threatening]," functions to reorient consciousness to become newly aware of the role that emotion plays in our attachment—or lack of attachment—to urban places. It is at this scale that the production of space must be challenged. In addition to further investigation of musical practices, a nuanced understanding of music as a cultural product and even a humanities "text" is crucial as we continue to gauge the theoretical resonance between emotions and cities.

CHAPTER 7

Representing Digital Spaces: Videogames and the Digital Humanities

This book's introduction presented a concise summary of the Snow–Leavis controversy, and in the first chapter it was asserted that "the divisions within and across the disciplines associated with the most inclusive iteration of urban studies do little more than perpetuate the disconnect between the humanities and the sciences famously addressed by C. P. Snow in a lecture delivered over 50 years ago." Building on issues of interdisciplinarity raised in that controversy, the first section of this chapter ("From Videogames to the Spatial/Geo-Humanities") posits study of the videogame as one area in which we might address the "antagonism" between the humanities and the social sciences. Specifically, the notion of (urban) space in the videogame presents an opportunity for the humanities scholar that both coincides with and diverges from the study of cinematic space. This section also argues that Lefebvre and the literary humanities are being left out of disciplinary collaborations, and notes one more time how Lefebvre's urban thinking complements the contemporary push to bridge geography and the humanities. The second section of this chapter ("Digital Humanities, Verso") builds on this broad discussion to advance a Lefebvrian take on the growing prominence of the Digital Humanities (DH), indicating that this new development may not be as emancipatory as some of its practitioners claim. It suggests that, in the end, it may be important to ask further questions regarding what the drive toward this specific form of collaborative digital work really entails. This questioning necessarily prompts exploration of the reconciliations between disciplinary knowledge, culture, politics, and economy at the heart of Lefebvre's thought and at the core of the urban cultural studies project more generally speaking.

From Videogames to the Spatial/Geo-Humanities

If there is reason to believe that the development of film and television profoundly affected the way we think over the course of the twentieth century, this shift cannot but be overshadowed by that which accompanies the ongoing rise of videogames. Addressing "the antagonist[ic] relationship" between the humanities and the social sciences with regard to videogame studies (Wolf and Perron 2009, 14; citing a personal e-mail from critic Jesper Juul), this section emphasizes the priority of a mobile knowledge of space as enacted in videogame play and subsequently establishes important connections with key ideas on knowledge and space from Lefebvrian philosophy and from the interdisciplinary field of spatial theory. In a way, this discussion returns to the notion of iconicity as elaborated in an earlier chapter with regard to film—but given the digital nature of the videogame, this pushes us one step further toward consideration of the DH that drives what is at once the subsequent section of this chapter and also the final chapter section of this book.

Videogames offer the scholar yet another perspective on reconciliations of art and life (everyday life, time, and space in the novel; iconicity-indexicality in film) in that they are interactive media. As one videogame scholar has put it, "In Pac-Man, as in other video games, no one tells the player the rules governing each monster's behavior; these rules must be induced from observation. In this way, Pac-Man is more like life than chess" (Greenfield 1984, 110). From a perspective that is simultaneously philosophical and cultural, the significance of the videogame lies in the way that it makes use of and encourages a particular epistemological approach to space. In contrast to the filmgoer's more passive reception of cinematic space, the videogame player's experience of space is interactive. As Mark J. P. Wolf (2001) compellingly argues in his book *The Medium of the Video Game*, we form knowledge of this space not through the passive absorption of images but rather through an active and largely self-directed process of exploration. In most cases, as Wolf recognizes, videogame space is seldom exhausted after one hour or even 400 hours of gameplay. Furthermore, it is the very nature of space in the videogame to be greater than any one player's experience. "Completing" a given videogame may no longer depend on an exhaustive knowledge of the game world—leaving no stone unturned, that is—but may instead develop along a number of possible routes. This is—continuing the metaphor—to necessarily leave quite a few "stones" untouched and more still unseen.

Certainly, as is well noted in historical accounts of the development of videogames, the use of space in their early manifestations (late 1950s, early 1960s) was much more limited and bordered on a simplistic flattened geometry (Wolf 2001). Yet nonetheless, the videogame player's exploration of space differed in its origins fundamentally from that of the cinematic spectator. Even early manifestations of videogame space entailed a self-directed process that—while perhaps not initially iconic or indexical in the same way as film space—already squared with a conception of knowledge as embodied, dependent on accumulated time and mobile. Intended as a contribution to the existing literature on videogame theory (e.g., Wolf and Perron 2003, 2009), this section seeks to complement approaches to interactive media grounded in psychoanalytic theory (Rehak 2003), aesthetics (Martin 2007), the trope of postmodernity (Filiciak 2003), gender and sexuality (Consalvo 2003), temporality (Crogan 2003), and literacy (Gee 2003; Zimmerman 2009) by fleshing out the more philosophical significance of the spatial epistemology of the videogame.

Ultimately, the study of videogames is relevant not only to the cultural or technological critic but also to the spatial theorist, who draws on a vast theoretical literature blending philosophy and geography on the way toward understanding how we perceive, conceive, and live space. From this perspective, videogames successfully create a more visible model of how we form knowledge of our spatial environment not merely through abstract modeling and static representation, but through their interactive qualities and the embodied experience of movement. There are two points that guide my analysis. Following on the heels of noted filmmaker and critic Pier Paolo Pasolini's (1988) assertion that "the semiotic code of cinema is the semiotic code of reality," I believe that "the epistemological mode of videogames is the epistemological mode of reality." In a sense, this is another way of highlighting an aspect of videogames that has frequently been pointed out by other scholars. Espen J. Aarseth, for example, has written that "in games, just as in life, the outcomes (winning, losing) are real and personal to the experiencer, unlike in stories," characterizing narrative in videogames as "architectural rather than sequential, enacted rather than related, experienced personally and uniquely rather than observed collectively and statically" (2004, 366).[1]

Moreover, the implication is that the form of spatial knowledge that underlies the phenomenon of the videogame is relevant to numerous other fields of enquiry. As a cultural product subject to the same inflections and interpretations as other visual and cinematic art forms, the videogame is significant as an object of cultural criticism in that it allows for a greater articulation of the key notions of the contemporary "mobility turn" in the hermeneutic practices of both the social sciences and the humanities. The videogame thus begs to be recognized as one of the most important focal points of philosophical and cultural inquiry in the twenty-first century. Significantly, videogames not only allow us to see how we form knowledge of space in general and of concrete places in particular, they also resonate with the theoretical foundations of contemporary research being done across disciplines under the name of urban spatial theory. Wolf and Perron point out that videogame theory "must be a synthesis of a wide range of approaches, but at the same time focus on the unique aspects of video games" (2003, 13)—and, clearly, one of the most unique aspects of the videogame is the player's experience of space. To this effect, Wolf has elaborated a now classic typology of space in the videogame (2001, 1997; cf. Fernández-Vara et al. 2005; Fernández-Vara 2009; Juul 2007), and James Newman asserts that "space is key to videogames" (2004, 31; also Keane 2007, 104; Aarseth 2007, 44). Wolf (2001, 55) even writes of the evolution of videogame space as consisting of a series of progressive innovations that paralleled the development of space in the cinema.

Videogame space is, of course, noticeably different from cinematic space, in that a game world consists of "entirely fabricated spaces" (Poole in Holland et al. 2003, 34) instead of indexical images of the extracinematographic world. Nonetheless, as Wolf notes, "Gradually as technology improved, designers strove for more representational graphics in game imagery, and today they still continue to pursue ever more detailed representations approximating the physical world" (2003, 47). Even if videogame space cannot be indexical in the same sense that the cinema can—and there is reason to believe that this may change down the road—in one key respect it goes far beyond what films can offer (see Grodal 2003, 139; cf. on film and videogames Keane 2007; King and Krzywinska 2002; Nitsche 2008). The most compelling case for a model of spatial production that is relevant to the study of both video game space and "real world" space is one advanced by spatial theorist, urban philosopher, and cultural studies pioneer Henri Lefebvre. In his landmark work *The Production of Space*, Lefebvre outlined not merely a dialectical understanding of spatial production but a triadic model comprising the complex relationships between representations of space, spaces of representation, and spatial practices (1991, 33). Importantly, the relevance of a Lefebvrian understanding of space to the study of videogames has already been recognized by a handful of scholars. Espen Aarseth explicitly seeks to "refine" Lefebvre's spatial theory in his essay "Allegories of Space" (2007, 45), and Stefan Guenzel in fact begins his essay "Eastern Europe, 2008" with a discussion of Lefebvre's "trialectic of spatial processes" (2007, 444). Nonetheless, the application of Lefebvrian terminology to the study of videogames has not been consistent. For example, Guenzel suggests that videogames be equated with Lefebvre's notion of "spatial practice" (2007, 444), and Aarseth writes that "computer games . . . are a type of spatial representation he did not anticipate" (2007, 45; even if Lefebvre "did not anticipate" the study of videogames, readers may be interested to see that the cover chosen for the third volume of his *Critique of Everyday Life* as republished in 2005 shows two children playing videogames using an Atari 2600).

I believe that a more thorough understanding of Lefebvre's work would suggest that there is a danger in reifying videogames as themselves one aspect or another of his triadic model of space. The key legacy of Lefebvre's work, in general terms, has been to support the notion of space as a process over the idea of space as a static representation. For example, geographer David Harvey (following explicitly in the Lefebvrian tradition) has drawn together absolute space, relative space, and relational space into a variegated theory ("Space as a Key Word," 2006c). Likewise, it is precisely an understanding of knowledge as active, mobile, embodied, and largely self-directed that is at the heart of the emerging shift in social science and humanities research that goes by "The Mobility Turn." What, in my estimation, differentiates the emerging emphasis on "mobility studies" (consider the recently formed journal *Mobilities*, established in 2006) from a significant portion of previous research on the "production of space" is merely that the approach is more carefully defined to prioritize movement. In the debut editorial from *Mobilities*, the authors in fact draw on Lefebvre and others in order to note that a "mobility turn" in research is emerging that calls for a renewed interest in content that "encompasses both large scale movements of people, objects, capital and information across the world, as well as the more local processes of daily transportation, movement through public space and the travel of material things within everyday life" (Hannam et al. 2006, 1). As argued elsewhere (Fraser 2010, 2011a), the philosophical roots of this mobility turn lie with the focus on movement (emphasized by Bergson 1912, 1998, 2001), on the complex fusion of rhythms (Lefebvre 2006a), and on the irreducible and ever-shifting forces that constitute the many contemporary urban worlds of the everyday (Lefebvre 1991b, 2002, 2003a, 2005). In the study of videogames, just as in the study of "real world" spaces, our approach must from the beginning emphasize space as a complex process, as a movement and as a relationship.

While earlier studies on videogames may have asserted that spatial skills transfer across the video game/"real world" divide (e.g., Gagnon 1985), contemporary work has advanced an even more sophisticated understanding of the connection of these two worlds, folding each into the other. In this way, some critics have even explored, for example, "the effects of software code on the spatial formation of everyday life" (Dodge and Kitchin 2005, 162) and, as the subtitle of an essay by Daniel G. Lobo (2007) puts it, "How SimCity influences Planning Culture." Given that we live in an increasingly urbanized world in which cities have had great effect on both physical and mental conditions of modern life (Wirth 1938; Harvey 1989; Simmel 1996; Lefebvre 2003a), the knowledge we form of space in videogames cannot be understood in isolation from larger processes of urban spatial production, in particular. It is important to recognize that much recent work on videogames has already begun to emphasize the theme of cities. For example, the 62 contributions to the volume *Space Time Play: Computer Games, Architecture and Urbanism* make it clear that videogames cannot be treated as cultural products isolated from the larger interdisciplinary discourses that shape both today's cities and our experiences in and of them (see also Nitsche 2008, 2).

As noted by Adriana de Souza e Silva and Daniel M. Sutko in their introduction to the volume *Digital Cityscapes*, the creation and use of video game spaces reflects a quintessentially modern "conceptualization of city spaces as places to be explored rather than circulatory spaces" (2009, 6). The marked increase in "'themed' spatial representations" (Lukas 2007) in videogames makes it possible to reconcile cities in videogames with extradiegetic urban spatial configurations. For example, in a book chapter titled "Visualizing the Mediterranean (From Goytisolo to the Video Game)," I have already written on various ways in which the Mediterranean has been represented in onscreen interactive space (Fraser 2011a). That publication detailed, in part, how in the videogame *Mario Kart Wii* (2008) players drive around a themed Mediterranean city trapped in a perpetual sunset evoking an entire tradition of touristic and leisure perceptions of cities such as Barcelona. Similarly, in *Monster 4x4* (2008), also for the Wii console, the myth of Barcelona as a city that has constantly reimagined itself (Resina 2008) is presented through an array of half-constructed urban buildings, complete with a glimpse of famed architect Antonio Gaudí's Sagrada Familia from privileged locations on the racetrack. Consider more generally the appeal of games such as *Grand Theft Auto* (Rockstar 1997–2011) that have presented fictionalized versions of American urban spaces—*GTA: San Andreas* as an amalgam of San Francisco, Las Vegas, and Los Angeles—with the experience of such urban centers heightening an appreciation of the game.

Michael Nitsche's *Video Game Spaces* (2008) makes a few lucid points that are relevant to the reconciliation of on- and off-screen spaces. His analysis fittingly prioritizes "the concept of space and spatial experience" in a reading of videogames (2008, 3). Key to this approach is Nitsche's insistence that there are "fundamental differences" between space in videogames and space in the "real world" (2008, 3). While this claim has a certain "commonsensical" appeal and perhaps does not deserve to be vitiated outright, his lucid assertion that interactive media spaces are "told to us using certain forms of presentation" (Nitsche 2008, 3) suggests the need for video game scholars to more thoroughly assimilate work being done in urban studies. Although even Nitsche is attentive to Lefebvre's seminal work *The Production of Space* (Nitsche 2008, 6, 16–17, 236), his appropriation of Lefebvrian spatial theory might be a tad more nuanced. For example, his assertion that "virtual spaces are highly directed in the way they can be used" (Nitsche 2008, 236)—which, given his argument (above), posits an implicit contrast with "real world" spaces—ignores a whole tradition of urban criticism whereby city spaces have themselves been created in certain interests for certain purposes, necessarily encouraging or discouraging certain uses of the built environment (Flusty 1994; Lefebvre 2003a, 1996; Mitchell 2003; Augé 2005; Fraser 2007a, 2008a). Nevertheless, these points do not detract from his analysis, but instead serve only to emphasize the need and importance of a more thorough reconciliation of video game studies with Lefebvrian spatial theory.

Nitsche's work succeeds in emphasizing that just like off-screen spaces, cyberspaces are diverse in nature (2008, 17). His astute observation that videogames take up progressively more of the player's attention ("Multilayered access and spatial referencing can demand so much attention that non-game-related information might be overpowered by the complexities of the virtual game world," 36) bears a curious resemblance to what early twentieth-century urban theorists described as a "chaotic" urban environment that required the savvy city-dweller to adopt a "blasé attitude"/"state of indifference" merely to cope with the conditions of modern life (e.g., Simmel 2010). Moreover, there are other similarities to consider. Just as with nondigital spaces, video game/virtual space is interesting also from the perspective of its "dialogic" qualities. Contemporary urban spaces are persistently being thought of in this sense, "as a meeting place, the location of the intersections of particular bundles of activity spaces, of connections and interrelations, of influences and movements" (Massey 1995, 59). Interestingly enough, this conception of space is increasingly emphasized in work on virtual spaces (Noveck 2006, 258; cf. Taylor 2006, 158–161, on the notion of online participatory cultures). Underlying these similarities, of course, there is the shared fundamental experience of the way our knowledge of space develops both inside and outside of the video game, speaking to a form of embodied knowledge of space that is equally applicable to both realms: one that is dependent on accumulated time and is mobile.

With this and other similarities in mind, the time is right to effect a thorough reconciliation of video game research and urban studies. While this chapter section has directed itself to making a general case for this reconciliation, it leaves open the question of how this reconciliation might be realized in future research. For instance, where do understandings of both virtual and "real" worlds as "rule-based spaces" (Nitsche 2008, 31–32) intersect? What similarities exist between the static conceptualizations of space employed by city designers (as denounced by Lefebvre 1996, 2003a) and by game designers? How do the intended uses of video game spaces as conceived by game designers compare to the intended uses of public spaces as conceived by city planners? In the end, discussion of these questions, although already under way (in *Space Time Play*, for example), will be enriched by a more sustained engagement with Lefebvrian spatial theory, and, moreover, by grappling with the spatial epistemology common to both realms of experience.

As scholars working in the field of videogames undoubtedly know, one of the biggest obstacles to this interdisciplinary reconciliation has been a reticence on the part of prior generations of scholars (in other fields) to take the videogame seriously (Wolf and Perron 2003, 1). In the broadly defined realm of cultural studies, many scholars have decried the lack of attention given to videogames. Wolf points out that "[d]espite three decades of development, there has been relatively little scholarly study of these games, or even an acknowledgment of the medium of the video game as a whole" (2001, 1), and James Newman suggests that even where this study has been undertaken, there is little agreement on how to go about investigating the videogame (2004, 10). Given the need to cultivate inter/multidisciplinary approaches to the videogame (expressed recently by Mäyrä 2009), it is important to see that one way to connect study of videogames to the larger humanities and social science fields is through recourse to spatial theory. This move may, in fact, "function to correct the antagonist[ic] relationship" between the humanities and the social sciences with regard to videogame studies as noted by Wolf and Perron (2009, 14).

Before moving on to consider the rise of the spatial humanities (and finally DH)—as part of the move to adopt a broad and inclusive definition of digital spaces—I return to an important question posed by Newman:

> Should we see videogames as continuations of other media such as film or television? Are they continuations of other non-computer games? Are they hybrids of both? Should we define them with reference to their uniqueness and dissimilarity from other entertainments, media or games, or as a consequence of their similarity? (2004, 10)

An urban cultural studies perspective entails that we read videogames both along with and against other media forms such as film and television—making sure to exploit their unique contribution to the interdisciplinary discussion on space and place. Lefebvre's nuanced spatial theory offers another way of getting to the idea that videogames "are not exclusively focused on representation" (Aarseth 2007, 47). The point is not merely to recognize that both videogame spaces and "real" spaces are caught up in Lefebvrian process of spatial production that includes "representational spaces, spaces of representation and spatial practices," but moreover to understand that the method through which we form knowledge of videogame space is in fact the very method through which we form knowledge of "real world" urban spaces. In making possible a discussion on the significant intersection of on- and off-screen space/place, videogames are important enough to warrant the full attention of spatial theorists and scholars working in the larger field of urban cultural studies. As videogames continue to evolve, technologically speaking, this connection cannot but prove to be of increasing importance.

Now, although videogames perhaps present their own challenges for urban cultural studies research, they may be more broadly considered as part of an effort to "digitize" the humanities. A necessarily cursory look at three recent edited volumes whose contributions cut across geography and the humanities can gauge how Lefebvre is both largely absent from and nevertheless deeply relevant to work that is currently being carried out in the relatively new area of inquiry that goes by the name *digital humanities*. First, *The Spatial Humanities: GIS and the Future of Scholarship* "proposes the development of spatial humanities that promises to revitalize and redefine scholarship by (re)introducing geographic concepts of space to the humanities" (Bodenhamer et al. 2010, vii). This is a strong and novel contribution whose connection to Lefebvrian ideas could certainly be more robust. Also of interest is that among the book's contributors—which include "three historians, a religionist, an archaeologist, and four geographers" (Bodenhamer et al. 2010, xiv)—there is not a single literary scholar. Although Lefebvre does not even figure in the index of the second book—*Envisioning Landscapes, Making Worlds: Geography and the Humanities* (2011)—this volume's 29 contributions (not counting the introduction) are perhaps marginally more attentive to the nuances inherent in aesthetic questions.[2] There are few contributions that go beyond the "history = humanities" equivalence to address literature and art directly; yet, overall, there is a real reticence on the part of the book's editors to seek out literary or artistic approaches. Ultimately, one has to wonder how novel it really is, in fact, to blend history with geography. In a third book, *GeoHumanities: Art, History, Text at the Edge of Place* (2011), we find many essays that emphasize what by now has become a familiar intent to embrace history as well as contributions on GIS. Nevertheless, *GeoHumanities* is refreshing in that here Lefebvre is mentioned specifically (2011, 5, 67, 72, 97–100, 104), and textual analysis of literary works acquires a privileged status of sorts. In particular, the seven essays in the section titled "Spatial Literacies"—merely part of the volume's total of 30 essays—delve into the reciprocal relevance of literary and geographical inquiries. In the end, however, all three of these volumes are not merely insufficient from the literary perspective, they are also insufficient from the urban perspective. Space is discussed outside of the context of urbanization; literature and aesthetic questions are a mere add-on to the historical-geographical foundation.

Looking beyond these three high-profile publications, however, there are reasons for hope; here I will mention two in particular. First, there is the potential extension of the Culture of Cities "interdisciplinary research program": "Bringing together scholars working in sociology, communications studies, English, art history, film studies, and several other disciplines and fields, the project has produced substantive studies of urban culture through its focus on the cities of Montreal, Dublin, Toronto and Berlin" (Straw and Boutros 2010, 4). The work this project has yielded so far—including the published books *The Imaginative Structure of the City* (Blum 2003), *Circulation and the City: Essays on Urban Culture* (Boutros and Straw 2010), and *Urban Enigmas: Montreal, Toronto and the Problem of Comparing Cities* (Sloan 2007)—is a step in the right direction (see particularly essays by Van Veen 2010—who looks extensively at Lefebvre—and Holmes 2010). Moreover, the HyperCities project is posed to make a game-changing contribution to DH scholarship that recognizes the importance of the traditionally literary. The website of the project explains that "HyperCities is a collaborative research and educational platform for traveling back in time to explore the historical layers of cityspaces in an interactive, hyper media environment" (http://hypercities.com). In fact, during the time I have spent working on this book, Todd Presner, Diane Favro, and Chris Johanson have directed an NEH Summer Institute at UCLA titled "Digital Cultural Mapping," in which 12 scholars explored how to develop innovative publications and course that privilege the "geohumanities."

These and other new directions in DH research are of great potential value to urban cultural studies scholars. Their potential stems from the fact that they offer—as if in homage to Lefebvre himself—an interdisciplinary reconciliation of science and art that recognizes, implicitly or explicitly, the primacy of the urban experience. Of course, if these projects are to succeed—if they are to prove disalienating, disciplinarily speaking—they must have a clear understanding of the value of humanities fields. Lefebvre is, in fact—as should be clear by now—a model thinker for such an endeavor given his reputation as a "genuinely interdisciplinary writer" (Parker 2004, 19), his emphasis on alieantion/disalienation, and his subsequent respect for the links between "culture, art and social transformation" (Léger 2006, 143).[3] Over all else, we must keep in mind Lefebvre's open philosophical (or better yet methodological) approach to the urban (as does Barth 2000, 23). The Snow–Leavis controversy outlined in this book's introduction showed how attempts at collaboration are often short-circuited by the same disciplinary boundaries that made those attempts necessary. And yet Lefebvre's urban thinking shows how we might forge a new, truly interdisciplinary field by pulling the humanities and the social sciences into a loosely structured pursuit of a common goal—that goal is to understand urbanized society in all of its complexity. Nevertheless, as this chapter's final section explores, DH must face its own demons: that is, we do well in moving forward into digital terrain cautiously and with a strong sense of the social relationships in which DH work necessarily operates.

Digital Humanities, Verso

It seems to me that during the period spanning 2012–2014 a most curious thing has occurred—far and wide scholars are all talking about DH. Humanities professors are talking about DH, social science professors are discussing it—and so are postsecondary administrators. This is not to say that all parties agree, of course; but all the same they talk, they fear, they rejoice, trumpet, wax poetic about, and even callously deride DH. This is admittedly a *slight* exaggeration. Those participating in these discussions are of many types. A crude and provisional typology of these parties might include the *newcomer*, the *simplifier*, the *early-adopter*, and the *new-wave DH-er*. That is, there is still someone who shouts from their office out to the group in the hallway "Just what is this DH thing you're talking about?" and "What does DH mean anyway?" The truth is that DH means many things to many different people. There are also those who would equate DH with the act of putting up a website. Strangely enough, this perception is voiced both by those who boast of practicing DH themselves and also by those who do not alike: the DH go-to site omeka.net is, in part, home to exhibits created by scholars who are posting text and images together on a topic of their choice.[4] There is a great variety among these DH projects, which range from simple displays to more complex and interactive, audiovisual, media-laden sites. Then there are those who, as Jerome McGann (2001) recounts in the Introduction of *Radiant Textuality*, have been riding the early wave of computerized literature since the 1990s and the creation of the World Wide Web. And now, finally, we have what I regard as the height of DH's evolutionary trajectory: the construction of massive and often spectacular online projects requiring large teams of highly skilled programers and web designers—that is, projects requiring massive investments. These are investments of personnel, of time, and—in a word—of capital: investments in a university brand, investments in a certain (changing) social function of education that deserves further scrutiny.

I must confess that, currently, I am in the group of *newcomers*—and also that I fully intend to get more involved with DH. So far: I have written a letter of support for a colleague at another university in search of a nationally competitive DH grant, I have created a profile for and joined DHCommons, I have posted a question at DH Q&A related to pedagogy, and I curated a specific DH project where members of a graduate Hispanic Studies class linked urban space and filmic representation of the city of Madrid.[5] I hope to continue to cultivate publicly available DH projects—in collaboration with the highly skilled DH practitioners now so frequently housed in university libraries.[6] I also run a multiauthored blog at urbanculturalstudies.wordpress.com ("the culture(s) of cities...space, time and everyday life") where posts deal quite frequently with the humanities and, at times, with DH. Even this rudimentary engagement with the DH has made me excited about its possibilities. I was even fortunate enough to receive start-up monies at a new academic position dedicated to reshaping an existing GIScience lab to accommodate DH projects by students and faculty.[7]

As an interdisciplinary scholar, I am an easy sell, of course. I am a member of both the Modern Languages Association and the Association of American Geographers. Like many scholars participating in and writing about DH, I continue to regard the inherent conservatism of disciplinary knowledge with suspicion. As an editor working with interdisciplinary journals (Managing Editor, *Arizona Journal of Hispanic Cultural Studies*; Executive Editor and Founder, *Journal of Urban Cultural Studies*) I have a working knowledge of what challenges tend to arise with interdisciplinary research. All this is to say that while I am interested and increasingly involved in DH—I have taken to teaching and digesting work by Jerome McGann, Kathleen Fitzpatrick, Lisa Spiro, and others—I believe there are some reasons to think more critically about what DH may mean for education, for universities, and for society. That is, it may represent not merely a pedagogical or methodological research shift but also a social change. The fact that this change is a social one does not stop it from having, also, economic and political consequences.

Let us quickly run through and accept the benefits of DH work, which are so frequently and rightly trumpeted: (A) Collaboration, on the production side of things—definitely a plus.[8] (People *should* talk to each other, they *should* share ideas. Down with the tyranny of the single-authored monograph!—but, of course, I would also ask whether the single-authored monograph really ever served as the expression of scholarly individualism). (B) The ability to put text, sound, and image—both still and moving images—together in unprecedented ways. (Journals such as *Vectors: Journal of Culture and Technology in a Dynamic Vernacular* and *Kairos: A Journal of Rhetoric, Technology and Pedagogy* continue to push the envelope regarding what is possible with DH publication). (C) The ability to work with questions of a larger scale. (The collaborative creation of massive databases certainly aids in the production of valuable single-author research). (D) Collaboration, on the consumption side of things—I look at the wonderful digital initiatives that already exist and have no doubt that these projects will prove to be of immense value to community members, students, professors, and school-age children of all levels.[9] There is undeniably a potential in DH work to which some would refer by employing the phrase "the democratization of knowledge." While I concede the above and other benefits of DH, I do not rush, however, to use that phrase myself.

I turn once again to twentieth-century social theorist and urban philosopher Henri Lefebvre as a way of thinking through the under-recognized and potential problems of DH. As Lefebvre wrote, every disalienation brings about new alienations—history itself, he argued in his *Critique of Everyday Life*, consists of the dynamic interplay alien-ation–disalienation–alienation. Technological changes clearly respond to and undoubtedly bring about social changes. It is somewhat silly to think that we can stem the tide of technological innovation—but we should neither accept such changes passively nor pretend that the adop-tion of new technologies will be inconsequential. The more I continue to reflect upon the problems and potential of DH, the more I am convinced that—at the very least—its proponents are not thinking it through as much as they should be. DH, for many, signals a sweeping and totalizing shift that will forever change the face of the university and of humanities research and instruction in particular—and for this reason alone, it is deserving of greater attention and more nuanced critique.

Recent articles published in *Digital Humanities Quarterly (DHQ)* reveal, perhaps appropriately, how hard people are pushing for DH—but it is important to note that these articles do not always adopt a dispas-sionate stance nor do they analyze the complex relations involved in DH work as thoroughly as they should. In Patrik Svensson's "Envisioning the Digital Humanities," for example, the author writes that "the uni-versity and the humanities need to change to accommodate this type of work"—but he does not address the problems that the humanities already face in the university. We should not forget that—as Alvin Kernan pointed out more than 15 years ago in the introduction to his edited volume *What's Happened to the Humanities* (1997)—"shifts in higher education have not, I think it is fair to say, been kind to the liberal arts in general, and to the humanities in particular" (5). In another *DHQ* article, Paul Rosenbloom's simplistic assertion that "the humanities naturally fit within the sciences as part of an expanded social domain" reveals how science-centered the (digital) humanities potentially may become—and, moreover, this on its own explains why institutions would be willing to invest in them—or encourage them with minimal investment, as is more common.

Although DH is subject to forces that originate both inside and out-side of the humanities, existing writing on DH tends to be tough on humanities scholars and easier on the larger forces shaping education today. In "New Media in the Academy: Labor and the Production of Knowledge in Scholarly Multimedia," for example, Helen J. Burgess and Jeanne Hamming affirm the notion that the biggest obstacle to DH is the fact that humanities scholars do not understand the "kinds of 'work' that go into producing scholarship in multimedia form." I, for one, find it very troubling that the word "work" appears in quotes; but more important is that this work is disguised as an emancipatory practice. The authors write that DH work "places scholars in an extended network that combines minds, bodies, machines and institutional practices and lays bare the fiction that scholars are disembodied intellectuals who labor only with the mind." These authors, and many proponents of DH, seem to think that as DH practitioners they are the oppressed minority within the university when the truth is that this situation (if there has ever been any truth to it) will certainly be changing soon. Bolstered by the almost utopian spirit of its supporters and pushed forward by the momentum of the frustration with economic and disciplinary pressures in the humanities that have built up over the last few decades—including the recent economic crisis—DH is currently poised to become the next big thing if not, as some would have it, to replace the humanities as they now exist.

Lest one believe in a positivistic timeline of history, it is crucial to admit that along with the triumphalist discourse of scholarly modernity there comes—as the case with modernity more generally—a darker side. David Perry—quoted in Svensson's article—exemplifies the totalizing approach of DH advocates, who "want the digital to completely change what it means to be a humanities scholar." For this reason alone we must think more thoroughly about what this change will involve. I must make clear that I do not intend my subsequent thoughts to be used as a case against DH—such an interpretation would merely reinforce the false opposition between "positive" and "negative" social/technological changes. Our contemporary world is more complex than such a categorization would allow. Moreover, as I have underscored above, I believe there are undoubtedly many benefits to DH work. But what is simultaneously clear to me is this—for a field that boasts so strongly of its commitment to interdisciplinary connections, discussion of how DH is situated in webs of educational capital is remarkably absent. It is to this last point that the present discussion is devoted—that is, to the social relations embodied in DH pedagogy and research that have, to date, received insufficient attention. To use a metaphor from print publishing—the social relationships inherent in DH in fact constitute a verso page, hidden by the digital world's vast expanse of dorso surface; to use a digital metaphor, social relationships seem to be the hidden html and xml code underlying DH's massive online projects. Behind these open-access projects lie complex questions relating to intellectual labor, knowledge, and the cultural logic of capital in an era of flexible accumulation.

As a way of dealing with those complex questions, the remainder of this chapter looks first at Kathleen Fitzpatrick's landmark book *Planned Obsolescence* (2011) as a way of questioning some of the key assumptions of DH work and of existing accounts of the digital turn in the humanities. This discussion will tease out the undertheorized implications of these assumptions, which are often in conflict with the way in which the humanities are being treated within universities, and it will also address the perennial challenges faced by professors as scholars positioned in university structures. This critique of Fitzpatrick's book—carried out by situating the latter within Henri Lefebvre's extensive capitalist critique as elaborated largely in the first major section of this book—can help us to see not only how knowledge and culture have been historically inflected by urbanized capital but also how DH, if unchecked, may turn out to be complicit with the logic of capitalist accumulation. The risk is that DH work—through its large scale and nonetheless novel method—may promote increasing collaboration not merely between students and among certain definitions of faculty and community, but also between education and corporate/business interests as well as between the humanities and the circuits of capital in which universities are increasingly enmeshed.

I might have subtitled this section "The Darker Side of DH"—but why? Can there be a darker side to something so exciting? "Surely not," many will say. "DH is, after all, a land of plenty where we can all be connected with one another; with disciplinary barriers lifted, communication and collaboration will now truly be possible"—so the thinking goes.[10] But we must ask, what exactly are the social relationships coded into DH research and pedagogy? What assumptions about education play themselves out in DH work? Is there another side to the collaborative aspect of DH? Does the discourse of collaboration, however valuable, dovetail nonetheless with existing myths about neoliberal democracy? Does DH work render capital flows more visible or does it hide them under the thin veneer of educational spectacle? These are, I argue, the questions that current DH praxis ignores, underanalyzes, or postpones.

Some of this avoidance of what I consider to be key questions—as such inextricable from the practice and analysis of DH—has to do with the positioning of DH within current universities. That is, there may be a conflict of interest generated by capital investments in DH projects through personnel, infrastructure, training, and so on. Furthermore, this process may not be unrelated to the increasing incursion of private capital into public university practice—whether that is through the search for postcrisis private endowment donations, partnerships with MOOC providers and (text)book publishers, or more generally the gradual erosion of publically funded postsecondary education. I also strongly believe there is a boosterism accompanying DH work online and in print, which tends toward the uncritical. I do, of course, undoubtedly identify with some of these triumphant and triumphalist sentiments. That is, DH *is* novel: it is transformative, it is potentially inclusionary, and in the end it is also "cool" and quite interesting. I understand the enthusiasm embodied in many accounts of DH work to be, in part, a natural response to decades of disciplinary conservatism in language and literature fields.[11] That is, why criticize something that is already held in low esteem by exponents of traditional disciplinary borders? But it is worth noting that this same lack of esteem continues to affect other relatively new ventures in humanities fields—ventures such as popular music studies, studies of the comic/sequential art/graphic novel, urban studies, and, strange as it may seem, even studies of film, which still occupy a relatively marginalized position in Hispanic Studies (on this see Brown, *Confronting*; Brown, *Constructing*; Brown and Johnson; and the response by Fraser et al. 2014).

Not all accounts of DH are uncritical, of course. It is illuminating to see how, where, and to what extent the social conditions inherent in DH work have already been commented upon in critical literature. For example, some of the most important publications on digital work from approximately the past decade—Jerome McGann's *Radiant Textuality* (2001), Johanna Drucker's *SPECLAB: Digital Aesthetics and Projects in Speculative Computing* (2009), and Kathleen Fitzpatrick's *Planned Obsolescence* (2011)—mention capital and capitalism explicitly.[12] These and other single-authored books, as well as the countless articles addressing DH that refer to them, are important contributions inasmuch as they grapple with the rapidly changing set of publishing expectations. Their collective strength is that they are global texts, written by well-informed and forward-thinking authors who truly and correctly believe in fostering improved communication among academics. In these books, there is a willingness to engage with issues of social power as they relate to disciplines and institutions: there are direct responses to the questions of authorship, scholarly editing, peer review, and university structures that routinely arise when discussing DH. And yet, their weakness lies in how they situate these arguments within contemporary society, more broadly speaking. One finds, for example, that the frequent invocation of the terms "capital" and "capitalism" in these books is often at odds with the fact that these terms are seldom contextualized in any depth.

In this respect, Fitzpatrick's *Planned Obsolescence: Publishing, Technology and the Future of the Academy* is an interesting and nuanced case—and, as such, it will be the focus of my comments here. The critic sees communication as a way of correcting the ills of "late capitalism" and links those ills to a rising emphasis on "supposedly more pragmatic fields," the replacement of "tenure-track lines...with more contingent forms of labor," and the lack of jobs for new graduates (2011, 5). This is an observable, widespread, and undoubtedly troubling phenomenon: one with which any department administrator is likely to be all too familiar. But there is something of a distance between the academy in her analysis and the capitalist context in which we are immersed: that is, she only takes on capitalist practice as it enters the sphere of the academy—perhaps, I am forced to presume, because she regards education as a relatively autonomous area of social life. Although we might like it to be, it is not—a point to which we will return anon. Apart from her awareness that professors are laborers and that scholarly publishing is increasingly regarded as a business platform—she also recognizes that the current economic crisis is affecting academic work in ways previously unseen—there is no global (nor historical) understanding of capitalism in the book. It might seem to some that this is a book launched not against capital accumulation strategies, the commodification of knowledge, and instrumentalization of education, but rather against the inherent conservatism of academic thinking in and across disciplinary contexts and the anxieties surrounding change in general. While I sympathize with aspects of that critique, I think Fitzpatrick misses an opportunity—as have many proponents of DH—to think more deeply about the problematic relationship between capital and education. Moreover, the problems plaguing this relationship cannot be attributed merely to the most recent economic crisis.

I say that I sympathize with aspects of Fitzpatrick's critique for this reason: many of her comments are quite astute. For instance, there are indeed many problems with peer review, and it has indeed gone undertheorized in many humanities areas. My own belief is that many of these problems can be fixed by tightening up existing peer review processes and making them more suitable for interdisciplinary research in particular (e.g., see Fraser et al. 2011). On the whole, Fitzpatrick's concerns tend to reflect the extent to which the practitioners in the field are perennially alienated from one another. I believe that this alienation, which certainly deserves our attention, says something about the way disciplinary knowledge has been constructed from the nineteenth century onward (in Lefebvrian terms), just as it also says something about the current conditions within the academy, conditions that undoubtedly heighten competitive behaviors, and anxiety about the worth of humanities disciplines. Her response to the specific issue of peer review—while certainly forward-looking—might be focused too narrowly. In Chapter 1 of her book, Fitzpatrick advocates leaving traditional peer review behind expecting—and here we have the technological determinism she attempts to distance herself from later on—that a change in the circumstances surrounding peer review will change relationships between the people who practice it. I would say, however, that Fitzpatrick reifies the peer review process as somehow external to existing social relationships, instead of seeing existing peer review structures also as an expression of those relationships. I assert that if peer review is flawed, it is because disciplinary specialization has been and continues to be a flawed way of conceiving of knowledge—not merely because academics are reticent to adopt new postures; it is because the disciplinary cultures of specialized expertise are ill-equipped to deal with non-canonical and interdisciplinary scholarship, not merely because people are unwilling to change; it is because the increased pressures leveed upon academics of all ranks encourage the same prejudicial judgments of scholarly quality that in previous decades were asserted in the name of canon, writing style or propriety—not only because the academy is by its very nature conservative.[13]

The question of authorship also deserves out attention. Single-authored publications—for many, it seems—have come to embody the individualistic myth of neoliberal capitalism. I am not sure where this notion comes from nor why it is so universally accepted. In Chapter 2 of *Planned Obsolescence* ("Authorship"), Fitzpatrick writes that "However critically aware we may be of the historical linkages among the rise of capitalism, the dominance of individualism and the conventionally understood figure of the author, our own authorship practices have remained subsumed within those institutional and ideological frameworks" (2011, 52–53). The single author is presumed to be some sort of tyrant. There is Barthes, who told us some variation on this theme in a single-authored publication; there is also Foucault, who did so in yet another single-authored publication; and now we have Fitzpatrick, who draws on both of these single-authored publications. I concede that all three of these single authors provide fascinatingly deep engagements with the themes they discuss—but I would make this objection: the single author in general is not (nor does s/he represent) pernicious capitalist relations.

Instead, as these texts themselves make clear, the single author is a comfortable fiction. Just as we use a director's name as a shorthand for the lengthy cast of characters who have contributed to the film we analyze (scriptwriters, actors, grips, sound engineers, editors, costumers, cinematographers), Fitzpatrick is right to reassert that the single-authored text is equally the product of a net of social and authorial relationships. The notion of single authorship is, however, a poor metaphor for the ills of capital. As Lefebvre is right to point out, capital has changed our understanding of knowledge and the way we relate to one another. For now, it is safe to say that what Fitzpatrick rails against in truth is "disdain" (2011, 13) by other academics and "anti-intellectualism" (2011, 14) by the larger society, not to mention what she describes as a universally held anxiety over authorship. Despite her mention of late-capitalism and her conflation of the single author with capitalist individualism, she does not explore in sufficient depth the threat posed to education by capital. In fact, her chapter on authorship—as she herself notes quite candidly in the text—is wholly conceived as a response to anxiety and not to the dynamics inherent in late-capitalism.[14] In sum, it is fetishistic to claim that the individual author who writes down their thoughts is merely fomenting the individualistic myth of neoliberalism—and yet this strange idea echoes throughout much DH scholarship, implicitly.[15]

In Fitzpatrick's text, one finds also another idea that is implicit in DH—or at least in digital publication—the emphasis on process over product (2011, "From Process to Product" is the subtitle of pages 66–72). That is, the book's description of the future of digital publishing paradoxically evokes the notion of an article as a final (if evolving) product. Digital publishing, many others similarly argue, allows for revisions to articles be suggested postpublication (in open-access formats, by anyone who reads it), and even for those revisions to subsequently motivate the author to change the article—the reader imagines authors willing to respond to those suggested changes, and to devote themselves to polishing the published piece over the course of years (decades?—I must wonder). Although the practicality of sustained authorial engagement with an individual article seems problematic, there is another problem I have with this idea. My personal view of publishing—borrowed from Henri Bergson's process-oriented philosophy of life—is that published pieces represent not the be-all and end-all of an author's thought, but rather that they are the static deposits left behind by an ever-mobile thought.[16] As such, they reflect the lived time and space of the author experienced during the course of that article's writing. If articles are continually updated—I do not think they will be, for a variety of reasons—where does that visible record go? Even given that there would be access to various historical "stages" of the article through online platforms (just as to various sets of reader comments), one must ask why an author should be forced to (or would want to) update a single digital publication over time during the precise moment at which technology—remember the massive database as one possible direction of DH work—renders the vast expanse of past, present, and future publications searchable? Part of the reasoning involved in stressing the "updating" of scholarly publications seems to be an anxious response to the *planned obsolescence* of technology with which we are becoming increasingly familiar. This anxiety has been met in some cases—it is clear to me—with the desire to create a more permanent publication, one that will endure and not merely fade away.[17] For all its forward-looking energy, *Planned Obsolescence* seems unaware of Marx's dictum that in the modern age "all that is solid melts into air." What DH seems to indicate—just as what all interdisciplinary scholarship seems to indicate about the literary canon—is that the seemingly unchanging (for Marx, what are in part perhaps traditionally religious; in this context, disciplinary, canonical) ideals have been exposed as alienations at the same time that the new alienations of capital threaten to bring even further changes.

In addition, the idea of collaboration invoked in Fitzpatrick's book (the subtitle of this section is titled "From Individual to Collaborative") is not without its own power dynamics.[18] The real way in which capitalist individualism rears its head in publishing is not on the author side of things but rather in the lack of interest in existing peer review processes. When Fitzpatrick bemoans, quite correctly, that people feel they get "no credit" for performing peer review, this is because today's scholars by and large may not feel part of an academic community. One major factor contributing to this state of things is easily identified as the increasing pressure to excel in all three areas (research, teaching, and service) at an ever-wider range of institution types. Another contributing factor would be that quantity is encroaching on quality in the evaluation of what is necessarily qualitative scholarly work in the humanities.[19] Scholars under such increasing pressures may have no other option than to ignore the traditional expectations regarding the relationship between publishing in a journal and serving as a peer reviewer for that same journal (on the exchange economy of peer review, see the article by Elden 2008). Mentoring others—which is what peer review at its best should be—is no longer a responsibility that many overburdened professors believe they can shoulder. This all points to a sea change in the field—where alienation, a social relationship subject to economic and other pressures of course, is rendered visible in certain areas of academic life. It is more than curious, I will add, that at the same time in which a movement is taking place to go beyond the perceived limitations of a single-authored model of publishing we are also witnessing a trend of scholarly individualism in this lack of interest in the peer review system[20]; that is, scholars must—for many reasons—now protect themselves and their time as never before, in the process sacrificing a long-operative notion of scholarly community.

As do others making similar cases, Fitzpatrick references collaboration as a hallmark of the scientific research culture.[21] I will say that think it is unfortunate when humanists use scientific models of collaboration to justify their thoughts on the future of the humanities. This is not because I believe that there are two existing cultures that should never be mixed (keep in mind the earlier discussion of the Snow–Leavis controversy).[22] Instead, it is because these two cultures are influencing academic culture and university procedure unevenly. I would venture a guess that no one on university tenure and promotion committees holds scientists to humanist standards or qualitative humanist metrics in their evaluations. On the other hand, however, it seems to me that the reverse is frequently all too true.

Moreover, as the topic of this book is the interdisciplinary field of urban cultural studies, I suggest that there is benefit to looking beyond the walls of the university to see how culture and the arts have been harnessed by strategies of capital accumulation (as a starting point, see the work of Sharon Zukin and David Harvey, for example). Within the academy, for example, there is an increasing attempt to "monetize" the humanities and hold them to scientific standards.[23] For example, in science programs, grants have long been used/required as a way to outsource university support of the science programs, to connect the sciences with corporate and business ventures, and also to bring prestige to professors, departments, and ultimately to the universities in which they are housed. The fact is that administrators are today increasingly seeking to apply this model to the humanities. The goals of this application are the same as in the sciences—increased funds through outsourcing, increased prestige for professors, departments, and universities—only that in this case the humanities do not dovetail as naturally with the scientific method nor do they accept collaborative work with corporations and businesses as cleanly. Nor either, of course, are grants as available for humanities projects, broadly speaking. It is worth remembering that Marx's theorizations on the circuits of capital held that investment in science was the second circuit of capital flow.

I will say it as clearly as possible: I fully support many of the motivations behind the battle which Fitzpatrick and others are fighting—among them, the desire to change existing peer review processes to account for the interdisciplinary era in which we find ourselves, to change the way humanists interact with each other, to change how we humanists are valued in the academy (by our peers and by others), and to allow for more flexibility regarding the notion of what scholarship is. In truth, however—and this is not a critique but an observation—much of Fitzpatrick's book is concerned not with the changing "digital" nature of the profession specifically but with the perennial (and alienating) conditions that govern our relationships with our colleagues and that regulate relationships within our departments and universities. That is, as I see it, faced with the somewhat universal reality that professors, departments, and administrators who know relatively little about (or, worse, who staunchly refuse to concede the value of) new directions in scholarly work nonetheless have great power in evaluating that work, Fitzpatrick subsequently imagines that technological change will even the playing field. The implications of her book (underscored by her title as well as her choice of introductory epigraphs[24]) are that the method of work associated with DH projects, over time, will alleviate the flaws embodied in the current peer review process, combat the tyranny of the single author thus bringing new respect to co-authorship, and even open up new possibilities for the creation, preservation, and publication of digital texts. These would all be welcome results.

What is not discussed, however, is that the widespread adoption of DH and of its methods is not necessarily as value-neutral as it appears to be. The critic writes of "knowledge advancement" and advocates "a broad communal framework"—but the problem is precisely that notions of knowledge and community require greater interrogation. In order to understand how and why writing on DH might grapple more thoroughly with these notions, we must digest Henri Lefebvre's interdisciplinary critique of how capital and knowledge have interacted since the nineteenth century.[25]

Others may disagree, but I believe that this is the most interdisciplinary time that has ever been in the academy. I have no doubt that it is the most interdisciplinary time that has ever been in Hispanic Studies—as can be confirmed by reflecting on the discipline's internal schisms.[26] DH is, in part, an expression of this movement toward innovation, this ongoing interdisciplinary tendency. But why is it that at the same time we see rising levels of interdisciplinarity in humanities fields, we also see universities and colleges under more pressure to get students to connect disciplines through such trends as learning communities and writing across the disciplines? One answer has to do with the externalization (and reification) of interdisciplinary connections. The understanding is that students today cannot do this on their own, that they must be instructed to do so (sacrificing further that scarce commodity of the faculty working day). In effect, such connections are seen as "things" and products in their own right, an additional intellectual specialization of sorts that needs to be transmitted as instructional content. Already we are getting into discussing the way in which disciplinary specialization is grounded in the specialized fragmentation of knowledge under capitalism, and of course of the specialization of labor to which it provides a complement—both of these being key components of Lefebvre's urban critique.

In this sense, Julie Thompson Klein's interesting book *Humanities, Culture and Interdisciplinarity* (2005) provides relevant reading; the way she explores the development of disciplinary specialization may be further tied to Lefebvre's own thought, not merely to displace literature as the center of the field, but simultaneously to contextualize knowledge within capitalist society. Klein writes, for example, that "The disciplining of knowledge was not a new phenomenon. Between the mid-seventeenth and late-eighteenth centuries, physics, biology and chemistry began assuming separate identities" and further traces this trend into the nineteenth and twentieth centuries (2005, 24). It is significant that this same segmentation of disciplines as "separate identities"—which is approached through an historical lens by Klein—is described by Henri Lefebvre with much more attention paid to the social context for this historical turn. To understand how knowledge and capitalism are connected, we have to return to Lefebvre's argument about the specialized— the *spatialized*—forms of knowledge supported by capitalist society.

For Lefebvre, the segmentation of knowledge that solidifies during the nineteenth century is inseparable from the larger socioeconomic dynamics accompanying an ongoing shift toward capitalism. The specialization of labor in capitalist environments for the French philosopher has its complement in the specialization of intellectual labor and of knowledge. In effect, the scientific model of knowledge promoting compartmentalization and segmentation of ideas functions as an ideology (Lefebvre 1982, 22–23). It fragments areas of a fluid world off into discrete specialized areas, and in so doing, it makes it impossible to understand how capitalist society functions as a whole. In brief, the bourgeois satisfaction with specialized knowledge obfuscates the Marxian notion of totality (see also Fraser 2011, 19–23). Building on Marx's thought (see Merrifield 2002; Fraser 2014), Lefebvre formulates the notion of totality as a threat to the varying alienations inherent to contemporary capitalism. Totality is, in effect, a disalienation. But we may ask a now-familiar question: what is alienation?

In a general sense, Lefebvre remarked that "The drama of alienation is dialectical . . . by producing them [objects], men are working to create the human; they think they are molding an object, a series of objects—and it is man himself they are creating (1969, 169).[27] Lefebvre, however, extended this Marxian premise to include multiple alienations, as discussed in his *Critique of Everyday Life*. Alienation could be social, philosophical, economic, ideological, and even urban. Another way to explain this is to point out that capitalist ideology obscures the relationships between the seemingly fragmented aspects of contemporary life—separating the political from the economic from the cultural from the social and prohibiting a holistic assessment of the way these areas are aspects of a variegated but organically interrelated capitalist mode of production. The notion of totality provides a way of understanding the effects of alienation.

Totality for Lefebvre suggests a move toward disalienating oneself and one's society from the effects of that capitalist ideology and experiencing contemporary urbanized life as an organic whole. Capitalism is not merely an economic system, but a social, philosophical, cultural, political, and urban system. As concerns us here, it is also a system of knowledge. Lefebvre writes that, "The problem remains: How can we make the transition from fragmentary knowledge to complete understanding? How can we define this need for *totality?*" (original emphasis; 2003a, 56). The answer, argues Lefebvre, is *not* to be found in simply grouping together objects of disciplinary (specialized) knowledge:

> Every specialized science cuts from the global phenomenon a "field," or "domain," which it illuminates in its own way. There is no point in choosing between segmentation and illumination. Moreover, each individual science is further fragmented into specialized subdisciplines. Sociology is divided up into political sociology, economic sociology, rural and urban sociology, and so forth. The fragmented and specialized sciences operate analytically: they are the result of an analysis and perform analyses of their own. In terms of the urban phenomenon considered as a whole, geography, demography, history, psychology, and sociology supply the results of an analytical procedure. Nor should we overlook the contributions of the biologist, doctor or psychiatrist, or those of the novelist or poet . . . Without the progressive and regressive movements (in time and space) of analysis, without the multiple divisions and fragmentations, it would be impossible to conceive of a science of the urban phenomenon. But such fragments do not constitute knowledge. (2003a, 48–49)[28]

Lefebvre thus writes specifically of the limitations of disciplinary structures in the context of the modern university (see 2003a, particularly 53–55; 1969, 41); but what is at stake is a more generalized (non–institution-specific) critique of fragmentary knowledge (see 1996, 95–96).[29] As long as disciplinary conceits structure our approach, no degree of systematic collisions will yield an understanding of the "totality" of the urban phenomenon (2003a, 53–54, 58–59); no "collection of objects—economy, sociology, history, demography" can reconstitute the complexity of the urban phenomenon (2003a, 57). Effectively allying himself with critics such as Paolo Freire and bell hooks who have denounced a style of "banking education" inflected by the capitalist reification of knowledge (see Freire 1998, 1970; hooks 1994; Rowland Dix 2010), Lefebvre similarly wrote that "An educator is not a mere conveyer, nor is the institution called 'university' a warehouse" (1969, 156) where learning can be reduced to a product in accordance with the capitalist logic of exchange (141).[30]

I reemphasize merely that there have always been insular and conservative forces in the academy—those who fear and vehemently oppose change. I am not—nor do I wish to be seen as—one of them.[31] On the other hand, to use a spatial metaphor, there have long been threats to the humanities from both the inside and the outside—threats that have always received their share of apologists. Neither will I be one of these. DH work should continue, but it must be noted that nothing about supporting DH precludes our being aware of and critically discussing the potential consequences it may bring. I imagine that critiques of this approach will not come from political economy approaches but instead from those who trumpet DH, something I will continue to do—even if I may feel ambivalently about the way it expresses a continuing change in the social relationships surrounding education, knowledge, and capital.

Conclusion

As pursued throughout this book, urban cultural studies is understood to be an inherently interdisciplinary field bringing humanities texts (literature, film, popular music, digital spaces, etc.) into close articulation with the urban phenomenon. It should be stressed that the field of urban cultural studies is inherently interdisciplinary. That is: because disciplinary knowledge itself has an historical and ongoing role in actively producing the disciplinary divisions that partition city-space from cultural production, an interdisciplinary method is the only method capable of approaching the urban phenomenon. To my mind, Henri Lefebvre stands out as one of the few single theorists whose extensive work has captured the spirit of this interdisciplinary inquiry.

What is needed—and what Lefebvre's work provides—is an understanding of how sociopolitical alienation is complemented by disciplinary alienation. We must return the humanities text to the urban world from which it has been separated. Put another way, we must admit that the urban phenomenon is shaped dialectically, in tandem with forces that are simultaneously material and immaterial. These forces are observable in today's cities, just as they are observable in cultural texts.

Henri Lefebvre's work is particularly suited to push us toward the formulation of an urban cultural studies method. This is so because of the attention he gives to the artistic and aesthetic dimensions of lived experience, but it is also due to other related reasons. Lefebvre's extensive and nuanced contributions contrast with the rather unnuanced materialist invocations of much previous and contemporary Marxian thought. His elaboration of Marxian insights into the multifaceted nature of alienation—and into the spatial nature of contemporary capitalism—are unavoidably significant. Moreover, his sense that everyday life serves as a site of both colonization and potential resistance signals the continuing importance of the cultural critic. Such cultural critique, of course, cannot remain isolated from the urban phenomenon as a whole. It is in Lefebvre's work that the urban phenomenon receives the full attention it is due.

The questions Henri Lefebvre raised continue to echo in the work of many, not least of all in the books written by David Harvey and Manuel Delgado Ruiz. And yet, Lefebvrian thought is not exhausted. Though fundamental, it is still relatively underappreciated. His assertion that capitalism survives by producing space remains just as relevant for the twenty-first century as it was for the twentieth century. New publications—not merely monographs and edited volumes dedicated to exploring the French thinker's work but also translations—appear on a regular basis. Just as before, we are still in need of a method that can articulate the relationship between what appear to be diverse areas of the human experience.

Bringing the humanities and the social sciences together in order to reach a greater understanding of the urban phenomenon is the very project that Lefebvre's work suggests to contemporary researchers. Lefebvre's work helps us to understand the interconnectedness of what seem to be disparate dimensions of the urban phenomenon. This book has attempted to ground the general reader in Lefebvre's thought with the understanding that this thought is adaptable to any range of geographical, linguistic, cultural, and political urban struggles. Lefebvre's method is merely one way of moving toward an urban cultural studies, but it is nonetheless significant.

By way of conclusion, we might ask the same question of the French urban philosopher that Lefebvre had asked of Marx:

"Should Lefebvre's thought be accepted today *en bloc*? Or should it be globally rejected?"

The answer to this question should be the same one that Lefebvre gave:

"Neither."

Notes

Introduction

1. David Harvey, for example, although he has gone beyond many of Lefebvre's specific analyses, first found the French theorist an invaluable point of reference in his early book *Social Justice and the City* (originally published 1973) and continues to dialogue with his work even in his most recent book *Rebel Cities* whose preface is titled "Henri Lefebvre's Vision" (Harvey 2012, ix–xviii). In *Social Justice*, Harvey had written that Lefebvre's work was instrumental in responding to the question "what insights and revelations do we gain through the use of Marx's method in the investigation of urban phenomena?" (2009, 302). On the next page he writes, "Lefebvre's work is more general than my own but it is also incomplete in certain important respects" (303). As Kofman and Lebas point out, Anglophone Geographers such as Gregory, Harvey, Merrifield, Smith, Soja, and Jameson, have built upon Lefebvre's insights (1996, 42–43). Merrifield points also to "second-wave interpreters like Rob Shields, Erik Swyngedouw, Stuart Elden, Stefan Kipfer, and Neil Brenner" (2006, 102–103).

2. It has been noted that Anglo-American approaches have tended to see Lefebvre "through the often mutually exclusive lenses of urban political economy and postmodern cultural studies" (Goonewardena et al. 2008, 6)—although each approach is certainly warranted, as is a fusion of both approaches. Also of interest is that while some have criticized Lefebvre for having little to say as regards gender, the body, and sexuality (a common misconception—see, e.g., Gottdiener 2000, 99–100), various studies (e.g., Kofman and Lebas 1996; Miller 2005; Simonsen 2005; Lim 2006) have made assertions to the contrary. In particular, Kofman and Lebas point out that "Lefebvre also frequently referred to sexuality and gender both in relation to the crisis of the 20th century and the role of psychoanalysis and Freudianism. He had read a number of the feminist classics, such as Kate Millet and Germaine Greer, and discussed the potential of contemporary feminism (1980b, 156–77)"—the reference "1980b" being to the Lefebvre's book *La présence et l'absence* (Casterman 1980), translated into Spanish (Lefebvre 2006b), but not yet into English. Consider, moreover, that Lefebvre is being seen as relevant to the field of Physical Cultural Studies—an area that comprises "sport,

exercise, fitness, leisure, health, dance, and movement-related active embodied practices" (Friedman and van Ingen 2011, who, in addition to Miller 2005, emphasized Lefebvre's relevance for LGBT struggles)—and also to the study of videogames (Nitsche 2008; Fraser 2011a, 2011c).

3. As Kofman and Lebas wrote, "However, it would be unfortunate if *Production of Space* were to be treated as the core of his work and other writing subordinated to it, for, as we have amply seen, his own production after the mid 1970s remained massive and, most significantly, represented a return to earlier passions and concepts which had in some cases lain dormant, though not forgotten" (1996, 43).

4. Snow and his colleague believed they hand found a way of producing vitamin A artificially. As Collini reports, "The discovery promised to be of immense theoretical and practical importance, and, following the announcement in *Nature*, the President of the Royal Society confirmed to the national press the significance of the findings. But alas, their calculations had been faulty, their 'discovery' had to be recanted amid considerable publicity, and, as his brother later put it, 'the trauma after all that publicity put Charles off scientific research irrevocably.' That Snow was a trained scientist was crucial to the authority with which he was later to treat the question of the 'two cultures,' but, as those scientists uneasy with this self-appointed champion of the scientific culture were to remark, his credentials were in fact somewhat shaky. By the time he came to give his Rede lecture, it was more than twenty years since he had been engaged in first-hand scientific research, and his achievement as a scientist had been patchy at best" (1993, xx).

5. Stefan Collini's substantial and thorough introduction to the 1993 edition of Snow's *The Two Cultures* explains how "Many of the preoccupations which surfaced in the controversy surrounding 'The Two Cultures and the Scientific Revolution' now appear to belong distinctively to the late 1950s and early 1960s. But in fact the germ of the argument and the tone of the lecture can be traced back to much earlier stages of Snow's career, and to a surprising extent they reflect facets of Snow's intellectual development which were shaped and fixed in the 1930s" (1993, xxii).

6. Even this initial formulation seems, to my mind, to be revealingly uneven; see Snow (1993, 5).

7. "The seriousness with which he takes himself as a novelist is complete—if seriousness can be so ineffably blank, so unware...as a novelist he doesn't exist; he doesn't begin to exist. He can't be said to know what a novel is. The nonentity is apparent on every page of his fictions" (Leavis 1972, 44–45). This is but a small token of the lack of esteem held by Leavis for Snow.

8. Leavis defends himself against the charge of literarism (1972, 97).

9. See also Leavis's statement (1972, 61) on how each culture is insufficient on its own.

10. Here there is a further point of comparison with Mumford, in that, in the process of defending against Snow's allegation of literary intellectuals as

Luddites, Leavis makes an implicit connection between Luddites and anti-urbanists (1972, 81).

11. "I am not suggesting that we ought to halt the progress of science and technology, I am insisting that the more potently they accelerate their advance the more urgent does it become to inaugurate another, a different, sustained effort of collaborative human creativity which is concerned with perpetuating, strengthening and asserting, in response to change, a full human creativity" (Leavis 1972, 156).

12. In particular, Mary Burgan's book, *What Ever Happened to the Faculty? Drift and Decision in Higher Education* (2006), points to the increasing reality of dispossession of the right to faculty governance by a new capitalist culture of university administration.

13. The 379-page proceedings from this conference are available online at urbanculturalstudies.wordpress.com.

14. See http://metropolitanstudies.as.nyu.edu/page/home; http://metrostudies .berkeley.edu/; and http://www.geschundkunstgesch.tu-berlin.de/fachgebiet _neuere_geschichte/menue/ueber_uns/parameter/en/?no_cache=1.

1 Why Urban Cultural Studies? Why Henri Lefebvre?

1. On base-superstructure, see Williams, *Marxism and Literature* (1977, 75). The literature on this subject dating from the 1970s is extremely vast—the following deserve mention (but are clearly neither exhaustive nor representative): Sharon Zukin's observation in her classic salvo *The Cultures of Cities* that "As I continued to think about cities, I began to think of their economies as based increasingly on symbolic production" (1995, ix); David Harvey's work on the relationship of culture to intercity competition (*Justice, Nature and the Geography of Difference* [1996]); and the essays in *State/Culture* (ed. George Steinmetz, 1999), particularly the introduction and the essay by Bob Jessop, where the author highlights "the discursive (or sociocultural) construction of political economic realities" (1999, 380). Lefebvre (2005) himself, of course—as will be discussed—goes beyond the base-superstructure model generally equated with traditional Marxism.

2. As discussed in this book's introduction, C. P. Snow was a scientist/physicist who thought of himself as a writer/novelist and who gave the Rede lecture at Cambridge in 1959, which was later published as the book *The Two Cultures*. The lecture and the book pointed to the distance between the humanities and the hard sciences—and since then, others have argued that there are in reality three cultures (humanities, hard sciences, and social sciences), each of which misunderstands the value of (and the values held by) the others. The introduction preceding this chapter uses the critique of Snow launched by F. R. Leavis (1972) to address contemporary issues of interdisciplinarity.

3. This view has been shaped by my own experiences as well, as I have attempted to engage two distinct but intersecting worlds of academic publishing over the better part of the last decade (through both humanities and social science venues).

4. For example, "The relationship between the town and the countryside is, for Lefebvre, an historical relationship, with the mediating role being played by industrialization and the advance of technology" (Elden 2007, 103).

5. Simmel's work was, of course, also influenced by Marx. Harvey references Lefebvre by name in the chapter "The Urbanization of Consciousness" in *The Urban Experience* (1989, 230), incorporating an explicit reference to what Lefebvre had written in *The Survival of Capitalism* (1976) and an indirect reference to his multivolume *Critique of Everyday Life* (Lefebvre 1991b, 2002, 2005).

6. See Elden (2001, 2004) on Lefebvre's identification as a Marxist philosopher; also Merrifield's *Metromarxism* (2002). Harvey, of course, has established an extensive dialogue with Lefebvre's work over a distinguished career, beginning with *Social Justice and the City* (1973) and even in his more recent *Rebel Cities* where he refers to "a restricted circle of Marxist urbanists and critical theorists (I count myself one)" (Harvey 2012, 35).

7. Park is also clear on the point that the city is both a material fact and a mental state; see "The City: Suggestions for the Investigation of Human Behavior in the Urban Environment" (1968, 1).

8. Clearly there are exceptions. The present book seeks not to explore those exceptions in depth, but rather to group together their central insights and offer them up for digestion to the relatively unacquainted by way of the eclectic and philosophical work of Lefebvre in particular.

9. For an example of the disagreement to this statement among cinema scholars, see especially David Clarke's edited volume *The Cinematic City* (1997).

10. To dismiss "culture" merely as alienating ideological veneer (as I believe Harvey does, at times, mostly against the spirit of his own readings) is also to ignore the emancipatory potential of alienating experiences (or alienated cultural products) to yield productive moments of disalienation (see Lefebvre 1991b, 2002, 2005; also *Critique of Everyday Life*).

11. See the books edited by Young and Holmes (2010) and also Prakash (2010) for an example of the breadth and depth of urban cultural studies approaches.

12. In Hispanic literature alone, there has been a surge in monographs spanning the humanities–social science divide, as evidenced by my own *Henri Lefebvre and the Spanish Urban Experience* (Fraser 2011a) but also *Constructing and Resisting Modernity* (2011) by Susan Larson, *Construyendo la modernidad* (2010) by Carlos Ramos, *Cultivating Madrid* (2008) by Daniel Frost, and *Constructing Spain* (2011) by Nathan Richardson, not to mention the numerous works by senior scholars and pioneers in this

regard, Edward Baker and Malcolm Alan Compitello (e.g., 2003; *Madrid. De la Fortunata a la M-40*).

13. The notion of totality—explored in later chapters of this book—is formulated by Lefebvre (building on its role in Marx's thought; see Merrifield 2002) as a response to the various alienations of contemporary capitalism. One way to explain this response is to point out that capitalist ideology obscures the relationships between the seemingly fragmented aspects of contemporary life—separating the political from the economic from the cultural from the social and prohibiting a holistic assessment of the way each of these areas is an aspect of a variegated but organically interrelated capitalist mode of production. Totality for Lefebvre suggests a move toward disalienating oneself and one's society from the effects of that capitalist ideology and experiencing contemporary (urbanized) life as an organic whole, refusing to live through alienation.

14. As contemporary cultural geographer Don Mitchell reflects, "Sauer's main purpose was to show that environmental determinism had pretty much got it backwards. It wasn't nature that caused culture, but rather [that] culture, working with and on nature, created the contexts of life" (2000, 21). Of course, from today's perspective, Sauer's understanding of culture was relatively simplistic: Mitchell continues: "'culture' was radically undertheorized in Sauer's own work...it was the taken-for-granted of human life" (2000, 29). Nonetheless, Sauer succeeded in placing "culture right at the center of geography's project" (2000, 21). In another essay, "The Fourth Dimension of Geography," he also clearly established that time "is and has been part of geographic understanding. Human geography considers man as a geographic agent, using and changing his environment in non-recurrent time and according to his skills and wants" (Sauer 1974, 192). Compare the above with, for example, Ira Katznelson's *Marxism and the City*, "Writing about the city in 1898, Vidal de la Blache proposed that the central problems of urban geography were twofold: 'Nature prepares the site, and man organizes it in such fashion that it meets his desires and wants'" (1992, 1).

15. In their highly readable "Henri Lefebvre in Contexts: An Introduction," for example, Neil Brenner and Stuart Elden (2001) provide (in effect) a concise bibliography outlining the applications of Lefebvre's thought—pointing to specific texts appropriating his thoughts on urban theory, sociospatial theory, the condition of postmodernity, the body and sexuality, everyday life, the production of scale, urban struggles, and the transformation of urban citizenship. See also Goonewardena et al. (2008).

16. From *Key Writings* (2003b, 7); originally from *L'Existentialisme* (1946). Lefebvre goes on there to talk about this taxi-driver (himself) in the third person: "The Paris underworld unfolded before him in all its sleazy variety and he began to discover the secrets of its brothels, knocking-shops and gambling dens, dance halls (for white and coloured), fancy hotels and greasy spoons, shady dealers, high and low-class pederasts, bookmakers,

armed robbers an police squads. I plumbed some of the smelly depths of 'existence' and what I dragged up would have sent the neo-existentialists of the Café Flore into transports of delight. But to what purpose? I want to remember only my contact with an infinitely more precious and more moving reality: the life of the people of Paris" (2003b, 7). See also Harvey (1991, 426); Merrifield (2006, xxi).

17. "Lefebvre the taxi-driver—like Lefebvre the urban philosopher—was no doubt aware of the shifting and negotiated relationship between material space and mental maps of the city, a relationship that was produced and reproduced through a mobile union of what he termed 'thought-action' (*Critique of Everyday Life*, vol. 1, 1991b)...the taxi ride comes to symbolize and even express the shifting nature of modernity" (Fraser 2011a, 124–125)—these words lead into a discussion of films (Martin Scorcese, Carlos Saura, Jim Jarmusch) and short stories (Juan José Millás) focusing on social relations as read through fictional taxi-rides.

18. "The philosophers have only interpreted the world, in various ways; the point is to change it" (Marx, *Theses on Feuerbach*, XI). See also Elden's "Some Are Born" wherein he writes: "That is, to change the world, rather than merely interpret it, is a change that is informed by and builds upon philosophy" (2006a, 191).

19. Stuart Elden has been insistent on seeing Lefebvre in this dual light. See, for example, Elden (2007) where Lefebvre's "is a simultaneously political and philosophical project and that it needs to be understood as such" (101).

20. See also Lefebvre (1996, 158). Readers of Fraser (2008a, 2010) will note that there is in his statement there a Bergsonian resonance.

21. This distinction is also of importance for Lefebvrian scholars such as Barcelona's Manuel Delgado Ruiz (2007, 182); see Fraser (2012c; also 2007a).

22. The notion of the practiced city reflects Lefebvre's assertion that the city should be "more or less the oeuvre of its citizens instead of imposing itself upon them as a system, as an already closed book" (1996, 117).

23. "To wit: the seventeenth century had seen the discovery of the circulation of blood (commonly attributed to the Englishman William Harvey), and to a certain degree the subsequent large-scale urban renovations of the nineteenth-century (by Haussmann, Cerdà and others) did little more than map this discovery onto existing cities through the rational, geometrical and even algebraic redesign of urban spaces" (Fraser 2011b, 185). As Richard Sennett explores in *The Craftsman*, "The scalpel had permitted anatomists to study the circulation of the blood: that knowledge, applied to the circulation of movement in streets, suggested that streets worked like arteries and veins" (2008, 204). As Harvey writes, Haussmann had "bludgeoned the city [of Paris] into modernity" (2006, 3). cf. Fraser (2011a, 2011b), both concerning Cerdà.

24. They thus ignored that, as Lefebvre put it, "the complexity of the urban phenomenon is not that of an 'object'" (2003a, 56).

25. See Lefebvre (1996, 167) on use-value and the nature of this urban revolution.

26. As Harvey points out, Lefebvre's viewpoint alerted scholars to the fact that urbanism had thus become the logical conclusion of industrialization (2009, 305–307). "Industrial society is seen not as an end in itself but as a preparatory stage for urbanism. Industrialization, he argues, can only find its fulfillment in urbanization, and urbanization is now coming to dominate industrial production and organization. Industrialization, once the producer of urbanism, is now being produced by it" (Harvey 2009, 306).

27. "It is worth remembering that the urban has no worse enemy than urban planning and 'urbanism,' which is capitalism's and the state's strategic instrument for the manipulation of fragmented urban reality and the production of controlled space... The urban, defined as assemblies and encounters, is therefore the simultaneity (or centrality) of all that exists socially" (Lefebvre 1976, 15).

28. Lefebvre was a member of the PCF from 1928 until 1957, when he was expelled. Even while a member, he was "restricted by the PCF from writing on more explicitly political or philosophical topics" (Elden and Lebas 2003, xiii).

29. Moreover, such an inquiry would beg the question of what Marxism itself, in fact, amounts to—particularly given the turbulent twentieth-century legacy established by experiments in state-socialism if not also the diversity of opinion surrounding not only its perceived strengths and weaknesses but in fact argument over its central tenets and even basic definition. There is, of course, no shortage of works that await the interested reader in this regard, but Leszek Kolakowski's *Main Currents of Marxism* is a good place to begin. In addition, for starters, there is the complicated question of "which Marx?"—that is, the relationship between the young Hegelian and the mature scientific Marx has itself been approached by widely divergent means. On the latter subject, "Lefebvre was one of the first to see Marx as a theorist of alienation and *contra* Althusser, to emphasize the continuity between the early and late works" (Elden 2007, 102).

30. See, for example, *The Sociology of Marx* originally published in 1966; and *Marx et la liberté*, *Le marxisme*, and *Marx*, untranslated into English and originally published in 1947, 1948, and 1964, respectively. This leaves out those many other books that deal almost exclusively with and elaborate upon Marxian ideas, such as *The Survival of Capitalism* (Lefebvre 1976).

31. As Merrifield has written, "Lefebvre's brand of Marxist-humanist urbanism demanded bread *and* freedom, ethics and aesthetics, praxis and poiesis" (original emphasis; 2002, 81).

32. This concise discussion runs over pp. 75–78; in it, Lefebvre points out that "There is not *one* Marxism but rather many Marxist tendencies, schools, trends, and research projects. Marxism does not have the same orientation in Germany, Italy, the Soviet Union, or China" (1988, 75), underscores that cultural expressions such as surrealism "have intersected with Marxism" (76), and addresses the question of "which Marx" (76; see previous note, this introduction); he also voices that a more nuanced understanding of

Marx must actually differentiate between "Marx and Engels" (76), potentially include Engels and also Lenin as constituent parts of Marxism (76), and see the echoes of Marxism "even in those who fought it or who diverged from it, like Schumpeter and Keynes" (76).

33. "Incontestably, something in Marxist thought persists. First and foremost is the imperturbable logic of the commodity; next, the analytic and critical understanding of relations of dependence, exploitation, and humiliation, not only of certain classes, but also of entire peoples" (Lefebvre 1988, 77).

34. "But what has happened is that capitalism has found itself able to attenuate (if not resolve) its internal contradictions for a century, and consequently, in the hundred years since the writing of *Capital*, it has succeeded in achieving 'growth.' We cannot calculate at what price, but we do know the means: *by occupying space, by producing a space*" (Lefebvre 1976, 21). The quotation from Burkhard refers not only to Lefebvre but also to his friend and collaborator Norbert Guterman.

35. As Lefebvre points out regarding this trinity: "Even from the Marxist standpoint there were confusions; much was staked on the two-term opposition bourgeoisie-proletariat, at the expense of the third term: the soil, agricultural property and production, peasants, predominantly agricultural colonies" (2006a, 11).

36. This spatial triad has also been applied to literary criticism in novel ways. See, for example, Watkins (2005).

37. "Lefebvre was always interested in the relationship between Hegel and Marx, and thus in idealism and materialism. Instead of matter being seen as the embodiment of mental constructs, or mind being seen as the reaction to matter, Lefebvre saw both material and mental together. It is the fusion of the idealist and materialist notions that enables an *idealist and materialist* approach to questions of life and lived experience" (original emphasis; Elden 2007, 102). On Hegel, see also Charnock (2010, 1285).

38. There is a philosophical dimension also, of course, to the writings of the late Marx, as the opening pages of *Capital* reveal.

39. Compare this to Manuel Castells' critique of Lefebvre: "Frankly I do not believe that it is possible to offer a theory of production of space on a strictly philosophical basis, without a profound knowledge of the economic and technological data about the processes of urbanization and about their social and political organization" (quoted in Stanek 2011, vii; cf. Merrifield 2002). Lefebvre maintained that Castells failed to understand space.

40. Stuart Elden, for one, has repeatedly insisted on the importance of philosophy for understanding Lefebvre: "I begin with philosophy, because Lefebvre was first a philosopher, and thinking this through is essential to understanding both his Marxism and his work on everyday life, urban and rural sociology and politics" (Elden 2007, 188; see also 2001, 809; 2004, 6; Fraser 2008a).

41. "When they first coalesced as a group in 1924, they were searching for a philosophic and religious solution to the *inquiétude* plaguing French

intellectuals after the Great War. Worse still, they embraced mysticism, in an effort to understand the world they lived in, directly, immediately and totally" (Burkhard 2000, 14). "Their preoccupation with the abstracted universal consciousness was transformed but retained as an analytic focus on social alienation, then a barely articulated or defined concept within Marxist theoretical frameworks" (Burkhard 2000, 72).

42. See Elden (2004, 65–109, Chapter 2).

43. Most important, of course, is that Bergson's method and antiphilosophical stance encouraged this connection in principle (Fraser 2008a, 2010).

44. The posthumously published volume titled *Rhythmanalysis* pursues a method originally elaborated in the second and third volumes of the *Critique of Everyday Life* and was originally intended to be a fourth volume of the *Critique*. Also, bear in mind that "The relationship between the town and the countryside is, for Lefebvre, an historical relationship, with the mediating role being played by industrialization and the advance of technology" (Elden 2007, 103) and, moreover, that "Lefebvre's writings on cities are intricately entwined with his writings on the critique of the everyday life. More specifically yet, we must note that quotidian existence in the city must be properly understood in terms of his rhythmanalysis" (Mendieta 2008, 150). See also Moran, who notes that "the everyday offers a corrective to the spectacularizing discourse of modernity" (2004, 54).

45. "Everyday Life, instead, possessed a dialectical and ambiguous nature. On the one hand, it's the realm increasingly colonized by the commodity, and hence shrouded in all kinds of mystification, fetishism, and alienation... On the other hand, paradoxically, everyday life is likewise a primal site for meaningful social resistance... Thus, radical politics has to begin and end in everyday life, it can't do otherwise" (Merrifield 2002, 79).

46. This interesting quote comes from the back cover of the 2008 re-edition of the 1991 translation of the *Critique of Everyday Life* (vol. 1).

47. Among the many books that deal specifically with art and culture are "*Rabelais et l'émergence du capitalisme* (written 1949–53, published 1955), *Contribution à l'esthétique* (1953), *Musset* (1955), *Pignon* (1956), *Trois textes pour le théâtre* (1972), and *La Présence et l'absence* (1980)" (Léger 2006, 143).

48. Léger also writes: "Through the theory of 'moments,' Lefebvre developed a concept of art that is related to historical process and economic alienation, but which also, in its dependence on the material basis of everyday life, and its difference from other registers of social life, represents a disalienation of the familiar through the fulfillment of species being, that is, through the creative transformation of the everyday" (2006, 144); "Lefebvre's ideas on art are still of interest today in that they provide an approach to aesthetics which is materialist but non-reductive and which is able to account for specificities of time, place and subjectivity within cultural production" (2006, 144).

49. "Critical pedagogue Paolo Freire provides such a dynamic pedagogy through his denunciation of 'banking education' through which students

are envisioned as passive receptacles for deposits of knowledge made by their teachers. Education, he says, cannot be seen as 'a set of things, pieces of knowledge, that can be superimposed on or juxtaposed to the conscious body of the learners' (1970, 72; see also 1998). Likewise, explicitly engaging this tradition articulated by Freire in *Pedagogy of the Oppressed*, bell hooks (1994) (the lowercase moniker under which Gloria Watkins has published numerous books) has argued that education should be the 'practice of freedom'" (Fraser 2009a, 272).

50. For example, "Either we affirm the irreducibility of the urban phenomenon with respect to the fragmentary sciences taken together, as well as the science of 'man' and of 'society'—which is not without risk—or we identify mankind (in general), society (in general), or the urban phenomenon with the residual whole" (Lefebvre 2003a, 56).

51. David Harvey in essence applies this critique to his home discipline of geography: "But in fact the structure of thinking within Marxism generally is distressingly similar to that within bourgeois economics. The urbanists are viewed as specialists, while the truly significant core of macroeconomic Marxist theorizing lies elsewhere" (2012, 35).

52. Lefebvre is often attentive to the way formations of knowledge impact classroom practices, for example, "Paradoxically, but in retrospect quite understandably, the new enquiry was in France inaugurated by *pedagogical critique*. This critique related both to teaching methods and to the content which was taught" (1976, 51; also 51–53). He was outspoken, of course, on the dogmatic nature of party Marxism—he once remarked that "it is simple and easily taught … it steers clear of complex problems, this being precisely the aim and meaning of dogmatism" (quoted in Merrifield 2002, 79).

53. "The attempt to separate technical knowledge (the applied sciences) from knowledge in general, from basic research, from philosophy or literary criticism (for example), has never really been successful, for it is a separation which immediately sterilises applied knowledge, shrouding 'the system' in a quasi-metaphysical uncertainty (hence the resurgence of philosophy and religion) and weakening it crucially" (Lefebvre 1976, 26; also 47).

2 Urban Alienation and Cultural Studies: Henri Lefebvre's Recalibrated Marxism

1. The recent anthology of Lefebvre's essays titled *State, Space, World* (eds. Brenner and Elden, 2009, originally published 1964–1986) underscores the theorist's wide-ranging interests and the varied application of his work since the 1970s: "From those early discussions of Lefebvre's urban theory through the critical engagements with his approach to socio–spatial theory during the 1980s, to the more recent appropriations of his work in the context of debates on the condition of postmodernity, the body and sexuality, everyday life, the production of scale, urban and antiglobalization

struggles, the transformation of citizenship, and the right to the city, Lefebvre's writings have served as central reference points within a broad range of theoretical and political projects" (2009, 1).

2. Rob Shields's foundational *Lefebvre, Love & Struggle: Spatial Dialectics* (2005, originally published in 1999) pushes for a totalizing view of Lefebvre's work, one that has been quite lacking: "The greatest problem in understanding his work is that his theories on particular subjects have often been studied without reference to his other works" (2005, 1). Stuart Elden's comprehensive book *Understanding Henri Lefebvre: Theory and the Possible* also "attempts to show how his work can be conceptualized as a whole" (2004, 7). Readers may also consult the work of Andy Merrifield, who has provided a compellingly readable look at the broad range of Lefebvre's interests both in a chapter from *Metromarxism* (2002, Chapter 4) and in his somewhat more lengthy scholarly biography titled *Henri Lefebvre: A Critical Introduction* (2006).

3. Among other evidence, see also Brenner (2000); Brenner and Elden (2001, 2009); Elden (2001, 2004, 2006); Goonewardena (2005); Kipfer (2009); Simonsen (2005); as well as the recent re-publication of his *Critique of Everyday Life* by Verso (Lefebvre 1991b, 2002, 2005).

4. This view obtains also outside of the humanities, of course. Until this point, Lefebvre has been invoked in the pages of journals such as *Culture, Theory and Critique*, for example, only when critics want to point to the existence of many kinds of space (Ridanpää 2010, 51) or more specifically to invoke Lefebvre's famed spatial triad (Filipcevic 2010, 68, 74, 81–82, 87).

5. See, for example, Harvey (1989, 1990, 1996, 2000, 2009a); Soja (1996); Delgado Ruiz (1991, 1999, 2001, 2006, 2007a, 2007b).

6. Lefebvre remarked succinctly that "Time is distinguishable, but not separable from space" (1991a, 175), and he returns again and again in his works to the relationship between space and time (e.g., see also Lefebvre 2003a, 73–74). This emphasis in his work has been pointed out by Elden (2004, 170; also Fraser 2008a).

7. In fact, as readers may be aware, Lefebvre has had much to say on the issue of disciplinary knowledge (e.g., see Lefebvre 2003a; 1969). See this book's Introduction.

8. This notion is developed in various ways in Lefebvre (1991b, 2002, 2005, 2008); Lefebvre's invocation of the notion of the "colonization of daily life" (e.g., 2002, 11; see also 2005, 26) owes to the thought of Guy Debord, with whom he had a falling out: see also Debord (1995); Knabb (2006); Merrifield (2005).

9. Marx is dealt with in depth, for example, in Lefebvre (1976, 1982, 1988, 2008); and Lefebvre's recalibrated Marxism is the focus on the first chapter of the book by Elden (2004, 15–64). Elden echoes the body text quotation from Lefebvre (1976) in his statement that: "His is a Marxist approach certainly, but not merely a Marxist approach" (2004, 8). Lefebvre also writes: "In short, Marx's work is necessary but not sufficient to enable us

to understand our time, grasp events, and, if possible, guide them. This is nothing new, but it is worth recalling" (1969, 23).

10. This, of course, purposely works against the periodizing thesis that distances the young from the older Marx (see Elden 2004, 7, 16–17, 50n.15; on alienation, see also Elden 2004, 39–43; a concise treatment of this thesis appears in Kolakowski 2005, 215–219). Significantly, Lefebvre himself supported such a "total" or unifying perspective of Marx's work (e.g., Lefebvre 1969, 34). Also of interest is that the publication of Lefebvre's *Dialectical Materialism* (originally in French, 1939), in fact, contributed to the characterization of Marx as a theorist of alienation; see Elden (2004, 41) who quotes Anderson (1976, 51) and Judt (1986, 180).

11. Here, Lefebvre clearly conceives of his exploration of alienation as part of a new reading of Marx. "Marx tended to push the many forms of alienation to one side so as to give it one specific definition in terms of the extreme case he chose to study: the transformation of man's *activities* and relations into *things* by the action of economic *fetishes*, such as money, commodities and capital. Reduced to economic alienation within and by capitalism, alienation would disappear completely and in one blow, through and historical but unique act: the revolutionary action of the proletariat" (Lefebvre 2002, 207).

12. "John Moore the translator of *Critique de la vie quotidienne* into English, has noted that one contribution [of Lefebvre's] was to extend alienation from the domain of work in particular to everyday life in general" (Shields 2005, 40).

13. "Henri Lefebvre's humanistic Marxism highlights the importance of the felt experience of dullness, boredom and estrangement as a source of Utopian inspiration and revolutionary resolve" (Shields 2005, viii).

14. "Although conceptions of the everyday can be found in the work of Nietzsche, Simmel, the Surrealists, Lukács and Heidegger, Lefebvre sought to align the everyday with the notion of alienation rather than the banal or the trivial. The everyday in this sense becomes dialectically bound up with the potential for disalienation, for an opening onto new possibilities" (Léger 2006, 149).

15. Marx famously asserted that "Frequently the only possible answer is a critique of the question, and the only possible solution is to negate the question" (1973, 127).

16. In *Introduction to Modernity*, Lefebvre writes also of the ironic thought of Socrates at length, finding the occasion to celebrate that: "He says loud and clear that he does not know—or rather, that he knows that he does not know...The Socratic ironist does not choose between 'knowing everything' and 'knowing nothing.' He knows something, and first and foremost that he knows nothing; therefore he knows what 'knowing' is" (1995, 10–11).

17. *Capital* continues: "Exchange value appears first of all as the quantitative relation, the proportion, in which use-values of one kind exchange for use-values of another kind. This relation changes constantly with time and

place. Hence exchange-value appears to be something accidental and purely relative, and consequently an intrinsic value, i.e. an exchange-value that is inseparably connected with the commodity, inherent in it, seems a contradiction in terms" (Marx 1977, 126–127). Of course, this is just the beginning of a much more nuanced discussion. See also Harvey (2010, 17).

18. "Money, currency, commodities, capital, are nothing more than relations between human beings (between 'individual,' qualitative human tasks). And yet these relations take on the appearance and the form of things external to human beings. The appearance becomes reality" (Lefebvre 1991b, 178). Harvey's comments on Marx's mobilization here of the distance between appearance and essence are, pardon the pun, *essential* (2010, 15).

19. See also *A Companion to Marx's Capital* (Harvey 2010, 15–53).

20. "More generally, at certain stages of its development, human activity spawns relations which masquerade as *things*" (Lefebvre 1991b, 179); "The theory of festishism demonstrates the *economic, everyday* basis of the *philosophical* theories of mystification and alienation. We say that goods are sold, that they are 'alienated'" (Lefebvre 1991b, 179).

21. Much could be written on how capitalist reification and alienation make a certain social use of what is also a biological evolution of mind—which according to Henri Bergson has developed by molding itself to the seemingly discrete forms of matter (*Creative Evolution*; also Fraser 2010). My own thought is that, in such an analysis, this correspondence between mind and matter would not necessarily need to be taken as philosophical escapism or as an ideology that distracts from the structuring role of relations of capital—and that it could be carried out much in the same way as Lefebvre has himself borrowed many insights from Bergson and disalienated them by reconciling them with political and economic analyses that are absent in his arguable influence (Fraser 2008a).

22. "A hundred years after Marx, the word 'production' has lost any clearly defined referential, and is used to mean production of whatever you like: production of meaning, signs, discourse, ideologies, theory, writing, literature, and even a kind of twice removed 'production of production.' . . . The more the content of the concept is diluted and gets lost in abstraction, the more profound the concept (which actually ceases to be such) appears to be" (Lefebvre 1976, 22).

23. To take one example, see *The Right to the City* (Lefebvre 1996, 177; see all of that work's Chapter 17, "Theses on the City, the Urban and Planning"). In *Everyday Life in the Modern World*, Lefebvre references the "doublefaceted proposition: *industrialization and urbanization*" (2007, 47); also "Industrialization can only find its fulfillment in urbanization—carried out according to the *idea* of the City and of urban society" (original emphasis; 2007, 134; see also 195).

24. As Harvey notes, urbanization played a role even in the development of industrial capitalism: he quotes Marx on urbanization, which "had to appear on the historical stage before the standard form of circulation of

capital through production could begin (*Capital* 1: 165)," and emphasizes that "A built environment potentially supportive of capitalist production, consumption, and exchange had to be created before capitalism won direct control over immediate production and consumption" (Harvey 1989, 24).

25. Harvey continues: "Again, the fiction of a national economy takes precedence because that is where the data can most easily be found and to be fair, where some of the major policy decisions are taken. The role of the property market in creating the crisis conditions of 2007–09, and its aftermath of unemployment and austerity (much of it administered at the local and municipal level), is not well understood, because there has been no serious attempt to integrate an understanding of processes of urbanization and built-environment formation into the general theory of the laws of motion of capital. As a consequence, many Marxist theorists, who love crises to death, tend to treat the recent crash as an obvious manifestation of their favored vision of the Marxist crisis theory (be it falling rates of profit, underconsumption, or whatever)" (2012, 35).

26. Moreover, as discussed earlier, Lefebvre's work itself offers a perspective on culture that is much more nuanced than Harvey's. More on this anon.

27. In Lefebvrian terms, strictly speaking (returning to his primary distinction between the city and the urban), it is proper to say that while our essence is not, in fact, urbanized, it is in a sense urban—a term that emphasizes potential and possibility over the exploitation, humiliation, and misery of the former.

28. For a critique of the limits of periodization, see Jameson's *The Political Unconscious* (1981, 27).

29. By this I mean to argue against an antiquated position, one that nevertheless remains entrenched in some language and literature departments and (incorrectly) views the move beyond textual analysis as a threat to the humanities themselves. Such views are usually found where there is skepticism regarding cultural studies research and are, lamentably, not all that uncommon. The opportunity is for humanists to internalize a lesson that has been expressed succinctly by Gilles Deleuze and Félix Guattari: "We will never ask what a book means, as signified or signifier; we will not look for anything to understand in it. We will ask what it functions with" (*A Thousand Plateaus*, 2002, 4). This quotation fits best in an endnote so as to avoid a more concerted introduction to Deleuze's work that might potentially be distracting. Readers may be interested to consider the degree to which Bergson's philosophy forms a common ground for approaching the work of both Deleuze and Lefebvre (see Fraser 2010).

30. See, for example, *The Production of Space*, where Lefebvre writes of "The current transformation of the perimeter of the Mediterranean into a leisure-oriented space for industrialized Europe" (1991a, 58; see also 122); that in spaces of leisure "a veritable feast of authenticity awaits the tourist" (84); that social space is "consumed (in such forms as travel, tourism or leisure activities) as a vast commodity" (349); and that in the twentieth

century "tourism and leisure become major areas of investment and profitability" (353). See also, of course, the *Critique* (vols. 1–3).

31. "By ignoring aesthetics, Marxists have left out the driving force behind much modern Marxist theory" (Lefebvre 1988, 83).

32. "For many Marxists, it seems that art is only a distraction, a form of entertainment, at best a superstructural form or a simple means of political efficacy. It is necessary to remind these people that great works of art deeply touch, even disturb, the roots of human existence... The highest mission of art is to *metamorphose* the real. Practical actions, including techniques, modify the everyday, the artwork transfigures it" (Lefebvre 1988, 82–83).

33. One scholar writes that Lefebvre "detested compartmentalization" (Merrifield 2006, xxxiii); see also Lefebvre (2003a) for a more thorough analysis of the fragmented nature of bourgeois knowledge and its functioning as ideology.

34. "Man is not just economic, or biological, or physiochemical, etc. And yet he is all of this. This is what makes him the total man. From each science, from each partial method of research, total humanism borrows elements for analysis and orientation (in varying proportions according to the moments and the problems...). The most extensive method of all, the dialectic, is the only one capable of organizing the 'synthesis' of all these elements and of extracting from them *the idea of man*" (Lefebvre 1991b, 159).

35. Consider that Richard T. LeGates and Frederic Stout, the editors of *The City Reader* (third edition), go so far as to say that, "Lewis Mumford's magisterial *The Culture of Cities* (New York: Harcourt Brace, 1938) was the first and remains the best book on the culture of cities" (2005, 10).

36. For example, Mumford's distinction between "producing cities and consuming cities: between the Five Towns, Pittsburgh, Lyons, Turin, Essen, on one hand, and London, New York, Paris, Berlin, Rome and their subsidiary pleasure resorts, on the other" (1970, 224) is insufficient not merely because of subsequent changes that fall under the perhaps inadequate moniker of postindustrialization but also because of the "colonization of everyday life" theorized by Lefebvre (and simultaneously by Debord).

37. See also his essay "What Is the City?" (originally from 1937) where he states that "The city in its complete sense, then, is a geographic plexus, an economic organization, an institutional process, a theater of social action, and an aesthetic symbol of collective unity. The city fosters art and is art; the city creates the theater and is the theater. It is in the city, the city as theater, that man's more purposeive activities are focused, and work out, through conflicting and cooperating personalities, events, groups, into more significant culminations" (Mumford 2005, 93–94; this was incorporated into *The Culture of Cities*, and the above quotation appears on Mumford 1970, 480).

38. See "Rise and Fall of Megalopolis" in Mumford (1970, 223–299), where the word "decentralization" is often used (e.g., 235, 297) as part of Mumford's insistence on "laying down the foundations for a new regional

order, based on the culture of life" (297). Also "The Regional Framework of Civilization" in Mumford (1970, 300–347), where he continues to reflect on "the human failure of metropolitan civilization" (300).

39. To mention just one brief example, see the section titled "The Non-Plan of the Non-City" (1970, 183–190), where Mumford emphasizes that "the reckless extension of the paleotechnic town was accompanied by the progressive destruction of open spaces" (1970, 186), "street planning was largely decorative" (187), "All over the Western World during the nineteenth century new cities were founded and old ones extended themselves along the lines I have just described" (187), "belief in unlimited growth was pervasive" (188), "these plans carried the system if absolutist abstractions even farther away from reality" (189), and concludes that "In short: as practical urban design, the dominant method of planning was simply a bad dream. Millions of people are still living in the midst of blighted areas, destitute of civic comeliness, paying bitter tribute day by day to the collective hallucinations that governed the layout of the paleotechnic town" (190).

40. "In recent years, culture has also become a more explicit site of conflicts over social differences and urban fears" (Zukin 1995, 2).

41. Mumford's is a call for "rational" city planning (1970, 9) whose time has come. As he writes in the Introduction to the 1970 re-edition of *the Culture of Cities*: "We have now reached a point where these fresh accumulations of historical insight and scientific knowledge are ready to flow over into social life, to mold anew the forms of cities, to assist in the transformation of both the instruments and the goals of our civilization" (1970, 10).

42. "Although Lefebvre perhaps arrived at an understanding of the life of city streets quite similar to that of Jacobs on his own terms and around the same time (Merrifield 2006, 64; Fraser 2009a), he nonetheless references her in his foundational works *The Urban Revolution* (2003) and *The Production of Space* (1991), thus making it clear that he is aware of and sympathetic to her contribution to urban studies" (Fraser 2012a, 27). That essay also provides two quotations from Lefebvre regarding Jacobs (see Lefebvre 2003a, 19; 1991a, 364).

43. Take, for example, the author's mention that "the ideas put forward in 'The Culture of Cities' continued to have an indirect effect upon the design of the British New Towns from 1947 onward, and had a direct effect upon the rebuilding of Coventry, not least its Shopping Center" (1970, xi), but that "more fashionable thought" grounded in modernist principles (Corbusier's radiant city) won out. His ideas on cities are quite lucid, even if incomplete from the present perspective. Zukin's book does not dialogue explicitly with planning traditions, but does deal with them indirectly and more concretely (in place) than does Mumford (see Zukin 1995, 7).

44. For example, "I began this work by assuming that the meanings of culture are unstable. I am not saying that the term 'culture' has many meanings. Anthropologists can count as many definitions of culture as the French make cheeses. I mean, rather, that culture is a fluid process of forming,

expressing and enforcing identities of individuals, social groups, or spatially constructed communities" (Zukin 1995, 288).

45. Another important, but generalized, similarity is the call to return from abstraction to life itself. Nevertheless, Mumford's call differs from Lefebvre's substantially in that, while he recognizes the material force of capitalism to disfigure cities in the industrial era, he paradoxically considers capital to be an abstraction: "Unfortunately, the fashionable political philosophies of the past century are but of small help in defining this new task: they dealt with legal abstractions, like Individual and State, with cultural abstractions, like Humanity, the Nation, the Folk, or with bare economic abstractions like the Capitalist Class or the Proletariat" (Mumford 1970, 9). Thus, in essence, his belief that capital is ideology perpetuates the ideology of capital. Although he deals with capitalism somewhat rationally, in his massive text he mentions Marx by name only once (in the context of child labor, p. 384) and capital/capitalism only a few unremarkable times.

46. Lefebvre's text draws attention to the sounds and smells of the city to counteract a visual bias of much thinking about the city. In addition, the future problem posed by Mumford—"One of the major tasks of the twentieth century is the re-settlement of the planet" (1970, 388)—is potentially answered by Lefebvre's reading of capitalism's twentieth-century occupation ("producing a space," Lefebvre 1976, 21).

47. In addition to invoking a generalized notion of human culture (above in text), he also makes universalizing statements, proposing, for example, that we pay more heed to "essential human values" over "the will-to-power and the will-to-profits" (Mumford 1970, 9); or that we create a "new set of working institutions, more consonant with a humane scheme of values" (391); the "human impulse to create everlasting monuments" (433).

48. The closest he gets to when he talks of dissociation (Mumford 1970, 8), which is, of course, alienation without its proper grounding in Marxian terms.

49. Note that one can see in Williams a tendency, similar to that of Lefebvre, to criticize a view that fragments "the social formation into relatively autonomous levels" and to emphasize the Marxian notion of totality as a way of disalienating us from the "culture"/"society" distinction (see Grossberg 2010a, 19). It is important to note that by urban context I mean to differentiate neither between urb and suburb, nor even between city and country (which as Williams 1975 notes are held in a dialectical tension; see also Jacobs 1970, 1984). As much urban theory has asserted over the last hundred years, the growth of cities and urban populations has resulted in a sea change of sorts in which consciousness has itself become urbanized. While such a recognition is a common element of now classic works on the urban (Simmel's "The Metropolis and Mental Life" from 1903; Louis Wirth's "The Urban as Way of Life" from 1938), it has also been reconsituted within Marxian frameworks, notably by Lefebvre but also by

Harvey's insistence on the twin processes of the "urbanization of capital" and the "urbanization of consciousness" (Harvey 1989, Chapters 1 and 8). The aforementioned classic article written by Wirth, a noted figure of the Chicago School of Urban Sociology, serves even today as a reminder that "The degree to which the contemporary world may be said to be "urban" is not fully or accurately measured by the proportion of the total population living in cities" (1938, 2).

50. At the beginning of his work *Sociedades Movedizas/Mobile Societies*, Lefebvrian urban theorist Delgado Ruiz effectively addresses this very need, calling for a scholarly reconciliation of what he calls "urban culture" with the "culture of urbanism" (2007a, 11).

51. Keeping in mind, of course, the Lefebvrian conceit that alienation and disalienation are aspects of a dialectical movement, Lefebvre writes that "Too often 'disalienation' has been taken as an absolute, and as the end of alienation in general"; "absolute alienation and absolute disalienation are equally inconceivable"; "alienation is not a 'state,' any more than disalienation is. Both are conceived as a movement" (2002, 207). Also, significantly as regards the risks of yielding unchanging critical definitions and assessments, "the 'alienation/disalienation' dialectical movement enables us to determine a structure within concrete, changing situations. Thus a disalienation can be alienating, and vice versa" (Lefebvre 2002, 208).

3   The Work (of Art): Putting Art at the Service of the Urban

1. As Andrew Hemingway writes in the Introduction to the anthology *Marxism and the History of Art*, "Two widely used anthologies published in the 1990s both assume that [Marxist art history] is obsolete" (2006, 1). Those anthologies are *Art History and its Methods*, edited by Eric Fernie; and *The Art of Art History*, edited by Donald Preziozi.

2. Although—as discussed throughout and at the end of this chapter— Lefebvre's reading (and Raymond Williams' reading) of Marx asserted the insufficiency of his thought for cultural or artistic matters—Chapters 4 and 5 of *Marx's Lost Aesthetics* by Margaret A. Rose point to the "ideal of a non-alienated 'artistic' form of production" as elaborated by Marx in his 1844 *Manuscripts* (Rose 1984, 79). The Lang and Williams anthology *Marxism & Art* does well in emphasizing that "a precise definition of Marxist aesthetics or Marxist criticism is impossible...Thus, there can be no such thing as *the* aesthetics of Marxism" (original emphasis; Lang and Forrest 1972, 13).

3. "Este libro no se dirige sino a quienes buscan a tientas un camino nuevo" (Lefebvre 2006b, 230).

4. "Pero los artistas y el arte forman parte hoy en día de la industria cultural, producción especializada a gran escala con un amplio mercado. La gran mayoría de los artistas juegan con la ambigüedad: 'obra-cosa-producto' y no tienen ningún interés en dilucidar las diferencias" (Lefebvre 2006b, 229–230).

5. "la distinción entre la cosa, el producto, la obra, se remonta a muy lejos si se sabe mirar"; "a) la mayoría, si no todos los filósofos, prefirieron un término, lo valoraron y lo elevaron a lo absoluto, de tal modo que: b) los tres términos en presencia no están todavía bien situados y restituidos después de esos análisis reductores" (Lefebvre 2006b, 234–235).

6. "c) no hay que establecer entre ellos ninguna separación ni discontinuidad" (Lefebvre 2006b, 235).

7. Lefebvre mentions that "Christianity distinguished between what was provided by nature, what came from humankind, what followed from God" (2006b, 234). He here also references the Kantian inheritance that distinguishes the thing in itself from the thing as it appears (noumenon/phenomenon) and notes that the thing as it appears to us ("cosa para nosotros") "is the product of an activity"—our use of the faculties of sensibility and of understanding (2006b, 235). Lefebvre's distrust of transcendent models of experience suggests, however, that he does not embrace this view and uses it merely for clarification of a historical chain of beliefs. Turning to the view he advances of the thing as part of the posthumously published *Rhythmanalaysis*: "*Things* matter little; the *thing* is only a metaphor, divulged by discourse, divulging representations that conceal the production of repetitive time and space (which the *thing* symbolises materially)" (2006a, 7).

8. It makes sense to mention here the more sophisticated if still similar understanding of nature vs. second nature, by which Lefebvre means that "Human praxis has produced a second nature which has become superimposed upon the first, penetrating it, covering it, clothing it" (1995, 89; see also 2006b, 220–221).

9. In *The Production of Space*, Lefebvre writes: "The successful unmasking of *things* in order to reveal (social) relationships—such was Marx's great achievement, and, whatever political tendencies may call themselves Marxist, it remains the most durable accomplishment of Marxist thought" (1991a, 81).

10. In such a way, he continues, that "d) el espacio (por ejemplo) es producido por la actividad económica y social pero trabajado por los proyectos arquitecturales y urbanísticos" (Lefebvre 2006b, 235). Moreover, the concepts of *work* and *value* in fact coincide for Lefebvre, begging the question of how value is produced and utilized in society (229).

11. "*El producto y la obra*. Las diferencias aparecen, sin romper el nexo. Producción y creación se distinguen considerablemente, pero la creación implica-explica la producción y el trabajo productivo" (Lefebvre 2006b, 267; see also 268).

12. "El capitalismo y el estatismo modernos han aplastado la capacidad creadora de las obras. Este aplastamiento acompaña el de lo social, atrapado entre lo económico y lo político. Inmensas fuerzas creadoras son rechazadas, marginadas. Contra ellas se establecen y se fortalecen las potencias dominantes. La estructura económica y política, a la vez opresiva y petrificada, estimula la producción y los productos; sustituye la capacidad

creadora por representaciones: la creatividad, el inventario, la exposición, el museo generalizado" (Lefebvre 2006b, 235–236).

13. "El producto se separa de la obra, la desplaza, la remplaza por sofistica-ciones técnicas. Relegadas a las periferias, creyendo a veces encontrar allí su lugar favorable, las fuerzas creadoras se condenan al fracaso: impoten-cia, esterilidad" (Lefebvre 2006b, 235–236).

14. "*because* of its connection": this is what routinely happens, as David Harvey makes clear in his work on 'The Art of Rent' (a subtitle in both Harvey 2012, 2001; the latter in Chapter 18). For example, Harvey writes that "By now critics will complain at the seeing economic reductionism of the argument. I make it seem, they will say, as if capitalism produces local cultures, shapes aesthetic meanings, and so dominates local initia-tives as to preclude the development of any kind of difference that is not directly subsumed within the circulation of capital. I cannot prevent such a reading, but this would be a perversion of my message. For what I hope to have shown by invoking the concept of monopoly rent within the logic of capital accumulation is that capital has ways to appropriate and extract surpluses from local differences, local cultural variations, and aesthetic meanings of no matter what origin ... But monopoly rent is a contradictory form ... It also leads to the valuation of uniqueness, authenticity, particu-larity, originality, and all manner of other dimensions to social life that are inconsistent with the homogeneity presupposed by commodity produc-tion" (2012, 109–110). See the edited volume *Marxism and Urban Culture* (Fraser 2014) for an introduction that delves into this text and a Foreword written by Andy Merrifield.

15. "Aun si hay mercado, la obra *escapa a lo económico de manera (siempre) ficticia-real*. El artista se realiza y realiza la obra a pesar de lo económico, lo social y lo político ... Así, *la obra restituye el valor de uso*" (original empha-sis; Lefebvre 2006b, 251). Lefebvre's remarks on kitsch—which he sees as a mixture of product and work (or in my view a work reclaimed by the mar-ket, degraded into product)—are also interesting, although they point to the need for an even more dynamic model of the "product–work" tension: "La obra difiere de lo *kitch* que no se separa ni del trabajo ni del mercado, que es por lo tanto un producto, o al menos una mezcla entre el producto y la obra" (original emphasis; Lefebvre 2006b, 251–252).

16. "¿Puede la obra, realidad y concepto nacidos del humanismo, cobrar figura nueva? Si es así, su concepto puede marcar la abertura de ese nuevo camino" (Lefebvre 2006b, 230). Of course as would be expected, Lefebvre asserts that the notion of the work is "necessary" but "not sufficient" (recalling his approach to Marxism itself; Lefebvre 1976, 1988).

17. "Lo individual es obra en el sentido más amplio. Como lo social y como la civilización. Eso fue lo que reconoció nuestro siglo XVIII. Estas obser-vaciones preparan y amplían el concepto de la obra y su teoría evitando reducirlos al arte, que sin embargo sigue siendo el caso ejemplar, el que hay que mantener en la meditación" (Lefebvre 2006b, 238).

18. Although he does not dialogue extensively with Lefebvre, it is worth noting that the notion of the city as a work of art in a not-un-Lefebvrian sense appears also in Alan Blum's *The Imaginative Structure of the City* (2003, 5). The present book is in fact linked to the questions Blum articulates there—"If the city is a work of art that is created and renewed in a constant struggle with the life that reminds its desire for the finality of truth of its groundessness, how can this work of art presence, how can the city appear as if a creative and vital set of practices?" (2003, 5); "If cities impress us as both material and ideal, as both matter and spirit, can we begin to unravel this relationship to make it more intelligible?" (2003, 189)—but in a different way. The major similarity across Blum's perspective, Lefebvre's perspective, and my own is that the notion of the city as a work of art is ultimately a way of viewing the city as totality (Blum 2003, 75).

19. "[We must also consider space the world over from the triple point of view of the thing (the land); the *product* (the division of labor on a planetary scale, the flows of exchange and communication, strategies, etc.); and finally as a *work* (urban centers; architectural and spatial projects, peripheral pre- and postcapitalist activities, etcetera)] También habrá que considerar el espacio mundial desde el triple punto de vista de la cosa (la tierra); del *producto* (de la división del trabajo a escala planetaria, de los flujos de intercambio y de comunicaciones, de las estrategias, etc.); y por último como *obra* (los centros urbanos, los proyectos arquitecturales y espaciales, las actividades periféricas pre y poscapitalistas, etcétera)" (Lefebvre 2006b, 238–39); "[A society is composed of concrete abstractions, of real fictions, of values rendered efficient and practical, blended together in a space. It is a construction, a construction, and as such a work] Una sociedad se compone de abstracciones concretas, de ficciones reales, de valores vueltos eficaces y prácticos, incorporados en un espacio. Es una construcción, un edificio, por lo tanto una obra" (Lefebvre 2006b, 242); "[No work—neither a work of art properly speaking nor the city and second nature, etc.—can be realized without bringing together [all of] the elements and moments, without constituting a totality] Ninguna obra—ni la obra de arte propiamente dicha ni la ciudad y la segunda naturaleza, etc.—puede realizarse sin reunir todos los elementos y momentos, sin constituir una totalidad" (Lefebvre 2006b, 244).

20. Lefebvre advocates: "mostrando cómo el arte, el proyecto, la obra, parten de la vivencia (la poesía, la música, el teatro, la novela, etc.) integrándole el saber y no al revés" (2006b, 237; see also 165).

21. "La teoría de la obra implica un respeto que tiene un alcance ético. Las obras, al igual que la vivencia, no deben tocarse sino con tiento y precauciones. Por lo tanto, nuestra teoría no se propone dar lecciones. Nada de estética normativa y pedagógica. Hay que elucidar una práctica creadora" (Lefebvre 2006b, 238).

22. Consider, for example, Lefebvre's rejection of Hegel's "system" as outlined in Schmid (2008, 32); and his approach to everyday life as "non-systemic"

in the words of Nadal-Melsió (2008, 171). This reaction against system is also an attribute to which I have devoted much attention in previous works by situating Lefebvre in relation to Bergson's own rejection of system more generally—see Fraser (2008a, 2010, 2011a,).

23. One can turn to any reader of literary theory to (re)familiarize oneself with the historical deployment of the specialized notion of "literariness"—and the resulting arguments over to what degree (if at all) this notion is compatible with social realities pertaining either to the time of the biographical author or that of the embodied critic (e.g., Selden 1986; Altamiranda 2001).

24. Williams continues, explaining that this distinction is inadequate for "advanced capitalism" (1977, 93).

25. Certainly culture was not untheorized by Marxist critics, as can be grasped most easily by reading one of many anthologies on the subject—for example, *Marxism and Art: Writings in Aesthetics and Criticism* (eds. B. Lang and F. Williams, 1972)—but the point that Lefebvre makes (among others), in general terms, is that Marxist theories of art suffered from their connections with specific political systems and sometimes also by valuing social realism to the detriment of other artistic strategies.

26. Clearly the theory of "art as reflection" is also more broadly accepted even by non-Marxian literary/art scholars.

27. Cf. Lefebvre (2006b, 268): "La obra hace corresponder una totalidad presente, actual con la totalidad rota o ausente; su relación no puede reducirse a un 'reflejo,' a una 'expresión,' como tampoco a una intención significante [The work creates correespondence between a present, current totality, and a broken or absent totality; its relation cannot be reduced to a 'reflection,' or to an 'expression,' nor even to a signifying intention]."

28. The full quotation is worthy of note (see Williams 1977, 99).

29. The full quotations are worthy of note (see Williams 1977, 150).

30. "Yet it is clear, historically, that the definition of 'aesthetic' response is an affirmation of 'creative imagination,' of certain human meanings and values which a dominant social system reduced and even tried to exclude. Its history is in large part a protest against the forcing of all experience into instrumentality ('utility'), and of all things into commodities" (Williams 1977, 151).

31. As Williams makes clear, "Literary theory cannot be separated from cultural theory, though it may be distinguished within it. This is the central challenge of any social theory of culture" (1977, 145).

32. "En cambio, el artista, el creador (no el productor) parte de la vivencia. Volvamos ahora a esta proposición para profundizarla y desarrollarla" (Lefebvre 2006b, 246). Williams himself interrogates the notion of creativity also in the last section of *Marxism and Literature* and suggests—among other things—that the creation of literary characters is not a move away from but rather a move toward what he calls "known persons" (1977, 208), a notion that is now wholly incompatible with Lefebvre's framework. This section is discussed further below.

33. "El creador de obras—entre las cuales la obra de arte, aunque hipercompleja, brinda el caso más fácilmente observable—no permancece en la vivencia; no la habita, no se queda en ella mucho tiempo, no se hunde en el flujo y lo vago. Cuando esto sucede, no hay obra, tan sólo gritos inarticulados, suspiros de dolor o de placer. El creador de obras halla en la vivencia la inspiración inicial, el impulso original y vital. Regresa a ella, la 'expresa' con las contradicciones y conflictos subyacentes, pero necesita emerger y más aún, asimilar el saber" (Lefebvre 2006b, 246).

34. One need not turn to Henri Bergson—Lefebvre's arguable precursor—to understand why this is so, for Lefebvre's own work makes this clear, and his "complex and open" definition of Marxism (Lefebvre 1988) indicates yet another source. Nevertheless, this is a connection I outline extensively elsewhere (Fraser 2008a, 2010).

35. "Las capacidades, obras en potencia, dejan de ser creadoras cuando se vuelven autónomas; y no pueden más que producir y reproducir las condiciones de su autonomía, volviendo a ésta cada vez más real, o sea cada vez más destructora" (Lefebvre 2006b, 244).

36. Lo que sólo *es* económico, tecnológico, lúdico, cotidiano, etc., no puede salir de las representaciones y de los productos, y se aparta de la obra" (original emphasis; Lefebvre 2006b, 244).

37. Gaia has attended the Maryland Institute College of Art, and interested readers can see a post on the blog treehuggingurbanism.wordpress.com—not Gaia's—for more information and images of his work.

38. The blogger who runs treehuggingurbanism.wordpress.com shares her name only as Megan. The Howard Street image of Harry Weinberg is available on her blog.

39. Williams's remarks on writing are worth consulting (1977, 211–212). On the whole, Williams seems to be much more skeptical than Lefebvre regarding creativity—suggesting its connections with mysticism (1977, 208).

40. "Así, el creador de obras realiza una doble creación: la de un saber por una vivencia, la de una vivencia por un saber. Lo cual excluye cualquier expropiación" (Lefebvre 2006b, 246).

41. "La obra de arte y el artista se proponen exaltarla, incluso transfigurarla [la vivencia]" (Lefebvre 2006b, 247).

42. "Esto: una totalidad anteriormente presente voló en pedazos; un centro invisible, acaso por ser 'espiritual' cedió su lugar a múltiples centros parciales; el libre juego de las representaciones y de las manipulaciones sustituyó la influencia decisiva de lo *civil*, que a su vez había remplazado lo religioso. Para ser más explícitos, una multitud de capacidades y potencias—una antiguas y otras más recientes—*se volvieron autónomas*, cada una yendo por su lado, afirmándose por su propia cuenta, imponiéndose o pretendiendo imponerse a las demás y totalizarse por su propia fuerza. Enumeremos esas capacidades y actividades. Lo económico se dice importante e incluso preponderante con los grandes ingleses Smith y Ricardo: luego Marx lo dice determinante. Lo *político* y luego lo *estatal* se afirman como la última y

suprema forma de lo absoluto desde Hegel hasta Stalin. La ciencia y el saber se autoproclaman *verdaderos* y apoderados de la verdad. El arte se hipostasia en "arte por el arte" y, más tarde, en arte abstracto" (original emphasis; Lefebvre 2006b, 240); also, "Nosotros (modernos) hemos asistido a esa fragmentación sin comprenderla a no ser por sus efectos tardíos" (Lefebvre 2006b, 242).

43. On the right to the city, see Lefebvre (1996, 173–174).

44. Fredric Jameson's view as outlined in *Postmodernism* suggests that he would be dismissive of Lefebvre's invocation of this Marxian discourse on nonalienated artistic production: "It used to be affirmed that art or the aesthetic in our time offered the closest accessible analogy to, constituted the most adequate symbolic experience of, a nonalienated labor otherwise unimaginable for us. This proposition in its turn derived from the preindustrial speculations of German idealist philosophy, where the experience of play offered a similar *analogon* to a condition in which the tensions between work and freedom, science and ethical imperatives, might be overcome.There are, however, good reasons why these propositions about hints, anticipations, or symbolic experiences of nonalienated labor should no longer be persuasive. For one thing, the very experience of art itself today is alienated and made 'other' and inaccessible to too many people whether it is a question of high art or of mass culture ... Specialization ... characterizes both" (1999, 146–147).

45. The full quotation is enlightening: "Although Marx had spoken of a future form of non-alienated labour in terms of artistic activity in his *Economic and Philosophic Manuscripts* of 1844, he had not yet offered a fully developed analysis of art as a form of economic production subject to the demands—and alienations—of other forms of production. As seen in the last chapter, the ideal of a non-alienated 'artistic' form of production functions for Marx in his 1844 *Manuscripts*, in contrast to his antagonist Adam Smith, as an as yet unrealised alternative to the economically productive— and alienated—forms of labour encouraged by industrial capitalism. In contrast, further, to Kant and Schiller, existing art did not for Marx represent an 'Ideal' separate from and transcending the real world of economic production, but a product of the same alienating conditions under which economic production has taken place. The liberation of the sense from their state of alienation is thus a problem which for Marx remains attached to that of ending the alienation of labour, and, as just seen, receives as little solution as that other problem in the *Manuscripts* as we now have them" (Rose 1984, 79).

46. Lefebvre does mention Marx's 1844 *Manuscripts*, in *La présence et l'absence* (2006b, 161–162).

47. "Se libra de la división del trabajo, aunque resulta de un trabajo. Por esta razón, no es un producto. El trabajo creador parece (ficticia-realmente) liberado de las coacciones, de los límites, de las separaciones. Aparentemente el artista hace todo por sí mismo; domina su tiempo y su espacio, por lo

tanto a través de la obra el espacio y el tiempo de todos. Trabaja (mucho, a veces sin descanso) sin que parezca que trabaje (como el poeta); actúa en un espacio de representaciones que no lo ata ni arrastra a una superficie ilusoria. La obra parece 'producir' su tiempo, su espacio, su afirmación y su fuerza" (Lefebvre 2006b, 251).

48. "In these terms, art is the product of a specific kind of work that characteristically struggles against the division of labour in an attempt to grasp the 'total' content of life and of social activity. This same struggle marks the relations of production, and the conditions of aesthetic production, as the site of alienation. Just as art's autonomy developed as a consequence of the commodification of cultural production, revolutionary art is the consciousness of this specialisation and separation of the artist from the general social activity of the age. Art is a specialised activity that resists specialisation. The artist struggles to overcome the impoverishing aspects of alienation in the process of participating in social life, and by adapting elements of play and fantasy to the elaboration of the language of art" (Léger 2006, 151; who cites Lefebvre's *Contribution à l'estétique* [1953], 40 [Paris Editions Socials]).

49. "Ninguna obra—ni la obra de arte propiamente dicha, ni la ciudad y la segunda naturaleza etc.—puede realizarse sin reunir todos los elementos y momentos, sin constituir una totalidad . . . Lo que sólo *es* económico, tecnológico, lúdico, cotidiano, etc., no puede salir de las representaciones y de los productos y se aparta de la obra. Ésta tiene 'condiciones' económicas y políticas pero explicarla por tal o cual de esas condiciones, es un esquema simplista y empobrecedor. La obra implica el juego y lo que está en juego pero es algo más y es otra cosa que la suma de esos elementos, de esos recursos, de esas condiciones y circunstancias. Propone una forma, que tiene un contenido multiforme—sensorial, sensual, intelectual—con predominio de tal o cual matiz de la sensualidad o de la sensibilidad, de tal o cual sentido, de tal o cual técnica o ideología, pero sin que ese predominio aplaste los demás aspectos o momentos" (Lefebvre 2006b, 244).

50. The full quotation is worth consultation (see Lefebvre 1991b, 199).

51. "Only the expression of the city as a work of art, in its blending of *praxis*, *poiesis*, and *techne*, can recover totality as its content-form. The realization of a non-philosophical totality in Lefebvre is always predicated on the overcoming of specialization, of the science of the fragment" (Nadal-Melsió 2008, 171).

52. "El carácter simultáneo de la obra fue estudiado entre otras cosas a propósito de la ciudad (*cf. El derecho a la ciudad*, p. 102). La forma urbana se caracteriza por el encuentro y la reunión de todo lo que constituye una sociedad, productos y obras. En este sentido, la ciudad fue y sigue siendo la obra suprema, la obra de las obras. De ahí la generalización de su rasgo esencial. No hay ciudad que no se presente como simultaneidad percibida desde lo alto de las torres, de las colinas y montañas, desde un avión, y que no se figure espacialmente en la trama de las calles y avenidas" (Lefebvre 2006,

261). This last sentence, of course, resonates with the views of the city viewed from above as simultaneity, structure, and/or abstraction evoked by Roland Barthes (1979), Michel de Certeau (1988), and David Harvey (1989). Philosophy is also, for Lefebvre, an oeuvre, with all that implies: "Philosophy (with art and works of art), a supreme *oeuvre*, says what is *appropriation*, not the technical mastery of material nature which produces products and exchange values" (1996, 175–76). In addition, of course, the city and the work of art are both objects of consumption: "Works of art and styles re distributed for prompt consumption and towns are devoured with such a remarkable show of pleasure that it seems to denote outstandingly imperative needs and frustrations" (Lefebvre 2007, 108).

53. Note that while Fredric Jameson remains skeptical of the notions of play and spontaneity in *Postmodernism* (1999)—coming to emphasize how these notions have been capitalized upon and appropriated by what is effectively the capitalist production of space through architecture and built environment (what he appropriately refers to as "the cultural logic of capitalism")—Harvey nevertheless echoes Lefebvre's position to a degree. In *Spaces of Hope*, he writes: "The lessons to be learned from the separate histories of utopianisms of spatial form and temporal process must not, however, be abandoned. Indeed there are even further insights to be had from a closer analysis of them. From the former, the idea of imaginative spatial play to achieve specific social and moral goals can be converted into the idea of potentially endlessly open experimentation with the possibilities of spatial forms" (2000, 182). Harvey makes explicit reference to Lefebvre's work here and pauses for a moment to discuss the opposition between "alternative and emancipatory strategies" and "closed authoritarianism" (2000, 182).

54. "As necessary as science, but not sufficient, *art* brings to the realization of urban society its long mediation on life as drama and pleasure" (Lefebvre 1996, 156–57). The lengthy discussion there is worth consultation.

55. "In other words, the future of art is not artistic, but urban, because the future of 'man' is not discovered in the cosmos, or in the people, or in production, but in urban society. In the same way art and philosophy must reconsider itself in relation to this perspective. The problematic of the *urban* renews the problematic of philosophy, its categories and methods. Without a need to break or reject them, these categories *accept* something else new: a meaning" (Lefebvre 1996, 173). That art and philosophy are linked has been recognized by other Marxist thinkers, of course; see, for example, G. A. Nedozchiwin's "What is Aesthetics"—"And there surely *is* a link between aesthetics and the other social sciences, most of all philosophy. Aesthetics is a philosophical discipline. It arose as a science within the bounds of philosophy. There is also even a link between the history of aesthetics and the history of philosophy" (1972, 132).

56. See "The Realization of Philosophy" (Chapter 16) for an instructive quotation regarding partial knowledge (Lefebvre 1996, 175).

57. Lefebvre, in fact, outlines three stages through which philosophy routinely moves with relation to the city (1996, 174).

58. As scholar Nadal-Melsió notes, the combination of art and philosophy is a central attribute of Lefebvre's thought generally speaking: "From very early on in his work, the collaboration, or rather the mutual inclusion, of the aesthetic and the philosophical is key to an understanding of the Lefebvrean project" (2008, 161). The reconciliation of art with science and technology recalls, of course, the Constructivist artists of the 1920s, some of whom, according to Rose, "best represent the original Saint-Simonist concept of the avant-garde as consisting of a union of artists, scientists and engineers able to pool their talents to produce artistic goods of technological as well as of economic value" (1984, 167n.1; also Chapter 7, 123–135).

4 The Urban Dominant: Everyday Life and the City in Textual Criticism

1. When properly situated within Lefebvre's extensive work, this theory affirms the central duality of the everyday—that just as everyday life is a battleground of commoditization it is simultaneously a site of resistance (Lefebvre 2005).

2. Elden writes that "Lefebvre made two main moves in his work: an assertion of the importance of space in tandem with that of time, and an analysis of the spaces of the modern age" (2004, 193).

3. "Marx largely limits *his* study of alienation to economic fetishism, but this does not mean that he, or we, should solely think it in that way. For Lefebvre, this notion of alienation will become 'the central notion of philosophy (seen as criticism of life and the foundation for a *concrete* humanism).' Alienation was certainly to become a central notion in Lefebvre's work...As Anderson and Judt have pointed out, Lefebvre's *Dialectical Materialism* and the best seller *Le Marxisme* were 'the first outright presentation in France of Marx as a theorist of alienation.' Such a reading was both novel and heretical" (original emphasis; Elden 2004, 41). The sources Elden cites are Lefebvre's *Critique of Everyday Life* (vol. 1), Perry Anderson's *Considerations on Western Marxism*, and Tony Judt's *Marxism and the French Left*.

4. Selden's opinion, for example, is that "the Russian Formalists were much more interested in 'method,' much more concerned to establish a 'scientific basis for the theory of literature... it remains true that the Formalists avoided the New Critics' tendency to endow aesthetic form with moral and cultural significance. They aimed rather to outline models and hypotheses in a scientific spirit to explain how aesthetic effects are produced by literary devices and how the 'literary' is distinguished from and related to the 'extra-literary.' While the New Critics regarded literature as a form of human understanding, the Formalists thought of it as a special use of language" (1986, 7). For his part, Jameson writes that "The unique claim

of the Russian Formalists is their stubborn attachment to the intrinsically literary" (1972, 43).

5. For this, the interested reader should consult *The Prison-House of Language* by Fredric Jameson (1972), beginning on p. 45.

6. For more recent essays on Jakobson's work and on "the dominant," see Gretchko (2003) and Sütiste (2008), both in the journal *Sign Systems Studies*.

7. "Writing in 1935, [Roman] Jakobson regarded 'the dominant' as 'the focusing component of a work of art: it rules, determines, and transforms the remaining components.' He rightly stresses the non-mechanistic aspect of this view of artistic structure. The dominant provides the work with its focus of crystallisation and facilitates its unity or *gestalt* (total order)" (Selden 1986, 15). Altamiranda locates this quotation also in *Language in Literature* (Jakobson 1987, 41) and specifies that Jakobson's definition of the term dates to a lecture delivered at the University of Masaryk in Brno in 1935.

8. Altamiranda traces the Russian Formalist concept of the dominant to a 1909 text on the *Philosophy of Art* by German philosopher Broder Christiansen and maintains that it is a "pillar of formalism" (2001, 42).

9. "Rather than look for eternal verities which bind all great literature into a single canon, the Formalists were disposed to see the history of literature as one of permanent revolution. Each new development is an attempt to repulse the dead hand of familiarity and habitual response. This dynamic notion of the dominant also provided the Formalists with a useful way of explaining literary history" (Selden 1986, 15). There is also a dynamic character to the dominant within Russian Formalism more generally speaking, as pointed out by Raman Selden: "Poetic forms change and develop not at random but as a result of a 'shifting dominant': there is a continuing shift in the mutual relationships among the various elements in a poetic system" (1986, 15).

10. This perspective in particular may perhaps be more prevalent among those who read Russian Formalism through their Anglophone counterparts, practitioners of the New Criticism. See Jameson (1972).

11. The full quote reads: "reject a mechanical formalism and attempt to reach beyond a narrowly literary perspective by trying to define the relationship between the literary 'series' (system) and other 'historical series.' The way in which the literary system develops historically cannot be understood, they argue, without understanding the way in which other systems impinge on it and partly determine its evolutionary path" (Selden 1986, 19–20). Consider also Mukarovsky's insight regarding the social function of aesthetics and the importance of extraliterary factors (Selden 1986, 20). See also Jakobson and Tynjanov (1985, 25). It is clear that a number of contemporary theorists—not just Lefebvre—have sought this balance between text and context, such as Fredric Jameson who writes: the "problem [of postmodernism] is at one and the same time an aesthetic and a political one" (1999, 55).

12. In fact, even despite how rigidly Jakobson holds to the notion of genre, he approaches it, as well, from a dynamic perspective. Krystyna Pomorska seems to regard this dynamic character of his thought as a hallmark feature, in fact beginning an introduction to his work with the sentence "Roman Jakobson was a thinker who approached every domain of human endeavor in a dynamic, integrated way" (Jakobson 1987, 1). Jakobson himself characterized "the question of invariance in the midst of variation" as the "dominant topic" of his career's work (1985, 3). To wit: his insistence on the liminal areas of genre classification—what he calls "an analysis of a transitional region between painting and poetry, such as illustration, or an analysis of a border region between music and poetry, such as the romance" (Jakobson 1987, 45)—both confirms his commitment to those static categories while suggesting that he found them to be inadequate at some level.

13. Jameson continues: "So even if everything is spatial, this postmodern reality here is somehow *more* spatial than everything else" (1999, 365). Despite the text's extensive length, Lefebvre figures on fewer than 10 pages, not all of which are listed in the book's index. The majority of these references, in fact, are in the book's conclusion.

14. Although this is not the place to discuss Jameson's ideas at length, it should be pointed out that despite the many lucid commentaries made in *Postmodernism*, urbanization is not directly theorized and appears only indirectly through discussions of space, architecture, and built environment. Interestingly, neither of the terms urban/urbanization or city figure into the book's index. He does, however, frequently repeat the use of the term dominant (Jameson 1999, 4, 6, 46, 68, 158–159, 299, 365).

15. That is, despite Jameson's extensive critical meditation on Russian Formalism in *The Prison-House of Language* (1972, 43–98), where he mentions the dominant specifically on pp. 42–43.

16. The thought of Mikhail Bakhtin is yet another source of potential interest for the literary scholar doing urban cultural studies work, especially because "he did not, as one might have expected, treat literature as a direct reflection of social forces, but retained a formalist concern with literary structure" and, like Lefebvre of course, was is "profoundly un-Stalinist!" (Selden 1986, 17). His notion of the chronotope in particular may dovetail nicely with an urban cultural studies method. On this, see Harvey's comments (1996, 269–271). Bakhtin's chronotope is also notably mentioned in an edited volume on *The Spatial Humanities* to be discussed in the final chapter of this book (see Ayers 2010, 4).

17. Elsewhere I have explained this aspect of Lefebvre's thought by reading it along with and against Henri Bergson's own frequently misunderstood emphasis on both space and time (Fraser 2008a, 2010). See Elden (2004) for an earlier formulation of Lefebvre as both spatial and temporal theorist.

18. This temporal problem has its complement in a spatial problem: "we fall into the trap of treating space 'in itself,' as space as such. We come to think in terms of spatiality, and so to fetishize space" (Lefebvre 1991a, 90).

19. "The objectivity of time and space is given in each case by the material practices of social reproduction, and to the degree that these latter vary geographically and historically, so we find that social time and social space are differentially constructed. Each distinctive mode of production or social formation will, in short, embody a distinctive bundle of time and space practices and concepts" (Harvey 1990, 204).

20. In fact, Harvey draws on Lefebvre so frequently from *Social Justice and the City* (originally published in 1973) to *Rebel Cities* (2012) that a full accounting of this influence is problematic here due to reasons of space.

21. From this perspective it is interesting that while praising Raymond Williams elsewhere (1990, 347), Harvey has taken him to task precisely on account of the perceived limitations of his cultural theory: "But Williams did not or could not put this mode of thought to work in confronting issues of place, spatio-temporality, and environment directly in his cultural theory" (1996, 47). It is instructive that Harvey imagines cultural theory as distinct from novelistic production, which he devalues almost despite himself: "The fact that Williams' dealings and concerns over space, place, and environment are voiced primarily in his novels suggests, however, a certain hesitancy if not an outright difficulty in getting this tripartite conceptual apparatus into the heart of cultural theory" (1996, 44).

22. "There is much to be learned from aesthetic theory about how different forms of spatialization inhibit or facilitate processes of social change. Conversely there is much to be learned from social theory concerning the flux and change with which aesthetic theory has to cope. By playing these two currents of thought off against each other, we can, perhaps, better understand the ways in which political-economic change informs cultural practices" (1990, 207).

23. My key complaint is that he reduces texts to content alone—as will be discussed in the text below. See the discussion of his textual analyses in the Introduction to this volume, just as (for example) at the end of *Condition of Postmodernity* (1990), throughout *Paris: Capital of Modernity* (2006), and at the beginning of *Justice, Nature and the Geography of Difference* (1996).

24. I am reminded specifically of the anecdote I shared earlier in this book of the geographer who saw nothing of value in close-readings of texts.

25. The quotation continues: "It is—and I make the point again in order not to be misunderstood—one thing to say that texts (discourses) internalize everything there is and that meaningful things can be said by bringing deconstructionist tactics to bear both upon actual texts (histories, geographies, novels) as well as upon a wide range of phenomena in which the semiotic moment has clear significance (such as movies, paintings, sculptures, buildings, monuments, landscapes, dress codes, and even a wide range of events such as religious rituals, political ceremonies, and popular carnivals). But it is quite another to insist that the whole world is nothing other than a text needing to be read and deconstructed" (Harvey 1996, 87). At this point in the text (1996, 87–88), Harvey invokes Lefebvre's own work as justification

of his point, but I think he in fact misreads Lefebvre's intention, specifically in light of what the French theorist has written on the city as a text in *The Right to the City*, discussed in the next paragraph of this chapter.

26. Lefebvre "thus turns to the concepts of city 'levels' and 'dimensions' (2003a, 77–102; 2002, 118–25 and 148–56; 1996, 111–17)—neither as rigid categorizations nor evidence of a strict hierarchy but rather as provisional "methodological tools" to be employed on the way to appreciating the complexity of the urban phenomenon. These levels and dimensions of the urban provide a way of reconciling the scope of differing scales of influence with the realities of life on the city streets. In *The Urban Revolution*, Lefebvre attempts to depict the three 'levels' he calls G, M and P: 'I distinguish a global level, which I'll indicate with the letter G; a mixed level, which I'll indicate with the letter M; and a private level, P, the level of habiting' (2003, 78)" (Fraser 2011a, 18). See also Brenner (2000); Marston (2000); Howitt (2003); Kipfer (2009).

27. A further point of contrast between Lefebvre's and Harvey's positions can be seen in the epilogue Harvey pens to his own *Spaces of Hope* (2000)— where a new society forms only as precipitated (caused?) by economic disaster: a somewhat reductively materalist explanation of social change that implicitly judges consciousness to be insufficient.

28. Harvey is correct to assert that "What is really at stake here, however, is an analysis of cultural production and the formation of aesthetic judgments through an organized system of production and consumption mediated by sophisticated divisions of labour, promotional exercises, and marketing arrangements. And these days the whole system is dominated by the circulation of capital (more often than not of a multinational sort)" (1990, 346); it is just that without the humanities-centered perspective, discussion of "aesthetic judgments" risks assuming the very capitalist (instrumentalist, reifying, alienating) logic that is to be disrupted.

29. I say *provisionally* as Lefebvre has yet to fully introduce his more nuanced, *triadic* model of spatial production (e.g., 1991a, 33) that has been so popular among Anglophone critics. I also employ the term provisionally as it is crucial to understand that Lefebvre's project—and any dialectical project—is somewhat cautious regarding the use of fixed terms to account for what are complex, dynamic relationships (see also Lefebvre's remarks on the inadequacies of language for reflecting upon urban reality; 1991a, 414). This reading certainly follows logically from the Lefebvre's general skepticism regarding dogmatic philosophical positions (e.g., Lefebvre 1988), but also from the similarity between Lefebvre's and Bergson's philosophical methods (Fraser 2008). Bergson, for example, routinely begins with provisional definitions of a number of concepts (space/time, intellect/intuition, and perhaps most captivatingly, matter/memory) only to arrive at a much more complex understanding of their entanglement or in his words, interpenetration. Thus, the use of the word provisional here implies the use of a certain philosophical method.

30. Continuation of quote: "Inasmuch as they deal with socially 'real' space, one might suppose on first consideration that architecture and texts relating to architecture would be a better choice than literary texts proper. Unfortunately, any definition of architecture itself requires a prior analysis and exposition of the concept of space" (Lefebvre 1991a, 15).

31. One should note that elsewhere, Lefebvre makes similarly substantial claims about the relevance of literature without fully exploring those claims—for example, "We cannot go into the concept of modernity and its critique in sufficient depth here to settle some rather serious questions. How should we assess what is called modern art, in its full range and diversity—painting, the novelistic literature often regarded as essential, but also music, architecture and sculpture—not forgetting poetry? And first of all, how it is to be situated?" (2005, 48).

32. There are likely many more ways of interpreting this statement that draw from anthropological, historical, sociological accounts, but given her importance for urban investigations, assertions by Jane Jacobs are crucial here: that cities have always been at the center of even preurban social formations and that the city may have made agriculture possible (Jacobs 1970, 1984)—a thesis that inverts a standard assumption that organized agriculture led to the formation of cities.

33. I have recently interrogated these notions at length in the realm of Hispanic Studies (and by extension in other Language and Literature fields) in a co-authored paper in the *ADFL Bulletin* responding to Joan L. Brown's 2010 book *Confronting Our Canons* (Fraser, Larson, and Compitello 2014).

34. Lefebvre continues, "*Ulysses* is diametrically opposed both to novels presenting stereotyped protagonists and to the traditional novel recounting the story of the hero's progress, the rise and fall of a dynasty or the fate of some social group. Here, with all the trappings of an epic—masks, costumes, scenery—the quotidian steals the show" (2007, 3).

35. See the discussion by Lefebvre (2007, 3–11). For a brief reference to *Ulysses*, see also Elden (2004, 183), who in turn also cites Lefebvre's *Everyday Life in the Modern World*.

36. Note Lefebvre's own remarks on this in *La présence et l'absence*, where he writes that the "work" cannot be reduced to a signifying intention: "La obra hace corresponder una totalidad presente, actual con la totalidad rota o ausente; su relación no puede reducirse a un 'reflejo,' a una 'expresión,' como tampoco a una intención significante" (2006b, 268).

37. In *The Production of Space*, Lefebvre asks a number of important questions that foreshadow his discussions of the product–work in *La présence et l'absence* and that once again draws attention to his vision that a theory of the work of art parallels an investigation of the city as a work of art and also the notion of living as itself an art (see chapter 3, this book; also Lefebvre 1991a, 74–75).

38. "In literature from Joyce to Simenon and Japrisot (a deliberate and somewhat ironic association), novelists seek to capture daily life at ever closer

range, in order to derive surprising effects from it. Not to mention American authors who systematically smuggle the extraordinary out of the ordinary (quotidian). Yet daily life is not counterposed in some *binary* opposition to the non-quotidian" (Lefebvre 2005, 3–4).

39. Consider, for example, Raymond Williams's assertion at the close of *Marxism and Literature* that literary characters are *necessarily* drawn from extraliterary life (1977, 208–211).

40. In Anglophone circles, studies such as Burton Pike's *The Image of the City in Modern Literature* (1981) or Blanche Housman Galfant's *The American City Novel* (originally published in 1954) seem to be fundamental. In my own home field of Hispanic Studies, attention to the city in literature is perhaps a more recent critical development, but grounded—as in other literatures—in the primacy of the nineteenth-century representation of cities by authors. In particular, my work has followed up on studies by Malcolm Alan Compitello and Edward Baker (2003) among others in looking at the urban context and representation in works by authors from the nineteenth century (Mariano José de Larra, Ramón de Mesonero Romanos; Fraser 2011a, 2012d), the twentieth century (Juan Goytisolo, Belén Gopegui; Fraser 2005, 2008c), and the twenty-first century (Agustín Fernández Mallo; Fraser 2012b); as well as films (Fraser 2006a, 2006b), graphic novels (Fraser and Méndez 2012), videogames (Fraser 2011c), music (Fraser 2011c), and more as the following chapters will make clear.

41. This view is criticized by Lefebvre directly in *The Urban Revolution* (2003a, 40) and, as I have argued elsewhere (Fraser 2008a), follows logically from his predecessor Henri Bergson's denunciation of the Kantian understanding of space (see Bergson 1970 [1889], Chapter 2; 1912 [1896], 307–309; 1998 [1907], 157).

42. For instance, this comment would fit well in discussions of the detective genre (see Fraser 2006c), in that the classical detective novel (at least in the 20 rules intuited and written down by S. S. Van Dine in the early twentieth century) eschewed description of "atmospheric conditions" while the hard-boiled novel turned to those conditions in widening the scope of the concepts of crime and justice and holding them to be synonymous with the urban problem. Applied to literature more generally, it seems to be problematic.

43. "The dazzling rapidity of success and ruin is the great theme of the nineteenth-century novel from Balzac to Maupassant: with it the city enters modern literature and becomes, as it were its obligatory context. Yet it is such precisely because the city as a physical place—and therefore as a support to descriptions and classifications—becomes the mere backdrop to the city as a network of developing social relationships—and hence as a prop to narrative temporality [that] "the urban novel . . . seeks to resolve the spatial in terms of the sequential" (2010, 309).

44. Interestingly, Moretti also misses an opportunity to mention how the protagonist of the novel he analyzes is in fact alienated from his urban environment (see Moretti 2010, 314). The quality of urban life that this passage

describes is, in my view, better described through recourse to Lefebvre's notion of urban alienation (2003a).

45. To the extent that Raymond Williams's perspective remains highly skeptical of bourgeois notions of literary value—in effect counteracting the Arnoldian notion of "great works" (1963)—I too remain suspicious of the notion of good/bad literature and more important of the possibility that this is a meaningful distinction for literary criticism in particular. On the other hand, perhaps there are some texts and/or types of texts that are better suited than others for urban cultural studies research. This matter can be left for future directions of Urban Cultural Studies to suss out, if it is indeed true (about this I have my doubts).

5   The Iconic-Indexical City: Visions of Place in Urban Films

1. The quotation continues: "What this focus has tended to displace is an appreciation of the iconic and mimetic aspect of certain categories of signs, namely pictorial signs, those most relevant to an understanding of the cinema. This stress upon the arbitrary nature of semiotic coding has had enormous consequences for the way film studies as a discipline has tended to frame questions about visual meaning and communication" (Prince 1999, 99).

2. From "Living Signs and Dead Poets" (1967; reprinted in Pasolini 1988). This idea is also found in the work of film critic Christian Metz, whose work holds that the images of cinema are always motivated (i.e., semiotically speaking). Although they may have agreed on certain issues, it is important to note that Metz and Pasolini were not always in agreement and had different perspectives on the double articulation of the cinematic image.

3. It is important to note that iconicity is not merely evident at the level of lexicon but, in fact, appears throughout the levels of analysis of spoken and written language, from the phoneme/grapheme through syntactical structures. The text *Syntactic Iconicity and Linguistic Freezes: The Human Dimension* (in which the Waugh and Newfield essay also appears) provides many such examples. Among them is the classic example stemming from Jakobson (1965): that of "veni vidi vici." Joseph H. Greenberg's contribution to the volume indicates this sequence is "the mapping of succession in language with succession in real time . . . the act of seeing follows the act of coming and the act of conquering follows the act of seeing" (1995, 59). The issue of iconicity in natural signed languages, for example, also deserves consideration, although it is much too complex to explore here without a proper introduction. Those interested might begin with Fraser (2007c, 2009c).

4. It should be noted that there is a strong historical bias among literary critics toward consideration of language as the preeminent system of signs. While I do not wish to uncritically accept or reject this perspective outright, it is significant that such a judgment is an easy sell for a given

set of critics (critics of written, verbal texts)—who can somewhat easily place themselves at the center of an hermeneutic paradigm. The Tartú School of semiotics that to some degree followed in the footsteps of the Russian Formalists (see Altamiranda 2001)—most notably I. Lotman and J. Uspenski—came to assert language as a primary modeling system, with the consequence that all other sign systems became secondary modeling systems that were in essence dependent on it.

5. "A basic principle of European aesthetics and art philosophy from the ancient Greeks to our own time has been that there is an external and internal distance and dualism between spectator and work of art. This principle implies that every work of art by force of its self-contained composition is a microcosm with laws of its own. It may *depict* reality but has no immediate connection and contact with it. The work of art is separated from the surrounding empiric world not only by the frame of the picture, the pedestal of the statue, the footlights of the stage. The work of art, by force of its intrinsic nature, as a result of its self-contained composition and own specific laws, is separated from natural reality and precisely because it depicts the latter cannot be its continuation. Even if I hold a painting in my hand, I cannot penetrate into the painted space of the picture. I am not only physically incapable of this, but my consciousness cannot do it either. It should be said here, however, that this feeling of insuperable distance was not always and everywhere present in all nations. For instance the Chinese of old regarded their art with a different eye" (original emphasis; Balázs 1970, 49–50; see also essays by Loewy 2006; Koch 1987).

6. "The concept 'flow of life,' then, covers the stream of material situations and happenings with all that they intimate in terms of emotions, values, thoughts. The implication is that the flow of life is predominantly a material rather than a mental continuum, even though, by definition, it extends into the mental dimension. (It might tentatively be said that films favor life in the form of everyday life—an assumption which finds some support in the medium's primordial concern for actuality)" (Kracauer 1968, 71–72).

7. See also Dear (2000, Chapter 9) for a lucid reconciliation of filmspace and cityspace. He also posits the intimate connection between the place of production and the production of place more generally. As Jeff Hopkins shows, also places are not merely reflected on screen—there is a more properly dialectical relationship operating across the boundary of the filmic text: "The cinematic landscape is not, consequently, a neutral place of entertainment or an objective documentation or mirror of the 'real', but an ideologically charged cultural creation whereby meanings of place and society are made, legitimized, contested and obscured" (1994, 47; also in Dear 2000, 182).

8. "This particular medium is not a traditional object of inquiry for geographers—as opposed to landscape or region—nor is it one of the usual

means through which instruction takes place. And yet, in articles and books, in lecture halls and seminar rooms, film has become one of the most popular sites for research and teaching. If we scan briefly the many forms this engagement has taken across the discipline, we can see the use of film as example, metaphor, as allegory, as a vehicle for querying the character of representation, and as a way of recording everyday perception of the world" (Cresswell and Dixon 2002, 1).

9. The reference to Siegfried Kracauer in particular seems to border on misunderstanding, in that by equating his theory of film with "mimeticism" in a simple sense, the authors disregard the incredibly complex notion of what he means by "reality"—one that I have elsewhere explained in greater depth by exploring the resonance between Kracauer's text and Bergsonian philosophy (Fraser 2010).

10. A recent review of the 2011 volume *GeoHumanities: Art, History, Text at the Edge of Place* (edited by Dear et al.; review written by Sullivan 2012) indicates that this general lack of awareness of previous work continues to operate even a decade later. Sullivan takes the editors to task for ignoring the way in which these discussions were initiated long ago by Denis Cosgrove. "One of the flaws of this collection has to do with the historiography of the relationship between geography and the humanities . . . On the historic side of things, it is with a gnawing sense of foreboding and a growing sense of trepidation to discover that the word 'new' is used eight times in the book's two-page introduction, along with the phrases 'novel approach,' 'radical break,' 'emerging zone of practice,' 'emerging forms of the geohumanities,' 'emerging geohumanities,' and, finally, 'a project that is just beginning.' Though the label of geohumanities may be relatively new, this is a project with a long and illustrious lineage" (Sullivan 2012, n.p.).

11. "By juxtaposing signs signifying other times and spaces, therefore, film promotes expansions and compressions in the viewer's temporal and spatial sensibilities; boundaries of time and space may become permeable and blurred. The viewer is simultaneously inside and outside the film, construing both fantasy and reality, switching back and forth across distances, visiting various settings and times, experiencing what Fell has termed a kind of 'geographic omnipresence' (1975, p. 63), without ever leaving his or her seat" (Hopkins 1994, 57).

12. Importantly, the film remains quite faithful to a strain of Spanish literature that has dramatized Barcelona as explicitly reshaped by touristic and capitalistic forces: Vázquez Montalbán's *Sabotaje Olímpico* (1993, treating the preparation for the 1992 Games), *Los mares del sur* (1997, in which a detective plot highlights the ills of urban speculation), Juan Goytisolo's *Señas de identidad* (1996, treating the 1929 Fair as well as the accelerating tourism of the dictatorship's 1960s). Eduardo Mendoza's *La ciudad de los prodigios* (2003) is of interest for its presentation of the 1888 Expo in Barcelona as well.

13. When Delgado writes of how the attempts to forge a "perfect Barcelona" will "desactivar para siempre lo urbano [disactivate the urban forever]" (2007b, 17), the reader familiar with his work understands not only that urban design is today more synonymous than ever with attracting tourism and international business but also that it is more and more geared toward reducing the possibilities for spontaneity and even democracy. This is, in fact, for some a legacy of modern urban planning in general: as Choay points out with reference to the case of Haussmann, "the Emperor [of France], wanted to put an end to riots by destroying the medieval structure of Parisian streets and replacing them with broad arteries along which the police could assemble and charge" (1969, 15); this critique may be applied also to the broad arteries of Cerdà's Eixample.

14. For reasons of space I have not covered the supernatural narrative arc of the film in the present chapter. My entire argument is available in the article from which this section is reproduced with publisher permission: *Studies in Hispanic Cinemas* (2012) 9.1.

15. Delgado writes of Jacobs in his own work: "My readings of *The Death and Life of Great American cities*, by Jane Jacobs ([published in Spanish translation by] Península, Barcelona, 1973), and *The Fall of Public Man*, by Richard Sennet [sic] (Península, Barcelona, 1974), were for me revelations, and the present book [*El animal público/The Public Animal*] would neither seek to, nor could it, hide this fact" (1999, 19; my translation). In *Sociedades movedizas/Mobile Societies*, he explores the "life of the sidewalk" similarly pronouncing that *Death and Life* is "a fundamental text" (Delgado 2007a, 245), and once again invoking and unpacking Jacobs' metaphor of street activities as dance (2007a, 135–136; my translations). For Delgado, the importance of the metaphor of the sidewalk ballet seems to lie in its potential to account for difference and multiplicity in the representation of urban spaces and activities.

16. In the original Spanish: "la integración de las incompatibilidades, donde se pueden llevar a cabo los más eficaces ejercicios de reflexión sobre la propia identidad, donde cobra sentido el compromiso político como consciencia de las posibilidades de la acción y donde la movilización social permite conocer la potencia de las corrientes de simpatía y solidaridad entre extraños."

17. Also, in line with a tradition of urban criticism that has questioned the existence of a "public space" that is not won through struggle (e.g., Lefebvre 1996; Staeheli 1996; Mitchell 2003), Delgado advances a skeptical view of the notion of public space, one that is helpful in understanding *Biutiful's* contribution to discourses of the urban (2007b, 225–226; also 2006).

18. As such, the film might be grouped alongside the critical urban vision of Bilbao-born Álex de la Iglesia, whose *El día de la bestia* (1995), *La comunidad* (2000), and *Crimen ferpecto* (2004) were also somewhat well-received denunciations of urban shifts in Spain (see Compitello 2003).

19. Even this shot might be interpreted as a reference to the way in which nineteenth-century cities—and Barcelona in particular—were redesigned over all else to promote the flow of traffic (even if not yet automobile traffic) and goods through the streets. The Plan Cerdà, for example, echoed the changes made by Haussmann in Paris in the construction of broad avenues and the widening of intersections with truncated corners (i.e., the *xamfrà*; see Cerdà 1867; Resina 2008, 22)—all to facilitate traffic. In fact, Cerdà's 1867 two-volume treatise, which he called the *Teoría general de la urbanización*, put forth a novel theoretical understanding of the city as evolving through stages that were dependent on the form of locomotion prioritized in each: *locomoción pedestre, locomoción ecuestre, locomoción rastrera, locomoción rodada (ordinaria y perfeccionada)*. See Fraser (2011a, 2011b).

20. The Torre Agbar, designed by French architect Jean Nouvel, opened in 2005 and lies at the boundary of the Poble Nou neighborhood, a district that has received much attention for being a hub of urban renewal schemes in the Catalan capital (see McNeill 1999).

21. Delgado continues Lefebvre's emphasis on the nineteenth-century shift that saw the triumph of exchange-value and, just as his influence, inflects this idea with a distinctly urban perspective. This shift, outlined by Karl Marx in *Capital* (1977), was for Lefebvre reflected in the uniquely modern construction of the city as an image to be consumed and visually possessed, and in the creation of needs to be satisfied through patterns of production and consumption (1996, 167–168).

22. In the original Spanish: "ciudad dramatiza, pues, el contencioso interminable entre dos modelos de sociedad urbana. Uno es el que encarna la ciudad burguesa, habitada idealmente y en exclusiva por una clase media autosatisfecha que detesta el conflicto...Una ciudad que se amolda dócil a los requerimientos de la fase del desarrollo capitalista en que se encuentra en cada momento y se muestra dispuesta a incorporarse a las grandes dinámicas de modernización urbana...Del otro lado, al otro lado del río, los explotados y los excluidos."

23. In the original Spanish: "El modelo de la ciudad politizada es el de una ciudad prístina y esplendorosa, ciudad soñada, ciudad utópica, comprensible, lisa, ordenada, vigilada noche y día para evitar cualquier eventualidad que alterara su quietud perfecta. En cambio, la ciudad plenamente urbanizada–no en el sentido de plenamente sumisa al urbanismo, sino en el de abandonada del todo a los movimientos en que consiste lo urbano–evocaría lo que Michel Foucault llama, nada más empezar *Las palabras y las cosas*, una *heterotopía*, es decir una comunidad humana embrollada, en la que se han generalizado las hibridaciones y en la que la incongruencia deviene el combustible de una vitalidad sin límites."

24. This type of parallel between humans and animals occurs also repeatedly in scenes where both moths and dead souls crawl on the ceilings of interiors.

25. We later learn that the ring was bought for Ana's mother Marambra.

26. As Zygmunt Bauman has argued, no-places are those characterized by the absence of difference "the comforting feeling of belonging—the reassuring impression of being part of a community" (2000, 99; see also Augé 2005; cf. Delgado 2004).

27. In *Sociedades movedizas*, building explicitly on Erving Goffman's idea of "desatención cortés [polite inattentiveness]" (2007a, 189), Delgado writes of the seeming lack of identity enjoyed by the urban pedestrian referencing as a refusal: "Esos seres han renunciado a proclamar quiénes son. Se niegan a identificarse [Those beings have declined to proclaim who they are. They refuse to be identified]" (2007a, 188; my translation; see also a particularly pertinent passage on p. 192).

6 Listening to Urban Rhythms: Soundscapes in Popular Music

1. Harvey notes that this emphasis is palpable "from the *Economic and Philosophical Manuscripts* onwards" and provides the following quotation from that work to illustrate his point: "*Sense-perception* must be the basis of all science. Only when it proceeds from sense-perception in the two-fold form of *sensuous* consciousness and of *sensuous* need—that is, only when science proceeds from nature—is it *true* science" (Marx 1964, 143; Quoted in Harvey 2000, 101; original emphasis). Note that I deal with this sensuous tradition of Marxism also in two contributions to the edited volume *Marxism and Urban Culture* (Fraser 2014) focusing on two different films and pulling more thoroughly there from the *Economic and Philosophical Manuscripts*.

2. Note Elden's remarks on the importance of music for Lefebvre: "Elsewhere in this writings, he deals extensively with the question of music. Aesthetics is, for Lefebvre, central to the way in which we perceive the world. It is clear that his work on music helped him to understand time, and his work on painting, including discussio of Picasso and an unjustly neglected study of Eduoard Pignon is a crucial stage in his understanding of representations of space. Lefebvre turned to these areas of study, particularly the work on literature, in a time of considerable political and intellectual / difficulty. Increasingly marginalised within the PCF, and prevented from publishing some of his more overtly political writings, Lefebvre wrote about the great figures of French literature" (Elden 2006a, 193–194).

3. In this respect his work resonates with that of Henri Bergson (Fraser 2008a, 2010; Bergson 2001, 2002).

4. "One could reach, by a twisty road and paradoxically beginning with bodies, the (concrete) universal that the political and philosophical mainstream targeted but did not reach, let alone realize: if rhythm consolidates its theoretical status, if it reveals itself as a valid concept for thought and as a support in practice, is it not this concrete universal that philosophical

systems have lacked, that political organizations have forgotten, but which is lived, tested, touched in the sensible and the corporeal?" (Lefebvre 2006a, 44–45; see also 67).

5. As Simpson points out: "However, much of the engagement with Lefebvre's rhythmanalysis has proceeded at a relatively abstracted level. Whilst many have called for or suggested the usefulness of rhythmanalysis in examining 'the city', little work has appeared in print which engages in detail in actual, specific, everyday practices and performances *in* these cities through the lens of the Rhythmanalayst. Few have in fact undertaken rhythmanalyses" (2008, 813).

6. Note that even in *Rhythmanalysis*, Lefebvre is similarly interested in the relationship between capital, time, and space. See particularly Lefebvre (2006a, 51–56).

7. There is a dualistic quality also in the dissonance between use of the terms "emotion" and "affect," as can be seen in the literature. See particularly McCormack (2003, 2006); Thien (2005); Anderson and Harrison (2006); Tolia-Kelly (2006).

8. One notable contribution in this area is an essay by Nichola Wood, which clearly explores the connection between emotion and a sense of place as galvanized through musical experiences. Wood highlights the "complexities of belonging to a national community" (2002, 58) through a look at the British tradition of summer promenade classical concerts known as The Last Night of the Proms. Whereas both emotion and music have been traditionally ignored in geographical scholarship, she argues, tuning in to listening practices can allow us to discern subjectivity formations in the process of being composed.

9. Lahusen (1993) warns the English-language reader of the paucity of sources on Basque culture in English, explores the relationship of Basque punk to Basque political divisions, and directs the reader to work on Basque Nationalism (Sullivan 1988; Ibarra 1989; Darré 1990; and especially Jáuregui 1986). Since Lahusen's article was published, many more English language articles of interest to scholars of Basque studies have appeared, most notably in the volume *Basque Cultural Studies* (Douglass et al. 2000) and other titles in Basque studies printed by the University of Nevada Press, but also in the *Journal of Spanish Cultural Studies*, the *Arizona Journal of Hispanic Cultural Studies*, and the *International Journal of Iberian Studies*, among others. See also Linstroth (2002); Kasmir (2002).

10. All lyrics cited throughout this chapter section will be in the original language, with English translations in brackets included exactly as they have been published in the liner notes to a given album—except where I have provided the accompanying note, "*my modified translation.*"

11. In Spain, the term has been used by Manuel Delgado Ruiz (2004, 2007a, 2007b; on Delgado, see Fraser 2007a, 2008a, 2011a).

12. As Certeau states in a section subtitled merely "Indeterminate" at the end of his *Practice of Everyday Life*: "every urban 'renovation' nonetheless prefers a *tabula rasa* on which to write in cement the composition created in the laboratory on the basis of discrete 'needs' to which functional responses are to be made... This is the logic of production... It rejects the relevance of places it does not create" (1988, 201). The univocal vision that characterizes this kind of instrumental spatial production has been critiqued thoroughly by Henri Lefebvre (1991a) and a number of other contemporary thinkers (David Harvey, Edward Soja, Jane Jacobs, etc.; see Fraser 2007a, 2008a, 2009a, 2012a).

13. "Bi minutu" begins: "Leku galduak. Garai bateko une bat, nahiz eta jendetza arrotzari begira, gogora ekarri nahi [Lost places. An instant of other time, though looking at the foreign crowd wanted to bring it to memory]." Pound's poem reads: "The apparition of these faces in the crowd / Petals on a wet, black bough" (1).

7 Representing Digital Spaces: Videogames and the Digital Humanities

1. As a way of discussing the "unique" properties of videogames as interactive media, the article from which this section is reproduced emphasizes the significant relevance of the Greek notion of *mētis* as embodied knowledge. "Video game playing involves a combination of the hand-eye coordination and the localized knowledge Scott attributes to *mētis*. As any seasoned game player knows, and as any novice game player soon finds out, practice makes perfect. Knowing the game board or the landscape of a given virtual world ahead of time may not be possible when playing a video game, and at best, even this knowledge will be a poor substitution for knowledge gleaned through direct experience" (Fraser 2011c, 98; drawing extensively on Scott 1998 and Detiene and Vernant 1978, but also De Certeau, Bergson, and Lefebvre).

2. It should be noted, of course, that the volume owes also to Edward Ayers of *The Spatial Humanities* "formerly of the University of Virginia (and now President of the University of Richmond), who co-hosted the AAG's 2007 Geography & Humanities Symposium at the University of Virginia" (2011, xi). I was fortunate enough to attend several of the sessions at that Symposium.

3. Note that alienation—absent from many accounts of Lefebvre's work is also absent in Parker's formulation (2004, 19–23). The full quotation from Léger indicates that "Lefebre's approach to culture, art and social transformation was always at the heart of his Marxism" (2006, 143). "Lefebvre's ideas on art are still of interest today in that they provide an approach to aesthetics which is materialist but non-reductive and which is able to account for specificities of time, place and subjectivity within cultural production" (Léger 2006, 144).

4. Not all of the sites hosted by omeka.net are so simple, of course. In addition, the plug-ins provided by Neatline allow for the creation of ever-more-complex DH projects fit for the individual working alone.

5. http://studentomeka.library.cofc.edu/exhibits/show/granviamadrid

6. See Fitzpatrick for the challenges faced by library staff and researchers in the era of digital publication. "And as Bethany Nowviskie pointed out in a paper delivered at the 2009 Modern Language Association Convention, these collaborations are frequently led by library and technical staff, whose intellectual property rights in the work they produce are often severely restricted by university policies that understand all of their production as 'work for hire'" (2011, 73).

7. I must thank John Sutherland, interim Dean of Arts and Sciences at East Carolina University, for his enthusiastic support for this project, as well as Burrell Montz, Chair of Geography; Cindy Putnam Evans, Associate Dean for Research; and Joseph Thomas, Assistant Director for Research and Scholarly Communication for their active support in assuring the success of this endeavor. While the monies dedicated for this purpose might seem meager in comparison to start-ups in the sciences, they are considerable for those of us working in the humanities.

8. Jonathan Arac provides terms that can help us to distinguish between collaboration (i.e., production, what he calls the "laboratory") and collection (i.e., consumption, the "shop window"): "These two sites, one for organizing research, the other for organizing consumption, both reached their first fully developed forms in the modern West about a century ago, at the same time that the American university achieved the form that it still maintains. None of these modes of organization—laboratory, shop window, or university—is my ideal, but by using two of them to think about the third, we may begin to find ways to break from all three toward a future" (1997, 117). Arac also makes the critique that interdisciplinary, many times, may be merely a shop window banner" (1997, 125).

9. For example, see those created by the team of DH practitioners at, for example, the College of Charleston via the Carolina Lowcountry and Atlantic Program (available online at http://prosper.cofc.edu/~atlantic/digital). The projects include: "After Slavery," "Voyage of the Echo," "Hortensia Mordecai's 1859 Travel Diary," "Civil War Timeline," "African Americans and Jews from Slavery to Civil Rights," "Free People of Color," "Willard Hirsch, South Carolina Sculptor," and more. See also those available at East Carolina University through the University Multimedia Center (at http://www.ecu.edu/cs-acad/umc/projects.cfm), including "The Sacred Center: Spenser, Raleigh and the Munster Plantation" and "Wilmington Race Riot of 1898."

10. This thinking was confirmed to some degree at the nonetheless important Chicago Summit on the Humanities at the Modern Languages Association I attended during January 2014.

11. For example, one of my own posts on urbanculturalstudies.wordpress.com relating to DH was met with firm, lengthy, and reasoned but enthusiastic responses by both an undergraduate student studying DH and another responder who wrote: "I currently work for Oxford University Press and I would like to point out that Digital Humanities should not be considered to only be an academic phenomenon. I think that a move towards the digital is present in academia, publishing, marketing, business, and much much more. It is likely to end up being the overall presence in how people do their jobs, no matter what their job is, in the next few years" (see the blog comment here: http://urbanculturalstudies.wordpress.com/2013/03/05/dh-in-general-4-points-and-a-rant-followed-by-a-question/#comments). This comment underscores the premise of the present article, in that, there are close existing and potential ties between DH and the processes of the accumulation of capital more generally speaking. I will not argue here whether those ties are similar to those generated by the personal computer—perhaps they are, and perhaps they are not. Nor will I attempt to make any larger case about the complex role of technology in human evolution and/or the development of contemporary capitalism. In any case, however, as the poster's comment reveals, DH is not merely about education or research but also about "publishing, marketing, business and much much more." The benefits of this and the appropriateness of adapting to these changes are clear—but I suggest there may be other consequences of this change that are less salubrious and equally ripe for analysis.

12. Beyond Fitzpatrick's book, capital(ism) is also referenced in other key works from the DH tradition. For her part, in the very last section of *SPECLAB*, titled "Digital Aesthetics and Critical Opposition" (2009, 189–199), Johanna Drucker looks specifically at (capitalist) ideology and digital projects. Therein she works through N. Katherine Hayles' posthumanism and Adorno's "profound pessimism" (2009, 190) regarding aesthetics (along with McLuhan, Horkheimer, Leibniz, Lyotard, Charlie Chaplin, Symbolist aesthetics) in order to synthesize art, technology, and capital/ism, a word she uses explicitly (2009, 190, 192). Readings of humanities scholarship—in general that explore the relationship between capital and knowledge formation—are also extremely scarce. Kronman's *Education's End* (2007) notes that the modern profession of the university professor emerged precisely during the historical period to be references in the next section of this article. Yet, although he notes on a single page that "Like the bureaucrat and the capitalist, the professional research scholar who emerged as a recognizable type in the German universities of the early nineteenth century worked not for his own sake but for the benefit of the discipline to which he belonged, distintuishing its interests from his own" (2007, 107), his book does not address capitalism with any depth.

13. Fitzpatrick also suggests that peer review might be replaced with peer-to-peer review, but she provides no assurance that traditional university

structures will be able to assmilate those changes—and my own experience as well as the experience of other academics in my generation tells me to distrust any party suggesting such assurance.

14. "[W]hat this chapter aims to do is less to disrupt all our conventional notions of authorship than to demonstrate why thinking about authorship from a different perspective—one that's always been embedded, if dormant, in many of our authorship practices—could result in a more productive, and hopefully less anxious relationship to our work" (2011, 56). In my view, this well founded call to re-examine authorship stems from the fact that this anxiety pervades departmental structures where members are alienated from each other—a situation tackled directly by the MLA 2006 report that underscored the value of co-authorship. DH may help people to learn to see the value co-authorship in the long-run, but I believe the problem is not related as much to individual scholarship itself as it is to the inherent conservatism of the academy. In any case, although Fitzpatrick connects single-authorship with capitalism, this amounts to little more than a fetishization of how capital actually affects the academy.

15. While he is more focused on class than its counterpart, alienation, Marxist urban geographer David Harvey (2006b) provides a much stronger argument of what capitalist individualism actually is in his book *A Brief History of Neoliberalism*. His influence, Henri Lefebvre, as discussed anon, allows us to better appreciate how alienation is a multifaceted relationship arising in tandem with class differentiation, the division of labor and advanced urban capitalism.

16. Recall Bergson's cone-model of time/memory/consciousness as explained in *Matter and Memory*. I have addressed Bergsonian philosophy and its relationship to interdisciplinary scholarship more substantially in my *Encounters with Bergson(ism) in Spain* (Fraser 2010).

17. Besides which, I find the idea (expressed by Fitzpatrick) that people today are producing "too-many" articles to be absurd. Is the idea that a professor should carfeully invest in a smaller number of online articles and sustain them over a lifetime, dedicating herself to continual changes and dialogues? This to my eyes seems to be yet another way in which anxiety plays into the very foundation of the author's approach to digital environments. People write what they write. The common-sensical notion that the more a person writes the more the quality of that work is diminished, is absurd, yet prevalent in discussions of online publishing. There is in this notion of a reduced intellectual corpus of work not merely an authorial anxiety but also a paean to golden times when authors produced few works but of an immense quality.

18. One of the potential problems with open-access and the 'democratization' of scholarly publishing is the naivety that prestige will cease to be a factor in which articles are read and which are not. It may even allow prestigious

authors and collaboratives to draw readerly attention unequally to the published works of a select few.

19. Bernard-Donals notes in an article that "fewer faculty members are working harder in an ever-broadening field with less support and with greater demands in all three areas of academic labor (teaching, research and service)" (2008, 173).

20. I will make clear that this individualistic attitude is not one I share. I have spent countless hours editing and peer-reviewing submissions, and have authored work of both an individual and also a collaborative type (the latter perhaps more that your average humanist). I have also argued for incorporating the Modern Languages Association recommendations on accepting co-authorship into a previous deparment's statement on tenure and promotion. Unfortunately (but predictably), this idea was not universally accepted, I would add, and did not make it through the deptartmental vote required of all changes to departmental procedure.

21. This is, of course, a classic trope of writing on DH: "In contrast to their counterparts in sciences and even in social science, humanists tend to be solo scholars and teachers, despite noteworthy exceptions" (Klein 2005, 72).

22. I discuss this in detail in the introduction to the present book. See also the video of a lecture delivered as an invited speaker at the University of Kentucky on September 12, 2012, which draws from this book project and discusses C. P. Snow and F. R. Leavis, specifically (68 minutes; watch full lecture at http://vimeo.com/50215247).

23. I note that the two "liberal arts" institutions at which I have worked so far have both wanted to foster a "culture of grant funding" in the humanities.

24. These are "The old stuff gets broken faster than the new stuff is put in its place" (quoted from Clay Shirky, "Newspapers and Thinking the Unthinkable") and "In many cases, traditions last not because they are excellent, but because inflential people are averse to change and because of the sheer burdens of transition to a better state" (quoted from Cass Sunstein, *Infotopia*; Fitzpatrick 2011, 1).

25. An alternative approach would look into the complexity of the notion of community as discussed by Harvey and Esposito. In addition, the work of critical pedagogues Paolo Freire and bell hooks fits easily with a Lefebvrian critique of contemporary education. See the Introduction and chapter 1 of the present book.

26. See the essays by Herzberger (2012), Pope (2012), and Ugarte (2012), which may constitute the most recent additions to literature on this subject. Also, Moraña (2005), Ortega (2010). Note that Brown's book follows up on two of her previous articles.

27. Another description is that: "Throughout history material forces have dominated human beings, and in considering capitalist society each separate element must be related to the whole and each phenomenon treated as a phrase in a developing process. In *Capital* Marx more than once recalls this

global aspect of his method of inquiry. No economic act, however trivial, such as the buying and selling that occurs millions of times a day, is intelligible except in the context of the entire capitalist system" (Kolakowski 2005, 256).

28. I have written elsewhere of the relevance of alieantion to urban life specifically, using Lefebvre's recalibrated Marxism. The following quotation is key to those endeavors: "Nor is it reasonable to assume that our understanding of the urban phenomenon, or urban space, could consist in a collection of objects—economy, sociology, history, demography, psychology, or earth sciences, such as geology. The concept of a scientific object, although convenient and easy, is deliberately simplistic and may conceal another intention: a strategy of fragmentation designed to promote a unitary and synthetic, and therefore authoritarian, model. An object is isolating, even if conceived as a system of relations and even if those relations are connected to other systems" (2003a, 57). Also, in *The Urban Revolution* he notes that the city is irreducible to a system or a semiology (2003a, 50) and bemoans the limitations of approaches that boast of being able to divide the urban phenomenon—defined in terms of its "enormity and complexity" (2003a, 46)—into a manageable if large number of subfields. He writes that the complexity of the urban phenomenon "makes interdisciplinary cooperation essential. [It] cannot be grasped by any specialized science" (2003a, 53).

29. Lefebvre after all, writes Merrifield, was a thinker who "detested compartmentalization" (2006, xxxiii).

30. "Critical pedagogue Paolo Freire provides such a dynamic pedagogy through his denunciation of 'banking education' through which students are envisioned as passive receptacles for deposits of knowledge made by their teachers. Education, he says, cannot be seen as 'a set of things, pieces of knowledge, that can be superimposed on or juxtaposed to the conscious body of the learners' (1970, 72; see also 1998). Likewise, explicitly engaging this tradition articulated by Freire in *Pedagogy of the oppressed*, bell hooks (the lower-case moniker under which Gloria Watkins has published numerous books) has argued that education should be the 'practice of freedom'" (Fraser 2009a, 272).

31. Take Ellis's disturbing book *Literature Lost: Social Agendas and the Cirruption of the Humanities*, which looks, among other things, at the "typical attitudes toward study of the humanities" (1997, 3) and is motivated by the conservative anxiety underlying changes in humanities research since the 1960s and 1970s (anxieties that have hardly gone out of fashion). I note too that the author's insistence that "Race-gender-class critics are by no means the first to have made the mistake of thinking that if a statement about a literary work is true, it must, by the same token, also be relevant and useful" (1997, 35) recalls statements by the closed-minded contemporaries whose insular conservativism was debunked by canonical Spanish

Enlightenment philosopher Benito Jerónimo Feijoo and Montenegro (1676–1764)—the Benedictine Monk in fact declares in his "Causas del atraso" (1745) that all true things are necessarily useful. On Feijoo's unique blend of literary and scientific concerns—one perhaps not irrelevant to the present article, see Fraser (2013). Ellis's complaints (on pp. 35–36) about a hypothetical resarcher who searches for references to "hunting" over a wide-swatch of medieval poems would indicate that he is opposed to digital humanities work just as he is to cultural studies and Marxist approaches and also "politicized critics" (1997, 60).

References

Aarseth, Espen. 2004. "Quest Games as Post–Narrative Discourse." In M.–L. Ryan, ed., *Narrative across Media: The Languages of Storytelling*, 361–76. Lincoln and London: University of Nebraska Press.

———. 2007. "Allegories of Space: The Question of Spatiality in Computer Games." In F. von Borries, S. Walz, M. Bottger, D. Davidson, H. Kelley, and J. Kücklich, eds., *Space Time Play. Computer Games, Architecture and Urbanism: The Next Level*, 44–47. Basel, Boston, Berlin: Birkhauser.

Aitken, Stuart, and Leo Zonn, eds. 1994. *Place, Power, Situation, and Spectacle: A Geography of Film*. Maryland: Rowman and Littlefield Publishers.

Aitken, Stuart C., and Deborah P. Dixon. 2011. "Avarice and Tenderness in Cinematic Landscapes of the American West." In *GeoHumanities: Art, History, Text at the Edge of Place*, eds., Michael Dear, Jim Ketchum, Sarah Luria, and Doug Richardson, 196–205. New York: Routledge.

Altamiranda, Daniel. 2001. *Teorías literarias*. 2 vols. Buenos Aires: Docencia.

Amin, Ash, and Nigel Thrift. 2002. *Cities: Reimagining the Urban*. Cambridge: Polity Press.

Anderson, B. 2005. "Practices of Judgment and Domestic Geographies of Affect." *Social and Cultural Geography* 6(5): 645–659.

Anderson, Perry. 1976. *Considerations on Western Marxism*. London: NLB.

Anderson, B., and P. Harrison. 2006. "Questioning Affect and Emotion." *Area* 38(3): 333–335.

Anderson, K., and S. Smith. 2001. "Editorial: Emotional Geographies." *Transactions of the Institute of British Geographers* 26(1): 7–10.

Anderson, B., F. Morton, and G. Revill. 2005. "Editorial: Practices of Music and Sound." *Social and Cultural Geography* 6(5): 639–644.

Arnold, Matthew. 1963. *Culture and Anarchy*, ed. J. Dover Wilson. Cambridge: Cambridge University Press.

Arac, Jonathan. 1997. "Shop Window or Laboratory: Collection, Collaboration and the Humanities." In *The Politics of Research*, eds., Ann Kaplan and George Levine, 116–126. New Brunswick: Rutgers Universities Press.

Attoh, Kafui A. 2011. "What *Kind* of Right is the Right to the City?" *Progress in Human Geography* 35(5): 669–685.

Atxaga, Bernardo. 1992. *Obabakoak*. Trans. Margaret Jull Costa. London: Hutchinson.

Augé, Marc. 2005. *Los no lugares. Una antropología de la sobremodernidad*. Trans. M. Mizraji. Barcelona: Gedisa.

Ayers, Edward L. 2010. "Turning toward Place, Space, and Time." In *The Spatial Humanities: GIS and the Future of Scholarship*, eds., David J. Bodenhamer, John Corrigan, and Trevor M. Harris, 1–13. Bloomington and Indianapolis: Indiana University Press.

Baker, Ed, and Malcolm Alan Compitello. 2003. *Madrid. De Fortunata a la M–40: Un siglo de cultura urbana*. Madrid: Alianza.

Baker, Houston A., Manthia Diawara, and Ruth H. Lindeborg, eds. 1996. *Black British Cultural Studies: A Reader*. Chicago, London: University of Chicago Press.

Balázs, Béla. 1970. *Theory of the Film. Character and Growth of a New Art*. Trans. Edith Bone. New York: Dover Publications, Inc.

Balsamo, Anne. 2011. "The Digital Humanities and Technocultural Innovation." In *Digital Media: Technological and Social Challenges of the Interactive World*, eds., Megan Winget and William Aspray, 213–225. Lanham, Toronto, Plymouth: The Scarecrow Press.

Barbaro, Umberto. 1972. "Materialism and Art." In *Marxism & Art*, eds., Berel Lang and Forrest Williams, 161–76. New York: David McKay.

Barker, Chris. 2008. *Cultural Studies: Theory and Practice*. 3rd ed. Los Angeles, London: Sage.

Barth, Lawrence. 2000. "Revisited: Henri Lefebvre and the Urban Condition." *Daidalos* 75: 23–27.

Barthes, Roland. 1979. *The Eiffel Tower and Other Mythologies*. Trans. Richard Howard. New York: Hill and Wang.

Bauman, Zygmunt. 2000. *Liquid Modernity*. Malden: Polity.

Berger, H. M., and M. T. Carroll, eds. 2003. *Global Pop, Local Language*. Jackson: University Press of Mississippi.

Bergson, Henri. 1912. *Matter and Memory*. 1896. Trans. Nancy Margaret Paul and W. Scott Palmer. London, G. Allen & Co; New York, Macmillan Co.

———. 1998. *Creative Evolution*. 1907. Trans. A. Mitchell. Mineola. New York: Dover Publications Inc.

———. 2001. *Time and Free Will. An Essay on the Immediate Data of Consciousness*. 1889. Trans. F. L. Pogson and M. A. Mineola. New York: Dover.

———. 2002. "Introduction to Metaphysics." 1903. In *The Creative Mind*, Trans. M. L. Andison, 159–200. New York: Citadel Press.

Bernard-Donals, Michael. 2008. "It's Not about the Book." *Profession*, 172–184.

Blum, Alan. 2003. *The Imaginative Structure of the City*. London: McGill-Queen's University Press.

Bodenhamer, David J. John Corrigan, and Trevor M. Harris, eds. 2010. *The Spatial Humanities: GIS and the Future of Scholarship*. Bloomington and Indianapolis: Indiana University Press.

Bondi, L. 2002. "Introduction." In *Subjectivities, Knowledges and Feminist Geographies*, eds., L. Bondi et al., 1–11. Lanham: Rowman & Littlefield.

Bowen, William M., Ronnie A. Dunn, and David O. Kasdan. 2010. "What Is 'Urban Studies': Context, Internal Structure and Content." *Journal of Urban Affairs* 32(2): 199–227.

Brenner, Neil. 2000. "The Urban Question as a Scale Question: Reflections on Henri Lefebvre, Urban Theory and the Politics of Scale." *International Journal of Urban and Regional Research* 24(2): 361–378.

———. 2004. *New State Spaces: Urban Governance and the Rescaling of Statehood.* Oxford: Oxford University Press.

Brenner, Neil, and Stuart Elden. 2001. "Henri Lefebvre in Contexts: An Introduction." *Antipode* 33(5): 763–768.

Brown, Joan L. 2010. *Confronting Our Canons: Spanish and Latin American Studies in the 21st Century.* Lewisburg: Bucknell Universities Press.

Bukharin, Nicholas I. 1972. "Art and Social Evolution." In *Marxism & Art*, eds., Berel Lang and Forrest Williams, 100–107. New York: David McKay.

Burgan, Mary. 2006. *What Ever Happened to the Faculty?: Drift and Decision in Higher Education.* Baltimore: Johns Hopkins University Press.

Burgess, Helen J., and Hamming Jeanne. 2011. "New Media in the Academy: Labor and the Production of Knowledge in Scholarly Multimedia." *Digital Humanities Quarterly* 5.3. http://www.digitalhumanities.org/dhq/vol/5/3/000102/000102.html. Accessed March 10, 2013.

Burkhard, Bud. 2000. *French Marxism between the Wars: Henri Lefebvre and the Philosophies.* Amherst: Humanity Books.

Casey, Edward S. 2011. "Do Places Have Edges? A Geo-Philosophical Inquiry." In *Envisioning Landscapes, Making Worlds: Geography and the Humanities*, eds., Stephen Daniels, Dydia DeLyser, J. Nicholas Entrikin, and Douglas Richardson, 65–73. Abingdon: Routledge.

Castells, Manuel, and John Mollenkopf. 1991. *Dual City: Restructuting New York.* New York: Russell Sage.

Cerdà, Ildefons. 1867. *Teoría general de la urbanización.* 2 vols. Madrid: Imprenta Española.

Charnock, Greig. 2010. "Challenging New State Spatialities: The Open Marxism of Henri Lefebvre." *Antipode* 42(5): 1279–1303.

Choay, Françoise. 1969. *The Modern City: Planning in the 19th Century.* Trans. M. Hugo and G. R. Collins. New York: George Braziller.

Clarke, David B., ed. 1997. *The Cinematic City.* New York: Routledge.

Cocola, Jim. 2011. "Putting Pablo Neruda's *Alturas de Macchu Picchu* in Its Places." In *Envisioning Landscapes, Making Worlds: Geography and the Humanities*, eds., Stephen Daniels, Dydia DeLyser, J. Nicholas Entrikin, and Douglas Richardson, 143–154. Abingdon: Routledge.

Collini, Stefan. 1993. "Introduction." In *The Two Cultures*, ed., C. P. Snow, vii–lxxi. Cambridge: Cambridge University Press.

Compitello, Malcolm Alan. 2003. "Del plan al diseño: *El día de la bestia* de Álex de la Iglesia y la cultura de la acumulación flexible en el Madrid del postcambio." In *Madrid. De Fortunana a la M–40. Un siglo de cultura urbana*, eds., E. Baker and M. A. Compitello, 327–352. Madrid: Alianza.

Connell, J., and C. Gibson. 2003. *Sound Tracks. Popular Music, Identity and Place.* London, New York: Routledge.

———. 2004. "World Music: Deterritorializing Place and Identity." *Progress in Human Geography* 28(3), 342–361.

Consalvo, M. 2003. "Hot Dates and Fairy–Tale Romances: Studying Sexuality in Videogames." In *The Video Game Theory Reader,* vol. 1, eds., M. J. P. Wolf and B. Perron, 171–194. New York, London: Routledge.

Cook, N. 1999. "Analysing Performance and Performing Analysis." In *Rethinking Music,* eds., N. Cook and M. Everist, 239–261. Oxford: Oxford University Press.

Corominas i Ayala, Miquel. 2010. *Los orígenes del Ensanche de Barcelona: Suelo técnica e iniciativa.* Barcelona: UPC.

Cosgrove, Denis. 2011. "Prologue: Geography within the Humanities." In *Envisioning Landscapes, Making Worlds: Geography and the Humanities,* eds., Stephen Daniels, Dydia DeLyser, J. Nicholas Entrikin, and Douglas Richardson, xxii–xxv. Abingdon: Routledge.

Cresswell, Tim, and Deborah Dixon, eds. 2002. *Engaging Film: Geographies of Mobility and Identity.* Lanham: Rowman and Littlefield.

Crogan, P. 2003. "History, Narrative, and Temporality in *Combat Flight Simulator 2.*" In *The Video Game Theory Reader,* vol. 1, eds., M. J. P. Wolf and B. Perron, 275–301. New York, London: Routledge.

Daniels, Stephen, Dydia DeLyser, J. Nicholas Entrikin, and Douglas Richardson, eds. 2011. *Envisioning Landscapes, Making Worlds: Geography and the Humanities.* London and New York: Routledge.

Darré, A. 1990. "Le parti nationaliste Basque. un mouvement péripherique et totalisant." *Révue Française de Science Politique* 40: 250–270.

Davidson, J., and C. Milligan. 2004. "Editorial: Embodying Emotion Sensing Space: Introducing Emotional Geographies." *Social and Cultural Geography* 5(4): 523–532.

Dear, Michael. 2000. *The Postmodern Urban Condition.* Oxford, Malden: Blackwell.

Dear, Michael, Jim Ketchum, Sarah Luria, and Doug Richardson, eds. 2011. *GeoHumanities: Art, History, Text at the Edge of Place.* Abingdon: Routledge.

Debord, Guy. 1961. "Perspectives for Conscious Changes in Everyday Life." *Internationale Situationiste* 6: 20–27.

———. 1995. *The Society of the Spectacle.* Trans. Donald Nicholson–Smith. New York: Zone.

de Certeau, Michel. 1988. *The Practice of Everyday Life.* Berkeley: University of California Press.

Degen, Mónica Montserrat. 2000. "Manuel Delgado, Capturing Public Life." Review of *El animal público. Space and Culture* 7/8/9.

———. 2004a. "Barcelona's Games: The Olympics, Urban Design and Glocal Tourism." In *Tourism Mobilities: Places to Play, Places in Play,* eds., J. Urry and M. Sheller, 131–142. London: Routledge.

———. 2004b. "Passejant per la passarel·la global: ciutats i turisme urbà." *Transversal* 23: 30–32.

———. 2008. *Sensing Cities: Regenerating Public Life in Barcelona and Manchester.* London, New York: Routledge.

Deleuze, Gilles, and Féliz Guattari. 2002. *A Thousand Plateaus: Capitalism and Schizophrenia II*. Trans. with Foreword by Brian Massumi. Minneapolis: University of Minnesota Press.

Deleyto, Celestino, and María del Mar Azcona. 2010. *Alejandro González Iñárritu*. Urbana: University of Illinois Press.

Delgado Ruiz, Manuel. 1991. "La ciudad cagada." In *Entre bichos anda el juego*, illustrated by José Luis Martín, 101–119. Barcelona: Puresa.

———. 1999. *El animal público*. Barcelona: Anagrama.

———. 2001. *Memoria y lugar: El espacio público como crisis de significado*. Valencia: Ediciones Generales de la Construcción.

———. 2004. "La no–ciudad como ciudad absoluta." In *La arquitectura de la no–ciudad*, ed., F. de Azúa, 121–154. Navarra: Universidad Pública de Navarra.

———. 2006. "Espacio público." (29 de mayo) *El País*. www.elpais.com.

———. 2007a. *Sociedades movedizas: pasos hacia una antropología de las calles*. Barcelona: Anagrama.

———. 2007b. *La ciudad mentirosa. Fraude y miseria del 'modelo Barcelona'*. Madrid: Catarata.

———. 2010. "La ciudad levantada: la barricada y otras transformaciones radicales del espacio urbano." In *Hacia un urbanismo alternativo* (*Architectonics, Mind, Land and Society* 19/20), 137–153. Barcelona: UPC.

Delgado Ruiz, Manuel, and Manuel Cruz. 2008. *Pensar por pensar: Conversaciones sobre el mundo y la vida*. Madrid: Aguilar.

D'Lugo, Marvin. 2003. "*Amores perros/Love's a Bitch*: Alejandro González Iñárritu, Mexico, 2000." In *The Cinema of Latin America*, eds., Alberto Elena and Marina Díaz López, 221–229. London: Wallflower Press.

DeNora, Tia. 2003a. *After Adorno. Rethinking Music Sociology*. Cambridge: Cambridge University Press.

———. 2003b. "Music Sociology: Getting the Music into the Action." *British Journal of Music Education* 20(2): 165–177.

Detienne, M., and Vernant, J.-P. 1978. *Cunning Intelligence in Greek Culture and Society*. Sussex: The Harvester Press Ltd.

Dodge, M., and R. Kitchin. 2005. "Code and the Transduction of Space." *Annals of the Association of American Geographers* 95(1): 162–180.

Douglass, W., J. Zulaika, C. Urza, and L. White. 2000. *Basque Cultural Studies*. Reno: University of Nevada Press.

Drucker, Johanna. 2009. *SPECLAB: Digital Aesthetics and Projects in Speculative Computing*. Chicago, London: University of Chicago Press.

Dubow, Jessica. 2011. "Still-Life, After-Life, *nature morte*: W. G. Sebald and the Demands of Landscape." In *Envisioning Landscapes, Making Worlds: Geography and the Humanities*, eds., Stephen Daniels, Dydia DeLyser, J. Nicholas Entrikin, and Douglas Richardson, 188–197. Abingdon: Routledge.

Edensor, T., and J. Holloway. 2008. "Rhythmanalysing the Coach Tour: The Ring of Kerry, Ireland." *Transactions of the Institute of British Geographers* 33: 483–501.

Elden, Stuart. 2001. "Politics, Philosophy, Geography: Henri Lefebvre in Recent Anglo–American Scholarship." *Antipode* 33(5): 809–825.

Elden, Stuart. 2004. *Understanding Henri Lefebvre: Theory and the Possible*. London, New York: Continuum.

————. 2006a. "Some are Born Posthumously: The French Afterlife of Henri Lefebvre." *Historical Materialism* 14(4): 185–202.

————. 2006b. "Rythmanalysis: An Introduction." In *Rhythmanalysis*, ed., Henri Lefebvre, trans. Stuart Elden and Gerald Moore, vii–xv. London, New York: Continuum.

————. 2007. "There Is a Politics of Space because Space Is Political: Henri Lefebvre and the Production of Space." *Radical Philosophy Review* 10(2): 101–116.

————. 2008. "The Exchange Economy of Peer-Review." *Environment and Planning D: Society and Space* 26: 951–953.

Elden, Stuart, and Elizabeth Lebas. 2003. "Introduction: Coming to Terms with Lefebvre." In *Henri Lefebvre: Key Writings*, eds., S. Elden, E. Lebas, and E. Kofman, xi–xix. New York, London: Continuum.

El-Khoury, Rodolphe, and Edward Robbins, eds. 2003. *Shaping the City: Studies in History, Theory and Urban Design*. New York, London: Routledge.

Ellis, John M. 1997. *Literature Lost: Social Agendas and the Corruption of the Humanities*. New Haven, London: Yale Universities Press.

Epps, Brad. 2001. "Modern Spaces: Building Barcelona." In *Iberian Cities*, ed., J. R. Resina, 148–197. New York, London: Routledge.

————, ed. 2002. "Barcelona and the Projection of Cataluña." Special Section of the *Arizona Journal of Hispanic Cultural Studies* 6: 191–287.

Esposito, Roberto. 2009. *Comunitas: The Origin and Destiny of Community*. Trans. T. C. Campbell. Stanford: Stanford University Press.

Ettlinger, Nancy. 2004. "Toward a Critical Theory of Untidy Geographies: The Spatiality of Emotions in Consumption and Production." *Feminist Economics* 10(3): 21–54.

Feaster, Felicia. 2011. "Life Isn't *Biutiful*: Alejandro González Iñárritu Turns Barcelona into Gomorrah." *Charleston City Paper* (February 9): 36.

Ferguson, Marjorie, and Peter Golding, eds. 1997. *Cultural Studies in Question*. London, Thousand Oaks, New Delhi: Sage.

Fernández–Vara, C. 2009. "The Tribulations of Adventure Games: Integrating Story into Simulation through Performance." PhD thesis, Georgia Institute of Technology, Atlanta.

Fernández–Vara, C., J. Zagal, and M. Mateas. 2005. "Evolution of Space Configuration in Videogames." *Changing Views: Worlds in Play (DIGRA 2005)*, Vancouver, BC, 16–20 June. http://users.soe.ucsc.edu/~michaelm/publications/fernandez–vara–digra2005.pdf. Accessed March 11, 2011.

Fernie, Eric, ed. 1995. *Art History and its Methods: A Critical Anthology*. London: Phaidon.

Filipcevic, Vojislava. 2010. "Urban Planning and the Spaces of Democracy: New York and the Great Depression in *42nd Street*, *Dead End* and *The City*." *Culture, Theory and Critique* 51(1): 65–91.

Filiciak, M. 2003. "Hyperidentities: Postmodern Identity Patterns in Massively Multiplayer Online Role–Playing Games." In *The Video Game Theory*

Reader, vol. 1, eds., M. J. P. Wolf and B. Perron, 87–102. New York, London: Routledge.

Fitzpatrick, Kathleen. 2011. *Planned Obsolescence*. New York, London: New York University Press.

Flusty, S. 1994. *Building Paranoia: The Proliferation of Interdictory Space and the Erosion of Spatial Justice*. West Hollywood: Los Angeles Forum for Architecture and Urban Design.

Fónagy, Ivan. 1999. "Why Iconicity." In *Form Miming Meaning: Iconicity in Language and Literature*, eds., Max Nänny and Olga Fischer, 3–36. Amsterdam: John Benjamins Publishing Company.

Ford, Larry. 1994. "Sunshine and Shadow: Lighting and Color in the Depiction of Cities on Film." In *Place, Power, Situation and Spectacle: A Geography of Film*, eds., Aitken and Zonn, 119–136. Lanham: Rowman & Littlefield.

Fortuna, C. 1998. "Images of the City: Sonorities and the Urban Social Environment." *Revista Critica de Ciencias Sociais* 51: 21–41.

———. 2001. "Soundscapes: The Sounding City and Urban Social Life." *Space and Culture* 11–12: 70–86.

Fraser, Benjamin. 2005. "On Mental and Cartographic Space: Belén Gopegui's *La escala de los mapas*, Bergson and the Imagined Interval." *España Contemporánea* 18(1): 7–32.

———. 2006a. "The Space in Film and the Film in Space: Madrid's Retiro Park and Carlos Saura's *Taxi*." *Studies in Hispanic Cinemas* 3(1): 15–33.

———. 2006b. "The Difference Space Makes: Bergsonian Methodology and Madrid's Cultural Imaginary through Literature, Film and Urban Space." PhD dissertation, Department of Spanish and Portuguese, University of Arizona.

———. 2006c. "Narradores contra la ficción: La novela detectivesca como estrategia política." *Studies in Latin American Popular Culture* 25: 199–219.

———. 2007a. "Manuel Delgado's Urban Anthropology: From Multidimensional Space to Interdisciplinary Spatial Theory." *Arizona Journal of Hispanic Cultural Studies* 11: 57–75.

———. 2007b. "Madrid's Retiro Park as Publicly–Private Space and the Spatial Problems of Spatial Theory." *Social and Cultural Geography* 8(5): 673–700.

———. 2007c. "Deaf Cultural Production in Twentieth-Century Madrid." *Sign Language Studies* 7(4): 431–457.

———. 2008a. "Toward a Philosophy of the Urban: Henri Lefebvre's Uncomfortable Application of Bergsonism." *Environment and Planning D: Society and Space* 26(2): 338–358.

———. 2008b. "Reconciling Film Studies & Geography: Adolfo Bioy Casares's *La invención de Morel*." *Mosaic: A Journal for the Interdisciplinary Study of Literature* 41(1): 153–168.

———. 2008c. "A Snapshot of Barcelona from Montjuïc: Juan Goytisolo's *Señas de identidad*, Tourist Landscapes as Process, and the Photographic Mechanism of Thought." In *Spain Is (Still) Different: Tourism and Discourse in Spanish Identity*, eds., E. Afinoguénova and J. Martí–Olivella, 151–184. Lanham: Lexington Books.

Fraser, Benjamin. 2009a. "'The Kind of Problem Cities Pose': Jane Jacobs at the Intersection of Philosophy, Pedagogy and Urban Theory." *Teaching in Higher Education* 14(3): 265–276.

———. 2009b. "The Bergsonian Link between Emotion, Music and Place: From the 'Motion of Emotion' to the Sonic Immediacy of the Basque band 'Lisabö.'" *Journal of Spanish Cultural Studies* 10(2): 241–262.

———, ed. and trans. 2009c. *Deaf History and Culture in Spain: A Reader of Primary Sources.* Foreword by Samuel J. Supalla. Washington: Gallaudet University Press.

———. 2010. *Encounters with Bergson(ism) in Spain: Reconciling Philosophy, Literature, Film and Urban Space* [Studies in Romance Languages and Literatures #295]. Chapel Hill: UNC Department of Romance Languages.

———. 2011a. *Henri Lefebvre and the Spanish Urban Experience: Reading the Mobile City.* Lewisburg: Bucknell University Press.

———. 2011b. "Ildefons Cerdà's Scalpel: A Lefebvrian Perspective on Nineteenth-Century Urban Planning." *Catalan Review* 25: 181–200.

———. 2011c. "Why the Spatial Epistemology of the Videogame Matters: Mètis, Video Game Space and Interdisciplinary Theory." *Journal of Gaming and Virtual Worlds* 3(2): 93–106.

———. 2011d. "Re-Scaling Emotional Approaches to Music: Basque Band Lisabö & the Soundscapes of Urban Alienation." *Emotion, Space and Society* 4: 8–16.

———. 2012a. "The 'Sidewalk Ballet' in the Work of Henri Lefebvre and Manuel Delgado Ruiz." In *The Urban Wisdom of Jane Jacobs,* eds., Diane Zahm and Sonia Hirt, 24–36. London, New York: Routledge.

———. 2012b. "On Nocilla and the Urbanization of Consciousness: Multiplicity & Interdisciplinarity in Agustín Fernández Mallo's Fragmented Trilogy." *Hispania* 95(1): 1–13.

———. 2012c. "A Biutiful City: Alejandro González Iñárritu's Filmic Critique of the 'Barcelona model.'" *Studies in Hispanic Cinemas* 9(1): 19–34.

———. 2012d. "Hacia un costumbrismo espacial: Larra y la ciencia–ficción de la vida cotidiana en *Sin noticias de Gurb* (Mendoza) y *Plutón BRB Nero* (De la Iglesia)." *Letras Hispanas* 8(1): 48–61.

———. 2013. "Feijóo on Mars: A Brief Note on the Literary Godfather of Spanish Science Fiction." *Dieciocho* 36(1): 37–50.

———, ed. 2014. *Marxism and Urban Culture.* Foreword by Andy Merrifield. Lanham: Lexington Books.

Fraser, Benjamin, and Abby Fuoto. 2012. "Manchester, 1976: Documenting the Urban Nature of Joy Division's Musical Production." *Punk & Post–Punk* 1(2): 139–154.

Fraser, B., and C. Méndez. 2012. "Espacio, tiempo y ciudad: La representación de Buenos Aires en *El Eternauta*." *Revista Iberoamericana* 78(238–239): 57–72.

Fraser, B., M.A. Compitello, and E. Romero. 2011. "An AJHCS Editorial Position Paper: A Modest Proposal on Peer Review." *Arizona Journal of Hispanic Cultural Studies* 15 (2011): 11–22.

Fraser, B., S. Larson, and M. A. Compitello. 2014. "Notes on the Renegotiation of a Hispanic Studies Canon." *ADFL Bulletin* 43(1).: 77–90.

Freire, Paolo. 1970. *Pedagogy of the Oppressed.* Trans. M.B. Ramos. New York: Continuum.

——. 1998. *Teachers as Cultural Workers. Letters to Those Who Dare to Teach.* Trans. D. Macedo, D. Koike, and A. Oliveira. Boulder: Westview.

Friedman, Michael Todd, and Cathy van Ingen. 2011. "Bodies in Space: Spatializing Physical Cultural Studies." *Sociology of Sport Journal* 28: 85–105.

Frith, S. 1988. *Music for Pleasure.* New York: Routledge.

——. 1996a. *Performing Rites. On the Value of Popular Music.* Oxford: Oxford University Press.

——. 1996b. "Music and Identity." In *Questions of Cultural Identity,* eds., S. Hall and P. DuGay, 100–127. London: Sage.

Frost, Daniel. 2008. *Cultivating Madrid.* Lewisburg: Bucknell University Press.

Gagnon, D. 1985. "Videogames and Spatial Skills: An Exploratory Study." *Educational Communication and Technology* 33(4): 263–275.

Galfant, Blanche Housman. 1970. *The American City Novel.* 1954. Norman: University of Oklahoma Press.

Gandy, Matthew. 2011. "The Texture of Space: Desire and Displacement in Hiroshi Teshigara's *Woman of the Dunes.*" In *Envisioning Landscapes, Making Worlds: Geography and the Humanities,* eds., Stephen Daniels, Dydia DeLyser, J. Nicholas Entrikin, and Douglas Richardson, 198–208. Abingdon: Routledge.

Gee, J. P. 2003. *What Video Games Have to Teach Us about Learning and Literacy.* New York: Palgrave Macmillan.

Gibson, Mark. 2007. *Culture and Power: A History of Cultural Studies.* Oxford, New York: Berg.

Goldston, Robert. 1969. *Barcelona: The Civic Stage.* London: Collier–MacMillan ltd.

González Iñárritu, Alejandro. 2010. *Biutiful.* Perf: Javier Bardem, Eduard Fernández, Luo Jin, Maricel Alvarez. DVD.

Goonewardena, Kanishka. 2005. "The Urban Sensorium: Space, Ideology and the Aestheticization of Politics." *Antipode* 37: 46–71.

Goonewardena, Kanishka, Stefan Kipfer, Richard Milgrom, and Christian Schmid, eds. 2008. *Space, Difference, Everyday Life: Reading Henri Lefebvre.* New York, London: Routledge.

Gopegui, Belén. 1993. *La escala de los mapas.* Barcelona: Anagrama.

Gorak, Jan. 1988. *The Alien Mind of Raymond Williams.* Columbia: University of Missouri Press.

Gottdeiner, Mark. 2000. "Lefebvre and the Bias of Academic Urbanism: What Can We Learn from the 'New' Urban Analysis." *City* 4(1): 93–100.

Goytisolo, Juan. 1999. *Señas de identidad.* 1966. Madrid: Alianza.

Greenberg, Joseph H. 1995. "On Language Internal Iconicity." In *Syntactic Iconicity and Linguistic Freezes: The Human Dimension,* ed., Marge E. Landsberg, 57–63. Berlin: Mouton de Gruyter.

Greenfield, P. M. 1984. *Mind and Media: The Effects of Television, Video Games and Computers.* Cambridge: Harvard University Press.

Gregori, Eduardo. 2006. "Geografías urbanas: La representación de la ciudad de México en *El sitio* y *Amores perros.*" *Espéculo: Revista de Estudios Literarios* 33.

Gregory, Ian. 2010. "Exploiting Time and Space: A Challenge for GIS in the Digital Humanities." In *The Spatial Humanities: GIS and the Future of Scholarship*, eds., David J. Bodehamer, John Corrigan, and Trevor M. Harris, 58–75. Bloomington and Indianapolis: Indiana University Press.

Gretchko, Valerij. 2003. "Aesthetic Conception of Russian Formalism: The Cognitive View." *Sign Systems Studies* 31(2): 523–532.

Grodal, T. 2003. "Stories for Eye, Ear and Muscles. Video Games, Media, and Embodied Experiences." In *The Video Game Theory Reader*, vol. 1, eds., M. J. P. Wolf and B. Perron, 129–155. New York, London: Routledge.

Grossberg, Lawrence. 2010a. "Raymond Williams and the Absent Modernity." In *About Raymond Williams*, eds., Monika Seidl, Roman Horak, and Lawrence Grossberg, 18–33. London, New York: Routledge.

———. 2010b. *Cultural Studies in the Future Tense.* Durham, London: Duke University Press.

Grossberg, Lawrence, Cary Nelson, and Paula A. Treichler, eds. 1992. *Cultural Studies.* New York, London: Routledge.

Guenzel, S. 2007. "Eastern Europe, 2008." In *Space Time Play. Computer Games, Architecture and Urbanism: The Next Level*, eds., F. von Borries, S. Walz, M. Bottger, D. Davidson, H. Kelley and J. Kücklich, 444–449. Basel, Boston, Berlin: Birkhauser.

Hall, Gary, and Clare Birchall. 2006. *New Cultural Studies: Adventures in Theory.* Athens: University of Georgia Press.

Hall, Thomas. 1997. *Planning Europe's Capital Cities: Aspects of Nineteenth–Century Urban Development.* London: E and FN SPON.

Hall, Stuart, and Tony Jefferson, eds. 1975. *Resistance through Rituals: Youth Subcultures in Post-War Britain. Working Papers in Cultural Studies No. 7–8.* Birmingham: University of Birmingham, Centre for Contemporary Cultural Studies.

Hall, Stuart, et al. 1978. *Policing the Crisis: Mugging, the State, and Law and Order.* New York: Palgrave Macmillan.

Harvey, David. 1989. *The Urban Experience.* Baltimore: Johns Hopkins University Press.

———. 1990. *The Condition of Postmodernity.* Cambridge, Oxford: Blackwell.

———. 1991. "Afterword." *The Production of Space*, ed., Henri Lefebvre, trans. Donald Nicholson–Smith, 425–434. Oxford: Blackwell.

———. 1996. *Justice, Nature and the Geography of Difference.* London: Blackwell.

———. 2000. *Spaces of Hope.* Berkeley: University of California Press.

———. 2001. *Spaces of Capital: Towards a Critical Geography.* New York: Routledge.

———. 2003. "City Future in City Past: Balzac's Cartographic Imaginary." In *After-Images of the City*, eds., Joan Ramon Resina and Dieter Ingenschay, 23–48. Ithaca, London: Cornell University Press.

———. 2005. "The New Urbanism and the Communitarian Trap: On the Social Problems and the False Hope of Design." In *Sprawl and Suburbia*, ed., William S. Saunders, introduction by Robert Fishman, 21–26. London, Minneapolis: University of Minnesota Press.

———. 2006a. *Paris, Capital of Modernity*. London, New York: Routledge.

———. 2006b. *A Brief History of Neoliberalism*. Oxford: Oxford University Press.

———. 2006c. "Space as a Key Word." In *Spaces of Global Capitalism: Towards a Theory of Uneven Geographical Development*, 117–148. London, New York: Verso.

———. 2009a. *Social Justice and the City*. Athens: University of Georgia Press.

———. 2009b. *Cosmopolitanism and the Geographies of Freedom*. Columbia: Columbia University Press.

———. 2010. *A Companion to Marx's Capital*. London, New York: Verso.

———. 2012. *Rebel Cities*. London, New York: Verso.

Henderson, V. L. 2008. "Is There Hope for Anger? The Politics of Spatializing and (Re)producing an Emotion." *Emotion, Space and Society* 1(1): 28–37.

Herzberger, David. 2012. "How Malcolm Compitello Discovered and Explained Juan Benet." *Capital Inscriptions: Essays on Hispanic Literature, Film and Urban Space in Honor of Malcolm Alan Compitello*, ed. B. Fraser, 53–64. Newark: Juan de la Cuesta.

Highmore, Ben. 2002. "Street Life in London: Towards a Rhythmanalysis of London in the Late Nineteenth Century." *New Formations* 47: 171–193.

———. 2005. *Cityscapes: Cultural Readings in the Material and Symbolic City*. New York: Palgrave Macmillan.

Holland, W., H. Jenkins, and K. Squire. 2003. "Theory by Design." In *The Video Game Theory Reader*, vol. 1, eds., M. J. P. Wolf and B. Perron, 25–46. New York, London: Routledge.

Holmes, Amanda. 2010. "Modern Heroics: The Flâneur in Adolfo Bioy Casares's *El sueño de los héroes*." In *Circulation and the City: Essays on Urban Culture*, eds., Alexandra Boutros and Will Straw, 240–257. Montreal, Kingston, London, Ithaca: McGill-Queen's University Press.

Hones, Sheila. 2011. "Literary Geography: The Novel as a Spatial Event." In *Envisioning Landscapes, Making Worlds: Geography and the Humanities*, eds., Stephen Daniels, Dydia DeLyser, J. Nicholas Entrikin, and Douglas Richardson, 247–255. Abingdon: Routledge.

hooks, b. 1994. *Teaching to Transgress. Education as the Practice of Freedom*. New York, London: Routledge.

Hopkins, Jeff. 1994. "Mapping of Cinematic Places: Icons, Ideology, and the Power of (Mis)representation." In *Place, Power, Situation, and Spectacle: A Geography of Film*, eds., S. Aitken and L. Zonn, 47–65. Lanham: Rowman and Littlefield Publishers.

Hughes, Robert. 1992. *Barcelona*. New York: Knopf.

Howitt, R. 2003. "Scale." In *A Companion to Political Geography*, eds., J. Agnew, K. Mitchell, and G. Toal, 138–157. Blackwell, Oxford.

Hudson, R. 2006. "Regions and Place: Music, Identity and Place." *Progress in Human Geography* 30(5): 626–634.

Ibarra, P. 1989. *La evolución estratégica de ETA*. Donostia.

Jacobs, Jane. 1970. *The Economy of Cities*. New York: Vintage.

———. 1984. *Cities and the Wealth of Nations: Principles of Economic Life*. NewYork: Random House.

———. 1992. *The Death and Life of Great American Cities*. New York: Vintage.

Jakobson, Roman. 1965. "Quest for the Essence of Language." *Diogenes* 51: 21–37.

———. 1985. "My Favorite Topics." In *Verbal Art, Verbal Sign, Verbal Time*, eds., Krystyna Pomorska and Stephen Rudy, 3–7. Minneapolis: University of Minnesota Press.

———. 1987. *Language in Literature*, eds., Krystyna Pomorska and Stephen Rudy. Harvard: Belknap.

Jakobson, Roman, and Jurji Tynjanov. 1985. "Problems in the Study of Language and Literature." In *Verbal Art, Verbal Sign, Verbal Time*, eds., Krystyna Pomorska and Stephen Rudy, 25–33. Minneapolis: University of Minnesota Press.

Jakobson, Roman, and Linda Waugh. 1979. *The Sound Shape of Language*. Bloomington: Indiana University Press.

Jameson, Fredric. 1972. *The Prison–House of Language: A Critical Account of Structuralism and Russian Formalism*. Princeton: Princeton University Press.

———. 1981. *The Political Unconscious*. Ithaca: Cornell University Press.

———. 1999. *Postmodernism: or, the Cultural Logic of Late Capitalism*. Durham: Duke University Press.

Jáuregui, G. 1986. "National Identity and Political Violence in the Basque Country." *European Journal of Political Research* 14: 587–605.

Jessop, Bob. 1999. "Narrating the Future of the National Economy and the National State: Remarks on Remapping Regulation and Reinventing Governance." In *State/Culture: State–Formation after the Cultural Turn*, ed., G. Steinmetz, 378–405. Ithaca, London: Cornell University Press.

Judt, Tony. 1986. *Marxism and the French Left: Studies on Labor and Politics in France 1830–1981*. Oxford: Clarendon Press.

Juul, J. 2007. "Variation over Time: The Transformation of Space in Single–Screen Action Games." In *Space Time Play. Computer Games, Architecture and Urbanism: The Next Level*, eds., F. von Borries, S. Walz, M. Bottger, D. Davidson, H. Kelley, and J. Kücklich, 100–103. Basel, Boston, Berlin: Birkhauser.

Juslin, P. N., and J. A. Slobada. 2001. "Music and Emotion: Introduction." In *Music and Emotion: Theory and Research*, eds., P. N. Juslin and J.A. Slobada, 3–21. Oxford: Oxford University Press.

Kantaris, Geoffrey. 2008. "Lola/Lolo: Filming Gender and Violence in the Mexican City." In *Cities in Transition: The Moving Image and the Modern Metropolis*, eds., Webber and Wilson, 163–175. New York, London: Wallflower Press.

Kasmir, S. 2002. "'More Basque than You!': Class, Youth and Identity in an Industrial Basque Town." *Identities* 9(1): 39–68.

Katznelson, Ira. 1992. *Marxism and the City*. Oxford: Clarenson Press.

Kay, Sarah. 2003. *Zizek: A Critical Introduction*. Cambridge: Polity.

Keane, S. 2007. *CineTech. Film, Convergence and New Media*, New York: Palgrave Macmillan.

Kelly, Michael. 1982. *Modern French Marxism*. Baltimore: Johns Hopkins University Press.

Kernan, Alvin. 1997. "Introduction." In *What's Happened to the Humanities*, 3–13. Princeton: Princeton Universities Press.

King, G., and T. Krzywinska, eds. 2002. *ScreenPlay: Cinema/Videogames/Interfaces*. New York, London: Wallflower Press.

Kipfer, Stefan. 2008. "Preface to the New Edition." In *Dialectical Materialism*, ed., Henri Lefebvre, xiii–xxxii. Minneapolis: University of Minnesota Press.

———. 2009. "Why the Urban Question Still Matters: Reflections on Rescaling and the Promise of the Urban." In *Leviathan Undone? Towards a Political Economy of Scale*, eds., Roger Keil and Rianne Mahon, 67–83. Vancouver: UBC Press.

Kitchens, John. 2009. "Situated Pedagogy and the Situationist International: Countering a Pedagogy of Placelessness." *Educational Studies* 45: 240–261.

Klein, Julie Thompson. 2005. *Humanities, Culture and Interdisciplinarity*. Albany: State University of New York.

Knabb, Ken, ed. 2006. *Situationist International Anthology*. Berkeley: Bureau of Public Secrets.

Koch, Gertrud. 1987. "Béla Balázs: The Physiognomy of Things." Trans. Miriam Hansen. *New German Critique* 40: 167–177.

Kofman, Eleonore, and Elisabeth Lebas. 1996. "Lost in Transposition—Time, Space and the City." In *Henri Lefebvre, Writings on Cities*, eds., E. Kofman and E. Lebas, 3–60. Malden: Blackwell.

Kolakowski, Leszek. 2005. *Main Currents of Marxism*. Trans. P. S. Falla. New York, London: W. W. Norton.

Kracauer, Siegfried. 1968. *Theory of Film: The Redemption of Physical Reality*. 1960. New York, Oxford: Oxford University Press.

Kronman, Anthony T. 2007. *Ecuation's End: Why Our Colleges and Universities Have Given Up on the Meaning of Life*. New Haven, London: Yale Universities Press.

Labanyi, Jo. 2000. "History and Hauntology; Or, What Does One Do with the Ghosts of the Past?: Reflections on Spanish Film and Fiction of the Post–Franco Period." In *Disremembering the Dictatorship: The Politics of Memory since the Spanish Transition to Democracy*, ed., J. R. Resina, 65–82. Amsterdam: Rodopi.

Lang, Berel, and Forrest Williams, eds. 1972. *Marxism and Art: Writings in Aesthetics and Criticism*. New York: David McKay Company.

Lahusen, C. 1993. "The Aesthetic of Radicalism: The Relationship between Punk and the Patriotic Nationalist Movement of the Basque Country." *Popular Music* 12(3): 263–280.

Larson, Susan. 2011. *Constructing and Resisting Modernity: Madrid 1900–1936*. Madrid: Vervuert/Iberoamericana.

Laurier, E. 2008. "How Breakfast Happens in the Café." *Time and Society* 17(1): 119–134.

Leavis, F. R. 1972. *Nor Shall My Sword: Discourses on Pluralism, Compassion and Social Hope*. New York: Barnes & Noble.

Lefebvre, Henri. 1946. *L'Existentialisme*. Paris: Editions de Sagittaire.

———. 1947. *Marx et la liberté*. Geneva: Editions des Trois Collines.

———. 1948. *Le marxisme*. Paris: Presses Universitaries de France.

———. 1964. *Marx*. Paris: Presses Universitaries de France.

———. 1969. *The Explosion: Marxism and the French Upheaval*. New York, London: The Monthly Review Press.

———. 1976. *The Survival of Capitalism: Reproduction of the Relations of Production*. Trans. Frank Bryant. New York: St. Martin's Press.

———. 1980. *La présence et l'absence: Contribution à la théorie des représentations*. Paris: Caterman.

———. 1982. *The Sociology of Marx*. Trans. N. Guterman. New York: Columbia University Press.

———. 1988. "Toward a Leftist Cultural Politics: Remarks Occasioned by the Centenary of Marx's Death." Trans. David Reifman. In *Marxism and the Interpretation of Culture*, eds., Lawrence Grossberg and Cary Nelson, 75–88. Chicago: University of Illinois Press.

———. 1991a. *The Production of Space*. Trans. Donald Nicholson–Smith. Oxford: Blackwell.

———. 1991b. *Critique of Everyday Life, Vol. 1*. Trans. John Moore. London; New York: Verso.

———. 1995. *Introduction to Modernity*. Trans. John Moore. London and New York: Verso.

———. 1996. *The Right to the City*. In *Writings on Cities*, eds. and trans., E. Kofman and E. Lebas, 63–181. Oxford: Blackwell.

———. 2002. *Critique of Everyday Life*. Vol. 2. Trans. John Moore. London, New York: Verso.

———. 2003a. *The Urban Revolution*. 1970. Trans. Robert Bononno. Minneapolis: University Minnesota Press.

———. 2003b. *Henri Lefebvre: Key Writings*, eds., S. Elden, E. Lebas, and E. Kofman, New York, London: Continuum.

———. 2005. *Critique of Everyday Life*. Vol. 3. Trans. Gregory Elliott. London, New York: Verso.

———. 2006a. *Rhythmanalysis*. Trans. S. Elden and Gerald Moore. London, New York: Continuum.

———. 2006b. *La presencia la ausencia: Contribución a la teoría de las representaciones*. Trans. Óscar Barahona and Uxoa Doyhamboure. México D.F.: Fondo de Cultura Económica.

———. 2007. *Everyday Life in the Modern World*. Trans. Sacha Rabinovich, introduction by Philip Wander. 11th ed. New Brunswick, London: Transaction Publishers.

———. 2008. *Dialectical Materialism*. Trans. John Sturrock with preface by Stefan Kipfer. Minneapolis: University of Minnesota Press.

———. 2009. *State, Space, World. Selected Essays*, eds., Neil Brenner and Stuart Elden, trans. Gerald Moore, N. Brenner, and S. Elden. London, Minneapolis: University of Minnesota Press.

LeGates, Richard T., and Frederic Stout. 2005. "How to Study Cities: Editors' Introduction." In *The City Reader*, 3rd ed, 9–18. London: Routledge.

Léger, Marc James. 2006. "Henri Lefebvre and the Moment of the Aesthetic." In *Marxism and the History of Art: From William Morris to the New Left*, ed., Andrew Hemingway, 143–160. London: Pluto Press.

Levitin, D. J. 2006. *This Is Your Brain on Music: The Science of a Human Obsession*. New York: Plume, Penguin Group.

Lilley, Keith D. 2011. "Digital Cartographies and Medieval Geographies." In *Envisioning Landscapes, Making Worlds: Geography and the Humanities*, eds., Stephen Daniels, Dydia DeLyser, J. Nicholas Entrikin, and Douglas Richardson, 25–33. Abingdon: Routledge.

Lim, Ming. 2006. "The (Re)Production of Organizational Time: Reading the Feminine through Henri Lefebvre." *Tamara Journal* 5(2): 125–137.

Lindner, Christophe. 2009. *Globalization, Violence, and the Visual Culture of Cities*. London, New York: Routledge.

Linstroth, J. P. 2002. "The Basque Conflict Globally Speaking: Material Culture, Media and Basque Identity in the Wider World." *Oxford Development Studies* 30(2): 205–222.

Lisabö. 2000. *Ezarian*. Irun: Esan Ozenki.

———. 2002. *Egan Bat Nonahi*. Madrid: Acuarela.

———. 2005. *Izkiriaturik aurkitu ditudan gurak*. Irun: Metak.

———. 2007. *Ezlekuak*. Irun: Bidehuts.

Lloyd, David. 1997. "Nationalisms against the State." In *The Politics of Culture in the Shadow of Capital*, eds., L. Lowe and D. Lloyd, 172–197. Durham: Duke University Press.

Lock, Gary. 2010. "Representations of Space and Place in the Humanities." In *The Spatial Humanities: GIS and the Future of Scholarship*, eds., David J. Bodenhamer, John Corrigan, and Trevor M. Harris, 89–108. Bloomington and Indianapolis: Indiana University Press.

Loewy, Hanno. 2006. "Space, Time, and 'Rites de Passage': Béla Balázs's Paths to Film." *October* 115 (Winter): 61–76.

Lotman, Iuri. 1976. *Semiotics of Cinema*. Ann Arbor: University of Michigan Press.

Loxham, Abigail. 2006. "Barcelona under Construction: The Democratic Potential of Touch and Vision in City Cinema as Depicted in *En construcción* (2001)." *Studies in Hispanic Cinemas* 3(1): 35–48.

Lukas, S. A. 2007. "The Themed Space: Locating Culture, Nation and Self." In *The Themed Space*, ed., S. A. Lukas, 1–22. Lanham: Lexington Books.

Luna, J. S. 2001. Lisabö: *Ezarian*. www.mondosonoro.com.

Luria, Sarah. 2011a. "Geotexts." In *GeoHumanities: Art, History, Text and the Edge of Place*, eds., Michael Dear, Jim Ketchum, Sarah Luria, and Doug Richardson, 67–70. Abingdon: Routledge.

———. 2011b. "Thoreau's Geopoetics." In *GeoHumanities: Art, History, Text at the Edge of Place*, eds., Michael Dear, Jim Ketchum, Sarah Luria, and Doug Richardson, 126–138. Abingdon: Routledge.

Marston, S. 2000. "The Social Construction of Scale." *Progress in Human Geography* 24(2): 219–242.

Martin, B. 2007. "Should Videogames Be Viewed as Art?" In *Videogames and Art*, eds., G. Mitchell and A. Clarke, 201–210. Intellect.

Massey, D. 1995. "The Conceptualisations of Place." In *A Place in the World?*, eds., D. Massey and P. Jess, 45–85. Oxford: Oxford University Press.

Marx, Karl. 1973. *Grundrisse*. Harmondsworth: Penguin Publishers.

———. 1977. *Capital*, vol. 1. Trans. Ben Fowkes, with introduction by Ernest Mandel. New York: Vintage.

Mäyrä, F. 2009. "Getting into the Game: Doing Multidisciplinary Game Studies." In *The Video Game Theory Reader*, vol. 2, eds., M. J. P. Wolf and B. Perron, 313–329. New York, London: Routledge.

McClary, S., and R. Walser. 1990. "Start Making Sense! Musicology Wrestles with Rock." In *On Record. Rock, Pop and the Written Word*, eds., S. Frith and A. Goodwin, 277–292. London, New York: Routledge.

McCormack, D. 2003. "An Event of Geographical Ethics in Spaces of Affect." *Transactions of the Institute of British Geographers* 28: 488–507.

———. 2006. "For the Love of Pipes and Cables: A Response to Deborah Thien." *Area* 38(3): 330–332.

McGann, Jerome. 2001. *Radiant Textuality: Literature after the WorldWide Web*. New York: Palgrave Macmillan.

McGaw, J., and A. Vance. 2008. "Who Has the Street–Smarts? The Role of Emotion in Co-Creating the City." *Emotion, Space and Society* 1(1): 65–69.

McNeill, Donald. 2002. "Barcelona: Urban Identity 1992–2002." *Arizona Journal of Hispanic Cultural Studies* 6: 245–262.

———. 1999. *Urban Change and the European Left: Tales from the New Barcelona*. London, New York: Routledge.

Mendieta, Eduardo. 2008. "The Production of Urban Space in the Age of Transnational Mega–Urbes: Lefebvre's Rhythmanalysis Or Henri Lefebvre: The Philosopher of May '68." *City* 12(2): 148–153.

Mendoza, Eduardo. 2003. *La ciudad de los prodigios*. Barcelona: Seix Barral.

Mennel, Barbara. 2008. *Cities and Cinema*. London, New York: Routledge.

Merrifield, Andy. 2002. *Metromarxism. A Marxist Tale of the City*. London, New York: Routledge.

———. 2005. *Guy Debord*. London: Reaktion Books.

———. 2006. *Henri Lefebvre: A Critical Introduction*. New York; London: Routledge.

Miller, Vincent. 2005. "Intertextuality, the Referential Illusion and the Production of a Gay Ghetto." *Social and Cultural Geography* 6(1): 61–79.

Mitchell, Don. 2000. *Cultural Geography: A Critical Introduction*. Oxford: Blackwell.

———. 2003. *The Right to the City: Social Justice and the Fight for Public Space*. New York: The Guilford Press.

Mogel, Lize. 2011. "Disorientation Guides: Cartography as Artistic Medium." In *GeoHumanities: Art, History, Text at the Edge of Place*, eds., Michael Dear, Jim Ketchum, Sarah Luria, and Doug Richardson, 187–195. Abingdon: Routledge.

Moran, Joe. 2004. "History, Memory and the Everyday." *Rethinking History* 8(1): 51–68.

Moraña, Mabel, ed. 2005. *Ideologies of Hispanism*. Nashville: Vanderbilt Universities Press.

Moreiras–Menor, Cristina. 2008. "Nuevas fundaciones: temporalidad e historia en *La comunidad* de Álex de la Iglesia." *MLN* 123(2): 374–395.

Moretti, Franco. 2010. "Homo Palpitans: Balzac's Novels and Urban Personality." In *The Blackwell City Reader*, 2nd ed., eds., Gary Bridge and Sophie Watson, 309–316. Malden, Oxford, Chichester: Wiley–Blackwell.

Morley, David, and Kevin Robins, eds. 2001. *British Cultural Studies: Geography, Nationality and Identity*. Oxford: Oxford University Press.

Morton, F. 2005. "Performing Ethnography: Irish Traditional Music Sessions and New Methodological Spaces." *Social and Cultural Geography* 6(5): 661–676.

Mumford, Lewis. 1934. *Technics and Civilization*. New York: Harcourt Brace and Co.

———. 1970. *The Culture of Cities*. 1938. New York: Harcourt, Brace Jovanovich.

———. 2005. "What Is a City?" 1937. In *The City Reader*, 3rd ed., eds., Richard T. LeGates and Frederic Stout, 92–96. London: Routledge.

Nadal–Melsió, Sara. 2008. "Lessons in Surrealism: Relationality, Event, Encounter." In *Space, Difference, Everyday Life: Reading Henri Lefebvre*, eds., Kanishka Goonewardena, Stefan Kipfer, Richard Milgrom, and Christian Schmid, 161–175. New York, London: Routledge.

Nedozchiwin, G. A. 1972. "What Is Aesthetics." In *Marxism & Art*, eds., Berel Lang and Forrest Williams, 131–136. New York: David McKay.

Newman, James. 2004. *Videogames*. London, New York: Routledge.

Nitsche, Michael. 2008. *Video Game Spaces. Image, Play and Structure in 3D Game Worlds*. Cambridge, London: MIT Press.

Noveck, B. S. 2006. "Democracy – The Video Game: Virtual Worlds and the Future of Collective Action." In *State of Play: Law, Games and Virtual Worlds*, eds., J. Balkin and B. Noveck, 257–282. New York: New York University Press.

Obert, J. C. 2008. "Sound and Sentiment: A Rhythmanalysis of Television." *Continuum: Journal of Media & Cultural Studies* 22(3): 409–417.

Olsen, Donald J. 1986. *The City as a Work of Art: London, Paris, Vienna*. New Haven: Yale University Press.

Ortega, Julio, ed. 2010. *Nuevos hispanismos interdisciplinarios y trasatlánticos*. Madrid: Vervuert/Iberoamericana.

Park, Robert. 1967. *On Social Control and Collective Behavior*. Chicago: Chicago University Press.

———. 1968. "The City: Suggestions for the Investigation of Human Behavior in the Urban Environment." In *The City*, eds., R. E. Park, E. W. Burgess, and R. D. McKenzie, 1–46. Chicago, London: University of Chicago Press.

Parker, Simon. 2004. *Urban Theory and the Urban Experience: Encountering the City*. London, New York: Routledge.

Pasolini, Pier Paolo. 1988. *Heretical Empiricism*, ed., Louise K. Barnett. Bloomington: Indiana University Press.

Perry, David. 2010. "The MLA, @briancroxall, and the Non-rise of the Digital Humanities." Blog entry, *AcademHack*. http://academhack.outsidethetext.com /home/2010/the-mla-briancroxall-and-the-non-rise-of-the-digital-humanities/. Accessed March 7, 2010.

Philo, Chris, and Gerry Kearns. 1993. "Culture, History, Capital: A Critical Introduction to the Selling of Places." In *Selling Places: The City as Cultural Capital Past and Present*, eds., Philo and Kearns, 1–32. Oxford: Pergamon.

Pike, Burton. 1981. *The Image of the City in Modern Literature*. Princeton: Princeton University Press.

Podalsky, Laura. 2011. "Migrant Feelings: Melodrama, *Babel* and Affective Communities." *Studies in Hispanic Cinemas* 7(1): 47–58.

Pope, Randolph. 2012. "Whereto Now? From *mezzo* to Messi, from *Don Quixote* to *2666*." *Capital Inscriptions: Essays on Hispanic Literature, Film and Urban Space in Honor of Malcolm Alan Compitello*, ed. B. Fraser, 93–104. Newark: Juan de la Cuesta.

Poster, Michael. 1975. *Existential Marxism in Postwar France: From Sartre to Althusser*. Princeton: Princeton University Press.

Pound, Ezra. 1913. "In a Station of the Metro." *Poetry* 2: 1.

Prakash, Gyan, ed. 2010. *Noir Urbanisms: Dystopic Images of the Modern City*. Princeton: Princeton University Press.

Preston, Peter, and Paul Simpson–Housley. 2010. "Writing the City." In *The Blackwell City Reader*, eds., Gary Bridge and Sophie Watson, 317–322. Chichester: Wiley–Blackwell.

Preziozi, Donald, ed. 1998. *The Art of Art History: A Critical Anthology*. Oxford: Oxford University Press.

Price, P. 2007. "Cohering Culture on *Calle Ocho*: The Pause and Flow of *Latinidad*." *Globalizations* 4(1): 81–99.

Prince, Stephen. 1999. "The Discourse of Pictures: Iconicity and Film Studies." In *Film Theory and Criticism*, 5th ed., eds., Leo Braudy and Marshall Cohen, 99–117. Oxford: Oxford University Press.

Purcell, Mark. 2002. "Excavating Lefebvre: The Right to the City and Its Urban Politics of the Inhabitant." *GeoJournal* 58: 99–108.

Ramos, Carlos. 2010. *Construyendo la modernidad: Escritura y arquitectura en el Madrid moderno (1918–1937)*. Lleida: Universitat de Lleida.

Rehak, B. 2003. "Playing at Being: Psychoanalysis and the Avatar." In *The Video Game Theory Reader*, vol. 2, eds., M. J. P. Wolf and B. Perron, 103–127. New York, London: Routledge.

Resina, Joan Ramon. 2008. *Barcelona's Vocation of Modernity. Rise and Decline of an Urban Image*, Stanford: Stanford University Press.

———. 2003. "From Rose of Fire to City of Ivory." In *After–Images of the City*, eds., J. R. Resina and Dieter Ingenschay, 75–122. Cornell: Cornell University Press.

Revill, G. 2005. "Vernacular Culture and the Place of Folk Music." *Social and Cultural Geography* 6(5): 693–706.

Richardson, Douglas. 2011. "Converging Worlds: Geography and the Humanities." In *Envisioning Landscapes, Making Worlds: Geography and the Humanities*, eds.,

Stephen Daniels, Dydia DeLyser, J. Nicholas Entrikin, and Douglas Richardson, xix–xxi. Abingdon: Routledge.

Richardson, Nathan. 2011. *Constructing Spain: The Reimagination of Space and Place in Fiction and Film, 1953–2003.* Lewisburg: Bucknell University Press.

Ridanpää, Juha. 2010. "Metafictive Geography." *Culture, Theory, and Critique* 51(1): 47–63.

Rihacek, T. 2006. "What Does a City Sound Like? The Urban Sonic Environment from Soundscape Concept Perspective." *Socialni Studia* 2: 155–171.

Riis, Jacob. 1890. *How the Other Half Lives.* New York: Charles Scribner's.

Rojek, Chris. 2007. *Cultural Studies.* Cambridge, Malden: Polity.

Rose, Margaret A. 1984. *Marx's Lost Aesthetic: Karl Marx and the Visual Arts.* Cambridge: Cambridge University Press.

Rosenbloom, Paul S. 2012. "Towards a Conceptual Framework for the Digital Humanities." *Digital Humanities Quarterly* 6.2. http://www.digitalhumanities.org/dhq/vol/6/2/000127/000127.html. Accessed March 10, 2013.

Ross, Kristin. 2004. "Lefebvre on the Situationists: An Interview." In *Guy Debord and the Situationist International: Texts and Documents,* ed., Tom McDonough, 267–284. Cambridge: MIT Press.

Rowland Dix, Hywel. 2010. "The Pedagogy of Cultural Materialism: Paolo Freire and Raymond Williams." In *About Raymond Williams,* eds., Monika Seidl, Roman Horak, and Lawrence Grossberg, 81–93. London, New York: Routledge.

Sacks, Oliver. 2007. *Musicophilia: Tales of Music and the Brain.* New York, Toronto: Knopf.

Sauer, Carl. 1925. "The Morphology of Landscape." *University of California Publications in Geography* 2: 19–54.

———. 1974. "The Fourth Dimension of Geography." *Annals of the Association of American Geographers* 64(2): 189–192.

Saussure, Ferdinand. 1983. *Course in General Linguistics.* London: Duckworth.

Schmid, Christian. 2008. "Lefebvre's Theory of the Production of Space: Towards a Three–Dimensional Dialectic." In *Space, Difference, Everyday Life: Reading Henri Lefebvre,* eds., Goonewardena, Kanishka, Stefan Kipfer, Richard Milgrom, and Christian Schmid, 27–45. New York, London: Routledge.

Scott, James C. 1998. *Seeing Like a State: How Certain Schemes to Improve the Human Condition Have Failed.* New Haven: Yale University Press.

Seidl, Monika, Roman Horak, and Lawrence Grossberg, eds. 2010. *About Raymond Williams.* London, New York: Routledge.

Selden, Raman. 1986. *A Reader's Guide to Contemporary Literary Theory.* Lexington: University Press of Kentucky.

Sennett, Richard. 1992. *The Conscience of the Eye: The Design and Social Life of Cities.* New York; London: W. W. Norton.

———. 1994. *Flesh and Stone. The Body and the City in Western Civilization.* London, New York: W. W. Norton.

———. 2008. *The Craftsman.* New Haven: Yale University Press.

Shepherd, J., and P. Wicke. 1997. *Music and Cultural Theory.* Cambridge: Polity.

Shiel, Mark, and Tony Fitzmaurice, eds. 2001. *Cinema and the City: Film and Urban Societies in a Global Context*. Oxford: Blackwell.

Shields, Rob. 2005. *Lefebvre, Love and Struggle: Spatial Dialectics*. London, New York: Routledge.

———. 2011. "Henri Lefebvre." In *Key thinkers on Space and Place*, eds., Phil Hubbard and Rob Kitchin, 279–285. London: Sage.

———. 2013. *Spatial Questions: Cultural Topologies and Social Spatialisation*. Thousand Oaks: Sage.

Simmel, Georg. 2000. "The Metropolis and Mental Life." In *Readings in Social Theory: The Classic Tradition to Post–Modernism*, 3rd ed., ed., James Farganis, 149–157. New York: McGraw Hill.

———. 2010. "The Metropolis and Mental Life." In *The Blackwell City Reader*, eds., Bridge and Watson, 103–110. Malden, Oxford, West Sussex: Wiley–Blackwell.

Simonsen, Kirsten. 2005. "Bodies, Sensations, Space and Time: The Contribution from Henri Lefebvre." *Geografiska Annaler, Series B: Human Geography* 87(1): 1–14.

Simpson, P. 2008. "Chronic Everyday Life: Rhythmanalysing Street Performance." *Social and Cultural Geography* 9(7): 807–829.

Sloan, Johanne, ed. 2007. *Urban Enigmas: Montreal, Toronto and the Problem of Comparing Cities*. Montreal, Kingston, London, Ithaca: McGill-Queen's University Press.

Smith, Neil. 1984. *Uneven Development: Nature, Capital and the Production of Space*. Oxford: Basil Blackwell.

Smith, Paul Julian. 2006. *Spanish Visual Culture: Cinema, Television, Internet*. Manchester: Manchester University Press.

Smith, Susan J. 1997. "Beyond Geography's Visible Worlds: A Cultural Politics of Music." *Progress in Human Geography* 21(4): 502–529.

———. 2000. "Performing the (Sound)world." *Environment and Planning D: Society and Space* 18(5): 615–637.

———. 2001. "Editorial: Emotional Geographies." *Transactions of the Institute of British Geographers* 26: 7–10.

———. 2005. "Performing the (Sound)world." In *Cultural Geography. Critical Concepts in the Social Sciences*, 90–119. London, New York: Routledge.

Snow, C. P. 1993. *The Two Cultures*. Cambridge: Cambridge University Press.

Soja, Edward W. 1980. "The Socio-Spatial Dialectic." *Annals of the Association of American Geographers* 70(2): 207–225.

———. 1996. *Thirdspace: Journeys to Los Angeles and Other Real–and–Imagined Places*. Cambridge: Blackwell.

Sontag, Susan. 1969. "Against Interpretation." 1964. In *Against Interpretation and Other Essays*, 13–23. Dell Publishing Co. Inc.

Souza e Silva, A., and D. M. Sutko. 2009. "Merging Digital and Urban Playscapes: An Introduction to the Field." In *Digital Cityscapes: Merging Digital and Urban Playscapes*, eds., A. Souza e Silva and D. M. Sutko, 1–17. New York: Peter Lang.

Staeheli, Lynn. 1996. "Publicity, Privacy, and Women's Political Action." *Environment and Planning D* 14: 601–619.

Stanek, Lukasz. 2011. *Henri Lefebvre on Space: Architecture, Urban Research, and the Production of Theory.* Minneapolis, London: University of Minnesota Press.

Steinmetz, George, ed. 1999. *State/Culture: State–Formation after the Cultural Turn.* Ithaca, London: Cornell University Press.

Straw, Will, and Alexandra Boutros. 2010. "Introduction." In *Circulation and the City: Essays on Urban Culture,* eds., Alexandra Boutros and Will Straw, 3–20. Montreal, Kingston, London, Ithaca: McGill-Queen's University Press.

Sturt, Fraser. 2006. "Local Knowledge Is Required: A Rhythmanalytical Approach to the Late Mesolithic and Early Neolithic of the East Anglian Fenland, UK." *J Mari Arch* 1: 119–139.

Sullivan, J. 1988. *ETA and Basque Nationalism. The Fight for Euskadi 1890–1986.* London, New York: Routledge.

Sullivan, Rob. 2012. Review of Dear Michael et al. 2011. *GeoHumanities: Art, History, Text at the Edge of Place. Environment and Planning D: Society and Space.* http://societyandspace.com/reviews/reviews-archive/dear-michael-et-al-2011 -geohumanities-art-history-text-at-the-edge-of-place-reviewed-by-rob-sullivan. Accessed June 4, 2012.

Sütiste, Elin. 2008. "Roman Jakobson and the Topic of Translation: Reception in Academic Reference Works." *Sign Systems Studies* 36(2): 271–314.

Svensson, Patrik. 2012. "Envisioning the Digital Humanities." *Digital Humanities Quarterly* 6.1. http://www.digitalhumanities.org/dhq/vol/6/1/000112/000112 .html. Accessed March 10, 2013.

Taylor, J. 1997. "The Emerging Geographies of Virtual Worlds." *Geographical Review* 87(2): 172–192.

Taylor, P. J. 1982. "A Materialist Framework for Political Geography." *Transactions of the Institute of British Geographers* 7: 15–34.

Taylor, T. L. 2006. *Play Between Worlds: Exploring Online Game Culture.* Cambridge: MIT Press.

Thien, D. 2005. "After or Beyond Feeling? A Consideration of Affect and Emotion in Geography." *Area* 37(4): 450–456.

Thorton, Niamh. 2003. "Finding a Place in a Megalopolis: Mexico City in *Amores perros.*" *Film & Film Culture* 2: 43–50.

Tierney, Dolores. 2009. "Alejandro González Iñárritu: Director without Borders." *New Cinemas: Journal of Contemporary Film* 7(2): 101–117.

Tiwari, R. 2008. "Being a Rhythm Analyst in the City of Varanasi." *Urban Forum* 19: 289–306.

Tolia–Kelly, D. P. 2006. "Affect – An Ethnocentric Encounter? Exploring the 'Universalist' Imperative of Emotional/Affectual Geographies." *Area* 38 (2): 213–217.

Turner, Graeme. 1990. *British Cultural Studies: An Introduction.* Boston: Unwin Hyman.

———. 2012. *What's Become of Cultural Studies.* Los Angeles, London: Sage.

Ugarte, Michael. 2012. "Hispanism's Crisis and the Compitello Generation." *Capital Inscriptions: Essays on Hispanic Literature, Film and Urban Sapce in Honor of Malcolm Alan Compitello,* ed. B. Fraser, 65–78. Newark: Juan de la Cuesta.

Van Veen, Tobias C. 2010. "Cities of Rhythm and Revolution." In *Circulation and the City: Essays on Urban Culture*, eds., Alexandra Boutros and Will Straw, 155–190. Montreal, Kingston, London, Ithaca: McGill-Queen's University Press.

Vázquez Montalbán, Manuel. 1990. *Barcelonas*. Trans. A. Robinson. London: Verso.

———. 1993. *Sabotaje Olímpico*. Barcelona: Planeta.

———. 1997. *Los mares del sur*. Barcelona: Planeta.

Watkins, Ceri. 2005. "Representations of Space, Spatial Practices and Spaces of Representation: An Application of Lefebvre's Spatial Triad." *Culture and Organization* 11(3): 209–220.

Waugh, Linda, and Madeleine Newfield. 1995. "Iconicity in the Lexicon and its Relevance for a Theory of Morphology." In *Syntactic Iconicity and Linguistic Freezes: The Human Dimension*, ed., Marge E. Landsberg, 189–221. Berlin: Mouton de Gruyter.

Webber, Andrew, and Emma Wilson. 2008. *Cities in Transition: The Moving Image and the Modern Metropolis*. New York, London: Wallflower Press.

Williams, Raymond. 1975. *The Country and the City*. New York: Oxford University Press.

———. 1977. *Marxism and Literature*. Oxford: Oxford University Press.

———. 2007a. "The Future of Cultural Studies." In *Politics of Modernism: Against the New Conformists*, 151–162. London, New York: Verso.

———. 2007b. "The Uses of Cultural Theory." In *Politics of Modernism: Against the New Conformists*, 163–176. London; New York: Verso.

Wirth, Louis. 1938. "Urbanism as Way of Life." *The American Journal of Sociology* 44(1): 1–24.

Wolf, M. J. P. 1997. "Inventing Space: Toward a Taxonomy of On- and Off-Screen Space in Video Games." *Film Quarterly* 51(1): 11–23.

———. 2001. *The Medium of the Video Game*. Austin: University of Texas Press.

———. 2003. "Abstraction in the Video Game." In *The Video Game Theory Reader*, vol. 1, eds., M. J. P. Wolf and B. Perron, 47–65. New York, London: Routledge.

Wolf, M. J. P., and B. Perron. 2003. "Introduction." In *The Video Game Theory Reader*, vol. 1, M. J. P. Wolf and B. Perron, eds., 1–24. New York, London: Routledge.

———. 2009. "Introduction." In *The Video Game Theory Reader*, vol. 2, eds., M. J. P. Wolf and B. Perron, 1–21. New York, London: Routledge.

Wollen. Peter. 1972. *Signs and Meaning in the Cinema*, 3rd ed. Bloomington: Indiana University Press.

Wood, N. 2002. "'Once More with Feeling': Putting Emotion into Geographies of Music." In *Subjectivities, Knowledges and Feminist Geographies*, eds., L. Bondi et al., 57–71. Lanham: Rowman & Littlefield.

Wood, N., and Susan J. Smith. 2004. "Instrumental Routes to Emotional Geographies." *Social and Cultural Geography* 5(4): 533–548.

Wood, N., M. Duffy, and Susan J. Smith. 2007. "The Art of Doing (Geographies of) Music." *Environment and Planning D: Society and Space* 25: 867–889.

X, Jorge. 2002. Entrevista a LISABÖ: sin darte cuenta. La factoría del ritmo. www. lafactoriadelritmo.com/fact13/entrevis/lisabo.shtml.

Young, Richard, and Amanda Holmes, eds. 2010. *Cultures of the City: Mediating Identities in Urban Latin/o America*. Pittsburgh: University of Pittsburgh Press.

Yuan, May. 2010. "Mapping Text." In *The Spatial Humanities: GIS and the Future of Scholarship*, eds., David J. Bodenhamer, John Corrigan, and Trevor M. Harris, 109–123. Bloomington and Indianapolis: Indiana University Press.

Zimmerman, E. 2009. "Gaming Literacy: Game Design as a Model for Literacy in the Twenty–First Century." In *The Video Game Theory Reader*, vol. 2, eds., M. J. P. Wolf and B. Perron, 23–32. New York and London: Routledge.

Zukin, Sharon. 1995. *The Cultures of Cities*. Malden: Oxford.

Index

9 781137 498557